The Victoria Tower at the Palace of Westminster, the
repository for the records of both Houses of Parliament

Guide to the
RECORDS OF
PARLIAMENT

MAURICE F. BOND

London
Her Majesty's Stationery Office
1971

Typographic design by HMSO

Printed in England for Her Majesty's Stationery Office
by William Clowes & Sons, Limited, London, Beccles and Colchester

SBN 11 700351 4*

PREFACE

This *Guide* describes the complete range of records preserved within the Palace of Westminster: the records of both Houses of Parliament; all documents which have been presented to the two Houses or purchased by them; and the papers which have accumulated in the various Parliamentary and non-Parliamentary offices of the Palace. The earliest in date are those of the fifteenth century, the latest those of the 1969–70 session of Parliament. Detailed attention is given to the manuscript material amongst the records, but descriptions are also included of those classes of Parliamentary record which have been published and are generally available, such as Journals of the Houses and the later Sessional Papers.

The arrangement of the *Guide* is in accordance with the *provenance* of the documents, and the records of each House and of each non-Parliamentary department are treated as separate archive groups. Within these groups each sequence or class of record corresponds to a particular function or aspect of work. The nature and content of the classes have been determined by Parliamentary procedure; brief historical notes on the relevant rules of procedure and their variations over the centuries have therefore been incorporated in the *Guide*.

Nearly all the materials described in this volume are accessible in the House of Lords Record Office Search Room at Westminster, which is open to the public throughout the year. In addition, typed or photographic copies of most of the documents can be supplied by that office. Further information concerning the records is provided by the Calendars and other publications listed below on pages 8–11.

The *Guide* is being published on the twenty-fifth anniversary of the establishment of the House of Lords Record Office, and its compilation has only become possible as a result of the work of the staff of the office since 1946. The initial preparation of lists of documents in individual classes has been carried out by the Office Assistants, and I would like especially to record my gratitude for the careful and thorough work both of past members of the staff, including the late Mr. J. R. Smith, Mr. H. A. Martins, and Mr. V. W. Meerabux, and of the present Chief Office Assistants, Mr. D. T. Gethin and Mr. F. C. R. Deacon, and Office Assistants, Mr. M. F. MacTavish, Mr. S. K. Ellison and Mr. J. A. Lamprell-Jarrett. Invaluable secretarial assistance has been given by Lady Trefgarne and Mrs. J. Wise. For help at every stage in the preparation of the descriptions of classes I have been indebted to the Assistant Clerks of the Records: to Mr. H. S. Cobb, Assistant Clerk since 1953, whose comprehensive knowledge of the records and their historical background has contributed richly to the *Guide*; to Miss E. R. Poyser, Assistant Clerk from 1950 to 1965, on whose pioneer work in the field of Private Bill records I have frequently drawn; and to Mr. D. J. Johnson, Assistant Clerk since 1965, whose patient scrutiny of successive drafts has improved both content and format. Mr. Johnson has, in addition, contributed a full general Index to the volume.

The *Guide* is issued with the approval and encouragement of the Officers of Parliament in whom the custody of the two main groups of records is vested:

Sir David Stephens, Clerk of the Parliaments, and Sir Barnett Cocks, Clerk of the House of Commons. I would like to express my thanks to them, and to all my colleagues in both Houses who have read and amended sections of the *Guide*. In particular, I am grateful for generous help in the House of Lords to Mr. R. W. Perceval, Clerk Assistant, Mr. C. S. A. Dobson, Librarian, and Mr. J. C. Sainty, formerly Clerk of the Journals; in the House of Commons, to Mr. S. C. Hawtrey, Clerk of the Journals, Mr. D. C. L. Holland, Librarian, and Dr. D. Menhennet, Deputy Librarian. I am also most grateful to many scholars for their helpful advice and especially to Master I. H. Jacob, Master of the Supreme Court, Miss Sheila Lambert, and Professor Elizabeth Read Foster, Dean of the Graduate School at Bryn Mawr College.

The latest accessions to be noted in the *Guide* were received in March 1971. All subsequent accessions will be listed in the annual *Reports* of the House of Lords Record Office. These are available on request to the Clerk of the Records, House of Lords, London SW1, to whom also all correspondence and enquiries should be addressed.

Record Office   Maurice F. Bond
House of Lords   *Clerk of the Records*
March 1971

CONTENTS

Preface   *page* iii
List of Illustrations   viii
List of Abbreviations   ix
Notes on using the Guide   x

General Introduction to the Records   1
The History of the Records   3
Facilities for students in the House of Lords Record Office   6
Publications relating to the Records of Parliament   8

Part One: Records of the House of Lords   13
List of Classes   15
The House of Lords   20
Members of the House of Lords   22
Lists of Parliaments 1242 to date   23
Records of Proceedings in the House of Lords   26
Records of Proceedings in Committees of the House of Lords   41
Records of Proceedings in Joint Committees of both Houses   57
Records of Proceedings in Conferences between the Houses   58
Records of Bills, Acts and Measures   59
  Procedure on Bills   59
  Message and Assent Formulae   62
  Public Bill Records, House of Lords   65
  Hybrid Bill Records, House of Lords   69
  Private Bill Records, House of Lords   70
  Acts of Parliament   93
  Church Assembly and General Synod Measure Records   104
Judicial Records, House of Lords   106
  Original Jurisdiction   107
  Impeachments   109
  Trials of Peers   111
  Appeal Cases   114
  Cases in Error   120
  Cases of Privilege   124

1*   v

Sessional Papers, House of Lords   127
  Returns   127
  Command Papers   128
  Act Papers   128
  Papers Laid pursuant to Subsidiary Legislation   130
  The Printing of Lords Papers   131
  Sessional Papers, House of Lords, 1641–1800   135
  Sessional Papers, House of Lords, 1801 to date   159
Peerage Records   160
  Records of Peerage Claims   160
  Records concerning Representative Peers for Scotland   165
  Records concerning Representative Peers for Ireland   167
Small Classes, House of Lords   170
Parliament Office Papers   181
Records of Black Rod's Department   195

Part Two: Records of the House of Commons   197
List of Classes   199
The House of Commons   201
Members of the House of Commons   202
Records of the House of Commons   204
Records of Proceedings in the House of Commons   205
Records of Proceedings in Committees of the House of Commons   218
Records of Bills, House of Commons   226
  Public Bill Records, House of Commons   226
  Hybrid Bill Records, House of Commons   227
  Private Bill Records, House of Commons   227
Sessional Papers, House of Commons   232
  Unprinted Sessional Papers   232
  Printed Sessional Papers   233
Department of the Speaker   237
Small Classes, House of Commons   238
Office Records, House of Commons   243
Records of the Serjeant at Arms Department   247

Part Three: Records of the Lord Great Chamberlain   249

Part Four: Records of the Clerk of the Crown   257

Part Five: Other Records of the Palace of Westminster   261
Statute Law Committee Papers   263

Scottish Commissions Records 264
The Shaw-Lefevre Papers 264
Exchequer Chief Usher Records 266

Part Six: Historical Collections within the Palace of Westminster 267
Historical Collections of the House of Lords Record Office 269
Historical Collections of the House of Lords Library 285
Historical Collections of the House of Commons Library 291

Appendices
I List of Clerks of the Parliaments 303
II List of Clerks of the House of Commons 305

Table of Acts of Parliament cited in the text 307

Index 313

ILLUSTRATIONS

frontispiece
The Victoria Tower at the Palace of Westminster

between pp. 98 and 99

1. Journal of the House of Lords, 1549
2. Minutes of the House of Lords, 1713
3. Minutes of Proceedings in Committee, House of Lords, 1797
4. Dundee Harbour Improvement Bill, Deposited Plan (House of Lords), 1814
5. Dundee Harbour Improvement Bill, Deposited Estimate of Expense and Estimate of Time (House of Lords), 1814
6. Barnet Market Bill, 1592
7. Linen and Hemp Manufactures Act, 1750
8. Appeal Case, Berkeley *versus* Cope, 1699
9. Writ of Error, MacDonnogh *versus* Stafford, 1624
10. Protestation Return from the parish of Covenham St. Bartholomew, co. Lincs., 1642
11. The Declaration of Rights, 1689
12. The Pedigree of 1st Lord Curzon of Penn, 1795
13. Journal of the House of Commons, 1624
14. Diary of Speaker Brand, 1881
15. Memorandum by Sir Herbert Samuel, 1931
16. Votes of the House of Commons, 1689

List of Abbreviations

c.	century, centuries
c.	[in titles of Acts] chapter
c.	*circa*
C.J.	Journal of the House of Commons
Calendar	The volumes of Calendars of the Manuscripts of the House of Lords, as listed on pp. 8–10 below.
co.	county
C. Priv.	Committee for Privileges
C.W.H.	Committee of the Whole House
Com.	Committee
Corr.	Correspondence
D.	Duke
doc.	document
Dss.	Duchess
E.	Earl
H.C.	House of Commons
H.L.	House of Lords
H.L.R.O.	House of Lords Record Office
H.M.C.	Royal Commission on Historical Manuscripts
H.M.S.O.	Her Majesty's Stationery Office
Kt.	Knight
L.	Lord
L.G.C.	Lord Great Chamberlain
L.J.	Journal of the House of Lords
M.	Marquess
M.P.	Member of Parliament
MS.	Manuscript
n.d.	no date
n.p.	not printed
N.S.	New Series
no.	number
occ.	occurs
P.	Prince
P.D.	*Parliamentary Debates*
P.H.	*Parliamentary History*
P.R.O.	Public Record Office
par.	parish
Pl.	Plate
Sel. Com.	Select Committee
S.O.	Standing Order
V.	Viscount
var.	various
vol.	volume
1a	First Reading
2a	Second Reading
3a	Third Reading

Notes on using the Guide

CLASSES

The basic entries in this *Guide* relate to individual classes of record. The titles of the classes are shown in heavy type. Summarised lists of them are printed on pp. 15–20 for Lords records, and on pp. 199–201 for Commons records. All classes are included in the general Index on pp. 313–352. Under the title of each class the limiting dates are shown, e.g. '1731 to 1800'. This indicates either a continuous or a moderately continuous sequence between the end dates; if there is an isolated item distant in date from those given, it is indicated separately, e.g. '1547, 1563 to 1849'. New Style dating is used throughout. Where possible, a count of individual items is also given, e.g. '200 docs.'. This count is normally exact for volumes, but only approximate for papers.

LISTS

The availability of lists of individual items within a class is indicated: some of the lists may be in published works, others are noted as typed or MS. lists in the House of Lords Record Office Search Room.

BIBLIOGRAPHIES

These are not intended to be complete general bibliographies, but are lists of relevant works of reference which are available to students in the House of Lords Record Office Search Room.

USE

Attention is drawn to the overall statement concerning the use of Lords documents (p. 20) and Commons documents (p. 204). Other rules relating to specific classes or other archival groups are noted in their appropriate sections.

GENERAL INTRODUCTION
TO THE RECORDS

GENERAL INTRODUCTION TO THE RECORDS

THE HISTORY OF THE RECORDS

The Parliament of the United Kingdom is composed of the Sovereign, the House of Lords and the House of Commons. Each of the two Houses has formed its own accumulation of official records, manuscript and printed. Those of the Lords date from 1497, those of the Commons from 1547. Both groups of records are preserved at the Palace of Westminster and, with a few exceptions, are there accessible to the public in the Search Room of the House of Lords Record Office. Parliamentary records of earlier date than 1497 are preserved today in the Public Record Office[1] and not at Westminster. This is because the mediaeval clerks of Parliament were recruited from Chancery; the petitions and bills that accumulated during a Parliament, together with the rolls of proceedings and of Acts, were therefore deposited with the records of Chancery.

The records of the House of Lords now preserved in the Palace of Westminster originated in March 1497, when the then Clerk, Master Richard Hatton, having prepared the Parliament Roll for that session for transfer to Chancery, retained in the House of Lords the complete series of sixteen enacted Bills, or 'Original Acts', from which he had made the enrolment. Since then, this class of enacted Bills has been preserved continuously among the records of the House of Lords. By 1509, the Clerk of the Parliaments and his assistants (today known collectively as the Parliament Office) had hived off from Chancery, and in the course of the 16th c. this newly independent Lords office gradually expanded and formalised its record keeping. In addition to the class of Original Acts already mentioned, the clerks preserved Journals of the House of Lords, now surviving from 1510, Petitions from 1531 and Bills from 1558. It seems, however, that the office was somewhat haphazard in its methods; Cardinal Wolsey, for instance, when Chancellor, is said to have removed all the Acts and Journals relating to one session. A more business-like administration began with the advent of two Clerks in the 17th c., Robert Bowyer (1609–21) and Henry Elsynge (1621–35). Under these diligent and scholarly men the Lords archive took its modern form. Petitions and many other forms of Papers coming to the Lords were carefully filed; extensive series of rough Minutes and of Committee Proceedings were preserved; and, not least in importance, the records were assigned a permanent home at the south-west corner of the Palace of Westminster, in a moated building (still surviving, and open to the public), the 14th c. Jewel Tower. Here the principal records of the Lords remained from 1621 to 1864, being available throughout this period for inspection by the public. The contents of some were given still wider currency in the 18th c. as certain Bills and Papers began to be printed, and when, in 1767, the Lords ordered the printing of their Journals.

Meanwhile, a second Parliamentary archive, the records of the House of

---

[1] They are described in *Guide to the Contents of the Public Record Office*, vol. i (1963); *see* the entries for Parliamentary and Council Proceedings, Parliament Rolls, Statute Rolls and Ancient Petitions respectively.

Commons, had been forming in another part of the Palace of Westminster. Initially, in the Middle Ages, it could be said that no formal records at all were made of the domestic proceedings of the House of Commons. From 1547, however, a Commons Journal survives, and, parallel with the formation in the Lords of the main Parliamentary records under Bowyer and Elsynge, separate series of domestic records of the Commons began to accumulate, of Petitions and Papers (from the reign of Elizabeth I), of Return Books of Elections (from 1625) and of Minute Books of Committees (from 1623). By the early 19th c. these documents were considerable in quantity, but on the night of 16 October 1834 almost the entire range—with the vital exception of the Commons Journals —was consumed in the 'tally-stick fire', which destroyed not only the enormous accumulation of wooden Exchequer tally-sticks but also a great part of the fabric of the Palace of Westminster.

The House of Lords archive survived the fire of 1834. This was in part due to the isolated position of the Jewel Tower where the main series of records had been preserved, but also in part owing to the efforts of a Lords clerk, Mr. Stone Smith, who threw out of the blazing windows of the main building into Old Palace Yard many hundreds of bundles of other Lords papers that had not been transferred to the Jewel Tower. These bundles for several decades after the fire led a confused existence, being virtually forgotten by those outside the Parliament Office, until, in 1870, the newly formed Royal Commission on Historical Manuscripts began to issue regular *Reports*. In them the Commission drew attention to the extent and variety of manuscripts preserved in the House of Lords. The first *Report* of the Commission brought to light a packet of letters which had been abandoned by Charles I at the battle of Naseby, as well as the 'annexed' Book of Common Prayer of 1662, the Declaration of Breda, and other 'public muniments' which had 'just been untombed from this mausoleum of historic remains' (as Duffus Hardy and his fellow Commissioners remarked). The succeeding *Reports* of the Commissioners were continued from 1900 onwards by calendars published by the House of Lords itself. The calendars have in recent years progressed to the end of the reign of Queen Anne and are now being continued into the reign of George I, but so great is the accumulation of modern Parliamentary records, that so far only about 2 per cent of the total bulk of Parliamentary records has been calendared. The rest, however, has been in part listed, and is described in the present volume.

During the time that the records were being identified and calendared on behalf of the Historical Manuscripts Commission they were also gradually being installed in a new repository. After the ancient Palace of Westminster had been burnt down in 1834, the House of Lords gave directions that a new building must contain *inter alia* two 'Fireproof Repositories for Papers and Documents'. Charles Barry's winning design, one bearing 'throughout such evident marks of genius and superiority of talent' and displaying 'so much taste and knowledge of Gothic Architecture' (in the opinion of the adjudicating Commissioners), had as its culminating feature a tower over the Royal entrance in which every storey included 'Record Rooms'. The height of this tower, the 'Queen Victoria Tower', steadily increased from that indicated in the original plan (of some 200 feet) until, in 1855, when the wrought iron flagstaff was at last put into position, the Tower was proudly claimed to be not merely 'the grandest feature of the building', but the largest and highest square tower in the world, 323 feet high to the base of the flagstaff and 395 feet high to the top of the crown at its summit.

Within the Tower, remarkable cast-iron spiral staircases of 553 steps linked twelve floors, and on most of the floors there were eight strong rooms—accommodation at that time so ample for the Parliamentary records that it is understandable that at one stage the Tower had been intended also to house the principal holdings of the Public Record Office.

During the present century two important developments have occurred in the preservation of the Parliamentary records. The first concerns the records of the Commons. In 1927 the Clerk of the House of Commons resolved to transfer to the Victoria Tower an extensive post-1834 series of Private Bill records, though still retaining ultimate ownership of them for the House. This precedent has been followed by succeeding Clerks of the Commons, and in 1957 the central records of the House of Commons, the series of some 241 original manuscript Journals, dating from 1547 to 1800, were deposited in the Victoria Tower, by authority of the Speaker of the House.

Secondly, in 1937, the then Clerk of the Parliaments, Sir Henry Badeley, initiated a survey of the entire Lords archive. The resulting report by Mr. V. M. R. Goodman revealed the necessity of a whole-time staff to undertake boxing, repair and production of the manuscripts. The second world war intervened, but in 1946 Sir Henry Badeley set up a House of Lords Record Office, under a Clerk of the Records who was to act as the deputy of the Clerk of the Parliaments in all record matters. To the Clerk of the Records was entrusted the care of the contents of the Victoria Tower, including both Lords and Commons documents and certain other small groups of records relating to the Palace of Westminster. A public Search Room was opened, and H.M. Stationery Office established a Bindery to enable the systematic repair of the documents to be undertaken. The publication of calendars, which had ceased in 1922, was resumed in 1949; and in the following year a series of *Record Office Memoranda* was initiated to include annual reports on work in progress, and, from time to time, handlists and sectional guides to the records. The present publication programme in addition comprises facsimile and other photographic reproductions of documents, together with illustrated booklets describing some of the more famous Parliamentary documents.[1]

The principal activity of the House of Lords Record Office, however, in the immediate post-war years concerned the reconstruction of the repository. The Victoria Tower, although ample in dimensions, was found in 1948 to be defective both in its structure and its equipment. In the course of the following years the interior of the Tower was therefore almost entirely rebuilt by the Ministry of Public Buildings and Works. The resulting repository is air-conditioned and contains $5\frac{1}{2}$ miles of steel shelving on twelve floors. It was declared open by the Viscount Hailsham, Leader of the House of Lords, on 3 July 1963, with the intention, as he said, that 'this new building may have a long and distinguished career . . . in the service of Parliament, history, and culture'.

Nearly all the records belonging to both Houses, which are described in this *Guide*, are in the immediate care of the House of Lords Record Office. A small proportion, however, is still preserved within the office of origin; and other manuscripts and printed records are cared for by the Librarians of the two Houses. The Library of the House of Commons was first established in 1818 and that of the House of Lords in 1826. In the subsequent century and a half each has

---

[1] A list of publications currently available is given on pp. 8-11 below.

become a reference library of great range and complexity, and each in addition has become the official place of deposit of certain records and documents. Since 1851 the Death Warrant of Charles I has been exhibited in the Lords Library, and since 1923 documents from the Victoria Tower have been displayed alongside it. Official copies of 'unprinted Papers' are deposited in the Commons Library, and both Libraries hold series of printed Parliamentary Papers, and have from time to time received gifts of manuscripts relating to Parliamentary history and procedure. By the kindness of the Librarians descriptions of all this material, now in their custody, are included in the appropriate sections of this *Guide*.

Finally, certain small groups of documents have accumulated within the Palace of Westminster which are to be distinguished from the records and the historical collections of the two Houses of Parliament. The most extensive of these small groups is the archive of the Lord Great Chamberlain. This dates from the 16th c. and relates not only to the fabric of the Palace of Westminster and ceremonies and trials held within it, but also to the arrangements made by the Lord Great Chamberlain for Coronations from 1689 onwards. This group of records has not previously been listed or described. In addition, the present *Guide* includes details of the records of the Clerk of the Crown in his capacity as an officer of Parliament; of the present Statute Law Committee and its 19th c. predecessors; of two 19th c. Scottish Commissions; of the Exchequer Chief Usher; and of a clerk who had held a number of public offices. Although distinct from the Parliamentary records proper practically all the documents in these smaller groups are likewise open to public consultation and access to them can be arranged by the Clerk of the Records.

BIBLIOGRAPHY

M. F. Bond, 'The Formation of the Archives of Parliament, 1497–1691', *Journal of the Society of Archivists*, vol. i, no. 6 (1957), pp. 151–8.
Second Report of the Royal Commission on Public Records, vol. ii, pt. i, Cd. 7544 (1914), pp. 15–16, 40; vol. ii, pt. ii, Cd. 7545 (1914), pp. 47–9, 104–7, 132, 174, 309; vol. ii, pt. iii, Cd. 7546 (1914), pp. 71–4.

FACILITIES FOR STUDENTS IN THE HOUSE OF LORDS RECORD OFFICE

THE RECORD OFFICE SEARCH ROOM

The Record Office Search Room is open to members of the public on weekdays (Saturdays and certain Public Holidays excepted) from 10 to 5. Approach to the office is *via* the Chancellor's Gate (which is near the Victoria Tower on the west front of the Houses of Parliament). At the gate, visitors are directed by those on duty to the House of Lords Record Office. All intending searchers are asked to telephone or write to the Clerk of the Records before their first visit, describing the nature of their research and, if possible, the specific documents they wish to consult. No special passes or introductions are required. All correspondence should be addressed to the Clerk of the Records, Record Office, House of Lords, London SW1. The telephone number is 01–930 6240.

CHARGES FOR SEARCHERS

A charge of 38p is made for the production of each document required for business or legal purposes. No charge is made for production for purposes of historical research except in connection with certain orders for photographic copies.

THE MAKING OF TYPED COPIES OF DOCUMENTS

Subject to the overriding needs of parliamentary business, the office can supply typed copies of documents at the following charges:

for copies of all documents, per folio of 72 words,
    if of later date than 1759   ...   . 5p per folio
    if dated 1759, or earlier   ...   . 10p per folio
    (plus production fee of 38p per document)
    if certified by the Clerk of the Parliaments, an additional fee of   £1

THE MAKING OF PHOTOGRAPHIC COPIES OF DOCUMENTS

Photographic copies can be supplied of those documents considered by the Clerk of the Records to be of suitable condition, size and format in the following media: xerox, microfilm, electrostatic prints from microfilm, black and white photographs, colour photographs, black and white slides, colour transparencies. Details concerning charges etc. are set out in the leaflet of *General Information*, obtainable on request from the Clerk of the Records.

STANDARD FORMS OF REFERENCE TO THE RECORDS

Students are asked to refer to documents in the charge of the House of Lords Record Office, when they quote them in printed works or in correspondence, so far as possible, in accordance with the following system. The name of the office is followed by that of the class of document, and that of the House concerned, and then by the date of presentation or first reading. The following examples typify both this general usage and certain necessary exceptions:

H[ouse of] L[ords] R[ecord] O[ffice]. Main Papers, H.L., 15 July 1942 (86th Report of Ecclesiastical Committee).
H.L.R.O. Parchment Coll., H.L., 10 Dec. 1660.
H.L.R.O. Original Act, 14 Geo. III, no. 4.
H.L.R.O. Committee Book, H.L., 11 May 1771 [date of entry] or [*after 1836*], 1850, vol. 156, p. 10.
H.L.R.O. Deposited Plan, H.L., 1846, London and North-Western Railway, p. 20.
H.L.R.O. Minutes of Evidence, H.C., 1846, vol. 3, London and North-Western Railway, p. 20.
H.L.R.O. Private Bill Office, H.L., Bill of Costs, 1846.
H.L.R.O. Braye MSS. 6, ff. 41–6.

PUBLICATIONS RELATING TO THE RECORDS OF PARLIAMENT

(*a*) CALENDAR OF THE MANUSCRIPTS OF THE HOUSE OF LORDS

The series of volumes in which the Lords Manuscripts are listed, described, and frequently printed in full, was begun by the Royal Commission on Historical Manuscripts (*see* nos. 1–13 below), and their Reports were published as Command Papers. From 1900 the House of Lords has continued the series as House of Lords Papers and the latest of these was published in 1962 (*see* nos. 14–24 below). Complete sets of the volumes are available for use in the Record Office Search Room and also in many public libraries.

List of Volumes

1. Description of the Records of the House of Lords, and transcripts of some of the Naseby Papers (1644–5).
   Pp. 1–10 of Appendix to *1st Report of the Royal Commission on Historical Manuscripts*, reprinted, 1874 [C.55].

2. Specimen Calendars for 1625 and 1634.
   Pp. 106–9 of Appendix to *2nd Report of H.M.C.*, 1871 [C.441].

3. Calendar of Manuscripts, 1450 (*rectius* 1498)–1625.
   Pp. 1–36 of Appendix to *3rd Report of H.M.C.*, 1872 [C. 673].
   (Includes the Mompesson Impeachment.)

4. Calendar of Manuscripts, 1625–41; with Supplementary Calendar, 1566–1625, Archbishop Laud's Visitations, 1634, etc., John Durye's Mission Papers, 1630–40, and Papers respecting 'The Incident', 1641.
   Pp. 1–163 of Appendix to *4th Report of H.M.C.*, 1874 [C.857].
   (This Report and subsequent volumes practically follow the daily entries in the Lords Journals.)

5. Calendar of Manuscripts, 1642–3.
   Pp. 1–134 of Appendix to *5th Report of H.M.C.*, 1876 [C.1432].
   (Includes Protestation Returns of 1642.)

6. Calendar of Manuscripts, 1644–7.
   Pp. 1–221 of Appendix to *6th Report of H.M.C.*, 1877 [C.1745].
   (Includes further Naseby Papers, letters of Essex, Hutchinson, Rushworth, Queen of Bohemia, etc.)

7. Calendar of Manuscripts, 1648–65.
   Pp. 1–182 of Appendix to *7th Report of H.M.C.*, 1879 [C.2340].
   (Includes papers relating to Act of Uniformity, the Regicides, the 'late King's goods', the Act of Indemnity, etc.)

8. Calendar of Manuscripts, 1666–71.
   Pp. 101–74 of Appendix to *8th Report of H.M.C.* (Re-issue), 1907 [C.4040 of 1881].
   (Includes Committee on Decay of Trade Papers, Clarendon's Impeachment and Skinner *v.* East India Company.)

9. Calendar of Manuscripts, 1670–8.
   Pp. 1–125 of Appendix Part ii to *9th Report of H.M.C.*, 1905 [C.3773 i of 1884].
   (Includes material concerning the Test Act, Habeas Corpus Act and Statute of Frauds.)

10. Calendar of Manuscripts, 1678–88.
    Appendix, Part ii to *11th Report of H.M.C.*, 1887 [C.5060 i].
    (Includes Popish Plot, Exclusion Bill and Habeas Corpus Act papers.)

11. Calendar of Manuscripts, 1689–90.
    Appendix Part vi to *12th Report of H.M.C.*, 1889 [C.5889 iii].
    (Includes material concerning the Revolution and the Bill of Rights.)

12. Calendar of Manuscripts, 1690–1.
    Appendix Part v to *13th Report of H.M.C.*, 1892 [C.6822].
    (Includes papers on the Lieutenancy of London and the French Trade Bill.)

13. Calendar of Manuscripts, 1692–3.
    Appendix Part vi to *14th Report of H.M.C.*, 1894 [C.7573].
    (Includes Naval Papers produced before the Committee on the State of the Nation.)

14. *Manuscripts of the House of Lords, 1693–1695.*
    New series, vol. i, 1900 (H.L.5). Reprinted, 1964.
    (Includes papers laid before the House concerning the Naval Miscarriages and Jacobitism.)

15. *Manuscripts of the House of Lords, 1695–1697.*
    New series, vol. ii, 1903 (H.L. 18). Reprinted, 1965.
    (Includes papers produced before the Committee on the State of Trade, and others concerning the establishment of an East India Company in Scotland.)

16. *Manuscripts of the House of Lords, 1697–1699.*
    New series, vol. iii, 1905 (H.L. 175). Reprinted, 1965.
    (Includes papers relating to the enquiry into Irish Appeals, and a text of the Irish 'Modus tenendi Parliamenta'.)

17. *Manuscripts of the House of Lords, 1699–1702.*
    New series, vol. iv, 1908 (H.L. 7). Reprinted, 1965.
    (Also includes Journal of the House 1658–9, then in the possession of Lady Tangye, now in the London Museum.)

18. *Manuscripts of the House of Lords, 1702–4.*
    New series, vol. v, 1910 (H.L. 62). Reprinted, 1965.
    (Includes papers relating to the Scottish Conspiracy.)

19. *Manuscripts of the House of Lords, 1704–1706.*
    New series, vol. vi, 1912 (H.L. 142). Reprinted, 1966.
    (Includes papers relating to the enquiry into Naval Affairs.)

20. *Manuscripts of the House of Lords, 1706–1708.*
    New series, vol. vii, 1921 (H.L. 1). Reprinted, 1966.
    (Includes records of the Lords enquiries into convoys and into privateers in the West Indies.)

21. *Manuscripts of the House of Lords, 1708–1710.*
    New series, vol. viii, 1922 (H.L. 40). Reprinted, 1966.
    (Includes papers relating to the French expedition of 1708.)

22. *Manuscripts of the House of Lords, 1710–1712.*
    New series, vol. ix, 1949 (H.L. 1947–8, 92).
    (Includes records of the enquiry into the defeat at Almanza and the Gertruydenberg Conference papers.)

23. *Manuscripts of the House of Lords, 1712–1714.*
    New series, vol. x, 1953 (H.L. 35).
    (Includes papers connected with the French and Spanish Commercial Treaties, the Demolition of Dunkirk, and the Jacobites. The early rolls of Standing Orders of the House are also printed.)

24. *Manuscripts of the House of Lords. Addenda, 1514–1714.*
    New series, vol. xi, 1962 (H.L. 1961–2, 123).
    (Includes records of the trials of Mary Queen of Scots, Archbishop Laud, and King Charles I; many Elizabethan and Jacobean Bills; and short Commons Journals or Diaries for periods in 1572, 1610 and 1625.)

FORTHCOMING. *Manuscripts of the House of Lords, 1714–1718.*

(*b*) HOUSE OF LORDS RECORD OFFICE MEMORANDA[1]

   1. *List of Main Classes of Records* (revised edition, 1969).

  11. *The Braye Manuscripts sold at Messrs. Christie, 23rd June 1954* (1954).

  13. *The Journals, Minutes and Committee Books of the House of Lords* (revised edition, 1957).

  16. *The Private Bill Records of the House of Lords* (1957).

  18. *Guide to the Parliament Office Papers* (1958).

  20. *Guide to the House of Lords Papers and Petitions* (1959).

  22. *Clerks in the Parliament Office, 1600–1900* (1960).

  26. *Hand List of Paintings, Drawings and Engravings, etc., of the House of Lords and House of Commons, 1523–1900* (1962).

  29. *Catalogue of the Records of Parliament displayed at the Opening of the Victoria Tower Repository by the Right Honourable the Viscount Hailsham, 3rd July, 1963* (1963).

  31. *Leaders and Whips in the House of Lords, 1783–1964* (1964).

  33. *Further Materials from an Unpublished Manuscript of the Lords Journals for Sessions 1559 and 1597 to 1598* (1965).

  35. *The Political Papers of Herbert, 1st Viscount Samuel* (1966).

  37. *The Financial Administration and Records of the Parliament Office, 1824 to 1868* (1967).

  39. *A List of Representative Peers for Scotland, 1707 to 1963, and for Ireland, 1800 to 1961* (1968).

  41. *The Personal and Literary Papers of Herbert, 1st. Viscount Samuel* (1969).

  43. *The Letters and Diaries of Speaker Brand* (1970).

---

[1] Memoranda not listed below are either annual Reports of the office, or Memoranda no longer available.

(*c*) OTHER PUBLICATIONS RELATING TO THE RECORDS

Historic Parliamentary Documents in the Palace of Westminster. Booklet with 21 illustrations (1960).

Historic Parliamentary Documents: Reproductions. No. 1, Tudor Royal Signatures (Postcard); No. 2, Commons Journal of 1621 (Postcard); No. 3, Commons Journal of 1642 (Postcard); No. 4, Commons Journal of 1653 (Postcard); No. 5, Lovelace Petition of 1642 (Postcard); No. 6, Banbury Patent with Charles I portrait (Postcard), 1627; No. 7, Death Warrant of Charles I, 1649 (Leaflet).

Historic Parliamentary Documents: Facsimile Reproductions. No. 1, The Petition of Right, 1628 (1 sheet); No. 2, The Declaration of Rights, 1689 (8 folded leaves, sewn).

Catalogue of the Exhibition Held in The Queen's Robing Room at the Houses of Parliament to Commemorate the Seventh Centenary of the Parliament of Simon de Montfort, 20th January 1265 (Booklet, iv + 20 pages).

The Seventh Centenary of Simon de Montfort's Parliament, 1265–1965: An Account of the Commemorative Ceremonies and an Historical Narrative ix + 92 pages, illustrated (1965).

M. Bond, *Acts of Parliament: Some notes on the Original Acts Preserved at the House of Lords, their Use and Interpretation* (1958). The British Records Association, Charterhouse, London EC1.

M. Bond, *The Records of Parliament: A Guide for Genealogists and Local Historians.* An introductory guide, explaining relevant Parliamentary procedure and available finding aids (1964). Messrs. Phillimore & Co. Ltd., Shopwyke Hall, Chichester, Sussex.

(*d*) PUBLICATIONS RELATING TO THE LIBRARIES OF THE TWO HOUSES

C. Dobson, *The Library of the House of Lords, A Short History*, privately printed (1960).

E. Gosse, *Catalogue of the Library of the House of Lords* (1908).

The Library of the House of Commons, a handbook, issued under the authority of the Speaker (1970).

See also the publications issued by H.M.S.O. in the series 'House of Commons Library Documents', referred to *passim*, below.

PART
ONE

RECORDS OF
THE HOUSE OF LORDS

RECORDS OF THE HOUSE OF LORDS

LIST OF CLASSES

Records of Proceedings in the House of Lords   *page*
    Original Journals, 1510–date   28
    Printed Journals, 1510–date   31
    Indexes to Journals, 1510–date   32
    Calendars of Journals, 1510–1826   32
    Minutes of Proceedings (MS. Minutes), 1610–date   33
    Printed Minutes of Proceedings, 1825–date   33
    Minutes of Proceedings (MS. Papers), 1610–44   34
    Draft Journals, 1621–90   34
    The Parliamentary History of England, 1066–1803   37
    Parliamentary Debates, 1803 date   38
    Television, Sound Broadcasting and Photographic Records, 1968   39

Records of Proceedings in Committees of the House of Lords
    Committee Appointment Books, 1610–1861   42
    Minute Books (Committee of the Whole House), 1828–55   42
    Minutes of Committees for Petitions, 1628–95   43
    Committee for Privileges Minute Books, 1660–1892   43
    Committee Minute Books, 1661–1836   43
    Committee Minute Books (Select and Estate Bills Committees), 1837–date   44
    Committee Minute Books (Standing Orders Committees), 1837–58   44
    Committee Minute Books (Committees of Selection and on Opposed Bills), 1837–58   44
    Committee Minute Books (Unopposed Private Bills and Appeal Committees), 1837–date   44
    Committee Minute Books (Opposed Private Bill Committees), 1859–date   45
    Committee Minute Books (Standing Orders Committees), 1859–date   45
    Committee Minute Books (Special Orders Committees), 1925–date   45
    Committee Minute Books (India and Burma Orders Committees), 1935–47   45
    Committee Minute Book Indexes, [1792]–1846   46

Evidence
    Manuscript Evidence, 1771–1834   47
    Evidence (Main Papers), 1835–1922   53
    Books of Evidence, 1835–date   53

Committee Papers, 1669–date   54

Records of Proceedings in Joint Committees of both Houses
    Minute Book, 1679–95   57
    Other records, 1864–date   57
Records of Proceedings in Conferences between the Houses
    Reports, 1610–1860   58
    Ancillary Conference Papers, 1610–78   58
Records of Bills, Acts and Measures
  Public Bill Records, H.L.
    Paper Bills, 1558–1849   65
    Engrossed Bills, 1547–1849   65
    Printed Bills, 1705–date   66
    Breviates, 1593–1849   67
    Amendments, 1542–date   67
    Petitions and 'Cases', 1572–date   67
    Miscellaneous Papers, 1584–1800   68
  Hybrid Bill Records, H.L.   69
  Private Bill Records, H.L.
    Affidavits, 1698–date   83
    Amendment Sheets, 1584–date   83
    Bill Books, 1910–35   83
    Bill Papers (Miscellaneous), 1819–date   84
    Paper Bills, 1584–1849   84
    Printed Bills, 1705–date   84
    Engrossed Bills, 1576–1849   84
    Book of Receipts, 1831–94   85
    Books of Reference, 1794–date   85
    Breviates, 1606–1849   85
    Certificates, Principal Secretary of State's, 1798–1911   85
    Certificates, Sacramental, 1621–1798   85
    Committee Office Amendment Book, 1905–20   85
    Committee Office Notice Books, 1898–1940   86
    Committee Office Petition Books, 1914–date   86
    Consents Lists, 1794–date   86
    Court Proceedings (Divorce), 1798–1922   86
    Declarations, 1794–date   86
    Demolition Statements, 1853–date   86
    Estimates of Expense, 1794–date   87
    Estimates of Time, 1814–date   87
    Examiners' Certificates, 1856–date   87
    Examiners' Evidence, 1859–date   87
    Examiners' Special Reports, 1856–date   88
    Judges' Reports, 1706–date   88
    Memorials, 1836–date   88
    Orders of Service, 1669–1922   88
    Orders of the House, 1621–date   88
    Parliamentary Agents (Appearance Registers), 1890–date   89
    Personal Bills, 1850–96   89
    Petitions, 1572–date   89

Plans, 1794–date 89
Private Bill Amendment Book, 1905–20 90
Public Notices, 1795–date 90
Registers of Petitions on Bills, 1914–date 90
Reports (Departmental) on Bills, 1841–date 90
Sections, 1795–date 90
Special Order Book, 1925–36 91
Special Orders, 1927–48 91
Subscription Contracts, 1794–1858 91
Subscription Lists, 1794–1858 91
Taxing Journals, 1847–1952 91
Trustees Acceptance Books, 1797–1842 92
Unopposed Committee Minutes, 1899–1927 92
Witness Books, 1641–1862 92

Acts of Parliament

Original Acts, 1497–1850 95
Printed Original Acts, 1849–date 96
Lists and Calendars of Acts, 1608–date 96
Church Assembly and General Synod Measure Records, 1920–date 104

Judicial Records, H.L.

Original Jurisdiction

Committee Order Books, 1640–63 108
Originating Petitions, 1621–93 108
Answers to Petitions, 1621–93 108
Ancillary Papers, 1621–66 109

Impeachments

Articles of Impeachment, 1621–1806 110
Answers of the Accused, 1621–1806 110
Petitions and Orders, 1621–1806 110
Evidential Documents, 1617–1795 110
Judgments, 1621–1806 111

Trials of Peers

Petitions, 1641–1776 112
Commissions Appointing the Lord High Steward, 1678–1935 112
Recognisances of Witnesses, 1678–1935 112
Orders of the House, 1641–1935 112
Miscellaneous Petitions and Orders, 1641–1935 113
Writs of Certiorari, 1678–1935 113
Indictments and Inquisitions, 1678–1935 113

Appeal Cases

Proceedings of Appeal Committees, 1849–date 116
Proceedings of Appellate Committees, 1948–date 116
Petitions, 1621–date 117
Respondents' Answers, 1624–date 117
Printed Cases, 1702–date 117
Ancillary Records, 1624–date 118
Registers of Judgments, 1839–date 119

Cases in Error

Originating Petitions, 1621–4   121
Writs of Error, 1621–1857   121
Transcripts of Record, 1621–1860   122
Transcripts of Proceedings, 1624–1852   122
Assignments of Errors, 1642–1854   122
Joinders in Error, 1670–1852   122
Printed Cases, 1702–1899   123
Ancillary Records, 1621–1877   123

Cases of Privilege

Committee for Privileges Minute Books, 1661–1885   125
Petitions, 1601–date   125
Registers of Protections, 1690–97   125
Ancillary Privilege Papers, 1610–date   125

Sessional Papers, H.L.

Returns, 1588–date   127
Command Papers, 1625–date   128
Act Papers, 1717–date   128
Papers Laid Pursuant to Subsidiary Legislation   130
List of Sessional Papers, 1641–1800   135
Sessional Papers, 1801–date   159

Peerage Records

Records of Peerage Claims

Minute Entry Registers, 1607–date   161
Manuscript Evidence Volumes, 1791–date   161
Manuscript Speeches, 1826–1908   162
Baronies by Writ Proceedings, 1836–1912   162
Printed Evidence, 1794–1858   162
Petitions of Claim, 1597–date   162
Attorney-General's Reports, 1718–date   163
Printed Cases (separate prints), 1734–date   163
Printed Cases (bound), 1720–1929   163
Peers' Pedigrees, 1767–1802   163
Peers' Pedigrees (Uncertified), *c.* 1770–84   164
Pedigree Proofs, 1767–1802   164
Original Petitions, Reports and Orders, 1663–date   164
Evidential Papers, 1708–date   164
Other Peerage Papers, 1628–date   164

Records concerning Representative Peers for Scotland

Evidence, 1850–77   166
The Long Roll, 1708   166
Certificates of Election, 1707–1963   166
Minutes of Proceedings at Elections, 1761–1963   166
Petitions concerning Elections, 1708–1880   166
Petitions of Claim to Vote, 1723–1877   166
Case, 1877   167
Additional Papers, 1828–77   167

Records concerning Representative Peers for Ireland
    Register of Claims, 1800–1916   168
    Evidence, 1812–1906   168
    Election Returns, 1801–1919   168
    Petitions of Claim, 1802–date   168
    Cases, 1826–1905   168
    Statements of Proof, 1822–41   169
    Additional Papers, 1802–1964   169
Small Classes, H.L.
    Accession Declarations, 1936, 1952   170
    Clerk of the Parliaments Rolls, 1825–date   170
    Garter's Rolls, 1621–1964   170
    Books of Orders and Ordinances, 1640–95   171
    Petitions, 1531–date   172
    Procedure of the House of Lords, 1850–1935   173
    Original Protest Books, 1831–date   174
    Protest Register, 1641–1779   174
    Proxy Books, 1625–1864   175
    Proxy Deeds, 1790–1864   175
    Royal Commissions (Letters Patent), 1542–date   175
    Royal Assent by Notification (Letters Patent), 1967–date   176
    Standing Orders, 1621–date   177
    Standing Orders (Companions), 1862–date   178
    Subsidies of the Clergy, 1543–1628   178
    Test Rolls, 1675–date   179
    Votes of Thanks, 1858–1919   179
    Writs of Summons, 1559–date   179
Parliament Office Papers
    Grants of Office, 1621–1856   184
    House of Lords Offices Committees (Office Papers), 1763–1902   184
    Establishment Papers, 1715–1902   184
    Fee and Account Records, 1619–1928   185
    General Parliament Office Administrative Papers, 1610–1934   186
    Parliament Office Book of Returns, 1813–49   186
    Officers' Personal Papers, 1583–1902   186
    Books of Ceremonial, 1950–date   187
    Deposited Papers (Library), 1896–date   187
    House of Lords Reform Papers, 1869–1952   187
    Journal Committee Papers, 1767–1863   187
    Journal Office Papers, 1825–date   188

Judicial Office Papers Relating to Appeals, Peerage Claims, etc.
1657–date   188

Library Papers, 1834–64   189

Lord Great Chamberlain Papers, 1804–date   189

Palace of Westminster (Fabric Papers), 1835–date   190

Palace of Westminster, Second World War Records, 1939–57   190

Palace of Westminster War Memorial Volumes, H.L., 1914–45   191

Parliament Rolls, 1610, 1844, 1856   191

Precedent and Procedural Papers, 1620–date   191

Private Bill and Committee Office Papers, 1767–date   192

Public Bill Office Papers, 1811–1921   192

Papers relating to Records, H.L. and Record Office, 1827–date   193

Refreshment Department Papers, 1905–date   193

Stray Papers, 1704–1934   193

Unpresented Papers, 1702–1911   194

Whips, 1909–date   194

Black Rod's Department Records   195

Use. All records of H.L. as listed above are available for inspection by the public unless restrictions are indicated in the descriptions of individual classes below.

THE HOUSE OF LORDS

Parliament originated in the Councils summoned by English kings in the 11th, 12th and 13th c. Assemblies of this kind, attended by varying numbers of archbishops and bishops, abbots, earls, barons, other lay magnates and royal ministers, met to give the King counsel on a wide variety of matters, and, in exceptional circumstances, to make special financial grants to him. By 1236 some of these councils were being called 'parliaments'. During the 13th c. representatives of the 'communities of the realm' from counties, cities and boroughs, were summoned with increasing frequency to assist, their attendance in Parliament becoming unvarying after 1327. By the end of the 14th c. they formed a separate house, the House of Commons, with its own Speaker and Clerk.

The lords similarly acquired identity as a separate House of Parliament, being usually known either as *domini* (*spirituales et temporales*) or as *domus superior* until, in the 16th c., the term 'House of Lords' became normal.

From the earliest times lords were summoned to Parliament by Writs of Summons issued out of Chancery. By 1341 it had become customary to summon certain lords consistently, Parliament by Parliament, and by 1377 the lists of spiritual and temporal lords had become almost unchanging, although that of temporal lords remained liable to modification, and royal discretion in the issuing of Writs of Summons was not finally declared unlawful until 1626. There are five degrees of peerage, the most ancient being those of Earl and Baron, the more recent of Duke (first creation, 1337), Marquess (first creation, 1385) and Viscount (first creation, 1440). In addition, from 1302 the Prince of Wales was summoned.

The creation of new peerages of all degrees except that of baron was by charter under the great seal[1]. 'Baron' at first simply meant 'peer', it denoted a status and not a rank. Therefore barons were not originally created by charter or letters patent, but simply received a Writ of Summons. In 1387, however, a barony was for the first time created by letters patent. Thereafter both methods of creation were employed for baronies until the early 17th c., when creation by Writ of Summons died out. Since 1482 sons have sometimes been called to sit in Parliament in the baronies of their fathers during the lifetimes of their fathers (a list of such summonses for 1482–1896 is printed in Appendix G, *The Complete Peerage*, vol. i (1910)). The instruments of summons are then known as Writs in Acceleration.

By the mid-15th c. the membership of the group of lords in Parliament is typified by those summoned for the 1453–4 session: 2 archbishops, 18 bishops, 27 abbots and priors, 5 dukes, 12 earls, 3 viscounts and 44 barons, 111 in all; the number summoned then declined, the total in 1485 being 78 and in 1509, 84.[2] The actual attendances in Parliament were often far fewer.[3]

After the suppression of the monasteries abbots and priors no longer sat. In 1640 the remaining Lords Spiritual were excluded from Parliament, and in 1649 the House itself, by Ordinance of the Commons, ceased to exist. An upper house again met in 1658 and 1659 under the title of the 'Other House'. The Convention Parliament of two Houses sat in 1660 without bishops, but the Parliament of 1661, by the Clergy Act, 13 Cha. II, sess. 1, c. 2, restored bishops to the House of Lords.

From 1707 until 1963 there were sixteen Representative Peers for Scotland in the House; since 1963 all holders of peerages in Scotland have had the right to be admitted to the House of Lords.[4] Similarly there were 28 Representative Peers for Ireland elected for life from the Union in 1800 until 1922, since when no further Irish peers have been elected. Four bishops also served in rotation for Ireland from 1800 until the disestablishment of the Irish Church in 1869.[5]

Until 1847, in addition to the Irish bishops, all the English and Welsh diocesan bishops and archbishops sat in the Lords. As a result of the Bishopric of Manchester Act, 1847, 10 & 11 Vict., c. 108, and later Acts, subsequent creations of dioceses have not led to an increase in the number of Lords Spiritual. The Archbishops of Canterbury and York, the Bishops of London, Durham and Winchester, and 21 other diocesan bishops, according to the seniority of their appointment to diocesan sees, have sat. The Welsh bishops ceased to sit as a result of the Welsh Church Act, 1914, 4 & 5 Geo. V, c. 91.

In 1856 a peerage for life was conferred on Sir James Parke in order to strengthen the judicial membership of the House; the House resolved that such a

---

[1] The post-1516 documents were enrolled on the Patent Rolls, but retained diplomatic features of the charter until 1927.

[2] An analysis of membership of the House at varying dates to 1963 is provided by S. Gordon in *Our Parliament*, 6th ed. (1964), app. i.

[3] Cf. J. S. Roskell, 'The Problem of the Attendance of the Lords in Medieval Parliaments', *Bulletin of the Institute of Historical Research*, vol. xxix (1956), pp. 153–204.

[4] *See* below, p. 165.

[5] *See* below, p. 167.

life peerage did not entitle the grantee to sit and vote in Parliament. The Appellate Jurisdiction Act, 1876, 39 & 40 Vict., c. 59, however, enabled the Sovereign to create four lords of appeal in ordinary, enjoying the rank of baron for life. Until 1887 their right of sitting and voting only continued so long as they exercised their office; since 1887 this right has lasted for life. The number of lords of appeal was increased to 6 in 1913, 7 in 1929, 9 in 1947 and 11 in 1968. The Life Peerage Act, 1958, 6 & 7 Eliz. II, c. 21, has enabled the Sovereign to grant by Letters Patent baronies for life, without limit of number, to persons of either sex, membership of the House having been hitherto restricted to men. Subsequently, the Peerage Act, 1963, c. 48, gave women holders of hereditary peerages of England, Scotland, Great Britain and the United Kingdom, the same right to receive writs as men.

The Peerage Act, 1963, also enabled disclaimers to be made for life of hereditary peerages. Instruments of Disclaimer are delivered by the peers to the L. Chancellor; the disclaimers are announced to both Houses and are recorded in the Journals.

Originally judges and others who were members of the Council might have places in attendance upon the King in Parliament, but in the course of the 15th c. these members 'gradually fall into a position of subordination to the peers.'[1] Judges of King's Bench and Common Pleas, barons of the Exchequer, the Master of the Rolls, the Attorney General, the Solicitor General and the King's Serjeants were summoned until 1873, though with somewhat varying regularity. Since then all the judges of the High Court of Justice and of the Court of Appeal have been summoned, together with the Attorney General and the Solicitor General, and 'such of the Privy Council as are called by Writ from the Crown to attend'. The Writs issued to them are 'Writs of Assistance'. Judges are now summoned by special order when their advice is required. The last attendance of the judges (except at State Openings) was in 1935. Masters in Chancery attended on the House, until the abolition of their office under the Court of Chancery Act, 1852, 15 & 16 Vict., c. 80, in order to carry messages and Bills from the Lords to the Commons; they were not summoned by Writ and were not legal assistants of the House, although they sat with the assistants upon the woolsacks in the House.

MEMBERS OF THE HOUSE OF LORDS[2]

(a) *Lists of Peerage Creations*

1. *To 1483.* Full transcripts of charters and Letters Patent of creation and of related documents, from Stephen to Edward IV, are printed in *Reports touching the Dignity of a Peer of the Realm*, H.L., 222 (1829).

2. *1485–1660.* Notes of creations with reference to Patent Rolls, etc., are given in *47th Report of the Deputy Keeper of Public Records* (1886), app.

[1] E. R. Adair and F. M. Greir Evans, 'Writs of Assistance, 1558–1700', *English Historical Review*, vol. 36 (1921), pp. 356–72.

[2] For references to peers and peerage matters before 1540, *see* J. Enoch Powell and K. Wallis, *The House of Lords in the Middle Ages* (1968).

3. *1702–83*. Lists are given of Peerage Creations in A. S. Turberville, *The House of Lords in the XVIIIth Century* (1927), app. A.

4. *1784–1837*. A similar list appears in Turberville, *The House of Lords in the Age of Reform* (1958), app. iii.

5. *1830–86*. List of Peerage Creations (typescript) by J. C. Sainty, available in H.L.R.O. Search Room.

6. *1880–1919*. *The Return of all Peerages created during the tenure of each Government from the year 1880 down to 31st December 1919*, H.L. 2 (1920), gives the names of each peer created during each administration with details of some of the peerages. Dates of creation within each administration are *not* given.

7. *1901–38*. Vol. xiii of G.E.C[okayne], *The Complete Peerage* (1940) (*see* below) gives details of creations chronologically.

See also BIBLIOGRAPHY for PEERAGE RECORDS, p. 161.

(b) *Lists of Membership of the House* (*sessional, annual, etc.*)

1. For mediaeval membership, see references in (a) above.

2. Garter's Rolls, 1621, 1628, 1660–1964, *see* p. 170 below.

3. Clerk of the Parliaments Rolls, 1825 to date, *see* p. 170 below.

4. Unofficial contemporary reference books, e.g. E. (later J.) Chamberlayne, *Angliae Notitia* (1669–1707), continued as *Magnae Britanniae Notitia* (1708–55); *The Court and City Register* (1742–1814); Vacher, *Parliamentary Companion* (1831 to date); Dod, *Parliamentary Companion* (1832 to date); J. Whitaker, *Almanack* (1869 to date).

(c) *Biographies of Peers*

A. Collins, *The Peerage of England* (1709, etc., ed. of 1812, ed. E. Brydges, 9 vols.) also provides details of families of peers.

G. E. C[okayne], *The Complete Peerage*, 8 vols. (1887–98); new ed., rev. by V. Gibbs, H. A. Doubleday *et al.*, 13 vols. (1910–59).

J. B. Burke *et al.*, *A Genealogical and Heraldic Dictionary of the Peerage and Baronetage of the British Empire* (1826, etc.). The earliest eds. are entitled *A General and Heraldic Dictionary*. Published at irregular intervals 1826–47, then annually to date.

J. Debrett, *The Peerage of England, Scotland and Ireland* (1802, etc.). Published almost annually to date.

LISTS OF PARLIAMENTS 1242 TO DATE

1. A 'List of Parliaments, 1258–1832' is printed as app. i of *Interim Report of the Committee on House of Commons Personnel and Politics 1264–1832*, Cmd. 4130 (1932). The list includes dates of writs, places and dates for which summoned, outside dates of elections, dates of sessions of the Commons with dates of dismissal, and statistics of names of M.P.s included in the *Official Return* (*see* p. 202 below) and of those since recovered.

2. A List of 'English and British Parliaments and related Assemblies to 1832' [from 1242] is printed in *Handbook of British Chronology*, ed. F. M. Powicke and E. B. Fryde, 2nd ed. (1961), pp. 492–544. Details are provided of dates and place of assembly, dates of summons and of initial prorogations, designation of the assembly in official records (to 1377), dates of sessional prorogations (from 1381) and terminating dates.

3. A List of 'Sovereigns, Prime Ministers and Parliaments since 1715' is app. 5 to S. Gordon, *Our Parliament*, 6th ed. (1964). It provides dates of assembly and dissolution. Similar information for 1900–66 is included in D. Butler and J. Freeman, *British Political Facts 1900–1968*, 2nd ed. (1969), pp. 124–5, together with statistics of business in the Commons.

GENERAL BIBLIOGRAPHY

The works listed here relate to the general history of Parliament as a whole or of the House of Lords. For similar works concerning the House of Commons, see pp. 203–4.

E. Allyn, *Lords v. Commons, 1830–1930* (1931).

P. A. Bromhead, *Private Members' Bills in the British Parliament* (1956).

P. A. Bromhead, *The House of Lords and Contemporary Politics, 1911–1957* (1958).

J. G. Edwards, *Historians and the Medieval English Parliament* (1960).

J. G. Edwards, '"Justice" in Early English Parliaments', *Bulletin of the Institute of Historical Research*, vol. xxvii (1954), 35–53.

C. H. Firth, *The House of Lords during the Civil War* (1910).

S. Gordon, *Our Parliament* (6th ed., 1964).

W. Holdsworth, 'The House of Lords, 1689–1783', *Law Quarterly Review*, vol. xlv (1929), pp. 307, 432.

W. Holdsworth, *A History of English Law*, vol. i (7th ed., 1956), vols. iv, v (3rd ed., 1956).

C. Ilbert and C. Carr, *Parliament, its History, Constitution and Practice* (3rd ed., 1956).

Ivor Jennings, *The British Constitution* (4th ed., 1961).

S. E. Lehmberg, *The Reformation Parliament* (1970).

K. Mackenzie, *The English Parliament* (5th ed., 1963).

A. Marongiu, *Medieval Parliaments: a comparative study* (1968).

Erskine May, *The Law, Privileges, Proceedings and Usages of Parliament* (17th ed,. 1964).

C. H. McIlwain, *The High Court of Parliament and its Supremacy* (1910).

E. Miller, *The Origins of Parliament* (Historical Association pamphlet, 1960).

H. Miller, 'The Early Tudor Peerage, 1485–1547', *Bulletin of the Institute of Historical Research*, vol. xxiv (1951), p. 88.

C. H. Parry, *The Parliaments and Councils of England . . . to 1688* (1839).

L. O. Pike, *A Constitutional History of the House of Lords* (1894).

A. F. Pollard, *The Evolution of Parliament* (2nd ed., 1934).

J. E. Powell and K. Wallis, *The House of Lords in the Middle Ages* (1968).

H. G. Richardson, 'The Origins of Parliament', *Transactions of the Royal Historical Society*, 4th ser., vol. xi (1928), pp. 137–83.

H. G. Richardson and G. O. Sayles, 'The Early Records of the English Parliaments', *Bulletin of the Institute of Historical Research*, vol. v (1928), pp. 129–154, vol. vi (1929), pp. 71–88, 129–155.

H. G. Richardson and G. O. Sayles, 'The Parliaments of Edward III', *Bulletin of the Institute of Historical Research*, vol. viii (1930–1), pp. 65–82, vol. ix (1931–2), pp. 1–18.

J. Roskell, 'The Problem of the Attendance of the Lords in Medieval Parliaments', *Bulletin of the Institute of Historical Research*, vol. xxix (1956), pp. 153–204.

J. C. Russell, 'Early Parliamentary Organization', *American Historical Review*, vol. xliii (1937), pp. 1–21.

M. P. Schoenfeld, *The Restored House of Lords* (1967).

G. Templeman, 'The History of Parliament to 1400 in the light of modern Research', *University of Birmingham Historical Journal*, vol. i, (1948), pp. 202–31.

A. Todd, *On Parliamentary Government in England*, 2 vols. (2nd ed., 1887–9).

R. F. Treharne, 'The Nature of Parliament in the Reign of Henry III', *English Historical Review*, vol. lxxiv (1959), pp. 590–610.

A. S. Turberville, *The House of Lords in the reign of William III* (1913).

A. S. Turberville, *The House of Lords in the Eighteenth Century* (1927).

A. S. Turberville, *The House of Lords in the Age of Reform, 1784–1837* (ed. R. J. White, 1958).

A. S. Turberville, 'The House of Lords under Charles II', *English Historical Review*, vol. xliv (1929), pp. 400–417, vol. xlv (1930), pp. 58–77.

C. C. Weston, *English Constitutional Theory and the House of Lords, 1556–1832* (1965).

N. Wilding and P. Laundy, *An Encyclopaedia of Parliament* 3rd. ed. (1968).

B. Wilkinson, *Constitutional History of Medieval England, 1216–1399* (1958).

B. Wilkinson, *Constitutional History of England in the Fifteenth Century, 1399–1485* (1964).

A. Wright and P. Smith, *Parliament Past and Present* (n.d.).

RECORDS OF PROCEEDINGS IN THE HOUSE OF LORDS

During the middle ages the only substantial record of proceedings in Parliament appears in the Petitions presented to Parliament and on the Parliament Rolls. The latter may record the opening of a session, the appointment of Receivers of Petitions, the presentation of the Speaker of the Commons, etc., that is, the essential framework of each session, together with full texts of certain petitions, with the responses given to them. There is no attempt to provide in the Parliament Rolls any journal of daily sittings. Copies of Journals of 1449 and of 1461 show, however, that in the 15th c. a separate record of the proceedings of the upper house was already being kept. The 1449 and1461 manuscripts each contain a list of lords present; to this the 1449 record adds a summary of speeches on a specific issue, and the 1461 manuscript some brief particulars of business transacted.

The surviving series of H.L. Journals at Westminster start in 1510 and consist of daily sheets which record the names of lords present and list the Bills read or other business done, normally without any comment or detail. The preparation of these Journal sheets was undertaken by the Clerk of the Parliaments as part of his domestic office routine. In 1597, however, the House took cognizance of the matter, ordering that the Clerk's Journal should be viewed and perused by a committee of lords, assisted by Garter King of Arms. In the early 17th c. this committee became a sub-committee of the Committee for Privileges, and in 1678 it was instructed every session to complete the examination of that session's Journal Book (Standing Order 73).[1] Many volumes of the 17th c. Journals bear the signatures of the peers who had thus inspected the entries. Similar sub-committees continued to meet in the 18th c., dealing for instance in 1767 with the printing both of the Rolls of Parliament and of the Journals, but although such a committee is still appointed each session it has not met for about a century. Immediate responsibility for compiling the Journal has continued to rest with the Clerk of the Parliaments, who, since 1610, has sworn, on appointment, to make 'true entries and Records of the things done' in the House. During the period of sinecure Clerks (1716–1855) the Journals came under the care of the Clerk Assistant. He from 1718 was helped by a Clerk of the Journals, with whom, during the subsequent two centuries, the initial responsibility for the compilation of the Journal has rested.

Behind the final Journal lies a varying number of preliminary records. These may be classified as Minutes or notes of proceedings made at the time of sitting or immediately after, either roughly in note form, or in a more extended and permanent form; and Draft Journals, in which the Minutes may be rearranged, with additions or omissions, in order to conform to established Journal precedent. The Minutes and Draft Journals may yield additional information not to be found in the final Journal. By the end of the 18th c., however, the Minutes acquired much of the formality of the Journal and seldom provide additional

[1] For the text of Standing Orders 1621–1712, see Calendar, 1712–1714, pp. 1–27.

information. In the course of the 19th c., owing to the congestion of Parliamentary business, an increasing proportion of what is recorded in the Minutes and Journals did not actually happen in the House, but consists of 'book entries'. Most transactions relating to Papers, and many of those in Judicial and Private Business, are of this kind; and at present these 'book entries' are much greater in number, (though not in importance), than those recording an actual event in the House.

The general principle is that what is *done* is recorded in the Minutes; what is *said* appears in Hansard. But Hansard also contains the text of amendments made or spoken to, and also Questions forWritten Answer. Forthcoming business of all kinds, and also particulars of Committees and Bills in Progress, are circulated with the Minutes.

The Lords Journal is a record to which all persons have right of access, and certified extracts from it are admitted as evidence. By the Evidence Act, 1845, 8 & 9 Vict., c. 113, copies of the officially printed *Journals* (*see* below) may be admitted as evidence in England and Wales without certification.

BIBLIOGRAPHY

M. F. Bond, ed., *The Manuscripts of the House of Lords*, vol. xi (N.S., 1962), pp. xiii–xvi.

H. S. Cobb, comp., *The Journals, Minutes and Committee Books of the House of Lords*, House of Lords Record Office Memorandum no. 13 (rev. ed., 1957).

E. J. Davis, 'An Unpublished Manuscript of the Lords' Journals, April and May, 1559', *English Historical Review*, vol. xxviii (1913), pp. 531–42.

Sir Simonds D'Ewes, *The Journals of all the Parliaments during the reign of Queen Elizabeth . . .* (1682, 1693).

W. H. Dunham, *The Fane Fragment of the 1461 Lords' Journal* (1935).

E. R. Foster, ed., *Proceedings in Parliament, 1610*, vol. i (1966).

E. R. Foster, 'Procedure in the House of Lords During the Early Stuart Period', *Journal of British Studies*, vol. v (1966), pp. 56–73.

M. A. R. Graves, 'The Two Lords' Journals of 1542', *Bulletin of the Institute of Historical Research*, vol. xliii (1970), pp. 182–9.

A. R. Myers, 'A Parliamentary Debate of the Mid-Fifteenth Century' [1449], *Bulletin of the John Rylands Library*, vol. xxii (1938), pp. 388–404.

[Sir H. N. Nicolas], 'Minutes of Proceedings of the House of Lords in the 3rd and 27th Henry VIII, supplying a Chasm in the First Volume of the Printed Journals', *Report on the Barony of L'Isle Peerage Claim* (1829), app. vi.

L. O. Pike, *Constitutional History of the House of Lords* (1894).

A. F. Pollard, 'The Authenticity of the "Lords Journals" in the Sixteenth Century', *Transactions of the Royal Historical Society*, Third Series, vol. viii (1914), pp. 17–39.

J. C. Sainty, ed., *Further Materials from an Unpublished Manuscript of the Lords Journals for Sessions 1559 and 1597 to 1598*, House of Lords Record Office Memorandum no. 33 (1965).

R. Virgoe, 'A New Fragment of the Lords' Journal of 1461', *Bulletin of the Institute of Historical Research*, vol. xxxii (1959), pp. 83–7.

[J. A. Woods, ed.] *A Bibliography of Parliamentary Debates of Great Britain*,
House of Commons Library Document no. 2 (1956); and works there
cited on 'Debates'.

See also BIBLIOGRAPHIES below concerning Bill Procedure, H.L., and Proceedings,
H.C.

Original Journals

1510 to date   395 vols.

See plate 1

Format. The earlier Journals, as they exist today, are the result of an Order of
the House in 1717 for 'such of the Journals of this House as necessarily require it
to be new bound, and Indexes to be made to all the Journals to which there are
none already'. By 1717, however, a number of Journals from between 1514
and 1598 had been lost, having disappeared before 1638. The sequence of some
32 vols, surviving in 1717, disparate in size and character and covering the period
1510 to 1614, were as a result of the Order bound into 8 vols, and provided with
indexes and additional marginal heads. The Journals from 1621 to 1640 had been
engrossed in vols. with parchment leaves as a result of the Order of the House in
1621, and were not rebound in 1717. The Journals from November 1640 onwards
had been written in paper vols.[1] and certain of these were rebound in 1717.

The Journal continued as a manuscript, in paper vols., until 1830. From that
date the Journals have been printed in the course of the session, so that the complete sessional vol. with index can be delivered to the House during the following
session. Since 1830 a special record copy of the Journal printed on blue paper
and bound in vellum has been deposited in the Victoria Tower.

Language. The early Journal entries are in Latin. As the memoranda of proceedings increased in quantity during the 16th c., new matter was entered in
English. The titles of Bills sent up from the Commons were entered in English
after 1542. Royal Commissions for Prorogation and Dissolution were entered *in
extenso* in Latin, the remainder of the entries of other Commissions being chiefly
in English. The record of the appointment of Joint Committees with the
Commons, the reports of such committees, and Messages from the Commons,
were also in English. From the beginning of the 17th c. all the proceedings are
in English, with the exception of the heading to each day's entry and the Lists
of Peers (both of which are still entered in Latin); the stages of Bills and the daily
adjournment (in Latin until 1850); and certain Royal Commissions and Letters
Patent (until 1733). The entries concerning Receivers and Triers of Petitions
were in Norman-French until they ceased in 1886.

Contents

Presents. From 1514 onwards the daily entries of business invariably commence
with the names of those lords present, except during the years 1628–9 and
1640–3.

---

[1] These Journals bear the signatures of the sub-committee members who inspected and
approved them. They were probably intended to be the Clerk's final draft before an engrossment (which he failed to make). He may have considered that his roughly written Journal
authenticated by the Lords would prove a more authoritative record than a subsequent fair-
copy engrossment.

Opening of Parliament. At the Opening of a new session (or of a new Parliament) the list of names is accompanied by some or all of the following entries, normally spread over several days' sittings, and arranged in varying order: List of Proxies (to 1628); Opening by Commission, with terms of the Letters Patent *in extenso*; Accession Declaration, and Declaration against transubstantiation until 1910, by the new Sovereign, if not already made at the Coronation (1837 onwards, but not entered *in extenso* until 1953); Order to the Commons to choose a Speaker; Return of Representative Peers for Scotland (from 1707 to 1960); List of lords who take the Oath or affirm; Entries of lords sitting for the first time; Writs of Summons and Letters Patent *in extenso* (the latter since 1850) of newly created and of promoted lords first introduced; Presentation of the Speaker chosen by the Commons and Approval of him by the Sovereign in person or by Royal Commission; Speech by the Chancellor or the Treasurer (in the 16th–17th c.), normally *in extenso*, although on occasion not entered; the King's speech *in extenso*; record of laying of Garter's Roll of Temporal Lords (to 1965); title of a Bill, now invariably the Select Vestries Bill, read *pro forma* 1a; Motion for Address of Thanks to the Sovereign for his Speech, with further proceedings; Appointment of Sessional Committees; Order to prevent Stoppages in Streets; Appointment of Receivers and Triers of Petitions (to 1886); the record of the laying of the Roll of Lords Temporal and Spiritual by the Clerk of the Parliaments (since 1825); List of Papers received during prorogation including Command Papers (since 1896) and Statutory Instruments (since 1948). The records of Judicial Sittings of the Lords of Appeal in the name of the House of Lords during prorogation or dissolution are generally inserted in the Journals before the record of a new Parliament or session.

Legislative Business. The stages in the progress of every Bill are entered; the text of the Bill, however, is not given. Amendments moved in Committee of the Whole House (since 1856), on Report, and on 3a are entered, but normally not those made in Select Committee; amendments made in Private Bill Committees were reported and entered in the Journals to 1873. Evidence given at the Bar on Public Bills, etc., may be entered *verbatim* to *c.* 1800.

Divisions. Unanimous assent, or the names of Dissentients, are sometimes noted in the 16th c., but the results of Divisions in Committee of the Whole House, and on other occasions in the House, are only entered from 1857; they are then accompanied by the names of those dividing and of those acting as Tellers. (Divisions from 1831 to 1857 are analysed with references to known lists of peers taking part, in a typescript available in H.L.R.O. Search Room.)

Committees. Proceedings in Committee of the Whole House have been included since 1856; Reports from Select Committees and Joint Select Committees to the House are generally entered in full; and transcripts or summaries of documents produced, and of evidence heard, may occasionally be entered. During the early 19th c. a considerable amount of Committee of the Whole House Evidence and Papers is printed *in extenso*, either in the body of the Journal or as Appendices, e.g. concerning the State of Ireland; the Coal Trade; the East India Company.

Judicial Business. Petitions are given in summary form or merely by title; hearings are noted; and the final Order and Judgment are given *in extenso*.

Further details must be sought in the Manuscript Minutes, in the original documents in the Main Papers, and in the Judicial records.

Accounts and Papers. The House from time to time calls for papers in connection with legislative or other business; other papers are laid before it by command of the Sovereign or under statute. These series of papers are noted in the Journal on being laid or presented, but except in rare instances, the text is not entered. (*See* SESSIONAL PAPERS, H. L. below.)

Orders and Ordinances. The full text of Orders of the House is entered as likewise of Ordinances made during the Civil War period (1642–9). *See* also, however, the separate class of ORDERS AND ORDINANCES (below).

Motions. The full texts of Motions are given. Speeches are not, however, recorded, with the exceptions of Official Speeches at the Opening, and Interrogations of witnesses (especially during the period 1603–49, and always for Divorce Bills). In general, Speeches (as also Questions to Ministers) may be found in Cobbett's *Parliamentary History*, Hansard's *Debates*, etc. *See* DEBATES.

Miscellaneous. Letters and petitions to the House are noted and, especially in the 17th and again in the early 19th c., their contents may be entered *in extenso* or in summary. The full texts of Protests by peers are always given, with names of those protesting and (to 1830) their signatures. From 1831 these are in the Protest Books.

Close of Session. Bills may receive the Royal Assent then, or at earlier dates; if passed by Commission (as they always were 1854–1966) the Letters Patent are entered *in extenso* as well as the Schedule of the titles of Acts passed. The Royal Speech and the Commission of Prorogation are printed *in extenso*. Lists of Bills received from the Commons and complete lists of Acts passed in the session occur in the 16th and 17th c. In the late 16th c. lists are also given of Writs sent by the Master of the Rolls for the certifying of Private Acts into Chancery.

Vacations. The House has sometimes ordered entries in the manuscript Journals (1510–1829) to be deleted or 'vacated'. Some vacations were done by erasure, by deletion, or by the Clerk writing the word 'vacat' in the margin. When the Journals were printed almost all vacated passages were omitted. They can often, however, be deciphered in the Manuscript Journals.

Contents of Original Journals, H.L., 1510–1614

Vol. 1. 21 Jan. 1510–31 Jan. 1547, comprising letter of John Browne to John Walker, 1683; note by Walker on the Journals, *c.* 1683; version of 'Modus Tenendi Parliamentum' entered by John Taylor (clerk 1509–23) (n.p.);[1] proceedings of the Parliaments of 1, 3, 6, 7, 25 and 35 Hen. VIII; Lists of Acts passed, 26 Hen. VIII; List of Proxies, 35 Hen. VIII; proceedings, 28 Hen. VIII; copy of grant of liberties to Westminster Abbey, 1066 (n.p.); Chronicle of the Kings of England (n.p.); original proxy of the Abbot of Shrewsbury, n.d.; proceedings 31, 32, 33, 34, 37 and 38 Hen. VIII, including second version for 33 Hen. VIII (n.p.); entries of proxies for 37 Hen. VIII and n.d., with memo. concerning Bishop of

[1] Cf. J. Taylor, 'The manuscripts of the 'Modus Tenendi Parliamentum', *English Historical Review*, vol. lxxxiii (1968), pp. 673–88.

Norwich's proxy, n.d. (n.p.). *See* also HISTORICAL COLLEC-TIONS, H.L.R.O. below.

Vol. 2. 4 Nov. 1547–31 March 1553. The Journal of 7 Edw. VI was the Speaker's copy, H. C.

Vol. 3. 2 April 1554–17 Nov. 1558 including Journals which seem to have been, respectively, copies supplied to the Recorder of London (the Journal for 1 Mary, sess. 2) and to the Speaker, H.C. (the remaining Journals for Mary's reign). No Journal survives for 5 Oct.–5 Dec. 1553.

Vol. 4. 23 Jan. 1559–2 Jan. 1567. The Journal for 1 Eliz. I was the Speaker's copy, H. C. Entries for certain days between 22 March and 6 May 1559, missing from the Original Journal, can be supplied from Bowyer's transcript (*see* HISTORICAL COLLECTIONS, H.L.R.O.) which has been printed by E. J. Davis and by J. C. Sainty (*see* Bibliography above).

Vol. 5. 2 April 1571–14 Sept. 1586. The printed Journal redistributes certain entries of Commissions, and omits a few clerk's notes.

Vol. 6. 15 Oct. 1586–19 Dec. 1601. The Journal for 28 & 29 Eliz. I contains some extensive deletions not noted in the printed Journals. Certain missing days between 3 Dec. 1597 and 9 Feb. 1598 can be supplied from Bowyer's transcript *ut supra*.

Vol. 7. 19 March 1605–9 Nov. 1608. 4 original papers are pasted in.

Vol. 8. 9 Feb. 1610–7 June 1614.

Note that vols. 1–8 were supplied with Indexes in 1717.

List. A typescript list of the MS. Journals is available in H.L.R.O.

Printed Journals

(i) 1510 to 1829   61 vols.

These vols. were printed from the original Manuscript Journals as a result of an order of the House made in 1767. The very substantial passages deleted or vacated by order of the House in the originals were not reproduced (except for certain of those concerning E. Strafford); side-notes added in 1717 were printed with no indication of the later origin. Punctuation and capitalisation follow 18th c. conventions. In vol. i, containing the Journals for 1510 to 1577, the editors omitted any original matter considered by them irrelevant, made minor emendations of their own, and omitted the variant Journal for 1541. Certain bound copies of vol. i also include the text of 'Rolls of Parliament to supply the deficiencies in the Journals of the House of Lords' [1513–53].

Students are recommended in cases of doubt to consult the original Manuscript Journals in addition to the printed Journals for the period 1510–1829.

(ii) 1830 to date   139 vols.

These vols. have been printed as soon as may be after the proceedings which they record, and are published during the Session following.

Indexes to Journals

    1510 to date   17 vols.

Manuscript Indexes for 1510–1628 and for 1660–1829 were added to the original Manuscript Journals, in accordance with an Order of the House, in 1717. General Indexes (Printed) were first ordered to be prepared in 1776. These afford the best single guide not only to the Journals, but also to the records of the House. Volumes for the following periods have been published:

        1510–1649
        1660–1714
        1714–1779
        1780–1820
        1820–33
        1833–53
        1854–63,   and thereafter decennially.

The General Indexes for 1833–53 and 1854–63 incorporate elaborate classifications of Bill entries, detailing each Parliamentary stage. A classified Index was also issued separately in parts as follows:

      I. General and Miscellaneous
     II. Public Bills
    III. Causes
  [IV. Not issued]
     V. Local and Personal and Private Bills.

Parts I–III were issued for 1833–63 and for 1864–73; part V for 1833–63 only.

Indexes have been printed at the end of each sessional volume of the Journals from 1820 to date.

Calendars of Journals

    1510 to 1826   26 vols.

(i) The official set of manuscript Calendars or 'Books of Tabulated Entries' under names and general subjects, 1510–1807, 6 vols. These were compiled pursuant to an order of the House of 1717.

(ii) Other manuscript copies. The 'Shelburne set' (previously in the ownership of the Earls of Shelburne): 1510–1728, 1771–1810, 5 vols. Other vols., 1510–1808, 5 vols.; 1510–1721, 2 vols.; 1640–2, 2 vols.; 1660–1776, 1 vol.; 1701–47, 1 vol.; 1753–64, 1 vol; 1774–5, 1 vol.; 1790–1813, 2 vols.

(iii) Printed versions. Vol. i, 1510–1808; vol. ii, 1808–26; with separate tables of Peers Introduced, Appeals and Writs of Error, the latter two being indexed.

Note that since *lacunae* and imperfections exist in the Manuscript Original Journals, recourse may be needed to transcripts in other offices and libraries which preserve additional material. (*See* also BIBLIOGRAPHY above.) The Braye MS. Journals, together with photographic or manuscript versions of transcripts of Journals held by H.L., are listed below under HISTORICAL COLLECTIONS, H.L.R.O.

Minutes of Proceedings ('Manuscript Minutes')

1610 to date   383 docs.

See plate 2

These vols. are the original central record of proceedings in the House. They have been compiled by Clerks at the Table during sittings of the House, usually by the Clerk Assistant, but sometimes by more than one Clerk. They are preserved in two separate series, the first for 1610 to 1827, the second for 1775 to date. In the first series the vols. for 1621–8 (sometimes known as 'Scribbled Books') contain many summaries of speeches, as do some later books up to 1714. All contain figures of voting in divisions (invariably after 1661); from 1661 onwards the speeches of counsel in Appeal Cases are given in some detail, together with the opinions of judges called in as assistants to the House. Throughout the period 1621–1826 details may be given on particular subjects which did not finally gain a place in the Journals, e.g. a series of speeches on a treaty, the examination of witnesses, etc. Certain extracts from the Minutes, notably for Appeal Cases, have been printed in the *Calendar* for 1678–1714, but no complete edition of the Minutes has been undertaken.

The second series of vols. of Minutes, 1775 to date, also known as the Clerk Assistant's Sheets, consists of separate sheets which have subsequently been bound into vols. for one session or for a group of sessions. From 1775 to 1808 this series includes Indexes to the MS. Journals, and sessional lists of printed Bills, of peers first sitting in Parliament, of Petitions for Private Bills, and of Appeals withdrawn.

Vols. of Minutes normally include lists of peers present, stages of Bills, judicial business, Papers laid, and details of divisions and tellers, of Motions and of Messages from the Commons. Since 1964 Marshalled Lists of Amendments dealt with in the House or in C.W.H. have been included.

An additional set of the daily lists of peers present for 1850–68 has been bound separately in 72 volumes and includes rough notes concerning business, and some pasted-in Minute entries.

Printed Minutes of Proceedings

1825 to date   149 vols.

The printed 'Minutes of Proceedings' of the House of Lords correspond to the 'Votes and Proceedings' of the House of Commons. They have been sent off to press at the rising of the House, and published the following morning. In principle they are printed copies of the Manuscript Minutes, but:

Command and Act Papers are more fully described in the printed version;

fuller details of Judicial Proceedings in the House (e.g. names of Counsel) are given in the MS. Minutes;

the names of peers present are not printed;

the 'marshalled lists' of amendments to Bills, which since 1964 have been incorporated in the MS. Minutes (the decision on each being noted), are not printed;

Commons Messages, which have been bound up with the MS. Minutes, are not printed in full, but the gist of them is given in both MS. and printed versions.

With the Minutes of Proceedings (and forming an unbound pamphlet which is colloquially called 'The Minute') there has been published each day other matter, as follows:

A 'Cause Sheet' showing judicial proceedings impending.

'Notices and Orders of the Day', showing the next month's programme of business in the House, so far as it is fixed.

'No Day Named' motions, in the order in which they come in; these correspond to 'Early Day' motions in the Commons, except that a fair proportion—perhaps a third—of No Day Motions are eventually moved in the House.

Questions for Written Answer.

Bills in Progress—a list of all Bills, both Public and Private, before the House, showing the stage reached.

Special Orders, and Special Procedure Orders, in progress—similar lists for these two types of Order.

The 'Committee Sheet', giving forthcoming meetings of Committees.

As necessary, there may also be included in 'The Minute':

Division Lists (since 1857) giving the names of peers voting on each side;
Leave of Absence Lists, since 1958;
Proceedings of Select Committees on Public Bills, since 1968.

The daily editions of 'The Minute', containing all the above matter, for office and library use are bound up, with the Speeches from the Throne at the Opening and Prorogation of Parliament, into sessional volumes.

Minutes of Proceedings (MS. Papers)

1610, 1640, 1644   3 docs.

Although the initial record of proceedings made at the Table in the early 17th c. was normally in a Minute or 'scribbled book', Minutes were also written on separate sheets of paper. Original rough Minute papers for 1610, 1640 and 1644, and photographic copies for 1640, 1641, 1660–3, 1667–80 and 1688, are preserved in the BRAYE MANUSCRIPTS.

The Parliament Office seems also to have prepared paper summaries of the Minutes for distribution to peers and others. In HISTORICAL COLLECTIONS, H.L.R.O. are preserved photographic copies of 20 Minute sheets sent in letter form to D. Somerset, 1696–7. In VOTES AND PROCEEDINGS, H.C. Lords MS. Minute sheets are included for the period 1735–1802. By 1786 H.L. Minute sheets were available daily from a London bookseller for purchase by the public.

Draft Journals

1621 to 1690   33 vols.

The Draft Journals represent the intermediate stage which existed in the 17th c. between the record made at the Table (in the Manuscript Minutes or Papers) and the final Journal. They may include details not preserved in the final Journal and represent more accurately the precise order in which business was taken. The series has almost entirely been formed from the collection of BRAYE MANUSCRIPTS; *see* the list below:

List of Volumes of Manuscript Minutes and of Draft Journals, 1610 to 1647

The List includes material preserved elsewhere.

Abbreviations

M.M.= Original Manuscript Minutes.

D.J. = Original Manuscript Draft Journal.

G.1 = Material printed in *Notes of the Debates in the House of Lords, officially taken by Henry Elsing, Clerk of the Parliaments, A.D. 1621.* Edited, S. R. Gardiner, Camden Society, vol. 103 (1870).

G.2 = Material printed in *Notes of the Debates in the House of Lords, officially taken by Henry Elsing, Clerk of the Parliaments, A.D. 1624 and 1626.* Edited, S. R. Gardiner, Camden Society, New Series, vol. 24 (1879).

R. = Material printed in *Notes of the Debates in the House of Lords, officially taken by Robert Bowyer and Henry Elsing, Clerks of the Parliaments, A.D. 1621, 1625, 1628.* Edited, F. H. Relf, Camden Series, 3rd Series, vol. 42 (1929).

24 Feb.–8 May 1610. M.M. Bowyer's Minutes of proceedings. Braye MS. 61.

30 Jan.–29 March 1621. M.M. Inner Temple Petyt MS. 538: 7 (R.).

12 March 1621. Elsynge's first D.J. Braye MS. 69.

2 March–27 March 1621. D.J. Braye MS. 11.

22 March–18 May 1621. M.M. H.L.R.O. MS. (G.1).

17 April–18 May 1621. M.M. B.M. Add. MS. 40085 (G.1). *Note* that B.M. Add. MSS. 40085–91 were originally part of the Carew Manuscripts (H.M.C. *4th Rept.* App. p. 369).

17 April–18 May 1621. D.J. Braye MS. 12.

14 Nov. 1621–8 Feb. 1622. M.M. B.M. Add. MS. 40086 (G.1).

12 Feb.–25 March 1624. M.M. B.M. Add. MS. 40087 (G.2).

12 Feb.–25 March 1624. M.M. H.L.R.O. MS.

1 April–29 May 1624. M.M. B.M. Add. MS. 40088 (G.2).

1 April 1624–15 March 1625. M.M. H.L.R.O. MS.

19 May 1624–15 March 1625. D.J. Braye MS. 13.

17 May–12 Aug. 1625. M.M. H.L.R.O. MS. (R.).

6 Feb.–29 April 1626. M.M. B.M. Add. MS. 40089 (G.2).

1 May 1626–15 June 1626. M.M. B.M. Add. MS. 40090 (G.2).

17 March–20 Oct. 1628. M.M. H.L.R.O. MS. (R.).

17 March–26 June 1628. M.M. B.M. Add. MS. 40091 (R.).

17 March–30 April 1628. M.M. Inner Temple Petyt MS. 538. 7 (H.L.R.O. photocopy) (R.).

17 March–30 April 1628. D.J. Braye MS. 14.

1 May–31 May 1628.   M.M.   Bodleian.   Rawlinson MS. A. 106 (R.).

1 May–26 June 1628.   D.J.   Braye MS. 15.

13 April–5 May 1640.   D.J.   H.L.R.O. MS.

13 April–5 May 1640.   M.M.   Braye MS. 16.

3 Nov. 1640–9 Feb. 1641.   D.J.   Braye MS. 17.

9 April–14 June 1641.   D.J.   Braye MS. 18.

11 Jan.–10 April 1641.   M.M.   H.L.R.O. MS.

15 June–29 June 1641.   D.J.   Braye MS. 19.

30 June–23 Oct. 1641.   D.J.   Braye MS. 20.

25 June–7 Aug. 1641.   D.J.   Braye MS. 21.

25 Oct. 1641–2 March 1642.   D.J. (2 vols.)   *Calendar, Addenda 1514–1714*, p. 514.   H.L.R.O. photocopy.   Braye MSS. 22, 23.

29 Nov. 1641–26 March 1642.   M.M.   H.L.R.O. MS.

4 March–1 April 1642.   D.J.   Braye MS. 24.

2 April–28 April 1642.   D.J.   Braye MS. 25.

17 Dec. 1642–22 April 1643.   M.M.   H.L.R.O. MS.

24 April–4 Dec. 1643.   M.M.   H.L.R.O. MS.

22 July 1644–3 March 1645,   M.M.   H.L.R.O. MS.

4 July 1646–15 Feb. 1647.   M.M.   H.L.R.O. MS.

RECORDS OF DEBATES IN BOTH HOUSES

As indicated in the sections describing the Journals and Minutes of the two Houses, it was customary for Clerks at the Table on occasion to note down speeches made in the House. The practice came to an end in the Lords *c.* 1714, and in the Commons it was forbidden in 1628. Even when Clerks noted speeches in their Minute Books or Journals, however, publication was considered a breach of privilege. The Lords S.O. 92 of 1698 declared it a breach of privilege 'to publish in print anything relating to the proceedings of this House without the leave of this House' and the Commons by various resolutions between 1642 and 1738 also condemned publication as a breach of privilege. In spite of this, debates in the Houses were sometimes published unofficially during the 17th and 18th c. From 1768 there was systematic newspaper reporting of debates and from 1771 no effective ban on parliamentary reporting was exercised. In spite of this relative freedom to report, the content of the speeches in the longer accounts in the 18th c. may be in part imaginary, the points made by the speakers were frequently marshalled in the wrong order, and the exact wording was seldom captured. In 1803 newspaper reporters obtained the right to sit in a specific part of the Commons Gallery and in 1831 they were assigned a section of the Lords Gallery. From 1878 Treasury grants were made in aid of publication, and from 1909 onwards each House published their own official verbatim reports of Debates; and the editors and reporters of Debates are now officials of their respective Houses.

The Parliamentary History of England
ed. W. Cobbett (1806–12) and T. C. Hansard (1812–20)

1066 to 1803   36 vols.

The *History* makes use of the Rolls of Parliament and the Journals of the two Houses, including Sir Simonds D'Ewes *Journal of the Votes, Speeches and Debates, both of the House of Lords and House of Commons throughout the whole reign of Queen Elizabeth* (1682). Substantial material is also incorporated from manuscript sources such as Archbishop Secker's notes on Lords Debates, 1735–43; from 18th c. monthly magazines, etc.; and from the following collections of debates (which still remain of value):

[Various editors], *The Parliamentary or Constitutional History of England* [The 'Old Parliamentary History'] (1751–61), 24 vols., relating to 1066–1660, and including material from the Parliamentary Journals, newsletters, separately published speeches, and a diary of the Convention Parliament of 1660.

[R. Chandler], *The History and Proceedings of the House of Commons* (1741–4), 14 vols. relating to 1660–1743.

[E. Timberland], *The History and Proceedings of the House of Lords from the Restoration in 1660* (1742–3), 8 vols. relating to 1660–1742.

Anchitell Grey, *Debates of the House of Commons, from 1667–1694* (1763), 10 vols.

J. Almon, *The Debates and Proceedings of the British House of Commons* (1766–75), 11 vols., relating to 1743–74.

J. Debrett, *The History, Debates and Proceedings of both Houses of Parliament* (1792), 7 vols., including a reissue of Almon's *Debates* and much additional material, some relating to the Lords, dealing with 1743–74.

Lists of Members of the Commons are sometimes included in the main text of the *Parliamentary History*, and 18th c. vols. may provide some details of divisions. Copies of treaties and of other papers laid on the Table may be reprinted. Certain vols. of the *Parliamentary History* have annexes reprinting political pamphlets. There are no indexes.

The *Parliamentary History*, although drawing on most of the sources then available, describes only a small proportion of parliamentary debate; thus, for 1770 a total of 40 hours debate is recorded for both Houses for the whole year. The *Parliamentary History* moreover does not reproduce all the contents of its source texts. Some speeches are cut, many debates on minor matters omitted, and the debates are not always given in chronological order.

For the period 1774 to 1803 the series of Almon and Debrett's Debates entitled *The Parliamentary Register*, published between 1775 and 1804 in 83 vols., supplies material not in the *Parliamentary History*. The *Register* was in part based on speeches supplied to the compilers by members. Newspapers, notably *The Morning Chronicle*, *The True Briton*, and *The Oracle*, often contain extensive reports for the post-1771 period.

Other useful sources for the later 18th c. and early 19th c. debates are:

[J. Stockdale], *The Debates and Proceedings of the House of Commons* (1785–8), 15 vols., dealing with 1784–8.

The Senator; or Parliamentary Chronicle, 28 vols., dealing with 1790–1801.

[W. Woodfall, et al.], *An Impartial Report of the Debates which occur in the two Houses of Parliament* (1794–1803), 33 vols., dealing with 1794–1803.

J. Stockdale, *The Parliamentary Register; or an Impartial Report of the Debates
that have occurred in the two Houses of Parliament* (1804–13), 29 vols., dealing
with 1803–12, and continuing Almon and Debrett's *Parliamentary Register.*

An extensive collection of debates from official and private records was
edited by L. F. Stock in *Proceedings and Debates of the British Parliaments respecting
North America* [for the period 1542 to 1754], 5 vols. (1924–1941).

See also the BIBLIOGRAPHY below, p. 39.

Parliamentary Debates

1803 to date   1,672 vols.

   1. *The Parliamentary Debates from the year 1803 to the present time*, published by
T. C. Hansard *et al.*, vols. 1–41 (22 Nov. 1803–28 Feb. 1820), 1812–20.

   2. *The Parliamentary Debates* [title to vol. 18]; thereafter *Hansard's Parliamentary Debates*, New Series, vols. 1–25 (21 April 1820–23 July 1830), 1820–30.

   3. *Hansard's Parliamentary Debates*, Third Series, vols. 1–356 (26 Oct. 1830–
5 Aug. 1891), 1831–91.

   4. *The Parliamentary Debates*, Fourth Series, vols. 1–199 (9 Feb. 1892–21 Dec.
1908), 1892–1908.

   5. *The Parliamentary Debates*, Fifth Series, House of Lords, vols. 1- 16 Feb.
1909– (1909–).

   6. *The Parliamentary Debates*, Fifth Series, House of Commons, vols. 1–
16 Feb. 1909– (1909–).

For reports of debates in Standing Committees, H.C., *see* pp. 220–1.

   The debates for 1803 to 1830 were prepared from matter previously printed
in newspapers, pamphlets, etc. From 1830 onwards T. C. Hansard also used his
own reporters and sent proofs to members for revision. Speeches supplied by
members are marked with asterisks. Until 1878, however, the vols. were still
mainly compiled from newspaper reports. The Treasury grant to the Hansard firm from 1878 onwards enabled them to employ four full time reporters
and to report more fully. No speech reported from 1878 on was normally less
than a third of its length as delivered; important speeches were in the first
person, others in the third. From 1909 the report became the 'Official Report' of
proceedings and its text 'full'. This had been defined by the Select Committee
on Debates, H.C., 1893, as one 'which, though not strictly verbatim, is substantially the verbatim report, with repetitions and redundancies omitted and
with obvious mistakes corrected, but which, on the other hand, leaves out
nothing that adds to the meaning of the speech or illustrates the argument'.

   The 1st and 2nd series included full texts of certain Papers laid on the Table.
Names of those taking part in divisions are given for each House with gradually
increasing completeness between 1803 and 1908; after 1908 the lists are complete.
Written answers to Questions are included after 1908.

   Each vol. has an index of speakers and subjects, and from 1830 onwards a
complete index for the session has been printed at the end of the session, either
as part of the final vol. or as an additional vol. A general index was published
in 1834 which covers all debates 1803–30 in the first two series.

   For the period 1828–41 reference should also be made to [J. Barrow], *The*

Mirror of Parliament, 60 vols., a contemporary record of debates in both Houses which is fuller than *Hansard* for the period 1828–33. Members at that time corrected their speeches for the editor of *The Mirror*.

The *Journals* and *Hansard* are supplemented by an unofficial publication which at one time received a Treasury grant, Ross's *Parliamentary Record* (1861–1939), 70 vols. This summarises 'Votes and Proceedings in Public Matters' in both Houses, session by session. From 1861 to 1863 the arrangement is diurnal; thereafter alphabetical. Lists of Divisions and of Private Bills are also included.

USE. The Libraries of the two Houses hold complete sets of the vols. of Debates, etc., mentioned above, and these may be consulted in the Search Room of H.L.R.O.

BIBLIOGRAPHY

A. Aspinall, 'The Reporting and Publishing of the House of Commons Debates 1771–1834', in *Essays presented to Sir Lewis Namier*, ed. R. Pares and A. J. P. Taylor (1956), pp. 227–57.

[H. H. Bellot *et al.*], 'General Collections of Reports of Parliamentary Debates for the Period since 1660', *Bulletin of the Institute of Historical Research*, vol. x (1932–3), pp. 171–7.

A Bibliography of Parliamentary Debates of Great Britain [ed. J. A. Woods], House of Commons Library Document no. 2 (1956).

P. and G. Ford, *A Guide to Parliamentary Papers*, 2nd ed. (1956).

M. Ransome, 'The Reliability of Contemporary Reporting of the Debates of the House of Commons, 1727–41', *Bulletin of the Institute of Historical Research*, vol. xix (1942–3), pp. 67–79.

P. D. G. Thomas, 'The Beginning of Parliamentary Reporting in Newspapers, 1768–74', *English Historical Review*, vol. lxxiv (1959), pp. 623–36.

P. D. G. Thomas, *Sources for Debates of the House of Commons, 1768–1774* (1959).

See also BIBLIOGRAPHY, pp. 27–8.

Television, Sound Broadcasting and Photographic Records, H.L.

H.L. conducted an experiment in televising its proceedings on closed circuit, 6, 7 and 8 Feb. 1968. At the same time, sound broadcasts were prepared from a sound tape, and photographers from press agencies, etc., were allowed to take still photographs of the proceedings. The following records of the experiment are preserved in H.L.R.O.:

Sound Tape (British Broadcasting Corporation), 6, 7, 8 Feb. 1968, 33 reels.

Film made from videotape (British Broadcasting Corporation), 6, 7 Feb. 1968 and the edited programmes relating to these days, 28 reels, master negative; 28 reels, viewing positive; (Independent Television News) 8 Feb. 1968, 9 reels telerecording, 9 reels, master negative; 9 reels, viewing positive.

Photographs, positives and negatives, 6, 7, 8 Feb., 11 files.

USE. The use of this material is at present restricted.

BIBLIOGRAPHY

1st Report by Sel. Com. on Televising the Proceedings of the House of Lords, H.L.
    Sess. Paper, 1966–7 (190).

2nd Report . . . ., H.L. Sess. Paper, 1966–7 (284), including memo. on television
    archives of parliamentary proceedings.

1st Report by Sel. Com. on Broadcasting the Proceedings of the House of Lords, H.L.
    Sess. Paper, 1967–8 (27).

2nd Report . . ., H.L. Sess. Paper, 1967–8 (159).

RECORDS OF PROCEEDINGS IN COMMITTEES
OF THE HOUSE OF LORDS[1]

The use of committees in the House of Lords originated in the middle ages but there is little information concerning them until the 16th c. The Journals, from the reign of Henry VIII onwards, occasionally record the commitment of bills to one or more lords, and Sir Thomas Smith (*ob.* 1577) observed that 'The committees are such as either the lords in the higher house, or burgesses in the lower house do choose to frame the laws upon such bills as are agreed upon, and afterward to be ratified by the said houses.' The H.L. S.O.s of 1621 provided for the appointment of committees both for bills, and also for general debate of 'great businesses'. Such committees were either of the Whole House (C.W.H.), or 'out of the House' (later called 'outdoor committees' or 'select committees'), to which particular members of the House would be appointed.[2] A third type of committee was an outdoor committee appointed to confer with a similar committee of the House of Commons (*see* p. 57 below).

Committees of the Whole House, Outdoor Committees and Committees for Conferences were usually ordered *ad hoc*. From 1621 onwards, however, certain Outdoor Committees were named at the opening of a session in order that they should deal with a specific category of business throughout that session. The first of these Sessional Committees was the Committee for Privileges, of which a sub-committee was appointed to peruse the Journals. A second, which played a particularly important part in the period 1640–9, was the Committee for Petitions. The most active Sessional Committee subsequently appointed was the Offices Committee, which originated in a series of Select Committees from 1717 onwards, and became sessional in 1824. Between 1889 and 1910 'Standing' Committees were appointed each session for Public Bills committed to them by the House (*see* below). Today Sessional Committees are regularly appointed as follows: the Committee for Privileges; one or more Appellate Committees; one or more Appeal Committees; Standing Orders Committee; Committee of Selection (for membership of Select Committees); H.L. Offices Committee; Special Orders Committee; Procedure Committee; Personal Bills Committee; Leave of Absence Committee.

Committees may only consider matters specifically referred to them by the House. Reports and papers may be referred to them to facilitate their discussions, and it is common practice for committees to proceed by the hearing of evidence. Witnesses are normally invited to attend by the clerk of the committee, but an Order of the House is needed to enforce attendance, or to cause the production of documents. All lords are entitled to attend Select Committees and to speak, but unless named as members of the committee they may not vote. Although

---

[1] For RECORDS OF JOINT COMMITTEES *see* p. 57 below and for RECORDS OF PROCEEDINGS ON CONFERENCES see p. 58 below.

[2] In the 18th and early 19th c., unless valid considerations, e.g., of security, suggested a need to restrict membership of the Outdoor Committee, all lords present were usually nominated, and subsequent Orders might add all other members of the House.

debate in committee is freer than in the House, every question in committee is determined in the same manner as in the House. The committee normally concludes its business by drafting and agreeing on a Report, and this is then presented, usually by the Chairman, to the House. The Report, the Evidence, and any relevant papers, may be ordered to be printed by the House (*see* SESSIONAL PAPERS). It has been customary for Private Bills to be referred to Select Committees, and Public Bills to Committees of the Whole House. This practice has not, however, been invariable, as when Standing Committees for legislative purposes were appointed for such classes of bill as the House determined, and every bill within these classses was to be committed to a Standing Committee unless otherwise ordered. The records of the Standing Committee proceedings were then included as appendices to the Minutes and the Journals for the appropriate days. Since 1968 a few Public Bills have been referred to Select Committees whose proceedings were likewise recorded in appendices to *Hansard*, the Minutes of Proceedings and the Journal respectively. The Bills were subsequently recommitted to C.W.H.

Occasionally the House has referred subjects 'of great delicacy and of much public importance' to Secret Committees of its members. Examples of such proceedings are those concerning the state of the Bank of England, 1818–19; Queen Caroline, 1820; and Commercial Distress, 1847–8. The reports were ordered to be printed (*see* SESSIONAL PAPERS).

LISTS. Typescript Lists are available in H.L.R.O. of all classes of Committee Books.

Committee Appointment Books

1610, 1621 to 1628, 1660 to 1664, 1690 to 1861   139 vols.

The vols. contain the names of lords appointed to Select and Sessional Committees and the times and places of meeting. The vol. for 1610 is amongst the BRAYE MANUSCRIPTS. Those for 1621–8 are prefaced by tables of Bills considered in committee. The vols. to 1628 contain the names of judges and other assistants ordered to attend the committee. From 1762 prints of Private Bill S.O.s are sometimes pasted in the vols. The series was discontinued in 1861. All appointments have usually also been entered in the Journals.

Minute Books (Committee of the Whole House)

1828 to 1855   10 vols.

Committee of the Whole House proceedings for 1621 to 1827 were entered in the Manuscript Minutes of the House; Amendments made to Bills in Committee of the Whole House were usually entered in the Journals. Between 1828 and 1855 separate Minute Books were kept in which were recorded: the name of the Chairman; the Order referring the matter to Committee of the Whole House; a list of the clauses, etc. considered, and of amendments made; and the Order to report to the House. Since 1856 all proceedings in Committee of the Whole House have been entered in the Journals, since 1909 in Hansard, and since 1964 fairly fully in the MS. Minutes.

Evidence given in Committee of the Whole House on Bills and general matters appears in the Minutes and in the Journals; from 1805 separate complete transcripts may survive (*see* p. 47 below).

SELECT AND STANDING COMMITTEE PROCEEDINGS
(1628 to date)

Note that the eleven types of Committee Book described below are arranged chronologically, in accordance with the dates of their inception.

Minutes of Committees for Petitions

  1628, 1660 to 1695   3 vols.

  Vol. 1 contains a summary record of proceedings on Petitions, vols. 2 and 3, entries of orders on Petitions, 1660–3; for other proceedings on Petitions *see* BOOKS OF ORDERS AND ORDINANCES, and the main COMMITTEE MINUTE BOOKS.

Committee for Privileges Minute Books

  1660 to 1885, 1890, 1892   46 vols.

  Appointments and Reports of the committee may be found in the Journals from 1621, but continuous Minutes of Proceedings only begin in 1660. These include proceedings in peerage claims, in claims to vote for Representative Peers, and in cases of breach of privilege of the House and of its members, together with proceedings relating to any other matters referred to the committee by the House. The Minutes normally include the name of the Chairman; lists of all Orders, papers, etc., read by the committee; summaries of Evidence given, of Judges' Opinions, and of Counsels' Speeches; texts of motions moved (but not of debates) in the committee, and of the final Order to report. Some of the material appearing in the Committee for Privileges Minutes is printed in the volumes of the *Calendar* for the period 1661–1714. Minutes of the Committee 1885 to date are printed as House Papers and are preserved amongst the SESSIONAL PAPERS. MS. Minutes, however, survive for 1890 (Precedence of D. Clarence and Avondale) and 1892 (Place in House of D. York).

Committee Minute Books

  1661 to 1836   95 vols.

  See plate 3

  These vols. contain, for all sittings of Select Committees, the name of the Chairman; for Bills, the record of clauses and of amendments considered, and of orders; for Bills, and also for general matters, the names of witnesses examined, a summary of their evidence (only occasionally verbatim), a note of all documents produced or read, a record of the number of 'contents' and 'not contents' on each question (though not consistently), a record of resolutions and of reports to be made to the House. Papers ordered to be reported may appear as appendices to the Minutes; occasionally, original letters, petitions and other documents produced in committee are sewn or pasted into the vols. Up to 1796 the signatures of trustees accepting trusts appear, thereafter they appear in the TRUSTEES ACCEPTANCE BOOKS.

  Much of the material to be found in the Committee Books, 1666 to 1714, has been printed in the *Calendar*.

Committee Minute Books (Select and Estate Bills Committees)

1837 to date   170 vols.

These vols. contain proceedings and evidence taken in Select and Standing Committees on Public Bills, Estate Bills and on other matters not specifically included in the subsequent categories below. Sometimes a sessional vol. has been formed which includes a single type of committee, e.g. the proceedings on Estate Bills or Personal Bills. The series includes proceedings of the H.L. Offices Committee and other subjects concerning the Palace of Westminster. From 1945 proceedings on Estate Bills and other Personal Bills have for the most part appeared in the vols. of Minutes of Personal Bill Committees.

Committee Minute Books (Standing Orders Committees)

1837 to 1858   23 vols.

Before the Second Reading of any Private Bill relating to railways, and before the sitting of the committee on any opposed Private Bill (not being an Estate Bill or a Divorce Bill), such Bills were referred to the Standing Orders Committee for proof of compliance with Standing Orders relating to notice, to the deposit of plans, sections, books of reference, etc. This procedure began in 1837 and ended in 1858. Thereafter Examiners took over the routine examination, and the Standing Orders Committee have only considered non-compliance and special reports from the Examiners (*see* the separate class of Minute Books noted below). The Minute Books contain printed statements and other evidence of compliance with the Standing Orders and also evidence taken before the committee.

Committee Minute Books (Committees of Selection and on Opposed Bills)

1837 to 1858   22 vols.

The Chairman of Committees and four other lords named by the House constituted a sessional committee to nominate five lords to form a Select Committee on each opposed Private Bill. Every opposed Private Bill, not being an Estate Bill, was referred to a Select Committee. The vols. contain (a) brief minutes of proceedings at the Committee of Selection; (b) more detailed minutes of the Committees on Opposed Bills, including summaries of petitions, records of counsel and others heard, occasional notes of arguments, details of amendments and the text of the final Order of the Committee. The series is continued from 1859 in the two classes noted below on p. 45.

See also EVIDENCE below.

Committee Minute Books (Unopposed Private Bills and Appeal Committees)

1837 to date (Appeal Committees to 1848 only)   121 vols.

Committees on unopposed Bills consist of the Chairman of Committees with any other lords who attend, but the business is principally transacted by the Chairman. Proceedings on the unopposed Bills mainly consist of statements concerning compliance with Standing Orders, proof of Allegations, holding of Public Meetings, etc., and the delivery of accounts and description of works.

Amendments, sometimes numerous, might be made to the Bills. The Appeal Committee Minutes, 1837–48, contain summaries of the Petitions considered (for further time, peremptory orders, etc.) and the texts of the committees' resolutions, usually without details of pleading. After 1848 the Appeal Committee Minutes appear amongst the Appeal Case records (*see* p. 116).

Committee Minute Books (Opposed Private Bill Committees)

1859 to date   100 vols.

This series continues that for 1837–58 noted above (p. 44). The Minutes include details of those present, the counsel appearing, the sequence of arguments presented by counsel, the names of witnesses examined, amendments made and the committee's Order. No further detail is included, and for each Bill it may be necessary therefore to consult the vols. of Evidence for fuller information.

Committee Minute Books (Standing Orders Committees)

1859 to date   99 vols.

This series continues that for 1837–58 noted above (p. 44). From 1859 the Clerks who served as Examiners of Petitions for Private Bills have reported upon all facts relating to the compliance or non-compliance with Standing Orders. Statements and evidence regarding compliance with Standing Orders from 1859 onwards are contained in vols. of Examiner's Evidence (*see* pp. 87–8). Cases of non-compliance with the Standing Orders are referred by the House to the Standing Orders Committee for its decision as to whether the Standing Orders should be dispensed with in such cases. Printed statements and evidence of the parties concerned are included in the vols.

Committee Minute Books (Special Orders Committees)

1925 to date   56 vols.

The Electricity (Supply) Act, 1919, 9 & 10 Geo. V, c. 100, and the Gas Regulation Act, 1920, 10 & 11 Geo. V, c. 28 provided for a new type of Order requiring approval by affirmative resolution of each House. The Lords by S.O. (Private Business S.O. 216) called these 'Special Orders' and required that they be reported on by a Committee. At first, Special Orders were mainly Private Business, but they were increasingly used also for Public Business and there have been no Private Business Special Orders since 1948.

The Minute Books include a record of those present, of those heard with reference to the Order, and of motions. In some instances transcripts of evidence may be bound in, as are also reports from, e.g., the Electricity Commissioners or a Minister, and petitions to the House.

On Special Orders, also see p. 91.

Committee Minute Books (India and Burma Orders Committees)

1935 to 1947   7 vols.

Between 1935 and 1947 the House appointed a sessional committee to consider Orders made under the Government of India Act and Government of Burma Act, 1935, 26 Geo. V & 1 Edw. VIII, cc. 1, 2, respectively. Debates on Motions for Addresses in H.C. to approve such orders were habitually adjourned until the Lords Committee had reported to the House. Any Amendments made by H.L. were then moved in H.C. before the Address was agreed. The Minute Books include Notes supplied by the India Office on each Order, printed copies of the Draft Orders, and printed sheets of proposed Amendments. Verbatim evidence is sometimes entered.

Committee Minute Book Indexes

[1792] to 1846   2 vols.

The vols. contain alphabetical indexes of Bills and other matters considered at committees. Individual vols. of Minutes of Proceedings, 1792 onwards, in the classes described above also contain short indexes.

Use. Certain Minutes concerning establishment are restricted for 30 years.

EVIDENCE

Witnesses have appeared before H.L. and its committees from the middle ages onwards in order to give evidence concerning matters which the House might choose to investigate. The Journals record appearances of witnesses in connection with Estate Bills and Bills of Attainder from 1548 onwards, and from 1585 counsel were frequently heard at the Bar of the House. A S.O. of 1705 ordered that all trustees named in Private Bill (what would now be called Personal Bill) proceedings should give evidence in committee of acceptance of trust. In 1706 another S.O. ordered that persons examined by the Judges on Private Bills should be sworn at the Bar of the House—the rule in fact customary for all witnesses. The ParliamentaryWitnesses Act, 1858, 21 & 22 Vict., c. 78 provided that any committee of H.L. could administer an oath to the witnesses before it.Witnesses may be summoned by an Order of the House, signed by the Clerk of the Parliaments; if after service of such an Order the witness does not attend he may be taken into custody. A witness at the Bar of the House or in Committee may be examined by counsel as also by lords. Further details concerning Evidence in the House or in committee may be found below in the sections dealing with Private Bill Records, Judicial Records and Peerage Records. In this section Evidence relating to legislation and general matters is described.

The records of such Evidence for the period to 1771 may be found in the Committee Books, or, in certain instances, in the Journals. After 1771 separate volumes of transcripts began to be kept,[1] but records may still be found in the Committee Books and in the Journals (in the case of Divorce Bill proceedings, verbatim accounts of Evidence are recorded in the Journals and MS. Minutes, as was also the Evidence given in 1835 on the Municipal Corporations Bill). Between 1771 and 1922 separate paper-covered vols. of records of Evidence given in Select Committee, Committee of the Whole House, at the Bar of the House, and in a few instances, in a Select Committee of the House of Commons, may have survived amongst the Main Papers, preserved at the end of the year's

[1] In 1789 Joseph Gurney was appointed to take verbatim notes of evidence and speeches at Warren Hastings' trial; W. B Gurney was appointed shorthand writer to H.C. in 1806, and to H.L. in 1813 (cf. W. H. Gurney Salter, *History of the Gurney System of Shorthand* [1924]).

papers. Pre-1835 vols. of this character are listed below, pp. 47–53. The greater proportion of evidence, 1835–date, however, is preserved in the class of Books of Evidence (see pp. 53–4 below). In certain instances the evidence was printed and may also be found (a) in the 11 vols. of Printed Evidence taken before Private Bill Committees, 1818–32; (b) incorporated in certain of the vols. of the Minutes of Proceedings at Committees on Private Bills and other matters for 1793–1817 or in the Minutes of Proceedings at Committees on Estate Bills and Select Committee (see above); (c) bound in the vols. of Sessional Papers, 1801 to date. Evidence may include papers delivered to the committee by the parties or witnesses, e.g. censuses of passengers on roads, railways or canals, statistics of trade, abstracts of balances of company's accounts, etc.

Manuscript Evidence

1771 to 1834   1,000 vols. and files

The following vols of MS. Evidence survive:

Manuscript Evidence on Public Bills

(*Unless otherwise noted: in H.L., on 2a until 1816, thereafter in C.W.H.*)

1775   Shaftesbury Election
1781   Sugar Warehousing
1782   Cricklade Election (Sel. Com.)
1788   Slave Trade
1789   Tobacco Duty
1790   Tobacco Duty
1792   Slave Trade
1794   Slave Trade
1794   Surgeons (Sel. Com.)
1799   Slave Trade Limiting
1800   Flour Company
1803   Nottingham Election
1804   Aylesbury Election
1805   Lancaster Justices
1805   Smuggling Prevention (C.W.H.)
1814 and 1815   Helleston Election (Sel. Com.)
1815   Gaol Fees Abolition (C.W.H.)
1816   Gas Light Company
1819   Cotton Factories
1820   Insolvent Debtors
         Queen's Degradation, printed, *L.J.*
1821   Grampound Disfranchisement, printed *L.J.*
1823   Weights and Measures (Sel. Com.)
         Scotch Linen Regulation (Sel. Com.)
         Silk Manufacture, 9 vols. (Sel. Com.)
1824   British and Foreign Life Assurance (Sel. Com.)
         Dublin Equitable Loan (Sel. Com.)
         Manchester Equitable Loan (Sel. Com.)
         Equitable Loan (Sel. Com.)
1825   Cotton Factory (Sel. Com.)   ·
         Equitable Loan (Sel. Com.)

1827   Leith Police (Sel. Com.)
1828   Penryn Disfranchisement, 19 vols., printed
          Wool Trade, 49 vols. (Sel. Com.)
          Game Laws, 9 vols. (Sel. Com.)
          Linen and Hemp, Ireland (Sel. Com.)
1829   Coal Trade, 21 vols. (Sel. Com.)
          British Gas Light (Sel. Com.)
          School for Indigent Blind (Sel. Com.)
1830   East India Company (Sel. Com.)
          East Retford Election
1831   Poor Law, 52 vols. (Sel. Com.)
          Baking Trade, Ireland (Sel. Com.)
1833   Woollen Trade (Sel. Com.)
          Court of Chancery Regulation, 15 vols. (Sel. Com.)
1834   County Rates, 13 vols. (Sel. Com.), printed, *L.J.*
          Abolition of Oaths, 8 vols. (Sel. Com.), printed, *L.J.*
          Warwick Disfranchisement, 28 vols., printed, *L.J.*
          Chimney Sweepers (Sel. Com.), printed, *L.J.*

Manuscript Evidence on Private Bills (Omitting Divorce Bills[1])
   (Unless otherwise noted, in H.L. Sel. Com.)

1771   Durham Yard, Middlesex, Embanking (Summary only), (C.W.H.)
1781   Isle of Man (C.W.H.)
          Phillips' Powder (C.W.H.)
1789   Cromford Canal (C.W.H.)
          Chelworth Inclosure (C.W.H.)
1791   Birmingham Canal (C.W.H.)
1793   Hollyn Inclosure
1794   Warwick and Braunston Canal
          Torquay Harbour
1797   Curwen's Exchange of Living
1798   Harston Inclosure
          Thornton and Geldart, Exchange of Lands
          Warboys, Hunts., Inclosure
1799   Poyntz *et Ux.*
1800   Aberdeen Streets
          Temple Bar Improvement
          London Docks (1799 H.C. Evidence, communicated with other papers)
          Ensham Inclosure
1801   Cartwright's Patent (C.W.H.)
          Koop's Patent (C.W.H.)
1803   Edinburgh Roads
          Worcester Roads
1805   Chalmorton Inclosure
1806   King's Lynn Paving
          Bath Common Leases
1809   Antingham Inclosure
          Queensferry Passage Improvement

[1] Divorce Bill Evidence is not listed as it was usually reproduced *in extenso* in *L. J.*

1809   Farrer's Estate
       Portsmouth Water
       Manchester Waterworks
       Kennet and Avon Canal
       Leeds and Liverpool Canal
       Bishopstone Inclosure
       Bermondsey Poor
       Strand Bridge
       Surrey Sewers
1810   Bletchingley Inclosure
       Lower Barrier Bank
       Leiston Inclosure
       Minsmere Level Drainage
       West Middlesex Water
       Surrey Sewers
       Eckington Inclosure
       London Docks
       Gayton Inclosure
       Romsey Paving
       Gas Light and Coke Company
       Kingston, Cambridge, Inclosure
       Bere Forest
       Weymouth Improvement
       Commercial Docks
1811   Southwark Bridge
       Grand Surrey Canal
       Harefield Inclosure
1812   Cupar Gaol
       Weald of Kent (Medway River) Canal
       Kent Street, Southwark, Lighting
       Windlesham Inclosure
       Nevin Inclosure
       Greenwich Ferry
       Cambridge Canal
       Margate Pier
       Paddington Canal (Regent's Canal)
       Penmorfa Inclosure
       Deptford Road
1819   St. Pancras Vestry
       Grand Junction Canal (Waterworks)
       Wear and Sunderland Navigation
1823   Thirsk and Yarm Roads
       Shadwell Church
       Ely Drainage
       London Bridge
       Limerick Regulation
       Cambridge Road
1824   Kensington Roads
       Glasgow and Portpatrick Roads
       Commercial Road

Fleet Market
Hammersmith Bridge
Thames Navigation
Plymouth Improvement
1825   South London Dock
Morgan's Estate
Rochdale Road
St. Katherine's Docks, 11 vols.
Oundle Improvement
Liverpool Buildings
Don Bridge
Renfrewshire Road
Doncaster and Thorne Road
Leith Reservoir
1825   Bristol Dues
Newbury Improvement
Oddie Estate
1826   Newport (Monmouth) Improvement
Witham Navigation
Macclesfield Gas
Tewkesbury Road
Liverpool and Manchester Road
Swineshead Road
Rugby Charity Estate
Birmingham Canal
Westminster Improvement
Charing Cross
Metropolis Turnpike Road
1827   Norwich Navigation, 6 vols.
Stirling Road
Redrow Road
Nene Outfall Improvement
Dunbar Harbour
1828   Stockton and Darlington Railway, 16 vols.
Charlwood Inclosure
Tees and Clarence Railway
Manchester and Salford Improvement
Surrey and Sussex Roads
Llanelly Roads
Aire and Calder Navigation
Tees Navigation
Commercial Roads
Wimbledon Poor
1829   Bath Road
London Bridge Approaches, 36 vols.
Covent Garden Vestry
1829   Clerkenwell Improvement
Nene Outfall
Langton's Discovery
Wilson's Road

Callan Common
Metropolis Roads
Clarence Railway
1830 Leeds and Selby Railway
Manchester Improvement
Hollingrake's Patent
Rickmansworth Road
Monks Risborough Inclosure
Meltham Inclosure, 7 vols.
Southwold Harbour
Holyhead Road
Glasgow Harbour
Birmingham Grammar School
Rotha Levels Drainage
Sheffield Water Works
Bute Ship Canal
Glasgow Road
Limerick Road
1831 Kidwelly Road
North Shields Road
Dublin Railroad
Wakefield and Austerlands Road
Warrington Railway
London Bridge
Llanelly Tithes
Preston and Wigan Railway
Manchester and Sheffield Railway
Belfast Harbour
Warrington and Newton Railway
Eau Bank Drainage
Frodingham Inclosure
1832 Five Oaks Road
Hartlepool Dock
Exeter and Crediton Railway
Metropolis Cemetery
London and Birmingham Railway, 7 vols.
Sunderland Dock, 11 vols.
Gravesend Pier, 24 vols.
1833 Moses Gate Road
Camberwell Poor
Leicester and Swannington Railway
Continental Gas
Farringdon and Bedford Road
Dublin Steam Packet Company
Thelluson's Estate
Stafford Bribery
London and Birmingham Railway
Gravesend Pier
Clackmannan and Kinross Parishes
1834 Sculcoates Small Tenements

North Union Railway
Calder and Hebble Navigation
London Bridge Approaches
Durham Railway
Upwell Tithes
Itchen Bridge
Welland Navigation
Liverpool Court of Passage
London and Southampton Railway, 30 vols.

Manuscript Evidence on Miscellaneous Matters

1779   Management of Greenwich Hospital (C.W.H.)
1781   American Prisoners in Mill Prison, Plymouth (C.W.H.)
1785   Irish Commercial Propositions (C.W.H.)
1791   Chandos Peerage (Com. Priv.)
1795   Chandos Peerage (Com. Priv.)
1797   Bank of England (Secret Com.), printed, *L.J.*
1800   Union with Ireland; Wool Trade (C.W.H.)
       Provisions (Sel. Com.)
1805   Hart and Dobson Trial; Complaint against Mr. Justice Fox (C.W.H.)
1812   Stafford Peerage (Com. Priv.)
       Barnewell Peerage (Com. Priv.)
       Roxburghe Peerage (Com. Priv.)
       Queensbury Peerage (Com. Priv.)
       Kilmore Peerage (Com. Priv.)
1819   Bank Cash Payments (C.W.H., Secret)
1820   Foreign Trade, 58 vols. (Sel. Com.), printed *L.J.*
1821   Foreign Trade, 33 vols. (Sel. Com.), printed *L.J.*
1824   State of Ireland, 42 vols. (Sel. Com.)
1825   State of Ireland, 24 vols. (Sel. Com.)
1826   State of Circulation of Papers, Ireland, 1804 (H.C. Sel. Com.)
       Promissory Notes, Scotland and Ireland, 38 vols. (Sel. Com.), printed,
       L.J.
1827   Fees on Private Bills, 35 vols. (Sel. Com.)
       Corn Importation, 27 vols. (Sel. Com.)
       John Bell, Doorkeeper (C.W.H.)
1828   V. Hawarden (Privilege) (Com. Priv.)
1830   State of the Coal Trade, 22 vols. (Sel. Com.).
       Mr. Gepp (County Rates, Western Division of Essex) (C.W.H.),
          printed, *L.J.*
       Office of the Clerk of the Parliaments (Sel. Com.)
       Sir Jonah Barrington (Judge of the Court of Admiralty in Ireland)
          (C.W.H.), printed *L.J.*
1831   Lieut. Woodcock's animadversion on speech in H.L. (Bar of House)
       Complaint concerning *The Times* (Bar of House)
1832   Assault of John Wright (C.W.H.)
       Slave Population and distressed condition of the West Indies Colonies,
          104 vols. (Sel. Com.)
       Tithes in Ireland, 56 vols. (Sel. Com.)

1833 Parliament Office, proceedings in execution of Reports of Lords
      Committees of 1824 and 1826 (Sel. Com.)
      Turnpike Road Trusts, 38 vols. (Sel. Com.), printed, *L.J.*
1834 Complaint concerning The *Morning Post*, 3 vols. (Bar of House), printed,
      L.J.

Evidence (Main Papers)

1835 to 1922   app. 290 files

This series continues the class of MANUSCRIPT EVIDENCE, 1771–1834,
listed above, and comprises Evidence which is stored with the Main Papers. It
contains Evidence given before Select Committees or Committees of the Whole
House, but excludes Evidence on practically all opposed Private Bills, which was
bound as a separate series from 1835 and is described below. There are four main
categories of subject: (a) Divorce Bill Evidence. This is also printed *in extenso*
in *L.J.*; (b) Evidence on Public Bills; (c) Evidence on general matters such as the
Sale of Bread, 1836; the New Houses of Parliament, 1841, etc.; the Navigation
Laws, 1848; (1 vol. of Evidence before the Select Committee on the Printing
of the Journals for 1841 is also preserved); (d) Evidence on a few Railway Bills,
such as the Taff Vale Railway, 1837. Some of the Evidence was also subsequently
printed either in an appendix to *L.J.* (until 1844), or as Sessional Papers; this last
method became increasingly common towards the end of the 19th c. and the
printed SESSIONAL PAPERS have now replaced the minutes of Manuscipt
Evidence as the official records for categories (a) to (c).

Books of Evidence

1835 to date   1,597 vols.

The series opens with 5 vols. of 'Evidence taken before Committees and other
Matters', 1835; continuing with 'Evidence taken before Committees', 1836 on.
Until 1843 the sessional vols. are divided into (a) Manuscript Evidence, (b)
Printed Evidence. From 1844 to 1917 the Evidence is manuscript only; from
1917 onwards it may be manuscript, typed, duplicated or printed.

The volumes for sessions 1835–42 contain evidence on general matters, e.g.
on the Destruction of the Houses of Parliament, 1835; Education in Ireland,
1837; the Operation of the Poor Law Amendment Act, 1837–8; the Supply of
Water to the Metropolis, 1840. From 1844 onwards the Evidence concerns
Opposed Private Bills only or those treated as opposed (i.e. referred to Sel.
Com.). Proceedings on unopposed Bills are described in COMMITTEE
MINUTE BOOKS (UNOPPOSED PRIVATE BILLS AND APPEALS)
noted above.

The report of evidence taken at each day's sitting on a bill or other matter
opens with the date and the name of the Chairman. It then contains a verbatim
account, directly taken from shorthand notes, of examination and cross-
examination of promoters, engineers and other expert witnesses, of property
holders and of other members of the public. The witnesses may be examined by
the Chairman, and by members of the committee, as well as by counsel for and
against the bill. The evidence gives information concerning the intentions of
promoters of new projects, and the evidence on later amending bills provides

detail of the subsequent history of the undertakings. As a whole the class of Evidence forms a principal source for the entire range of Private Bill legislation relating to transport, public works and town improvement.

COMMITTEE PAPERS

Select Committees in the course of their sittings may have papers and other records referred to them, and they may formulate and consider memoranda and drafts of their own; also, if authorised by the House, they may send for or have presented to them reports, memoranda, and other types of papers. In addition, the chairman, the clerk appointed to serve the Committee, and individual members, may have correspondence relating to the business transacted. At the conclusion of their deliberations the Committee normally prepares a report. The only separate papers, apart from the petitions referred to them, emerging from the business of Committees are the reports made by the Committees and any specific documents which may be laid before the House by the Committees as annexes to their reports. It should be noted that a certain number of original draft and final reports, with annexed papers (including some not transcribed in the Journals), survive amongst the Main Papers. Prior to 1801, the most important Committee reports (with, on occasions, such annexes) were incorporated in the Lords Journals; others were only noted there. Between 1826 and 1844 much of the evidence and many of the documents produced in Select Committees were printed *in extenso* in the Journal or in appendices to it. By S.O. of 18 May 1865, all Select Committee Reports were to be laid on the Table and ordered to be printed. It is now usual to present some or all of the evidence to the House in addition to the report. Papers laid before the Committee may still be reported to the House as an appendix to the evidence.

The papers reported to the House belong to the class of SESSIONAL PAPERS. Those produced in Committee but not reported to the House, have only intermittently been preserved in the Parliament Office. Select lists of such Committee Papers are appended, in chronological order (relatively few papers are preserved for 1801–1906).

Committee Papers I (1669 to 1801)

Date	Committee on	Number of docs.
1669–70	Decay of Trade	5
1670–1	Assault on Duke of Ormonde	59
1675–7	Printers of Libels	38
1675–9	Impeachment of Lords in the Tower	1
1680	Commissions of the Peace	61
1689	Courts of Justice (irregularities)	103
1689	Inspections (Dispensations, Pardons, Charters, etc.)	20
1690	Impeachment Precedents	18
1697	State of the Trade of the Kingdom	46
1698	Appeals from Court of Chancery in Ireland Enquiry	39
1698	Suits in the Courts of Law and Equity	15
1698	Exchequer Bills	7

1699	Newfoundland Expedition	25
1699	Fleet and Fortifications	6
1703	Price of Coals	12
1704	Navy	196
1704	Keeping of Records in Offices	9
1707	Trade (Privateers in West Indies)	44
1707	Navy (Building of Ships, etc.)	5
1719	Public Records	70
1719	Writs of Error	50
1723	Conspiracy	2
1732	Courts of Chancery	4
1765	Dearness of Provisions	103
1767–77	Printing of the Rolls of Parliament and of the Journals of the House	60
1774	Massachusetts Bay Disturbances	6
1793	East India Company	30
1794	Warming and Ventilation H.L. (John Soane's plans)	8
1797	(Secret Committee) The Order in Council of 26 February 1797	1
1800	Pensions relating to India	7
1800	Dearth of Provisions	2

Committee Papers II (1907 to date)

Files are preserved for various Joint Committees and H.L. Select Committees, including the following:

Date	Type of Committee	Subject
1907–8	Select	Reform of H.L.
1912–43	Select and Joint	Public Utilities, etc.
1919–32	Select	Peers' War Memorial
1920–date	Joint	Ecclesiastical
1926	Select	Peerages in Abeyance
1933–4	Joint	India
1935–6	Joint	Water Resources and Supplies
1936	Joint	Public Sewers
1945	Select	Private Bill S.O.s
1948–56	Offices (sub-com.)	Peers' War Memorial
1951–6	Offices (sub-com.)	Windows in H.L. Chamber
1954	Select	Procedure of the House
1954–5	Select	Private Bill Procedure
1955–6	Select	Attendance of Peers
1958	Select	Leave of Absence
1959	Joint	Promotion of Private Bills
1962	Joint	Reform of H.L.
1963	Privileges	Scottish Peerages
1966	Privileges	Irish Peers
1966–7	Joint	Theatre Censorship

Files are also preserved for Special Orders Committees, 1937–date, which include prints of the Orders and Memoranda from Ministers.

All papers presented to Committees, 1801–52, are registered in the MS. Register of Committee Papers.

Use. The use of Committee Papers is restricted for 30 years.

RECORDS OF PROCEEDINGS IN JOINT COMMITTEES OF BOTH HOUSES

Joint Committees of the two Houses were occasionally appointed from 1641 onwards in order to save double enquiries and to enable members of H.C. to share the special privilege of H.L. of hearing evidence taken on oath. The number of Commons present was always double that of the Lords. This enabled the Commons to control the Lords and contributed to the disuse of the system after 1695.

Joint Committees were revived in 1864 and became an established element in the committee system, the numbers appointed by each House now being equal. Consolidation Bills are referred to a Sessional Joint Committee. Joint Committees are from time to time set up to consider Private Bills in the following categories: competing Bills; a number of Bills on the same subject; Bills in respect of which the promoters and a substantial body of the opponents ask for such reference; and Bills on which the Government announce that a Joint Committee would be in the public interest. Matters of domestic interest to both Houses, such as Parliamentary procedure and accommodation in the Palace of Westminster, may likewise be referred to a Joint Committee.

Joint Committee Minute Book

1679 to 1695   1 vol.

The Minute Book contains entries for 1679 (Popish Plot), and 1695 (Sir Thomas Cooke and the East India Company). An original H.C. Resolution of 26 May 1679 is annexed.

Joint Committee Records

1864 to date

The H.L. records of post-1864 Joint Committees may be found in COMMITTEE MINUTE BOOKS and in SESSIONAL PAPERS. It is usual for the Report, Minutes of Proceedings and some or all of the Evidence given to be printed as Sessional Papers of each House.

For JOINT COMMITTEE PAPERS see above, pp. 54–5.

RECORDS OF PROCEEDINGS IN CONFERENCES BETWEEN THE HOUSES

From the fourteenth c. it was customary for delegations from the two Houses to confer together. The earliest reference in the Lords Journal to a Conference between the two Houses is in 1514, and the earliest S.O.s (of 1621) show that Conferences were a normal part of the business of the House. A Conference could arise from a request by either House made in a Message to the other House. If the Message was agreed to, each House then named 'Managers' or deputations of its own Members who were to meet together; those from the Commons were twice the number of those from the Lords. The Conference normally took place in the Painted Chamber; Members of both Houses who were not Managers could attend but not speak. Otherwise the deliberations were secret, except that at their conclusion Reports would be made back to each House. While a Conference met the Houses did not sit. Most frequently Conferences were held to offer reasons for disagreeing to amendments to bills, or in connection with the process of Impeachment, but more general issues might be dealt with, and if the Conference was specifically named as a 'Free Conference' there was free debate and further argument. The last Free Conference was in 1835 on the Municipal Corporations Bill, the last Conference on any subject was in 1860 on an Address relating to the French Commercial Treaty. Conferences on Amendments and Reasons have now been replaced by Messages between the Houses.

Reports of Conferences

1610 to 1860

The only official record of proceedings was the report to the Houses by the Managers; this might contain extensive versions of speeches made at the Conference, or might be confined to the statement of a conclusion or of a Message from the Commons. It was entered in the Journals, and comparable material will normally be found in the extant Minute Books. A few manuscript Reports have been preserved amongst the Main Papers. *See* also HISTORICAL COLLECTIONS, p. 280 below.

Ancillary Conference Papers

1610 to 1678

Amongst the SESSIONAL PAPERS and the BRAYE MANUSCRIPTS may be found certain ancillary papers such as Heads for a Conference, Reports in preliminary note form of a Conference, copies of individual speeches and Messages between the two Houses concerning Conferences. These have been calendared.

RECORDS OF BILLS, ACTS AND MEASURES, HOUSE OF LORDS

PROCEDURE ON BILLS

The first Parliament for which 'Original Acts'[1] have been preserved at Westminster is that of 12 Henry VII (16 Jan.–13 March 1497);[2] the procedure on Bills which was customary at that date became more complex during the course of the 16th c. and it acquired elaborate refinements for the passage of Private Bills in the 18th and 19th c. During the years 1849 and 1850 the use of manuscript texts for Bills and Acts was abandoned in favour of printed texts, and the outline survey of archival and legislative procedure which follows is therefore divided into two periods: (a) 1497–1849; (b) 1849 to date.

From at least the 17th c. Bill procedure in the Lords was generally identical with that in the Commons, except as to the method of dividing. The survey therefore refers to both Houses unless a specific exception is made, and it includes Private Bill procedure, except for the special features described separately in the section on PRIVATE BILL RECORDS below, pp. 70–2.

(A) 1497 TO 1849

The Drafting and Introduction of Bills

The initial texts of Bills were usually drafted under the direction of a Minister of the Crown, or by the interested parties (for Private Bills), or by or on behalf of a private Member of either House. Any surviving records relating to such drafts may be found in departmental records, in the records of local authorities, or in records still in private custody. Except for the period 1800–49 (*see* p. 192) no such 'pre-Parliamentary' classes of records have been preserved at Westminster.

Lambarde, *c.*1586, described Subsidy Bills as originating only after the subsidy had been voted in H.C. and the matter had been 'committed to divers, who agree upon the articles'. The Commons ruled by S.O.s made in 1703 and 1772 that propositions for Bills relating to religion or trade must first be considered in C.W.H. The practice of receiving Private Bills only after the presentation of a Petition praying for the Bill was gradually established during the 17th c. and a S.O. to that effect was made in 1699. Erskine May in 1844 recorded the long-standing custom that 'the exclusive right of the Commons to grant supplies, and to impose and appropriate all charges upon the people, renders it necessary to introduce by far the greater proportion of bills into that house'. Estate Bills,

---

[1] I.e. Engrossed Bills to which Royal Assent has been given. This class of record was given the title of 'Original Act' in the Parliament Office from at least 1621.

[2] The ancestry of the Original Acts at Westminster has been traced by M. F. Bond in 'Acts of Parliament', *Archives*, vol. iii (1958), pp. 202–3.

Divorce Bills and those concerning restitution of honours and blood, however, normally began in the Lords. Bills for general pardons began with the Crown and were sent ready engrossed to Parliament, there being read once only in each House; they could not be amended except by licence from the Crown.

The First House

1. *Motion to Introduce.* In H.C. a motion to introduce the Bill (unless it was a Bill already ordered by C.W.H. to be drawn up) was proposed by a Member. In H.L. a peer introduced without a motion. The text of the Bill on paper (the 'Paper Bill'), together with a summary, 'brief' or 'breviate' of it, and (in H.C.) the Order of leave to introduce were handed in.

2. *First Reading* [1a]. Although general debate might occur at this stage, by 1621 1a was usually formal, apart from the reading of the breviate.

3. *Second Reading* [2a]. After a second reading of the breviate, the second reading general debate could take place, and counsel might be heard at the Bar of the House. After 2a the Bill would be committed, or, the Committee stage being omitted, it would be ordered to be engrossed.[1]

4. *Committee Stage.* The Committee might be of the Whole House [C.W.H.], or of part, 'out of the House', i.e. an 'Outdoor Committee' to which specific members were appointed. In Committee counsel could be heard and witnesses examined, the speeches being recorded either summarily or *in extenso*. Amendments to the Bill and new clauses were incorporated in the paper text in the 17th c., but subsequently they were written on separate sheets of paper.

5. *Report Stage.* The Chairman reported from the committee; amendments were read once and agreed or disagreed; new clauses were read twice, agreed or disagreed. Further amendments could be made by the House, the Bill's text and the breviate both then being amended. Re-commitment was possible in either House at this point, but normally the altered text was ordered to be engrossed on parchment, thus producing the 'engrossed Bill'.

6. *Third Reading* [3a] and *Passing.* The breviate, engrossed Bill, paper Bill and amendments, tied together, were brought to the Table of the House. The third reading was proposed and the breviate read. The Bill could then again be amended, new clauses being engrossed on parchment (and known as 'riders') and then read 3 times; simple amendments were written on paper. After the Bill's third reading the question was put that the Bill do now pass. On passing, the engrossed Bill had its title endorsed, and 'soit baillé . . .'[2] inscribed. Then, together with the breviate, it was sent to the second House.

Note that three readings did not become invariable practice in both Houses until the later 16th c.

The Second House

7. *First Reading* [1a]. This stage, again, was usually formal.

8. *Second Reading* [2a]. The amended breviate would be read, and the general principle of the Bill debated. Counsel might be heard at the bar.

---

[1] For the various motions that might occur at this and later stages in the 18th c. *see* P. D. G. Thomas, *The House of Commons in the Eighteenth Century* (1971), pp. 45–64.
[2] *See* the description of Messages, p. 62 below.

9. *Committee Stage.* Normally, though not necessarily, the Bill would be committed, as in the first House. All amendments made here, or on Report or 3a, were written on paper with references to the 'press' (or skin of parchment) and the line of the engrossment. Evidence again might be heard and recorded in the proceedings of the committee.

10. *Report Stage.* The Chairman would report from the committee, and further amendments could be made.

11. *Third Reading* [3a] and *Passing.* After 3a and passing, the engrossed Bill, if unamended, remained in the Lords, or was sent to it, as appropriate, to await Royal Assent. Supply Bills, however, were returned to the Commons. If amendments had been made, the engrossed Bill was returned to the first House with the paper of amendments.

Concluding Stages

12. *Consideration of Amendments.* Any amendments in the second House had to be agreed by the first House, or, alternatively, the second House might not insist on their amendments. The first House might make further amendments, to which the second House then needed to agree.

13. *Conferences.* If disagreement persisted, a Conference could be desired by the House which disagreed to an amendment, at which that House stated its reasons. If these were not convincing to the first House, a further Conference could be called, at which the House resisting amendments would state its reasons. If this Conference failed, one or more 'free Conferences' could be called for general discussion. If the two Houses failed ultimately to agree, the Bill failed and the engrossed copy would be kept in the custody of the House then holding it.

14. *Royal Assent.* When Bills were finally agreed, the amendments were transferred from the papers of amendments to the engrossment, being written on to the engrossed roll, or on to separate parchments tacked on to the roll at appropriate points. Assent was given either by the Sovereign in person or by Royal Commission (*see* below, pp. 175–6). Until 1849, the engrossed roll (the 'Original Act'), together with the enrolment (if any) on the Parliament Rolls, provided the texts of the law. From these texts certified copies were issued. The Original Acts were preserved in the custody of the Clerk of the Parliaments in the Jewel Tower at Westminster until, in 1864, they were removed to the Victoria Tower.

(B) 1849 TO DATE

By Resolution of H.L., amended and accepted by H.C. on 12 February 1849, printed book form was substituted for engrossment in the making of fair texts of Public Bills and Acts.[1] In the same year an analysis of the several clauses of a Bill began to be printed at the head of the Bill's text. The various types of separate manuscript amendment sheets and riders were replaced by manuscript insertions in interleaved and printed copies of 'House Bills'. Thus, the classes of Breviates, Paper Bills, Engrossed Bills, Amendment Sheets and Riders end

---

[1] *See First Report from the Select Committee on Printing; together with the Minutes of Evidence.* Sessional Papers, H.C. 1847–8, xvi, pp. 65–102.

in 1849, and are succeeded by Printed Bills in the categories described below (pp. 66-7).

Other alterations in Public Bill procedure since 1849 have not had major archival effects. They may be traced most fully in the various editions of Erskine May's *Treatise*. The greater proportion of Public Bills still originate in the Commons, and the general sequence of readings, Committee stages, etc., remains as outlined above. From 1966, however, Public Bills can be given a second reading in the Commons not in the House itself, but in a Second Reading Committee. Attention should also be drawn to the procedural consequences of the two Parliament Acts. By that of 1911, 1 & 2 Geo. V, c. 13, a Bill certified by the Speaker of H.C. as a Money Bill, if not passed by H.L. without amendment within one month, was to be enacted without the consent of the Upper House; other Bills, if passed by H.C. in three successive sessions (two years having elapsed between the first and third occasion), after a third rejection by H.L. were likewise to be enacted. The Parliament Act, 1949, 12, 13 & 14 Geo. VI, c. 103 (itself passed under the 1911 Act) reduced the time from three to two successive sessions with a minimum of one year.

For details of the new type of enactment made under the Church of England Assembly (Powers) Act, 1919, 9 & 10 Geo. V, c. 76, *see* the section on CHURCH ASSEMBLY AND GENERAL SYNOD MEASURE RECORDS, below, pp. 104-5.

MESSAGE AND ASSENT FORMULAE

The formulae inscribed by the clerks on Bills (normally at the head of the text) indicate the main procedural stages through which the Bills have passed and, at Royal Assent, the categories of the Bills. These formulae derive from the 14th and 15th c.; their use was not standardised until the later 16th c., and spelling has varied somewhat. The present usage may be summarised as consisting of the following standard phrases, with appropriate variations:

Communication of the Bill to the other house: 'Soit Baillé aux Seigneurs (Communes).'

Passing of the Bill in a house: 'A ceste Bille (avecque des Amendemens) les Seigneurs (Communes) sont assentus.'

Agreement to amendments: 'A ces Amendemens les Seigneurs (Communes) sont assentus.'

Royal assent to all Bills except Personal Bills and Supply Bills: 'La Reyne (Le Roi) le veult'; 'Soit fait comme il est désiré'—Personal Bills; 'La Reyne (Le Roi) remercie ses bons sujets, accepte leur Benevolence, et ainsi le veult' —Supply Bills.[1]

Royal refusal: 'La Reyne (Le Roi) s'avisera' (last used in 1708).

---

[1] For Acts of grace or pardon (which had Royal assent before they were agreed to by the two Houses) the ancient form of assent was 'Les prelats, seigneurs, et communes, en ce present parliament assemblées, au nom de tous vos autres sujets, remercient très humblement vostre majesté, et prient à Dieu vous donner en santé bonne vie et longue'.

BIBLIOGRAPHY

A list of works on Parliamentary procedure, arranged chronologically by dates of compilation, or, where indicated, of publication.

14th c.   *Modus Tenendi Parliamentum*, ed. T. D. Hardy, Record Commission, 1846. Cf. texts of the 'Modus' in M. V. Clarke, *Medieval Representation and Consent* (1936); and V. H. Galbraith, 'The Modus Tenendi Parliamentum', *Journal of the Warburg and Courtauld Institutes*, vol. xvi (1953).

c. 1562–6   Sir Thomas Smith, *De Republica Anglorum, The Maner of Government of England*, 1st ed., 1583; also, ed. L. Alston (1906).

1575, pub.   John Hooker, *alias* Vowell, *The Order and Usage of the Keeping of a Parliament in England* (reprinted in Lord Mountmorres, *History of the Principal Transactions of the Irish Parliament*, vol. i (1742); in R. Holinshed, *Chronicles*, vol. ii (1586) and in *Somers Tracts*, vol. i (1809), pp. 175–83).

c. 1586–1601   [William Lambarde], *Orders, Proceedings, Punishments and Priviledges of the Commons House of Parliament*, pub. 1641; reprinted, *Harleian Miscellany*, vol. v, pp. 258–67.

c. 1604   [Anon.] 'Policies in Parliament', pub. 1951, ed. C. S. Sims, *Huntingdon Library Quarterly*, vol. xv, pp. 45–58.

1610 or 1611   William Hakewill, *The Order and Course of passing Bills in Parliament* (unauthorised edition); *The Manner how Statutes are enacted in Parliament* (with author's preface), pub. 1641.
Further chapters of Hakewill's collections on procedure have been published recently; *see* C. S. Sims, 'The Speaker of the House of Commons, an early 17th century tractate', *American Historical Review*, vol. xlv (1939–40), pp. 90–5; and E. R. Foster, 'Speaking in the House of Commons', *Bulletin of the Institute of Historical Research*, vol. xliii (1970), pp. 35–55.

1625   Henry Elsynge, *The Ancient Method and Manner of holding Parliaments in England*, pub. 1660; subsequent editions, 1663, 1675 (enlarged), and 1786, 'corrected and enlarged' by T. Tyrwhitt. *See* also the forthcoming essay by E. R. Foster, 'The Painful Labor of Mr Elsyng'.

c. 1625   Henry Elsynge, *The Method of passing Bills in Parliament*, pub. 1685; re-printed, *Harleian Miscellany*, vol. v., pp. 226–34.

c. 1625   [Henry Elsynge, 'A Tract on Procedure of the House of Lords'], a précis of the section on Judicature, ed. F. H. Relf, in *Notes of the Debates in the House of Lords ... 1621, 1625, 1628* (1929), pp. ix–x.

c. 1625   Henry Elsynge, *The moderne forme of the Parliaments of England*, pub. by C. S. Sims, *American Historical Review*, vol. liii (1948), pp. 288–305.

c. 1625–32   [Henry Elsynge], *Expedicio Billarum Antiquitus*, ed. C. S. Sims (1954).

1628, pub.   [Anon.], *The Priviledges and Practice of Parliaments in England*.

c. 1628–34	E. Coke, *The fourth part of the Institutes of the Laws of England*, c. 1, 'Of the high and most honourable Court of Parliament', pub. 1644, etc.
1656, pub.	Henry Scobell, *Memorials of the Method and Manner of Proceedings in Parliament in Passing Bills.*
1657, pub.	Henry Scobell, *Remembrances of some Methods, Orders and Proceedings heretofore used and observed in the House of Lords.*
1685, pub.	R. C., *Arcana Parliamentaria, or Precedents concerning Elections, Proceedings, Privileges and Punishments in Parliament.*
1690, pub.	George Petyt, *Lex Parliamentaria, or, a Treatise of the Law and Custom of the Parliaments of England.*
1692, pub.	Henry Scobell, *Rules and Customs which … have obtained the name of Orders of the House.* [Abridged version of his *Memorials.*]
1707, pub.	[Anon.] *The Original Institution, Power and Jurisdiction of Parliaments.*
1762–3	[Anon.] *The Liverpool Tractate*, ed. by C. Strateman (1937).
1776–96, pub.	John Hatsell, *Precedents of Proceedings in the House of Commons*, 4 vols. 4th ed. (1818), with additions by Charles Abbot, L. Colchester (previously Speaker, H.C.)
1844 pub.	Erskine May, *A Treatise on the Law, Privileges, Proceedings, and Usage of Parliament*, and later editions as follows:

1851	2nd ed.	1893	10th ed.
1855	3rd ed.	1906	11th ed.
1859	4th ed.	1917	12th ed.
1863	5th ed.	1924	13th ed.
1868	6th ed.	1946	14th ed.
1873	7th ed.	1950	15th ed.
1879	8th ed.	1957	16th ed.
1883	9th ed.	1964	17th ed.

See also Procedural Manuals preserved amongst the H.L. and H.C. Records, and, for recent procedural changes, C. J. Boulton, 'Recent developments in House of Commons Procedure' [1964–70], *Parliamentary Affairs*, vol. xxiii (1969–70), pp. 61–71.

PUBLIC BILL RECORDS, HOUSE OF LORDS

(i) For Records of Proceedings on Public Bills *see*:

> COMMITTEE APPOINTMENT BOOKS, 1610 to 1861, p. 42.
>
> COMMITTEE BOOKS, 1661 to date, pp. 43–6.
>
> PARLIAMENTARY HISTORY and PARLIAMENTARY DEBATES, pp. 37–9.
>
> MANUSCRIPT MINUTES, etc., of the House, 1610 to date, pp. 33–6.
>
> JOURNALS OF THE HOUSE, 1510 to date, pp. 28–32.

(ii) Other Records relating to Public Bills

Note that with the exception of the failed Engrossed Bills (which are preserved in the Parchment Collection) the following Public Bill Records are preserved in the Main Papers, H.L. (*see* p. 127 below).

Paper Bills

> 1558 to 1849
>
> *See* plate 6

Paper Bills contain the full text of the Bill written large on single sides of paper sheets which are secured at the top. The text is that as introduced in the first House. Amendments made in that House up to report stage may be incorporated. The Bill is endorsed with its long title and a note of its progress up to and including the report stage in the first House. Paper Bills survive for most Bills introduced into the Lords from 1620, but Commons Paper Bills survive only in some instance for the period 1558–1649. In the *Calendar*, Paper Bills have been described as 'drafts of acts'.

Engrossed Bills

> 1547, 1563 to 1849
>
> *See* plate 7 showing an Enacted Bill

Engrossed Bills consist of the full texts of the Bills, written large on vellum membranes. The membranes, if necessary, are stitched together in order to form a roll (the length of the rolls varies from a few inches to about 550 yards). The text is that as amended after the report stage in the first House. Amendments made in the first House on 3a were also entered on the engrossed rolls, but additional clauses were engrossed on separate pieces of parchment (known as 'riders') which were then stitched to the roll. All amendments in the second House were written on separate pieces of paper, and were not added to the roll until they had been agreed by both Houses. The engrossed roll is endorsed with the long title and a note of the stages in its further progress. Because Engrossed

Bills, from 1497 to 1849, became, after Royal Assent, the Original Acts themselves, and are therefore preserved in that class, the class of Engrossed Bills preserved in H.L.R.O. is merely that of certain Bills which failed to receive the Royal Assent. The earliest Bill engrossment preserved which did not receive Royal Assent is of a Chantries Bill (1547). The texts of some unenacted Bills, to 1714, have been printed *in extenso* in the *Calendar*. (Engrossed Bills which failed in the Commons were kept in that House, but were destroyed in the fire of 1834.)

Printed Bills

1705 to 1849

The need to provide members with texts that could be referred to during debates caused prints to be made of Public Bills from 1705 onwards, although it is not until the 1740s that the practice became fairly general, and even in 1800 certain Public Bills were not ordered to be printed by the Lords. Prints were usually headed 'A Bill intituled an Act for . . .' and might contain the text of any particular stage in the progress of the Bill. The printed endorsement (if any) may not indicate at which stage the print was made, or whether the print was ordered by H.L. or H.C. When the print is of the Bill as introduced, an entry may be found in the Journal of an Order to print by the House; but such Orders were not essential. No regular file of printed Public Bills has been kept, but a few survive for important bills among the Main Papers, and many are preserved in the British Museum and elsewhere. (*See* S. Lambert, *List of House of Commons Sessional Papers, 1701–1750* (1968), pp. v–ix.) In the 19th c., the clerks used the prints of the Bills for collating amendments; prints, sometimes annotated, pasted up or clipped as a consequence, may survive for Bills between 1800 and 1849. Printed Bills also appear among the SESSIONAL PAPERS of the House after 1800 (*see* p. 159). Prints of some Commons Bills between 1731 and 1800 are bound in the Abbot Collection of Parliamentary Papers. It should be noted that for the period 1800–49, unusually, there survive in the Main Papers certain prints of Bills which may be regarded as the final Cabinet draft of the Bill, before introduction. These printed texts are headed 'Draft of a Bill', and are the texts, appropriately amended, which had been presented and read 1a in the House and then sent to the printer for the preparation of the first Parliamentary prints of the Bills.

1849 to date

The sequence of published prints continues throughout the recent period, and the Bills are published. They may most easily be consulted in the volumes of SESSIONAL PAPERS.

In addition, new classes of printed Bills appear in 1849, as the result of the disuse of manuscript texts for the official copies. Those preserved for H.L. are: *Table Bills*, prints of each Bill as it received a first reading in H.L. The prints are interleaved with blank pages coloured blue upon which amendments made on subsequent stages in H.L. are entered;
House Bills, which are similar prints made after 3a in H.L. and then sent to H.C. These copies normally return from H.C. with or without amendments, and provide the authoritative copies from which the final Acts are prepared.

The House Copy of any Bill which starts in H.C. contains the text of the Bill as passed by that House, interleaved with blank pages coloured blue, upon which amendments made by H.L. can be written.

Breviates (Briefs)

1593 to 1849

This class of document comprises summaries of the texts of Bills suitable for reading aloud in the House; they are usually known as 'briefs' or 'breviates', sometimes as 'abstracts'. They have not been preserved consistently, and, after prints of Public Bills came into general use in the 18th c. (*see* above) few were saved by the Clerks. Breviates were finally replaced, after 1849, by 'the analysis of the several clauses, which is now prefixed to the bill' (*Erskine May*, 2nd ed., 1851).

Amendments

1542, 1584 to date

Papers or parchments on which one or more amendments to Bills are written may be found in the Main Papers or with the engrossed Original Acts to which they refer. Amendments on parchment are known as riders and consist of new clauses offered to an engrossed Bill; those on paper consist of other amendments offered in either House. These amendments may be as proposed by an individual member or members, or may be a complete and 'marshalled' list. References in these lists of amendments are given to the current text of the bill (*see* PRINTED BILLS above) and this class of document can therefore only be interpreted in relation to that text. The amendments, if accepted, were incorporated in the relevant text to the bill. Since 1947 amendment sheets have been preserved in 'Public Bill Files' assembled in the Public Bill Office for each Public Bill. In these files may also be found relevant copies of *Hansard*, additional copies of the interleaved Bill and other Papers.

Petitions and 'Cases'

1572 to date

Petitions may be presented relating to a Public Bill about to be considered or in course of consideration in the House. Such Petitions are recorded in the Minutes of Proceedings and the Journals, but the originals have not in the past usually been preserved. For the period from 1572 onwards, however, a certain proportion survives in the Main Papers. Their general format and character are similar to those of Public Petitions (*see* pp. 172-3). The Petitions relating to Public Bills are usually manuscript, but some are printed.

Arguments or statements relating to a Public Bill were sometimes circulated to Members in the form of a 'Case'; these omitted all petitionary forms and rehearsed the arguments that might be put forward perhaps by counsel or witnesses heard at the Bar of the House. Some Cases of this type were preserved by the Clerks with the papers of the Session and survive in the Main Papers from 1621 onwards, although in the 17th c. they may bear varying titles, e.g. 'Objections on . . .', 'Representation against . . .', 'Reasons for . . .', etc. (*See* also HISTORICAL COLLECTIONS, H.L.R.O. for a bound set of Cases.)

Miscellaneous Papers

   1584 to 1800

For the 17th and 18th c. the H.L. Main Papers frequently contain one or more of the following subsidiary Bill classes:

   Lists of Committees on Bill, H.C., 1584 on (to which a summary of Proceedings in Committee, H.C., may be annexed, 1621 on).

   Lists of Committees on Bill in H.L., 1606 on.

   Orders and Draft Orders relating to progress of the Bill and procedure on it, 1606 on.

   Reports, Evidential Material, etc., of a statistical character to support Petitions and Cases, as noted above.

HYBRID BILL RECORDS, HOUSE OF LORDS

It has always been regarded as a fundamental principle in Parliament that a person particularly affected by a Bill, whether Public or Private, should be allowed to petition against the Bill and, generally speaking, to develop his case at the Bar of the House or in Committee. During the first half of the 19th c. however, restrictions began to be imposed upon appearance on petition at the Bar of the House and on petitioning against Public Bills, and as a consequence persons wishing to petition on such Bills found themselves, under what became known as 'Hybrid Bill procedure', compelled first to prove that they had a special, as opposed to a general, interest in the subject-matter of the Bill, and secondly to make use of the Private Bill procedure in prosecuting their petitions. Accordingly, Bills upon which it is thought that particular interests may exist, have been referred after 1a to the Examiners; if the Examiners certify that certain Private Business Standing Orders apply, i.e. that such interests do exist, the Bill is subject to a certain part of the Private Bill procedure; a petitioning time is set, and after 2a the Bill goes to a Select or Unopposed Bill Committee. Thereafter it is recommitted to a Committee of the Whole House and proceeds as a Public Bill. There is no procedural limit other than public expense upon the matters with which a member may seek to deal by Public Bill. If, however, his Bill is aimed at or affects any interest too particularly, it will be treated as a 'hybrid', so that those concerned may petition upon it. The earliest Hybrid Bill records concern the Metropolitan Water Supply Bill (1851); these and subsequent records will be found in the appropriate Public or Private classes.

GENERAL PRIVATE BILL PROCEDURE

Private legislation is defined by Erskine May as 'legislation of a special kind for conferring particular powers or benefits on any person or body of persons—including individuals, local authorities, statutory companies, or private corporations—in excess of or in conflict with the general law.' It contrasts with public legislation 'which is applicable to the general community'. In practice, however, Parliament has on occasion dealt with private matters by Public Bill, and public matters by Private Bill, and the distinction between the two types of legislation originally concerned method of procedure rather than subject matter. A Private Bill was (as it remains) a petition to Parliament by someone outside Parliament; a Public Bill was (as it still must be) one moved by a member of either House. A further consequent distinction between the two categories was that by the 16th c. it was established that fees were levied on Private Bills by the Parliamentary officers but not on Public Bills. During the reign of Elizabeth I procedure on Private Bills began to diverge in increasing detail from that on Public Bills until in later centuries, as Erskine May comments, Private Bill procedure became marked 'by much peculiarity', which included elaborate arrangements, of a judicial nature, for enquiring into the effect of the proposed legislation on the rights of private individuals and corporations. The developments in procedure from 17th c. onwards may be summarised as follows:

1. *Petition to introduce.* During the 17th c. it became the practice to receive Private Bills only after a separate Petition had been received praying leave, and in 1685 this was made a S.O. in H.C. Thereafter the Petition for leave was referred to a committee, which might examine witnesses upon the Petition and report back to the House. From 1706 until 1941 Estate Bills were referred not to a committee of the House, but to two judges. Since 1941 Petitions for non-Scottish Estate Bills in H.L. have been referred to a standing committee of the House which, from 1945 onwards, has dealt with all categories of Personal Bills, i.e. those relating to 'the estate, property, status or style or otherwise relating to the personal affairs, of an individual'. Such Bills were usually first introduced into H.L., but Bills involving any pecuniary charge or burden on the people, by way of tax, rate, toll, fine or forfeiture were usually brought first into H.C. Since 1858 Private Bills have been divided between the two Houses by agreement.

2. *Commitment* of a Private Bill in H.L. was almost invariably to a Sel. Com. and not to C.W.H. Public notices of such committees had to be given from 1698.

3. *The Printing of Private Bills.* In 1705 both Houses ordered that Private Bills should be printed before 1a. *The Liverpool Tractate*, however, indicates that this order was not enforced for the classes of Naturalisation, Change of Name or Scottish Twopence Duty Bills.

4. *Private Bill Deposits.* From 1794 it became necessary for promoters of Canal or Water Bills involving new works to submit Plans of any land that might be needed for compulsory purchase under the Bill, together with a Book of Reference to the owners and occupiers of such land (and usually to the lessees as well); a List of owners, occupiers and lessees consenting; a Statement of any sums subscribed for the undertaking; and an Estimate of its expense. Similar deposits were required for docks and harbours (from 1800), railways and tramways (from 1802), town improvements, streets and paving (from 1811), and turnpike roads and bridges (from 1814). From 1838, the deposit of small-scale Maps of the whole project, and of enlarged Plans of built-up areas and Sections of the whole works for all Railway Bills became obligatory, together with a copy of the Subscription Contract itself (from 1837). From 1853 Statements concerning demolitions in 'working class areas' were added to the deposits (see the contemporary printed editions of S.O.s for the full list of deposits required in any specific session).

5. *Preliminary Investigation for Private Bills, other than Estate Bills.* In 1824 H.C. and in 1837 H.L. appointed a Standing Orders Committee to consider dispensation from S.O.s in specific instances and to hear proofs of compliance with S.O.s.[1] The hearing of proofs was transferred in 1846 (H.C.) and 1856 (H.L.) to the Examiners, each of whom is an officer of both Houses. These Examiners issue certificates of compliance with Standing Orders; cases of non-compliance are referred to the Standing Orders Committee.

6. *Replacement of Engrossed Bills by Printed Bills,* as described above for Public Bills, took place for Private Bills on 31 July 1849 (i.e. began to operate for the 1850 session). It should be noted that Breviates or briefs of Private Bills continued in use until 1850 (few, however, have survived).

7. *Parliamentary Agency.* The business of promoting Private Bills and of conducting proceedings upon petitions against such Bills is now carried out by Parliamentary Agents. Until 1835 much of this Private Bill business was conducted by officers of the two Houses, who themselves actively promoted the interests of the private individuals and corporations employing them. In 1835 H.C. required its officers either to cease acting as agents in this way, or to resign their clerkships. From then on Private Bills have been promoted by outside agents operating under rules approved by the two Houses. Registers of the persons entitled to practice as Parliamentary Agents are kept in the two Private Bill offices.

8. *Provisional Orders.* From 1845 onwards various statutes gave authority to commissioners, government departments, etc., to make Provisional Orders, the objects of which could otherwise only have been obtained by Bill. Bills for confirming Provisional Orders were treated as Public Bills, except for proceedings before the Examiners in order to ensure that adequate notice had been given to persons affected, and for proceedings upon any petition against an Order. In such matters Private Bill procedure was, broadly speaking, followed. By 1882 the departments had issued 3,554 Provisional Orders or Certificates, of which 3,142 were confirmed without opposition, and considerable numbers

---

[1] This compliance had previously been investigated by the Select Committee on the Bill itself. The new H.L. Committee at first dealt with only Railway Bills; from 1839 its sphere included all other Private Bills that were opposed, except Estate and Divorce Bills.

of Provisional Order Confirmation Bills continued to be passed annually until
the 1950s. By 1964, however, few Bills were being passed.

Provisional Orders in Scotland have been governed by the Private Legislation
Procedure (Scotland) Act, 1899, 62 & 63 Vict., c. 47, and subsequent Acts,
under which, instead of presenting a petition for a Private Bill, parties proceed
by presenting a petition to the Secretary of State, praying him to issue a Provisional Order in accordance with the terms of a draft Order submitted to him or
with such modifications as shall be necessary (for details of procedure, see Erskine
May, *Treatise*, 17th ed., chapter xl).

The Records of Provisional Order Confirmation Bills are kept with those
of Public Bills.

9. *Special Orders.* See the note on Special Orders procedure, on p. 45, above.

For records of Special Orders see the COMMITTEE MINUTE BOOKS
(p. 45) and the SPECIAL ORDER BOOK and SPECIAL ORDERS (p. 91).

10. *Special Procedure Orders.* The Statutory Orders (Special Procedure)
Acts, 1945, 9 & 10 Geo. VI, c. 18, and 1965, c. 43, provided a further alternative
to procedure by Private Bill. The 1945 Act applied to Orders made under
certain existing Acts and to those made under any subsequent Act which
provides that such Orders shall be 'subject to special parliamentary procedure'.
By Address to the Queen this procedure can also be applied to Orders made
under earlier Acts. Special Procedure Orders subsequently largely replaced
Provisional Orders.

Copies of Special Procedure Orders are presented in both Houses; petitions
of 'general objection' or of 'amendment' may then be presented. These are
examined by the L. Chairman and the Chairman of Ways and Means, who
report to their respective Houses on the petitions, which may then be considered
by a Joint Committee of the two Houses. The committee either (1) reports the
Order without amendment, the Order then becoming law, or (2) reports the
Order with amendment, the Order so amended becoming law unless the
Minister withdraws it, or (3) reports that the Order be not approved, in which
case it does not come into force. In the case of (2) or (3) the Minister may introduce a Bill to confirm the Order, which is treated as a Public Bill. Special
Procedure Orders may also be annulled by a Motion in either House.

The records of Special Procedure Orders are to be found among COMMIT-
TEE PROCEEDINGS and SESSIONAL PAPERS.

BIBLIOGRAPHY

M. F. Bond, 'Materials for Transport History amongst the Records of Parliament', *Journal of Transport History*, vol. iv (1959–60), pp. 41–5.

G. Bramwell, *The Manner of proceeding on Bills in the House of Commons* (1809,
etc.).

F. Clifford, *History of Private Bill Legislation*, 2 vols. (1885–7).

H. S. Cobb, 'Sources for Economic History amongst the Parliamentary
Records in the House of Lords Record Office', *Economic History Review*,
2nd Series, vol. xix (1966), pp. 158–68.

C. T. Ellis, *Practical Remarks and Precedents of proceedings in Parliament ...
relative to the applying for, and passing, Bills for inclosing or draining lands ...*
(1802). See also C. T. Ellis, *The Solicitors Instructor in Parliament* (1799).

Report from the Select Committee on Proceedings in relation to Special Orders, H.L. Sess. Paper (1970) III.

S. Lambert, *Bills and Acts: Legislative procedure in eighteenth century England* (1971).

H. Newbon, *The Private Bill Reports*, sessions 1895–9 (1896–1902).

O. C. Williams, *Historical Development of Private Bill Procedure and Standing Orders in the House of Commons* (1948).

LISTS. Lists are available in H.L.R.O. Search Room of Private Bill Plans and other deposits, 1794 to date. It is intended to publish vols. containing annotated Lists of Private Bill Records for both Houses, 1794 onwards. A list of Irish Plans, 1794–1850 is included by B. Dietz in 'A Survey of Manuscripts of Irish Interest for the period 1715–1850 in the House of Lords Record Office', *Analecta Hibernica*, no. 23 (1966), pp. 237–43.

CATEGORIES OF PRIVATE BILLS

The archival history of Private Bills from the 18th c. onwards has differed according to the character of their subject-matter, e.g. the records made in connection with the promotion of a Bill to construct a railway are different in character from those concerning naturalisation. A description of the main categories of Private Bills has therefore been prefixed to the analysis of record classes now surviving at Westminster. The numbers given in brackets after the heading to each record class on pp. 83–92 below refer to the appropriate categories of Private Bill. The categories 1–9 are arranged alphabetically and numbered as follows:

1.	Canal, River and Navigation Bills	*page* 73
2.	Divorce Bills	75
3.	Estate Bills	75
4.	Highway and Turnpike Bills	76
5.	Inclosure Bills	77
6.	Name Bills	78
7.	Naturalisation Bills	79
8.	Railway Bills	79
9.	Restitution and Reversal Bills	81
10.	Local Government Bills	81
11.	Other Private Bill Categories	82

1. CANAL, RIVER and NAVIGATION BILLS

Canal building in England has been regarded as beginning with the Duke of Bridgwater's Canal Act of 1759, 33 Geo. II, c. 2 (Private), but many earlier harbour and navigation acts entailed similar construction work. The Bridgwater Act was followed by an increasing number of Bills, culminating in some 81 canal and navigation Bills passed between 1791 and 1794.

From 18th c. onwards the construction of canals was closely connected with
that of railways; some early railways or tramroads were built solely for bringing
goods to the quayside, and in 1832 the Manchester, Bolton and Bury Canal
Company obtained an Act for building a railway, 2 & 3 Will. IV, c. lxix. By
1847 the emphasis was reversed and a number of Acts had been passed to enable
railway companies to absorb or amalgamate with canal companies. In 1873
disputes between railway and canal companies on certain subjects were placed
within the jurisdiction of the Railway Commissioners by the Regulation of
Railways Act, 36 & 37 Vict., c. 48, and these Commissioners were reconstituted
with enlarged powers as the Railway and Canal Commissioners in 1888 by the
Railway and Canal Traffic Act, 51 & 52 Vict., c. 25. In 1919 all powers over
canals possessed by existing Government departments were transferred to the
newly created Ministry of Transport by the Ministry of Transport Act, 9 &
& 10 Geo. V, c. 50. In 1947 the British Transport Commission, with few exceptions, took over all canals (whether they were independent or were owned by
railway companies) under the Transport Act, 10 & 11 Geo. VI, c. 49. In 1962
the Transport Act, 10 & 11 Eliz. II, c. 46, transferred the management of canals
to the British Waterways Board, and in 1968 the Transport Act, c. 73, amended
the powers of the Waterways Board.

Because canal Bills contained clauses for levying tolls for the upkeep of the
canals and for the profit of their makers, the bills were introduced, by petition,
into H.C. Their progress was then governed until 1794 by the usual procedure
for Private Bills. From 1794 it was necessary under S.O. to deposit various
documents for canal, navigation and water Bills, and for Bills for variations of
existing undertakings, if they involved compulsory acquisition of land. Promoters were required to submit an exact plan of the land to be taken—but not a
section of the works proposed—together with a book of reference of the
names of owners and occupiers of each parcel of land, a consents list of owners
and occupiers, a list of the sums individually subscribed if money was to be raised
for the undertaking, and an estimate of the expense of the proposed works.
Compliance with these and other S.O.s was investigated by the committee on
the Bill.

In 1813–14 consents became necessary from owners and occupiers of streams
which might be affected, and the deposit of an estimate of the time required to
complete the project was ordered. In 1814, plans, etc. for Scottish projects were
ordered to have annexed to them an affidavit, taken before the local sheriff or his
deputy, that the conditions of local publicity had been complied with, and also
a certificate of the sheriff that he had examined the person making such affidavit
and that the latter was a person competent to make it.

Canal Bills were affected by the general reorganisation of S.O.s in 1837.
The investigation of proof of compliance with S.O.s was transferred from the
Committee on the Bill to the Standing Orders Committee and, later, to the
Examiner of Petitions for Private Bills. Other elaborations in the S.O.s for
railways were applied to canal Bills where they were relevant (see the section
below on Railway Bills).

LISTS. *Index to Local and Personal Acts . . . 1801–1947*, H.M.S.O. (1949).
  Index to the Local and Personal and Private Acts: 1798–1839, Thomas
  Vardon (1840), and subsequent eds. to 5th., for 1801–65 (1869).

BIBLIOGRAPHY

H. S. Cobb, 'Parliamentary Records relating to Internal Navigation', *Archives*, vol. ix (1969), pp. 73–9.
C. Hadfield, 'Sources for the History of British Canals', *Journal of Transport History*, vol. ii (1955–6), pp. 80–9.

2. DIVORCE BILLS

After the proceedings concerning 1st M. Northampton in the 16th c., no Divorce Act was passed until 1670. The object of promoting Divorce Bills in the following period was usually the remarriage of the promoter. Parliamentary divorce proceedings concerned only English, Irish and colonial marriages, as petitioners against Scottish marriages could find their remedy in the consistorial courts of Scotland. In 1857 by the Matrimonial Causes Act, 20 & 21 Vict., c. 85, divorce by legal process without enactment became possible, and ecclesiastical matrimonial jurisdiction was replaced by that of the secular courts. The rare Divorce Acts since 1857 have dealt with Irish or Indian marriages (or other marriages beyond the jurisdiction of English courts) or have given relief on grounds not covered by the 1857 Act.

The earlier Divorce Bills established two precedents, that divorce was granted on the grounds of adultery alone, and that only in exceptional circumstances was it granted to a woman petitioner. Adultery was a ground for separation (*a mensa et thoro*) in the ecclesiastical court and also for damages in a civil court. Divorce Bills had to be commenced by petition to H.L. By Lords S.O. 141 of 1798 copies of proceedings in the ecclesiastical court had to be produced before any Bill could be presented, and these copies were subsequently retained. By S.O. 214 of 1831, a report of any civil proceedings, made by a judge or undersheriff, had to be laid on the Table before 2a. Counsel could be heard on behalf of both parties, and orders of service for the attendance of witnesses were asked for at 1a. Before 2a, the petitioner and witnesses appeared at the Bar of the House for examination, and records of this appear in the Minutes and Journals. The difficulty of notifying witnesses, etc., frequently led to secondary petitions. Divorce Bills were Personal Bills and so were not referred to Standing Orders Committees or to the Examiners, but were normally committed to C.W.H.

LISTS. *Index to Local and Personal Acts, etc.* (as above).

BIBLIOGRAPHY. J. Macqueen, *Appellate Jurisdiction of the House of Lords and Privy Council together with the Practice on Parliamentary Divorce* (1842).

3. ESTATE BILLS

The series of Private Bills to regulate the tenure of property in the post-mediaeval period begins in 1512 and concerns six different types of subject:

(1) Bills to enable entailed estates to be sold in order that debts might be paid, infants provided for, estates consolidated, mineral rights developed, etc.; (2) Bills to unite or disunite livings, to settle rights of presentation, to

enable new churches to be built, to annex benefices, etc.; (3) Bills to authorise the legally disabled, such as minors, to carry out their aims; (4) Bills to enable boundaries of parishes to be ascertained or changed; (5) Bills to appoint new members to statutory trusts or to implement the purposes of private deeds and wills; (6) Bills to establish, regulate, etc., charitable institutions.

S.O. 103 of 1706 required all parties concerned in an Estate Bill to sign the petition for leave to bring in the Bill. Estate Bills were usually first introduced by petition into H.L., unless some money clause or other reason made H.C. the appropriate House. It was the practice from 1706 to refer Estate Bills to two judges, who were to consider the allegations in the Bill (previously the work of the Select Committee) and to certify their accuracy. For this purpose they examined (on oath, under S.O. 108 of 1706) the persons principally involved. The judges' report was to be produced before 1a, and it was expected to contain further comment, for example on the suitability of the Bill in relation to general principles of law and to the rights of widows, infants and those interested in remainders. If the judges were adverse to the Bill, proceedings on it were not continued. After the Acts of Union with Scotland and with Ireland, the personal attendance of witnesses and the taking of their consents became inconvenient and expensive, and the work was delegated to judges in Scotland (in 1792) and in Ireland (in 1801). Personal attendance of trustees in charitable trust Bills was dispensed with in 1840. After 1843 the judges confined themselves to legal points, leaving the examination of the allegations in the Bill and of witnesses to the usual Parliamentary procedure.

The judges reported to the House; the Bill then followed the usual course. The committee on the Bill received the consents of interested parties and saw that S.O.s were observed. In addition, for Bills to exchange or sell settled lands, the committee sought to ascertain the value of the lands concerned; in 1799 (S.O. 151) it was laid down that such Bills should have attached to them a schedule of the annual rent of the estate and the value of timber growing there.

Reference to the judges for a report was abolished in 1941 in the case of Bills relating to England or Wales, the judges' work now being carried out by a Personal Bills Committee of the House, which reports to H.L. on the Petition for the Bill. For Scottish Bills, however, a judges' report is still required and is made to this committee.

LISTS

G. Bramwell, *Analytical Table of Private Statutes* (1813), which contains a Table
    of Estate Acts, 1727–1812; vol. ii (1835) continues listing for 1813–34.
Index to Local and Personal Acts, etc. (as above).

BIBLIOGRAPHY. M. F. Bond, *Estate Acts of Parliament*, Short Guides to Records
    no. 9, Historical Association (1964), and in *History*, vol. xlix (1964), pp.
    325–8.

4. HIGHWAY AND TURNPIKE BILLS

The greater proportion of English roads until the 19th c. were subject to parochial administration, governed by common law and certain public Acts (which were codified by the Highway Act, 1835, 5 & 6 Will. IV, c. 50). The first turnpike Act is generally considered to be that of 1663, concerning the London and York road in the counties of Hertford, Cambridge and Huntingdon; the main period of expansion was the reign of George III. The turnpike trusts were created by local Acts[1] but the general conduct of the trustees was also governed by a series of public general Acts concerning the qualifications of trustees, provision of weighing machines, imposition of tolls, etc. (e.g. Turnpike Roads Act, 1822, 3 Geo. IV, c. 126). Tolls were generally specified for a period of 21 years so that continuation Acts were usually necessary. The Annual Turnpike Acts Continuation Act of 1871, 34 & 35 Vict., c. 115, fixed terms for the abolition of many trusts, all of which ultimately came under the local authorities.

Road Bills were introduced first into H.C. partly because of their local interest, and partly because the clauses imposing tolls were reckoned to be a form of taxation. In 1813 revised S.O.s were applied to all Bills for new roads and for all deviations above 100 yards. Lists of assents, dissents and neuters, however, were not demanded, although they were often handed in, together with the plans which were from then on required to be deposited. The Orders concerning affidavits and certificates for Scottish Bills of 1814 were also applied to Scottish road Bills. In 1822, by the Turnpike Roads Act, 3 Geo. IV, c. 126, turnpike trustees were empowered to purchase land for the widening or diversion of existing roads on certain conditions. The reorganisation of S.O.s in 1837 was applied to road Bills, and thereafter, in general, the procedure and the documents required were as for railway Bills.

LISTS. *Index to Local and Personal Acts, etc.* (as above).

BIBLIOGRAPHY

S. and B. Webb, *English Local Government: the Story of the King's Highway* (1913).
Annual Reports of the Secretary of State on Turnpike Trusts, from 1851. Abstracts of accounts, reports on individual roads, etc., from 1820 printed in Sessional Papers.

5. INCLOSURE[2] BILLS

In the 16th c. Private Bills to inclose were usually concerned with drainage and inclosure in marshland areas. The majority of inclosure Bills enacted in the 18th and 19th c. dealt with waste, common lands or open fields. Inclosure Bills became so numerous that public general Acts were passed to obviate, in certain circumstances, recourse to Parliament (e.g., 6 & 7 Will, IV, c. 115). In 1845 by the Inclosure Act, 8 & 9 Vict., c. 118, Inclosure Commissioners were appointed and authorised to issue Awards and Orders for inclosure, after a local enquiry had been held, without submitting them to Parliament for approval. This procedure did not, however, apply to inclosures of wastes of manors, or of lands subject to indefinite rights of common, nor to a few other specific categories. These excepted categories were subsequently included in single general

---

[1] Many important roads, however, came under public Acts, e.g. Regent Street and Whitehall; the London and Holyhead Road; Highland (Scottish) Roads, etc.
[2] 'Inclosure' and not 'Enclosure' is the Parliamentary spelling of the word.

Acts passed annually. The Inclosure Act of 1852, 15 & 16 Vict., c. 79, made it necessary for all orders for inclosure to be confirmed by Act. The Commissioners submitted an annual Report to Parliament, and, from time to time, Reports on individual proposals (*see* SESSIONAL PAPERS). The powers of the Inclosure Commissioners (later termed the Land Commissioners) were taken over by the Board of Agriculture in 1889 under the Board of Agriculture Act, 52 & 53 Vict., c. 30, and since then few Inclosure Bills have been promoted.

Inclosure Acts did not divide up the lands in question among claimants, but named Commissioners who were to do so within a given period of time. Therefore, in order to ascertain the actual division of land, the Inclosure Awards of the Commissioners must be consulted. None of these Awards is preserved in H.L.R.O.; some may be found at the Public Record Office, others may be found locally, amongst parish records, in County Record Offices, etc. The Parliamentary Bills do, however, normally indicate the outer limits of the area dealt with, and also the rights of various individuals, e.g. of the incumbent with his tithe and glebe, and of the lord of the manor.

LISTS

Return of all Inclosure Awards, or copies, at present deposited or enrolled with Clerks of the Peace of England and Wales. H.C. 50 (1904), lxxviii, gives lists of parishes, arranged alphabetically under counties, with date of Act and date of Award.

Return of all Acts passed for Inclosure of Commons or Waste Lands in England and Wales. H.C. 399 (1914), lxii, gives list of Acts (including chapter numbers) arranged chronologically under counties.

Annual Reports of the Inclosure Commissioners, 1846–83; continued by the Land Commission 1883–89, and by the Board of Agriculture from 1890, printed in Sessional Papers.

G. Bramwell, *Analytical Table of Private Statutes* (1813) gives a Table of Inclosure Acts, 1727–1812; vol. ii (1835) deals with 1813–34.

Index to Local and Personal Acts, etc. (as above).

6. NAME BILLS

Bills to effect changes of name are few in number, the last being in 1907. They were usually the result of testamentary dispositions whereby the heir, to gain his full inheritance, must change his name and assume the coat of arms of the testator. Change of name could also be effected by Royal Licence and by deed poll.

Change of name Bills could be begun, by Petition, in H.L., and followed the normal procedure for Personal Bills.

LISTS

An Index to changes of name, 1760–1901, ed. W. P. W. Phillimore and E. A. Fry (1905).

Index to Local and Personal Acts, etc. (as above).

7. NATURALISATION BILLS

Until 1844 naturalisation could only be obtained by Act of Parliament, either through Public Acts naturalising specific classes of persons (e.g. the Foreign Protestants Naturalisation Act, 1708, 7 Anne, c. 5), or through a Private Act naturalising named persons.[1] From 1844 naturalisation could also be obtained by certificate from the Secretary of State; this obviated the necessity of recourse to Parliament except in those cases in which persons wished to be relieved of certain remaining disabilities (such as inability to sit in Parliament or to hold land from the Crown). After 1844, therefore, few Naturalisation Bills have been presented; the last was in 1911.

A Bill was introduced on petition into either House, though it became increasingly usual to introduce it into H.L. From 1609, under the Naturalisation and Restoration of Blood Act, 7 Ja. I, c. 2, it was essential that the petitioner should be in communion with the Church of England. He had, therefore, to produce a certificate that he had received the Holy Communion, signed by a priest of the Church of England, and suitably witnessed by parish officials. He was also required to take the Oaths of Supremacy and Allegiance in both Houses. (These conditions effectually prevented all Roman Catholics from applying for naturalisation until 1829.) From 1798, in accordance with S.O.s originally made for the duration of the French war, the petitioner had to produce a certificate of good conduct signed by one of the principal Secretaries of State. In 1825 (by the Naturalisation and Restoration of Blood Act, 6 Geo. IV, c. 67) it became no longer necessary to receive the Holy Communion, but the Oaths of Supremacy and Allegiance were still compulsory, until new oaths were substituted for Roman Catholics by the Roman Catholic Relief Act, 10 Geo. IV, c. 7. At no time were naturalisation Bills referred to the Standing Orders Committee or to the Examiners, being Personal Bills.

LISTS

Index to Local and Personal Acts, etc. (as above).
Card Index in H.L.R.O.

BIBLIOGRAPHY

John Cutler, *The Law of Naturalization as amended by the Naturalization Act, 1870* (1871).
Memorandum on Naturalisation Laws, House of Lords Record Office.

8. RAILWAY BILLS

In the 18th c. some canal companies constructed tramroads for which they obtained legislation (e.g. in 1776 the Trent and Mersey Navigation Company was authorised to make a line from Froghall to Caldon). The first railway Act in the modern sense was that for the Croydon and Wandsworth line in 1801, in which horse power was employed. The number of Bills for creating companies to construct and run lines from one point to another was further augmented in

---

[1] Certain members of the Royal Family, however, were naturalised by Public Act.

19th c. by Bills to deviate from the original project, to add branch lines, to extend the time to be taken in construction, to alter the charges laid down, etc. There were also many public general Acts to regulate railways (e.g. the Abandonment of Railways Act of 1850, 13–14 Vict., c. 83). Railways came under Government supervision in 1840 when a Railway Department was set up in the Committee for Trade, as a result of the Railway Regulation Act, 3 & 4 Vict., c. 97.

Meanwhile the Harbour Department of the Admiralty had been concerned with projects near tidal waters from 1842, and this department was transferred to the Board of Trade in 1864. In 1896 the Light Railway Commission was set up by the Light Railways Act, 59 & 60 Vict., c. 48, and continued to function separately, also under the Board of Trade, until the creation of the Ministry of Transport in 1919, by the Ministry of Transport Act, 9 & 10 Geo. V, c. 50. Finally, the railways were nationalised and brought completely under the control of a British Transport Commission in 1947 by the Transport Act, 10 & 11 Geo. VI, c. 49. In 1962 the Transport Act, 10 & 11 Eliz. II, c. 46, transferred the management of the railways to the British Railways Board, and the Transport Act, 1968, c. 73, changed the composition of the Railways Board.

In 1803 the existing S.O.s for canal Bills (of 1794) were applied to railway Bills, and the same Orders continued to be applied to both types of Bill until 1836, when both Houses drew up an elaborate procedure for railway Bills, to be operative in the following session. For new works, the deposit of enlarged Plans of built-up areas and Sections of the whole works was made compulsory; for the first time the consents of lessees of property were to be taken (though they had often been provided before) and a subscription contract, as well as a list of subscriptions, submitted. Since Plans, etc., had now to be deposited with the Clerk of the Parliaments before the session began (and not, as previously, before the Bill came from H.C.), any H.C. amendments had to be notified on a second set of Plans, etc., for H.L.

A Standing Orders Committee was set up to deal with all railway Bills from the session of 1837, and the respective spheres of this Committee and the committee on the Bill were defined.

From 1838 a second set of Plans, Sections and Books of Reference was lodged with the Clerks of the Peace, to be sealed and sent to either House if called for. From 1849 copies of the compulsory notices in *The London Gazette* were regularly preserved in H.L. though earlier examples may be found. Demolition statements were first submitted in 1853.

Reports of various bodies and departments on railway Bills became a feature of the preliminary investigations, of which Parliament took account in considering Bills for new works. There were general Reports from the Railway Department, from 1841, as well as many reports on individual projects; these were regularly sent to the committee on the Bill after 1848. From 1849 Admiralty officers reported on lines along foreshores or tidal waters. From 1853 it was ordered that a report should be sent by the Attorney-General of England or Ireland upon any Bill involving the lands of any charity not covered by the Lands Clauses Consolidation Act, 1845, 8 & 9 Vict., c. 18. Nowadays, reports submitted by any department on any Bill are always considered by the committee on the Bill.

LISTS. *Index to Local and Personal Acts*, etc. (as above).

BIBLIOGRAPHY

M. F. Bond, 'Materials for Transport History amongst the Records of Parliament', *Journal of Transport History*, vol. iv (1959–60), pp. 37–52.
D. B. Wardle, 'Sources for the history of Railways at the Public Record Office', *Journal of Transport History*, vol. ii (1955–6), pp. 214–34.
Annual reports and reports on individual Bills are often found printed in Sessional Papers.
See also G. Ottley, *Bibliography of British Railway History* (1965).

9. RESTITUTION AND REVERSAL BILLS

There were three types of Bill to mitigate the effects of attainder: (1) Bills for reversal of attainder, whereby the person attainted regained all his rights; (2) Bills for restitution in blood, whereby persons attainted or their relatives could regain their civil rights; (3) Bills for restoration of honours and lands, whereby either those attainted or their heirs could regain their titles or other positions in the State, and their property.

Bills of all three types could only be introduced with the consent of the Crown. They were normally introduced into the Lords but Bills for restoring some civil rights (e.g. enabling to sue) could be introduced in H.C. Although no petition for leave to introduce a Bill was required, the preamble to the Bill was in petition form. Thereafter the Bill usually pursued the normal course of three readings in each House and Royal Assent; it was rarely amended. From 1609, under the Naturalisation and Restoration of Blood Act, 7 Ja. I, c. 2, it became necessary for every beneficiary to take the Oaths of Allegiance and Supremacy in the House before the second reading of the Bill.

LISTS

There is a list of restitution, etc. Bills in F. Clifford, *History of Private Bill Legislation*, vol. i, (1885), pp. 361–9.
See also *Index of Local and Personal Acts* (as above).
Return of all Acts . . . passed during the last two hundred years by which a Peerage has been restored . . ., H.L. 161 (1884–5), vol. xii, p. 543.
Report by the Lords Committees appointed to search for precedents of Bills for reversal of attainders . . ., H.L. 86 (1824), vol. clxviii, pp. 1–14.

10. LOCAL GOVERNMENT BILLS

Private Acts relating to local authorities were relatively infrequent in the 16th and 17th c. In the 18th c. increasing numbers of Bills were promoted, e.g. for the paving, lighting and cleansing of cities or towns, but the great period of expansion in legislative activity on behalf of local authorities was between 1882 and 1906, and local government bills have since constituted a principal category amongst Private Bills. From 1882, Private Bills promoted by local authorities and relating to police or sanitary regulations were referred by H.C. to a Select Committee known as the 'Police and Sanitary Committee'; from 1909 onwards the matters referred were somewhat extended, and the committee was known as the 'Local Legislation Committee'. After 1930 the committee lapsed (but cf. O. C. Williams, *Private Bill Procedure*, vol. i, pp. 246–51).

Acts relating to counties have not been numerous; their subject matter has frequently concerned boundaries, finance, or education. Many Acts, however, have been passed relating to cities and boroughs. The topics dealt with are diverse; a useful classification is that used in the *Index to Local and Personal Acts* for London: 1, Improvements; 2, Markets, Exchanges, etc.; 3, Parish Affairs, Poor Relief, etc.; 4, Courts of Justice, Prisons, Police, etc.; 5, Miscellaneous; 6, Superannuation.

LISTS. *Index to Local and Personal Acts*, etc. (as above).

11. OTHER PRIVATE BILL CATEGORIES

The previous sections have dealt with those classes of Private Bill of particular historical interest and those with the most complex archival history. The remaining categories may be grouped as follows:

Ecclesiastical Bills (e.g. exchange of advowson, or compensation for tithe).
Trading and other company Bills (these may involve the deposit of copies of deeds of partnership and declarations of capital, shares and shareholders).
Fishery Bills.
Construction of bridges, ferries, roads, subways and tunnels Bills.
Road and miscellaneous transport Bills (e.g. omnibuses, air transport).
Construction of harbours, docks, ports, piers and quays Bills.
Water supply and drainage Bills.
Lighting Bills (gas and electricity).

LISTS. *Index to Local and Personal Acts*, etc. (as above).

PRIVATE BILL RECORDS

(i) For Records of Proceedings on Private Bills *see*

COMMITTEE APPOINTMENT BOOKS, 1610 to 1861, p. 42.
COMMITTEE BOOKS, 1624 to date, pp. 43–6.
EVIDENCE, 1771 to date, pp. 48–54.
EXAMINERS' EVIDENCE BOOKS, 1859 to date, p. 87.
PARLIAMENTARY HISTORY and PARLIAMENTARY DEBATES, pp. 37–9.
MANUSCRIPT MINUTES OF THE HOUSE, 1610 to date, pp. 33–6.
JOURNALS OF THE HOUSE, 1510 to date, pp. 28–32.

(ii) Other Records relating to Private Bills.

Note: that the numerals in brackets after the titles of classes of documents on pp. 83–92 refer to the categories of Private Bill as listed above (e.g. Railway Bills) for which these particular classes exist.

LISTS. In H.L.R.O. MS. lists of Plans, Books of Reference, Subscription Contracts etc. 1794 to date, 100 vols. The other classes may be found listed among the Main Papers or in the Parchment Collection. *See* also p. 192

Affidavits   (Categories 1, 3, 4, 8, 10, 11 above)

1698 to date

S.O. 90 of 1698 ordered that committees should only notice Consents to Bills if they were given in person, or if affidavits had been made both of consent and of inability to attend personally. Affidavits under this S.O. were usually on separate sheets of paper, were given most frequently in connection with Estate Bills, and are preserved in the appropriate Bill bundles amongst the Main Papers. (In the *Calendar* they are classified as 'Consents'.) Affidavits might also exceptionally be given by letter (as on 26 December 1691). From 1814, S.O.s provided that affidavits could be submitted to Private Bill Committees in proof of allegations (*see* the present S.O. 126). These affidavits may be preserved in the appropriate Bill bundles, but from 1954–5 onwards they are found, together with the original Petitions, in the Minutes of Proceedings of Select Committees, or of Unopposed Bill Committee proceedings. When Examiners of Private Bills were appointed they were empowered to receive Affidavits in proof of compliance with S.O.s (present S.O. 80). This series of Affidavits was not preserved until a separate class of Examiners' Affidavits was formed in 1963.

Amendment Sheets   (1–11)

1584 to date

Amendments made in committee were usually written on a sheet of paper and reported to the House together with the Paper Bill or (since 1849) the Printed Bill, complete clauses being written on separate sheets and similarly reported. The texts of Private Bill Amendments, etc., are not recorded in the Journals after 1873. As in the case of Public Bill Amendments, Amendment Sheets need to be read in conjunction with the then current text of the bill.

Bill Books

1910 to 1935   13 vols.

These registers contain alphabetical lists of Bills, followed by a record of progress through H.L., under 23 headings, from the date on which the Examiner's Certificate was laid on the Table to the date of Royal Assent. Memoranda indicate the dates on which Bills were withdrawn or preambles not proved, and on which Bills were suspended pursuant to resolutions, or were thrown out in committee. Consents may also be noted. (*See* also REGISTERS OF BILLS, H.C.)

Bill Papers (Miscellaneous)   (1–11)

See PARLIAMENT OFFICE PAPERS (PRIVATE BILL OFFICE PAPERS, 1819–date).

Paper Bills   (1–11)

1584 to 1849

These contain the full text of H.L. Bills as read in that House (*see* the general description for Public Bills above, p. 65).

Printed Bills   (1–11)

1705 to date

The printing of Bills by those petitioning for them became obligatory in 1705 (S.O. 101), but the prints did not supplant either the Paper Bills (above) as the official text up to the Report Stage in the first House, or the Engrossment (below) as the official text thereafter. Since 1849, however, two official series of printed Private Bills have been preserved: *Table Bills* and *House Bills* (cf. p. 66 above). Occasionally after 1849, and continuously from 1936, the following three additional classes of prints have been preserved, either with the Main Papers or as separate classes: *Precedent Bills* in which the precedents for each clause are noted in the margin for the use of the Lord Chairman; *Proof Bills* produced before the L. Chairman containing consents and proofs that the preamble has been approved;[1] and *Filled Bills* in which the Parliamentary Agent has entered amendments made during the passage of the Bill.

Many Private Acts before 1815 and a few between 1815 and 1922 were never officially printed and published after receiving the Royal Assent. Consequently prints of the Bill at earlier stages, made under the 1705 S.O., have often been the texts most readily available for use by students; it should be observed, however, that many of these texts may be incomplete or misleading so far as the text of the final act is concerned. A collection of printed Private Bills and Private Acts has been formed by the H.L. Library of 200 vols., 1713–1867, which is fairly complete from about 1760 (the 18th c. vols. principally contain Bills, the 19th c., Acts). A similar but rather shorter set in 46 vols is preserved in the H.C. Library for 1779–1819. A bound set of Private Bills, 1860–date, includes prints of various stages. Individual prints may also be found amongst the Main Papers.

Engrossed Bills   (1–11)

1576 to 1849

As is the case of Public Bills (*see* p. 60), the text of Private Bills was engrossed on parchment after report stage in the first House. Until 1849 this engrossment became the authoritative Act after Royal Assent. The class of Engrossed Bills now preserved in H.L.R.O. consists of those Bills which did not reach Royal Assent. Their general format, etc., is that described below for ACTS OF PARLIAMENT.

---

[1] A bound set of 9 Proof Bills, 1767, is preserved separately in the PARLIAMENT OFFICE PAPERS.

Book of Receipts (3)

1831 to 1894   1 vol.

Receipts are noted for the return of Registers produced in Sel. Com. on Estate Bills.

Books of Reference (1, 4, 5, 8, 10, 11)

1794 to date

By S.O. of 11 March 1793 it was ordered that maps or plans of proposed canals and the lands through which they were to pass must be deposited with the Clerk of the Parliaments 'together with a Book of Reference containing a List of the Names of the Owners or reputed Owners and also of the Occupiers of such Lands respectively'. This was extended to railway and tramway Bills in 1803, and to turnpike road Bills in 1813, and it was elaborated as regards railway bills in 1836, becoming a general order in 1838. Each parcel of land is numbered to correspond with the plan, and general descriptions are given of the properties, e.g. 'arable field', 'sheep down', etc. The names of lessees may also be given, invariably so from 1838.

Breviates (Briefs) (1–11)

1606 to 1849

The Breviates or Briefs for Private Bills are similar to those for Public Bills and summarise the texts of the Bills. Few have been preserved. A Breviate for the Ross and Cromarty Jurisdiction Bill is amongst the PARLIAMENT OFFICE PAPERS.

Certificates, Principal Secretary of State's (7)

1798 to 1911

This class of Certificate originated with the requirement of S.O. of 20 April 1798 that no naturalisation Bill should be read 2a until the petitioner had produced a Certificate from 'one of His Majesty's principal Secretaries of State' (in practice, the Home Secretary) that the Secretary was satisfied that the petitioner had proved he had conformed to the laws relating to aliens and was well affected to the Crown and government. The Certificates are formal in character and are under the signature and seal of the Secretary of State.

Certificates, Sacramental (7)

1621 to 1798

Produced in connection with naturalisation Bills, Sacramental Certificates contain the name of the church in which Holy Communion was received, of the officiating priest, and of the witnesses.

Committee Office Amendment Book

1905 to 1920   1 vol.

A register of Private Bills for which amendments were deposited in the Private Bill Office.

Committee Office Notice Books   (1–11)

1898 to 1940   3 vols.

These books provide chronological lists of sittings of committees on Bills, together with notes as to Cards and other Notices sent out to members of the committee (under the dates of issue).

Committee Office Petition Books   (1–11)

1914 to date   19 vols.

These books contain alphabetical lists of Bills together with names of Petitioners and Agents, with the dates on which counsel were to appear in committee on opposed Bills. (*See* also H.C. REGISTERS OF PETITIONS.)

Consents Lists   (1, 4, 8, 10, 11)

1794 to date

Consents required in the case of Private and Personal Bills were usually given orally in committee, and the signatures of those concerned were then appended to the entries in the Committee Book or endorsed on a print of the Bill, unless Affidavits of consent (*q.v.*) were accepted. From 1794 onwards Lists of Owners and Occupiers of property which was to be acquired compulsorily had to be deposited with the Clerk of the Parliaments showing whether each individual had consented to, dissented from, or was neuter concerning the Bill. From 1836 Lists of Lessees were added, although such lists might often have been included earlier. Consents Lists are usually in the form of paper booklets; they are usually preserved with deposited Plans, but may sometimes be preserved separately in connection with Bills for extending the time limit for construction.

Court Proceedings (Divorce)   (2)

1798 to 1922

In accordance with a S.O. of 1798, petitioners for a Bill of Divorce delivered to H.L. an official copy of the proceedings and the sentence of divorce *a mensa et thoro* given in the ecclesiastical court. These have been preserved with the Main Papers.

Declarations   (1, 4, 8, 10, 11)

1794 to date

Declarations are formal statements that the company or authority promoting the Bill is able to provide the money to carry it out from its own resources. They have frequently been submitted, usually in connection with public works Bills, instead of Subscription Contracts.

Demolition Statements   (1, 4, 8, 10, 11)

1853 to date

Demolition Statements give the number, description and situation of the houses, and the number of persons to be displaced, together with a statement of any provision for rehousing. They are also known as 'working class statements', or 'rehousing statements'. From 1853 it has been required that such Statements should be deposited before 1a for all Bills involving the compulsory acquisition and demolition of '30 houses or more inhabited by the labouring classes in any one parish or place'. From 1899 statements were required where the total number of persons to be displaced in any area was more than 30 (cf. the present S.O. 47).

BIBLIOGRAPHY

H. J. Dyos, 'Some Social Costs of Railway Building in London', *Journal of Transport History*, vol. iii (1957–8), pp. 23–30; and 'Railways and Housing in Victorian London', *ibid.*, vol. ii (1955–6), pp. 13–14, 98–9.

Estimates of Expense   (1, 4, 8, 10, 11)

1794 to date

See plate 5

S.O. 136 of 1793 ordered the deposit of signed Estimates of Expense for all projects including provisions for raising money to defray expense. The Estimates have usually been made by the engineer responsible, and are signed either by him or by the chairman of the authority submitting the Estimate. Between about 1835 and 1865 the Estimates were brief, but both before and after that period they may be detailed, including, e.g. the cost of land per acre, the cost of excavating so many cubic feet of earth, and the individual costs of locks, wharves, bridges, etc. The Estimates are filed with the other deposits.

Estimates of Time   (1, 4, 8, 10, 11)

1814 to date

See plate 5

Estimates of the probable time within which the whole of the projected works would be completed were ordered in 1813. These were signed by the engineer or by the chairman of the authority. Most Bills had a clause limiting the time for compulsory acquisition of land and for the completion of the works, after which time certain powers given by the Bill would lapse unless extended by a further Bill.

Examiners' Certificates   (1, 4, 5, 8, 10, 11)

1856 to date

Since 1856 the Examiners have laid on the Table of the House Certificates that S.O.s have (or have not) been complied with in the case of each Petition for a Private Bill (*see* also EXAMINERS' SPECIAL REPORTS below).

Examiners' Evidence   (1, 4, 5, 8, 10, 11)

1859 to date

Minutes of evidence before the Examiners of Petitions for Private Bills are preserved in bound vols. and consist largely of verbatim evidence taken on petitions. The evidence may include confirmation or correction of points of detail in the original deposited plans and other documents.

Examiners' Special Reports   (1, 4, 5, 8, 10, 11)

1856 to date

In case of doubt about the application of a S.O. to a particular case the Examiner makes a special report to the Standing Orders Committee. The Reports, and proceedings on them, are in COMMITTEE BOOKS.

Judges' Reports   (3)

1706 to date

Until 1706 Estate Bills were examined in detail in committee, and proceedings were recorded in COMMITTEE BOOKS (*q.v.*). In 1706, S.O. 104 ruled that all Petitions for Bills then described as Private Bills (i.e. what are now known as Personal Bills) should be referred to two judges, who were to summon all parties before them, and then report to the House the 'state of the case and their opinion thereupon'. In 1843, however, a new S.O. limited the judges to legal points; they no longer investigated the truth of the allegations of the petitioner. In practice, references to judges has been confined almost entirely to Estate Bills; in these instances the Reports, until 1843, have sometimes been lengthy and detailed.

Memorials   (1, 4, 5, 8, 10, 11)

1836 to date

Memorials are statements alleging non-compliance with S.O.s by the promoters of Private Bills. They are deposited in the Private Bill Offices, H.L. and H.C. Those in H.C. were considered by the S.O.s Committee from 1836–46 and by the Examiners after 1846. Some Memorials in H.L. have been bound in the Committee Books; from 1966 a separate class has been formed of Memorials, H.L.

Orders of Service   (2)

1669 to 1922

These original copies of Orders of the House, served on those concerned in Divorce Bill proceedings, were signed by the Clerk of the Parliaments and returned to the House with notice either that the Order had been obeyed, or, that for reasons stated, it had not been obeyed. The Order and endorsed reply are entered in the Journal.

Orders of the House   (1–11)

1621 to date

These are copies of Orders made by the House, concerning Private Bill proceedings, which were usually made to order the attendance of witnesses, the production of documents, or the reference of petitions to judges. They are entered *in extenso* in the Journal.

Parliamentary Agents (Appearance Registers)

1890 to date   47 vols.

The vols. include: (1) Alphabetical list of Agents with addresses, and references to the Bills promoted by them; (2) A chronological record of Appearances on the Bills by the named Agents; (3) A chronological list of Appearances on memorials or petitions. Printed copies of 'Rules to be observed by the Officers of the House and by all Parliamentary Agents and Solicitors engaged in prosecuting proceedings in the House of Lords upon any Petition or Bill', or of Declarations by the Agents may be prefixed to the Registers.

Personal Bills (2, 3, 6, 7, 9)

1850 to 1896   1 vol.

A vol. containing prints of Personal Bills with notes of amendments and other entries.

Petitions (1–11)

1572 to date

Petitions in relation to Private Bills belong to three broad classes: (1) to initiate legislation for the purposes set out in the petition; (2) to object to proposed legislation or to seek amendments thereto; (3) concerning the progress of the Bill, e.g. for leave to proceed, for additional provisions, against alterations in Bills, etc. Petitions concerning Private Bills in the 17th and 18th c. were usually lengthy, but subsequently have been briefer and more formal. Petitions may be entered in the Journal.

Plans (1, 4, 8, 10, 11)

1794 to date

See plate 4

S.O. 136 of 1793 ordered that Plans of projected canals, cuts, navigations, etc., should be deposited, showing the line of such canals, etc. In 1795, S.O. 140 ordered that these plans or maps should be engraved or printed on a scale of at least $\frac{1}{2}$ inch to the mile. In 1803 railways and tramroads were brought within the same S.O.s (S.O. 169). In 1813 maps or plans were required also of tunnels, archways, bridges, ferries, docks, piers, ports and harbours (S.O. 185), and these were to be at least 1 inch to the mile in scale (S.O. 186). Plans of docks and harbours have in fact been preserved from 1800, and for town improvements from 1811. Plans for turnpikes were also to be deposited from 1813 onwards (S.O. 190). Maps or Plans of railways from 1836 onwards were to be on a scale of not less than 4 inches to the mile, with enlarged Plans of built-up areas on a scale of $\frac{1}{4}$ inch to 100 feet (S.O. 216). From 1837, Plans were to be deposited before the beginning of each session and not, as formerly, before the Bill came from the Commons. Until the appropriate Ordnance Survey sheets were available certain Deposited Plans were manuscript drawings on paper or parchment; by the mid-19th c. they were often specially printed or consisted of manuscript additions to Ordnance Survey sheets. The class provides extensive information not only concerning the works projected but also relating to the topography and utilisation of the area. The Plans are normally accompanied by annexed BOOKS OF REFERENCE (*q.v.*).

In addition to Plans deposited at the beginning of Parliamentary proceedings on a Bill, there is a separate category of 'Signed Plans' which have been produced in evidence during committee proceedings. The chairman signs each such plan and initials any alterations on it (and in the accompanying Book of Reference) which may be agreed upon by the committee.

Private Bill Amendment Book   (1–11)

1905 to 1920   1 vol.

The volume contains a chronological list of Private Bills received from H.C. with initials of clerks who have checked amendments made in H.L.

Public Notices   (1, 4, 8, 10, 11)

1795 to date

S.O. 134 of 1793 provided that no Canal Bill should be read 3a unless notice had been inserted three times in the *London Gazette*, and in one newspaper in each county affected. This provision was later applied to other categories of Private Bill. Copies had to be deposited from 1849 onwards. The surviving series of Notices from *Gazettes*, etc., is imperfect.

Registers of Petitions on Bills   (1–11)

1914 to date   13 vols.

The vols. contain alphabetical lists of Bills, with lists of Petitioners and of the Agents through whom they were presented.

Reports (Departmental) on Bills   (1, 4, 5, 8, 10, 11)

1841 to date

From 1841 the Railway Department of the Committee for Trade began to submit reports on Bills to Parliament, and S.O. of 8 August 1844 made it obligatory to refer such reports to the committee on the Bill. Other departments subsequently reported similarly on Bills within their own spheres of responsibility. Some of these reports survive amongst the Main Papers; certain Reports were ordered to be printed, and appear in SESSIONAL PAPERS.

Sections   (1, 4, 8, 10, 11)

1795 to date

Prints or drawings of sections through proposed works, showing the level of the ground in relation to the height or depth of the works, have normally been deposited with the Plans. S.O. 216 of 1836 provided that sections for Railway Bills should be drawn to the same horizontal scale as the Plan and to a vertical scale of not less than 1 inch to every 100 feet.

Special Order Book

1925 to 1936   1 vol.

The Register contains alphabetical lists of Special Orders, followed by a record of proceedings on them.

Special Orders

1927 to 1948   18 vols., 7 files

Before 1927 individual copies of Special Orders were treated as SESSIONAL PAPERS and are preserved with Main Papers. From 1927 to 1935 Special Orders were bound in sessional vols. which have now also been placed with Main Papers (18 vols.). From 1937 to 1948 individual Special Orders and Special Procedure Orders are also preserved in 7 box files. Duplicated explanatory notes and departmental memoranda are included in the box file for 1948. *See* also p. 45.

Subscription Contracts   (1, 4, 8, 10, 11)

1794 to 1858

The deposit of copies of Subscription Contracts began in 1794 and was made compulsory for Railway Bills by S.O. 216 of 1836. This provided for Subscription Contracts to be printed and delivered to the Clerk of the Parliaments before the introduction of the Bill. All such Contracts contain the names, occupations and residences of those who have subscribed to the proposed works, the amount of subscription, the names of those witnessing the contract, and its date. The obligation to deposit ended in 1858. (*See* SUBSCRIPTION LISTS following.)

Subscription Lists   (1, 4, 8, 10, 11)

1794 to 1858

S.O. 136 of 1793 provided that if money were to be raised by subscription for building a canal, an account of the money subscribed and the names of subscribers should be annexed to the deposited Plan or map. This provision was extended later to cover other classes of public works including railways. The obligation ended in 1858.

BIBLIOGRAPHY. H. Pollins, 'The Swansea Canal', *Journal of Transport History*, vol. i (1953–4), pp. 135–54; and 'The Finances of the Liverpool and Manchester Railway', *Economic History Review*, 2nd series, vol. v (1952), pp. 90–7.

Taxing Journals, etc.   (1, 4, 8, 10, 11)

1847 to 1952   19 vols.

The Journals (1886–1952) are records made by the Taxing Officer to the House of Lords for taxations of Private Bills. They contain considerable detail, with occasional lengthy reports and statements from the Taxing Officer to the Clerk of the Parliaments relating to memorials; and also with texts of certificates of taxation prepared on the request of official liquidators and others. One vol. relates to the taxing of Light Railway Bills (1904–33). Preserved with this class are 8 vols. of Precedents, Acts, Taxing Notes, Lists of Charges, etc., 1847–1922; and 2 vols. of Fee Receipt Books (Light Railway Commission), 1904–28.

Trustees Acceptance Books   (3)

1797 to 1842   4 vols.

Before 1797 and after 1842 the names and signatures of those accepting a trust appear in the appropriate COMMITTEE BOOKS. Between these two dates they are recorded in separate vols. The greater number of the trustees were concerned with Estate Bills.

Unopposed Committee Minutes   (1, 4, 8, 10, 11)

1899 to 1927   5 vols.

Rough entry books kept by the clerks of committee concerning the consideration of Unopposed Bills. Attendances and proceedings are briefly noted in chronological order.

Witness Books   (1–11)

1641 to 1862   136 vols.

Vol. 1, for 1641–8, is a book of Warrants, in which the complete texts of the Orders summoning witnesses are recorded; subsequent vols. list the Bill or other matter being dealt with, the names of the witnesses called, and the date on which they were sworn. No vols are preserved for 1690–1704.

From 1846 the vols. consist of bound printed forms, one form for each Bill or proceeding, and include the names of the Parliamentary agents for the Bills.

ACTS OF PARLIAMENT

From the 13th c. onwards formal decisions made by the King in Parliament which effected a permanent change in the law of the land were incorporated in a text known as a 'statute'. The statute was drawn up, on behalf of the King, by judges and other members of his Council at the conclusion of each Parliament or each session. The statute included all individual enactments of this type made during that Parliament or session, and each separate enactment was a 'chapter' of the statute.[1] No original texts of the earliest statutes, 1235–76, have been preserved in official custody, but from 1278–1468 statutes were enrolled in the Chancery series of Statute Rolls now preserved in the Public Record Office (cf. *Lists and Indexes*, P.R.O., no. xxvii). There was probably a further Statute Roll covering the period 1468–89, but this has not survived; and a gap also now exists from 1431 to 1445; for both of these periods, however, reference can be made either to contemporary texts made for annexing to Writs of Proclamation, or to texts preserved in the Exchequer. Public Acts, either in the form of Petitions and Responses, or of the official draft Acts, were entered on the Parliament Rolls; from 1483 they were regularly enrolled in their final enacted form.

Within mediaeval Parliaments decisions which were made relating to individuals or localities, of the type subsequently regarded as being appropriate for 'Private Acts', were not usually incorporated in statutes but were enrolled on the Parliament Rolls. These decisions were set out on the Rolls at the foot of the text of the petition to which they referred and from which they began. The Exchequer series of Parliament Rolls runs only from 1290 to 1322, but the Chancery series begins in 1327, then forming a uniform and continuous series to 1850. By the end of the 15th c. it had become increasingly common for these decisions on private matters also to be drawn in legislative form, i.e. for texts of 'Private Acts' to be composed. These texts might be enrolled on the Parliament Rolls for a fee, but the titles alone, without the texts, of Private Acts appeared on the Rolls from 1593.

The original text of each individual petition was the starting point in the legislative process, both for statutes later to be inscribed on the Statute Rolls, and also for decisions on private petitions eventually recorded on the Parliament Rolls. These original petitions survive today at the Public Record Office for the 13th–16th c. in three separate classes: Parliamentary and Council Proceedings in the Chancery records; the smaller miscellany of Parliamentary and Council Proceedings (Exchequer); and, in considerable quantity in the artificial class of Ancient Petitions. During the 15th c. certain petitions reveal a significant development in Parliamentary procedure. It had been customary for the King when he initiated legislation, to introduce complete bills in the modern sense, i.e. texts in final legislating form. The same practice was adopted by the Commons in the case of money bills, and then by both Commons and Lords in all instances in which legislation was initiated by them. This development was under way in the earlier 15th c. and became general during Henry VI's reign,

[1] From 1389 each chapter forms a separate public Act, or Statute in the modern sense.

between 1422 and 1461. As a result, although late 15th c. Bills might still open in petitioning form, they then continued with such formulae as 'Be it therefore ordained', that is, they were *petitiones formam actus in se continentes*. Thus the document handled in Parliament, which had previously been merely the starting point for the composition of the text of the final Act, became (when the Royal Assent was given) the Act itself, any amendments made during debate in Parliament being incorporated in the original text.

These 'evolved petitions' (now known as Engrossed Bills) were transferred to Chancery in the same way as the earlier petitions had been, and there are at least 411 original texts of this type surviving at the Public Record Office for the period before 1483. From 1483 to 1497 there is a gap, when no single document of the evolved type survives, but in 1497 the series of Engrossed Bills preserved in the House of Lords begins and continues to 1850, there being known, when enacted, as the 'Original Acts'. Those Engrossed Bills which did not receive the Royal Assent are preserved separately (*see* BILLS above). During the years 1849–50 the system of engrossment was replaced by printing. The printed text which had been used during debate (the House Bill) was replaced by a new print (the Vellum) for preservation in continuation of the series of Original Acts.

The general procedure for the enactment of a Bill and the preparation of the Original Act in the period since 1497 is as follows:

After a bill has passed both Houses the authoritative text (i.e. the Engrossed Bill until 1849–50; thereafter the House Bill) remains in the custody of the Clerk of the Parliaments,[1] except that Bills for granting aids and supplies are returned to the custody of the Commons until the Royal Assent is about to be given, when they are brought up by the Clerk of the House of Commons.[2] At a Royal Assent the Clerk of the Crown reads out successively the short titles of the Bills, and the Clerk of the Parliaments pronounces on behalf of the Sovereign (whether the Sovereign is present or not), the appropriate formulae (*see* p. 62 above). This procedure has remained fairly constant since the 16th c. From 1967 onwards, however, under the Royal Assent Act, 1967, the Royal Assent can be notified to each House, sitting separately, by its Speaker. The power to refuse a Bill was last exercised on 11 March 1708. The first occasion on which the Sovereign was not present, but gave assent by commission, was on 11 February 1542; the last occasion on which the Sovereign gave assent in person was on 12 August 1854. Since then all assents have been by commission or by notification. For the class of ROYAL COMMISSIONS, *see* pp. 175–6.

Until 1849–50, after assent or refusal had been given, the Clerk of the Parliaments superscribed the formula of assent or refusal at the head of the engrossed roll, thereby authenticating it as the 'Original Act'. He endorsed the roll with its Parliament Office number, which was assigned in strict order of assent and regardless of the classification of the Bill. From 1793 onwards he likewise endorsed the roll with the date on which assent was given, under the provisions of the Acts of Parliament (Commencement) Act, 1793, 33 Geo. III, c. 13. The Act was then listed in the Parliament Office List of Acts (*see* below, pp. 96–7); and subsequent enrolments and certifications were made from it by the Clerk of the Parliaments.

[1] In fact, until 1849, in the hands of an assistant, the Clerk of Inrollments.
[2] This is no longer necessary, however, if Royal Assent is given by notification (*see* p. 176 below).

It should be observed that no seals were appended to the engrossments, unless the engrossments in certain instances were presented together with the appropriate Royal Commission, in which case the tag of the Commission's seal might be passed through a slit at the foot of the Engrossed Bill. The Royal Sign Manual was superscribed by the Sovereign with decreasing regularity between 1497 and 1558; thereafter it only appeared as a mark of royal licence or consent for a Bill affecting the Crown to be read. The Sign Manual does not appear to have been treated as authentication of the text. This was guaranteed by the superscribed or endorsed formula of assent and by continuous custody in the Office of the Clerk of the Parliaments.

From 1849–50 onwards the Original Act has been newly printed, after assent, from the House Bill. The formula of assent is still superscribed on the Original Act on behalf of the Clerk of the Parliaments; and as an additional form of authentication, the Act is signed at its conclusion by the Clerk of the Parliaments or his deputy.

Original Acts

1497 to 1850[1]   25,836 rolls

See plate 7

Acts from 1497 to *c*. 1558 consist usually of a single membrane of parchment, cut according to the length of the Act, and varying from a small slip, 12 inches × 3 inches, to a large skin, 42 inches × 34 inches. Acts comprising lay subsidies are in the form of indentures, but from 1535 are in roll form, the membranes being sewn head to tail. From about 1558 this 'Chancery roll' format is followed for all Acts, those of post 1660 date being invariably 12 inches in width, but varying greatly in length, some of them reaching about a quarter of a mile.

The language is English. The handwriting at first diverse, although usually of Secretary type, became in about 1660 stereotyped in a sloping mixed Secretary-Italic hand, written large and open. This 'Parliamentary hand' was ordered to be used generally in recording all court proceedings by the Proceedings in Courts of Justice Act, 1730, 4 Geo. II, c. 26.

As noted in the section on Bills, the engrossments may have interlineations, deletions and interpolated annexes on parchment. From these the various stages in the progress of the Bill through Parliament may sometimes be reconstructed.[2]

All the Acts for 14 & 15 Hen. VIII and for 21 Hen. VIII have been lacking from the class since the 16th c. Certain other Acts have been lacking since at least 1850.

The following documents of particular constitutional importance belong to the class of Original Acts:

Act of Supremacy, 1558, 1 Eliz. I, c. 1; Original Act, 1 Eliz. I, no. 1.

Petition of Right, 1628, 3 Cha. I, c. 1; Original Act, 3 Cha. I, no. 2. Photographic facsimiles are available in H.L.R.O. for purchase.

[1] Omitting the period 1642–60, for which *see* p. 96 below.
[2] Cf. S. T. Bindoff, 'The Making of the Statute of Artificers' in *Elizabethan Government and Society*, ed. Bindoff *et al.* (1961), pp. 56–94.

Act of Uniformity, 1662, 14 Cha. II, c. 4; Original Act, 14 Cha. II, no. 3. The
    Book of Common Prayer originally annexed to the Act is now preserved
    separately in the Library, H.L.
Habeas Corpus Act, 1679, 31 Cha. II, c. 2; Original Act, 31 Cha. II, no. 3.
The Bill of Rights, 1688, 1 Will. & Mary, sess. 2, c. 2; Original Act, 1 Will.
    & Mary, sess. 2, no. 2 (for the *DECLARATION OF RIGHTS see*
    SESSIONAL PAPERS).
The Act of Union with Scotland, 1706, 6 Anne, c. 11; Original Act, 6 Anne,
    no. 7 (for the *ARTICLES OF UNION see* SESSIONAL PAPERS).
The Reform Act, 1832 (Representation of the People Act), 2 & 3 Will. IV,
    c. 65; Original Act, 2 Will. IV, no. 147.

From the 15th to the 17th c. certain documents other than Acts were classified
with them, e.g. the Articles against Thomas Yatten, 1497 have also been
preserved with the Acts, and numbered as 12 Hen. VII, no. 14; the Declaration
against Dr. Manwaring (3 Cha. I, no. 14); the Protestations of the Lords (16 &
17 Cha. I, no. 36); and the Charges and Answers concerning E. Strafford (16 &
17 Cha. I, no. 37).
    Note that for the texts of Ordinances, 1642–1660, it is necessary to see
JOURNALS, H.L. and ORDERS AND ORDINANCES. Printed texts of
Acts and Ordinances appear in C. H. Firth and R. S. Rait, *Acts and Ordinances of
the Interregnum, 1642–1660*, 3 vols. (1911), as well as in contemporary vols. of
Acts and Ordinances.

Printed Original Acts (Vellums)

1849 to date   31,500 docs.

    The authentic text of each Public Act, from 1849, and of each Private Act
from 1850, has been printed separately. Each doc. is composed of one or more
gatherings of vellum with leaves of about 8 inches × 12 inches. The gatherings
are pierced by three holes in the margin, and bound by a red silk tape passed
through them and tied on the front cover. In 1955, for economy, it was decided
to print Private Acts on hand-made paper instead of vellum, but in 1957 it
was agreed that the covers should be again of vellum to give greater protection.
In 1957 it was also decided that the complete text of Public Acts should continue
to be printed on vellum. As from 1849–50 a duplicate has been made of each
Original Act; this is transmitted to the Public Record Office and is there placed
amongst the records of Chancery.

Lists and Calendars of Acts

1608 to date   23 docs.

    This class of document consists of guides to the accumulation of Original
Acts made for the use of the Parliament Office. 'The Long Calendar' and 'the
Short Calendar' had an especially authoritative status; the remainder are copies
or working papers relating to the checking of Acts. The notes on missing Acts
provide a guide supplementary to that in appendix C to the Introduction of
Statutes of the Realm, vol. i.
    *Unless otherwise indicated, all the following MSS. refer to Acts by their Parliament
Office number.*

The Short Calendar: Alphabetical list of short titles of Acts,[1] 3 vols., 1497–1903, compiled contemporaneously from 1706 onwards. (Short titles for Acts may differ from those noted for the same Bills, e.g. in the margin of the Journals.)

The Long Calendar: Chronological list of long titles of Acts, 6 vols., 1497–1863. Compiled contemporaneously from *c.* 1608 onwards. Vol. i contains lists signed by Clerks, 1607–60, and to it is prefixed a list of 'The severall Journalls in the Parliament Office', showing the make-up of the present vol. i of the manuscript Journals in 1660.

Other Calendars:
'A Calendar of all the Acts of Parliament in the Office', 1497–1735, compiled 1735, 1 vol.

'Calendar of Acts in the Parliament Office', 1497–1784, compiled 1731–84, 1 vol.

'An Alphabet to the Calendar of the Acts of Parliament in the office at Westminster', 1497–1739, compiled for William Cowper, Clerk of the Parliaments, 1735–9, 1 vol.

Index of Acts by short title, 1818–26, 1 vol.

Draft Index of Acts, 1865–70, 1 vol.

Index of Acts, 1871–4, 1 vol.

'Index to Local Personal and Private Acts in the Library, House of Lords', 1722–1840, 2 vols.

Index to the Statutes, (printed). Pt. i, Public General Acts (1801–44); pt. ii, Local and Personal, Local and Private Acts (1801–59).

Collection of Tables of Statutes, 1860–69, annotated with Parliament Office numbers.

Lists of Acts by Regnal Years:
Annotated List of 'Acts in Castle [Jewel] Tower and Strong Room', 1850.

Annotated List of 'Original Acts in the Tower belonging to the Parliament Office', 1497–1858, with Survey, 1963, including notes on those missing.

2 Lists of 'Acts missing in Castle', 1858, 1861.

List of 'Acts of Parliament deposited in the Victoria Tower,' 1864, with tables of regnal years, Sovereign, duration of Parliaments and lists of Calendars.

Annotated list of Acts, indicating those missing, 1870, with lists of Acts missing and found, 1871.

* * * * *

THE NUMBERING, CLASSIFICATION AND PRINTING OF ACTS

(i) *Numbering of Acts of Parliament*

Until 1962 Acts were described by reference to the session of Parliament in which they were passed, and the session of Parliament was described in terms of the regnal year or years during which it occurred. Thus, an Act was described as having been passed in the Parliament of 3 Geo. II, or of 4 & 5 Geo. V. If two sessions were wholly within one regnal year their Acts were numbered

---

[1] Each Act has a 'long title' which sets out in general terms the purposes of the Act. This from 33 Hen. VIII is consistently endorsed on the Original Act, and it appears in printed

separately as belonging to either 'session' 1 or 2, e.g. to 1 Geo. I sess. 1. If the
sessions were not of the same Parliament, and so could not be numbered consecutively, the Acts were described as 'statute' 1 or 2 of that regnal year. From
1963 however, under the Acts of Parliament Numbering and Citation Act, 10 &
11 Eliz. II, c. 34, the calendar year has been substituted for the regnal year and
the session. An Act is now, therefore, described as '1964, c. 34', etc.

   Within the Parliament Office, between 1497 and 1902 all original Acts
received consecutive numbers in a single series for each session and the manuscript or printed Original Act of that period is most accurately referred to as, e.g.
5 Anne, no. 23. After 1902 the Original Acts are numbered as in the published
texts (*see* below p. 101). The published texts and lists of titles of Acts have since
the 18th c. used a numeration which treats each class of Act, Public, Private, etc.
as a separate sequence, and each Act within that class as a chapter of the whole,
thus: 47 Geo. III, sess. 1, c. cliii. This type of numeration is still followed, apart
from the substitution of the calendar year for the regnal year from 1963 onwards.

(ii) *Classification of Printed Acts of Parliament*

The broad division of Acts is that between Public Acts and Private Acts; a
division which in general corresponds with that between Public Bills and Private
Bills. Public Acts contain a part of the law of the land, and it is the law that
they are known by the judges and by the people. A Private Act, on the other
hand, while it is an instrument having legal effect by authority of Parliament,
needs to be brought before a court of law, as does a private document, before it
can be recognized. It was this point of law which led those drafting Private Bills
to insert with increasing frequency after 1700 a clause to the effect that the Act
resulting from the Bill was to be deemed and taken to be a Public Act.[1]

   In general, Private Bills containing this clause received the Royal Assent in
the form 'Le Roi le veult' and therefore became, strictly speaking, Public Acts.
But they have not usually been so referred to, even though the Interpretation of
Acts Act, 1850, 13 & 14 Vict., c. 21, and the Interpretation Act, 1889, 52 & 53
Vict., c. 63, provided that all Acts are Public Acts unless they declare that they
are not. In the present century the only Acts which have declared that they are
not public are those which resulted from Personal Bills, that is, those dealing
with the estate or other personal affairs of an individual.

   The best general guide to the classification and numeration of Public Acts is
in the official *Chronological Table of the Statutes* (see p. 102 below) which lists the
short titles from the 13th c. to date. After 1714 the system of classification and
numbering is relatively clear; before then difficulty arises. The *Chronological
Table* indicates that for Acts before 1714 there have been two principal systems of
classification and numeration in use, the official one (used in *Statutes of the Realm*)
and that followed by the various editions of Ruffhead's *Statutes*. Broadly

---

texts. The clerks from the 15th c., however, also used abbreviated or short titles (of perhaps
3 or 4 words) for some acts, as in the Short Calendar. From 1849–50 onwards the printed
Original Acts have the long titles printed on the covers and at the opening of the text,
and short titles at the heads of the covers and of each page of text. From *c.* 1866 the Acts
themselves may contain a 'short title clause' and the Short Titles Act, 59 & 60 Vict., c. 14,
and subsequent Acts have conferred official short titles, some of which may not be the same
as those used contemporarily in the Parliament Office for Acts passed before 1866.
   [1] At first these clauses were confined to Bills which did make a substantial, albeit local,
change in the law—for example, Bills for the creation of turnpike roads, evasion of
the tolls on which was a crime.

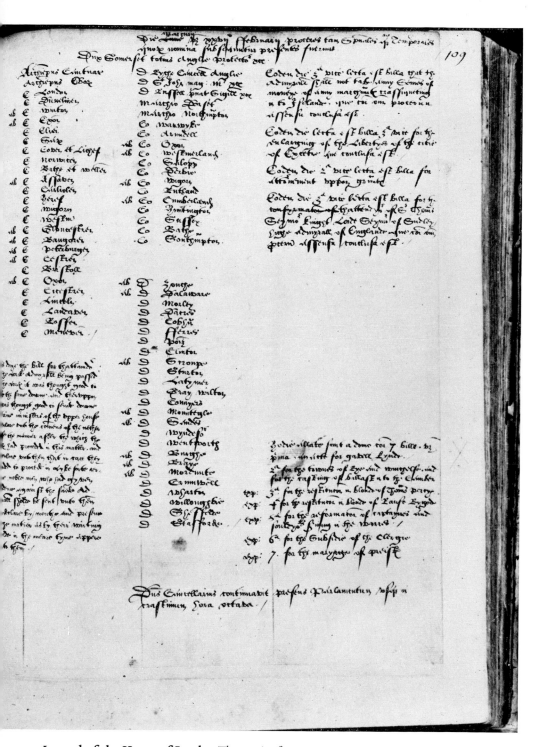

1. Journal of the House of Lords The entries for 27 February 1549 comprise lists of peers, with absentees marked, and (*in the right hand column*) notes of business done, with (*bottom left*) the record of a message sent to the Commons concerning the attainder of Thomas Seymour. 28 cm × 38 cm (see p. 28)

2. Minutes of the House of Lords showing entries for 1 June 1713. The division concerning the dissolution of the Union with Scotland is recorded on the right-hand page, those present voting 'content' or 'not content', and proxies being counted subsequently. 38 cm × 31 cm (see p. 33)

27ᵈ Martii 1797.

Lord of the Manor, Impropriator of the Rectory, Owner of the Great Tithes & Patron of the Vicarage of Iving, the Revᵈ Henry Jerome De Salis D.D. Vicar of the said Vicarage & Parish Church of Iving, Sir Jonathan Lovett Bart. Wardbook T. Pykes, Mrs. Stuart, the other Proprietors, according to the &c great Majesty & the other Proprietors, according to the Instrument mentioned above, signifying their Consents to this Measure before Dance that it may pass into a Law.

The Preamble is agreed to.

Mr. John Hare proves the Allegations in the several Clauses of the Bill.

The Enacting Clauses are severally read & agreed to.

The General Saving Clause read & agreed to.

The Title again read & agreed to.

Ordered

That the Bill be reported without Amendment.

Eodem Die.

Curatum, Manor & Lord Bishop of Bangor in the Chair.
Fakstone Bills

Order of Reference read.

The Title read and postponed.

The Preamble is read, & Mr. Edmund Armstrong is called in, who proves all the Allegations thereof to the Satisfaction of the Committee.

The same Witness produces a State of the Property on the some is rated for the Poors Rate, which State amounts to the Sum of £9 : 16 : 7¾ And being asked who after all the Parties have consented, says the Owners of Property rated to the Sum of £8 : 16 : 3¾ have signed their Consents to the Bill, and that the Owners of Property rated at £1 : 0 : 4¾ make no Objection, but did not chuse to sign the Bill.

The same Witness produces two written Copies & two printed Copies of the Bill, & proves the signing thereof by the Most Honble the Marquis Cornwallis K.G., Thomas Brandram Esqⁿ the Guardians of the Right Honble James Earl Waldegrave an Infant Lord of the Manor of Chewton Mendip, Impropriator &c.? Agent for the behalf of the Rt honourable Earl Waldegrave of his Majesty's Fleet, Lord of the Rectorage, Manor of Chewton Mendip, & Patron of the Rectorial impropriate of Iving, the same

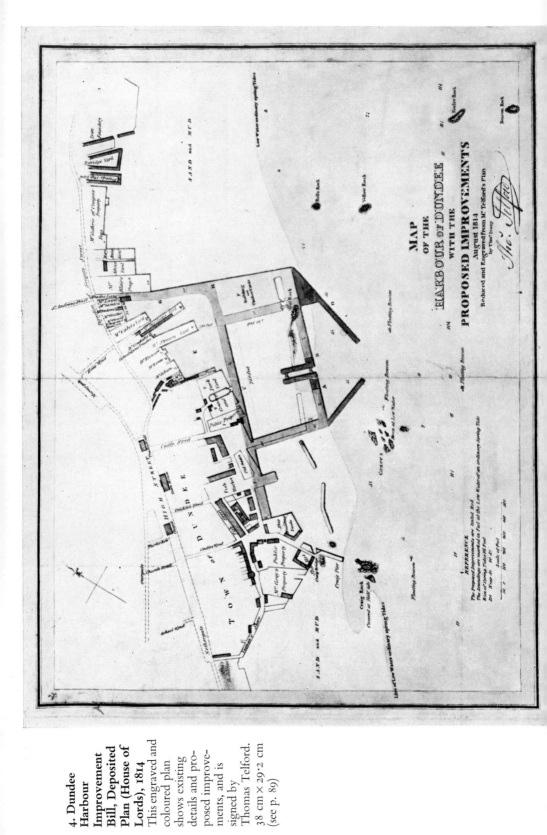

MAP
OF THE
HARBOUR OF DUNDEE
WITH THE
PROPOSED IMPROVEMENTS
August 1814
Reduced and Engraved from Mr Telford's Plan
by Tho? Imray

Tho? Telford

REFERENCE

The Proposed Improvements are tinted Red.
The Soundings are marked in Feet at the Low Water below an ordinary Spring Tide
Rise of Spring Tide 18 Feet

4. Dundee Harbour Improvement Bill, Deposited Plan (House of Lords), 1814 This engraved and coloured plan shows existing details and proposed improvements, and is signed by Thomas Telford. 38 cm × 29·2 cm (see p. 89)

An Estimate of the Expences of
improving the Harbour of Dundee

1	Improving the Quays of the Old Harbour and excavating the Bottom of do	2405	12	-
2	Increasing the Breadth, extending the length and returning the Main Pier to **A** on the Plan - Underbuilding the Eastern side of do - building a Quay Wall from root of do to the Eastern side of the Graving Dock and deepening the Harbour between the Main Pier and the Line marked **AC**	10915	16	6
3	Extending the Quay wall from the Graving Dock to opposite Mr Stewarts Yard, returning it South to the West Rock and again westward to the Letter **B** on the Plan and deepening that part of the Harbour, also making up and protecting the ground adjacent to the Eastern End of the Harbour and forming a Communication with Trades Lane and St Andrews Street	23486	2	6
4	For making an Entrance Lock to Wet dock making up Quays between **A** and **B** on the Plan and constructing protecting Piers on each side of the Entrance	27328	14	6
	Allow for Surveys, Plans, Act of Parliament Superintendance and Contingencies 10 ⅌ Cent	6403		
	Tho.ˢ Telford £	70439	5	6

I am of Opinion that the whole of the above
work may be probably completed in the span
of twelve years if not prevented by unavoidable accidents

Tho.ˢ Telford

5. Dundee Harbour Improvement Bill, Deposited Estimates of Expense and Time (House of Lords), 1814
The estimate includes the cost of works, surveys and plans, and of passing the Bill. It is signed by Thomas Telford. An Estimate of Time is appended. 20·6 cm × 32·8 cm (see p. 87)

6. Barnet Market Bill, 1592 to alter the day on which weekly markets were held at Barnet. The first sheet is shown of the Paper Bill as introduced into the Commons. 27·5 cm × 34·5 cm (see p. 65)

7. Linen and Hemp Manufactures Act, 1750, 24 Geo.
II, c. 31. The first membrane of the Original Act,
engrossed in the House of Commons, and bearing the
appropriate superscriptions, including the Royal Assent
'Le Roy le Veult'. 30 cm × 46 cm (see p. 95)

8. Appeal Case, Berkeley v. Cope, 4 January 1699,
showing (*lower document*) Petition and Appeal of John
Berkeley *et al.* for the reversal of a decree in Chancery;
(*upper document*) Answer of Jonathan Cope *et al.*; each is
counter-signed by the counsel of the party.

66·6 cm × 61·7 cm (see p. 117)

9. Writ of Error, MacDonnogh v. Stafford, 28 May 1624.   The upper document is the Writ addressed to the Chief Justice of the King's Bench ordering him to bring into Parliament the record of the case; the lower document is the first membrane of the roll of transcript from the Plea Rolls of King's Bench brought in by the Chief Justice. 31 cm × 5 cm; 22·4 cm × 31 cm (see p. 122)

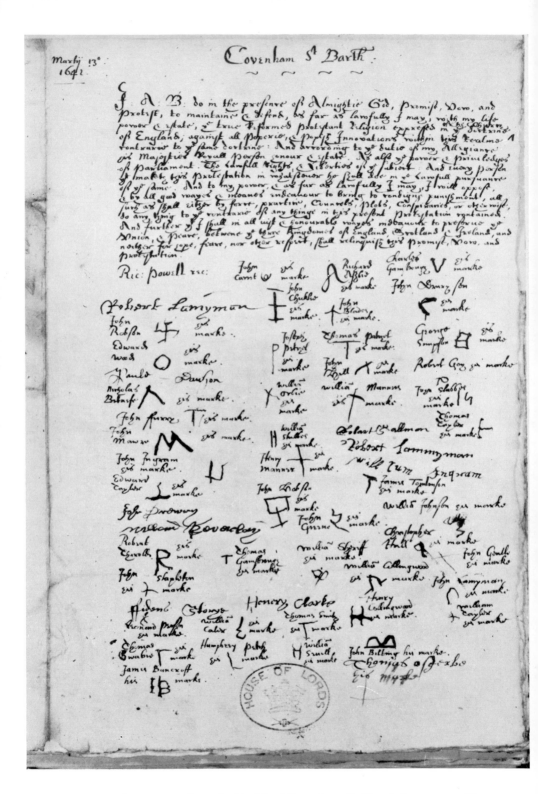

10. Protestation Return from the Parish of Covenham St. Bartholomew, co. Lincs.,
13 March 1642. The text of the oath 'to maintain the true Reformed Protestant Religion'
is followed by the signatures or marks of those taking it. 20 cm × 30 cm (see pp. 154–5)

Die Martis 12° February 1688

The Declaration of the Lords Spirituall and Temporall and Comons Assembled at Westm[inster]

Whereas the late King James the second by the assistance of diverse evill Councellors Judges and Ministers imployed by him did endeavour to subvert and extirpate the Protestant Religion and the Lawes and Libertyes of this Kingdome.

By assumeing and exerciseing a Power of dispencing with and suspending of Lawes and the execution of Lawes without consent of Parliament:

By committing and prosecuteing diverse worthy Prelates for humbly petitioning to be excused from concurring to the said assumed Power

By issueing a Commission under the Great Seale for erecting a Court called the Court of Comissioners for Ecclesiasticall Causes

By levying money for and to the use of the Crowne by pretence of Prerogative for other time and in other manner then the same was granted by Parliament:

By raiseing and keeping a standing Army within this Kingdom in time of Peace without consent of Parliament. and quartering Souldiers contrary to Law

By causeing severall good subjects being Protestants to be disarmed at the same time when Papists were both armed and imployed contrary to Law

By violateing the freedome of Election of Members to serve in Parliament

By causeing ... and prosecuted in the ... for matters and causes ... and by divers other illegall courses: By Prosecut... in the Court of Kings Bench for matters ... causes cognizable only in Parliament and by divers other Arbitrary & illegall Courts

11. The Declaration of Rights by both Houses, 12 February 1689. The first page of the text, written in the Commons, shows amendments made in the House of Lords, and incorporated in the text by the Clerk at the Table, the large ink blot being made at the time. 22·5 cm × 34 cm (see p. 152)

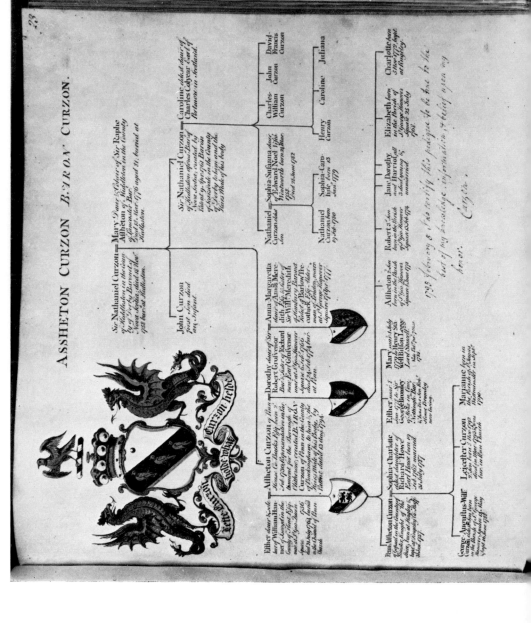

12. Pedigree of Assheton Curzon, 1st Lord Curzon of Penn certified by Lord Curzon, 5 February 1795, and delivered into the House of Lords in accordance with the Standing Order of 11 May 1767. 44 cm × 40 cm (see p. 163)

13. Journal of the House of Commons showing entries for 13 May 1624, including a report from the Conference with the Lords on Monopolies; cf. the printed version, *C.J.*, i, pp. 703–4. 38 cm × 31 cm (see p. 207)

I wish shortly to state the circumstances which led up to this remarkable Parliamentary incident.

The Debate on the application for leave to introduce the Bill for the Protection of Property & Person in Ireland had already lasted many days –; the House was boiling over with indignation at the apparent triumph of obstruction; and Mr. Gladstone, yielding to the pressure of his friends, committed himself, unwisely as I thought, to a continuous sitting on this day, Monday the 31st of Jan'y, in order to force the Bill through its first stage —.

On Tuesday, after a sitting of 24 hours, I saw plainly that this attempt to carry the Bill by continuous sitting would fail, the Parnell Party being strong in members discipline & organization, & with great gifts of the power of speech —.

I reflected on the situation, & came to the conclusion that it was my duty to extricate the H. out of the difficulty, by closing the debate of my own authority, &

14. Diary of Speaker Brand, vol. xi, showing entry for 31 January 1881 recording his decision to close the Coercion Bill debate on his own authority.
18·7 cm × 22·5 cm (see p. 291)

Memorandum written at the Conference at Buckingham Palace, August 24th 1931 between Mr. Ramsay MacDonald, Mr. Baldwin & H.S. after the King had withdrawn.

(11)

BUCKINGHAM PALACE.

1. That a Nat. Govt. be formed to deal with the present financial emergency.

2. It will not be a coalition in the ordinary sense of the term but a cooperation of individuals.

3. When the emergency is dealt with the Govt's work will have finished and parties will return to their ordinary position.

4. The economies and imposts shall be equitable and shall generally follow the lines of the ~~Memorandum~~ b.d. suggestions attached, designed to enable a loan to be raised in ~~America~~

---

15. The Samuel Papers A Memorandum by Sir
Herbert Samuel at the Conference at Buckingham Palace
concerning the formation of a National Government,
24 August 1931. 19 cm × 24·2 cm (see p. 283)

16. **Votes of the House of Commons**

showing pages from the issues for 14 and 15 November 1689 respectively, bound as part of vol. ii in the official set.

31 cm × 27·5 cm (see p. 213)

A Message from the Lords, That the Lords had sent down a Bill for Punishing Officers and Soldiers, that should Desert Their Majesties Service, and for Preventing of False Musters.

Sir *John Guise* acquaints the House, That he had Attended His Majesty with the Address for sending Persons into *Ireland*, to take an Account of the Number of the Army there, and of the State and Condition of the same; And that His Majesty was pleased to give this Answer: *That He would send some Persons forthwith into Ireland, according to the Desires of the House.*

The aforesaid Bill sent down from the Lords was Read the First time, and Ordered a Second Reading to Morrow morning.

Then the House Resolved into a Committee of the whole House, according to the Order made Yesterday, to Consider of the State of the Nation; and after some time spent therein, Mr. Speaker Resumed the Chair, and Mr. *Grey* Reported, That the Committee had come to this following Resolution, *Viz.*

That the want of a Guard, or Convoys for the Merchants for the last Year, hath been an Obstruction of Trade, and an Occasion of great Losses to the Nation.

Ordered,

That all Committees be Adjourned.

And then the House Adjourned till to Morrow morning Nine of the Clock.

H. Powle, *Speaker.*

I Do Appoint Charles Bill, and Thomas Newcomb, *Their Majesties Printers, to Print these Votes; and that no other do presume to Print the same.*

H. Powle, *Speaker.*

L O N D O N,

Printed by *Charles Bill* and *Thomas Newcomb,* Printers to the King and Queens most Excellent Majesties.

1 6 8 9.

V O T E S

O F T H E

House of Commons,

Veneris 15° *die Novembris,* 1689.

A Petition of *Thomas Bush,* in Custody of the Serjeant at Arms for a Breach of Priviledge, in Arresting the Servant of the Lord *Sherrard,* a Member of this House, acknowledging his Offence, and craving Pardon for the same, was Read, and Ordered, That the said *Thomas Bush* be Discharged out of Custody, paying his Fees.

Mr. *Grey* Reports from the Committee of Priviledges and Elections, The Case touching the Election of a Member to serve in this present Parliament for the Borough of *Stockbridge* in the County of *Southampton,* in the room of *Oliver St. John* Esq; lately deceased; That there had appeared very Undue Practices, in Giving and Promising several sums of Money for procuring Voices at the said Election: Whereupon the said Committee had come to three Resolutions, *viz.*

Resolved,

1. That *William Montague* Esq; is not duly Elected a Burgess to serve in this present Parliament for the said Borough.

2. That *William Strode* Esq; is not duly Elected a Burgess to serve in this present Parliament for the said Borough.

3. That the said Election is a void Election.

To all which Resolves the House Agreed.

T   *Ordered,*

speaking, Ruffhead followed a system of numeration and classification ultimately based on the Statute Rolls up to 1468 and, from 1483, on the original printed Sessional Volumes. The Statute Rolls (*see* p. 93 above) did not contain the text of any Public Acts which were not intended to make a permanent change in the law. Thus, Bills which conferred a subsidy or those which regulated the affairs of the King, the Royal Family, or the Government, although they were Public Bills, were not inserted in the Statute Roll. Such Bills were, however, recorded in full in the Parliament Roll, as were also those Private Bills, promoters of which were prepared to pay the necessary fee.

For certain years in the 15th c. no Statute Roll has survived; and although there were other sources, such as the Book of the Exchequer or the Parliament Roll, for the texts of some Acts, it was not certain that these texts were precisely the same as those that would have been engrossed on the Statute Roll for the year, or even that the same Acts would have been included. When therefore the Record Commissioners, between 1810 and 1828, came to compile the authoritative edition of all the Acts of Parliament up to 1714 (*The Statutes of the Realm*) and went to the best original sources available, they did not in all cases follow the arrangement and selection which it is probable would have been followed in the missing Statute Rolls. Furthermore, the editors of *Statutes Revised* and of the *Chronological Table* (see p. 102) did not in all cases (for example in the years 1463 to 1474) follow the system of chaptering and numeration employed by the compilers of the *Statutes of the Realm*.

A further complication is added from 1483. At this point printed Sessional Volumes of Acts began to appear; but the selection of Acts included in the volume was somewhat capricious. In general, anything which would have been on the Statute Roll seems to have been included in the sessional printed volumes; but certain Acts (such as 6 Hen. VIII, c. 17) which were by any standard 'Private Acts' were also printed. In addition, there are among the early Sessional Vols. of Henry VIII's reign a number of Acts which in modern terms would be called 'hybrid' (*see* p. 69). From the 1530s, moreover, subsidies came to be regarded as statutes and were regularly included in the printed Sessional Volume.

Apart from those Private Acts which were, apparently arbitrarily, included in the early Sessional Volumes of Henry VIII, no attempt was made to publish information about Private Acts until the reign of Queen Elizabeth. From 1571, however, a list of the Private Acts, numbered in arabic numerals, was prefixed to the Sessional Volume; and after 1593 the system of enrolling certain Private Acts on the Parliament Roll was discontinued, the titles only of Private Acts being given on the Parliament Roll until 1757.

The following table shows the system of numeration and classification followed in the printed versions since the Restoration (the numbers given in roman or italic numerals are merely examples):

Year	Public Acts	Private Acts
1660–1752	Sessional Volumes, printed from pamphlet type but with numbered pages, of 'Public General Acts' and 'Local and Personal Acts declared Public' in one series indiscriminately; cc. I–IX.	Lists of Private Acts numbered 1–9. None printed, except privately from 1705 and unnumbered. Parliament Roll gives Titles only of 'Private Acts' till 1757.

1753–1797	Ditto, but Public Acts in Volume I (cc. I–IX), 'Local and Personal declared Public' in Volume II (cc. IX–XL).	Listed in Sessional Volume and numbered 1–9. Separate private prints unnumbered.
1798–1802	Public Sessional Volumes as above (cc. I–IX), 'Local and Personal declared Public' in separate volume cc. 1–9.	Listed in Sessional Volume numbered 1–9. Separate private prints unnumbered.
1803–1814	Public as above. Local and Personal declared Public, and Local and Personal to be judicially noticed. } One volume cc. 1–9	Private listed in Sessional Volume and numbered 1–9. Separate private prints unnumbered.
1815–1868	Public as above (including Provisional Orders). Local and Personal declared Public in one volume, cc. i–ix.	Private printed (at parties' expense by King's Printer) 'the printed copies of which may be given in evidence'. Private unprinted } One series 1–9
1869–1875	Public (excluding Provisional Orders) cc. 1–9. Local Acts* (including Provisional Orders, which henceforth are noted as 'Public Acts of a Local character) cc. i–ix. (* 'Local and Private' in 1869 only.)	†Private printed as above. †Private unprinted. [†Private henceforth in effect= personal] } One series *1–9 in italics.*
1876–1922	Public as above.	Local. Private printed as above and numbered *1–9 in italics.* } One volume‡ ‡ Private unprinted and unnumbered listed in this volume.
1923–1947	Public as above.	Local as above. Private (if any) as above } One volume
1948 onwards	Public as above.	Local as above. Personal (if any) as above. } One volume

Two particular difficulties arise in connection with this system. First, it became (as explained above) the custom for certain Private Acts to declare that they were Public; and this might have been expected to give rise to a class of 'Private Acts declared Public'. Evidently, however, this was felt to be too paradoxical a description, and accordingly the expression 'Local and Personal' was substituted for the word 'Private'. Generally speaking, 'Local and Personal Acts' is a satisfactory equivalent for 'Private Acts'; but it should be noted that 'Personal Acts' were not 'declared Public', so that the expression 'Local and Personal Acts declared Public' is confusing. In the second place, the compilers of the *Chronological Table* have prefixed the word 'Local' or 'Private' to certain Acts, but explain in their preface that 'the terms "Local", "Personal", "Private" are not here used in any technical sense but merely to describe the subject-matter of the Acts'. These descriptions therefore may well run counter to the rest of the system of classification adopted in the *Chronological Table*.

(iii) *Printing of Acts of Parliament*

Sessional Volumes of Statutes (or Public Acts)

1483 to date

From 1483 onwards the Public Acts of each session have been officially printed. Until 1662 they were printed directly from the Original Act itself before the document was laid up for permanent preservation in the Parliament Office. Until 1793 the text was in gothic, i.e. 'black letter' type, and the vols. are therefore sometimes called black letter vols. These vols. are of high authority as texts. Few sets exist for the 16th and 17th c., but H.L. Library holds 26 vols. dating from the 16th c., 8 from the 17th c. and a set for 1702–13. For the sessions from 1714 onwards H.L. and H.C. Libraries each hold complete series. From 1940 onwards the vols. have been annual instead of sessional.

From 1798 onwards the varying classes of Local Acts, etc., have appeared in separate series of printed vols. (*see* below). The vols. of statutes normally include lists of all types of Acts passed during the period in question and may also comprise elaborate indexes of legislation and classified lists of Local and Private Acts.

Sessional Volumes of Collected Local and Personal Acts

1798 to 1875

This series of collected separate prints, available in H.L.R.O. and certain libraries,[1] provides complete texts of the majority of Local and Personal Acts for the years indicated; but the contents vary as noted in section (ii) above. The vols. also contain printed lists and indexes similar to those in the Statute vols.

Sessional Volumes of Collected Local Acts

1876 to date

These vols. continue the foregoing series of separate prints and contain all Local Acts. They are also supplied with printed lists and indexes.

Sessional Volumes of Collected Private Acts

1815 to date

This series of separate prints, lists and indexes, in spite of its title, only contains the residuum of those printed texts of Private Acts not included in the

---

[1] As are also the following two series of vols.

series of Local and Personal, or Local Acts. Amongst them are many Inclosure Acts in the earlier vols., together with a number of Tithe Acts, but the principal contents are Estate Acts. There remain certain categories of Private Acts which are not printed, such as Divorce, Name and Naturalisation Acts. In these instances the record copies (Original Acts) in H.L.R.O. and, after 1849, also in the Public Record Office, are usually the only available official texts of the Acts.

Statutes Revised

1st ed., 1870–85, in 18 vols.; and subsequent editions, each of which presents the texts of those Public Acts in force at the date of publication.

Statutes of the Realm

11 vols., ed. A. Luders, T. E. Tomlins, J. Raithby *et al.* for the Record Commission (1810–28). This series contains the full texts of Charters of Liberties, 1101–1301 and of all Public Acts and similar legislative material from 1235 to 1713. The texts of the Acts were derived in part from earlier private collections, and include variant readings. In appendix (F) to the Introduction the Editors discuss the relation of the Parliament Office originals to the Rolls of Parliament for the period 1497 to 1640. Lists are included of all Acts to 1713, and in these lists the numeration in the Parliament Office series and in the Chancery and other enrolments is set out. The Acts and Ordinances of 1642–60 are not printed in *Statutes of the Realm* but their texts are included in C. H. Firth and R. S. Rait, *Acts and Ordinances of the Interregnum, 1642–1660*, 3 vols (1911) (*see* also ORDERS AND ORDINANCES, p. 171).

The Statutes of the Realm were based in part on earlier 'booksellers'' collections, which they wholly replaced for scholarly purposes for the period to 1713. For the period after 1713, however, reference should be made to the printed Annual Volumes. Texts also appear in various private collections. Of these, the most important is: *Statutes at Large of England and of Great Britain from Magna Charta to the Union*, ed. by T. E. Tomlins and J. Raithby, 1800, quarto edition, 10 vols.; octavo edition, 20 vols.; continuations to 1869 in 29 vols., quarto; 69 vols., octavo. These vols. contain complete lists of long titles of all categories of Acts, and full texts of most Public Acts, but Acts repealed or obsolete may be summarised or completely omitted, annual Acts such as Land Tax Acts are usually omitted, and Private Acts are largely excluded.

(iv) *Lists and other Guides to Acts of Parliament*

Index to the Statutes in Force, 1st ed., 1870, in 1 vol.; now annual in 2 vols. This begins with a Table of Statutes which are in force at the date of publication, and then, in an index, analyses the main provisions of these Acts under such headings as 'Air Force', 'Alien', 'Aliment, Scotland', 'Alkali, etc., Works'. It provides similar information for Church Assembly Measures. This *Index* is an official publication, as are the two following works.

Chronological Table of the Statutes. 1st ed., 1870, now annual in 1 vol. This work includes an important 'Table of Variances between the Statutes of the Realm and Ruffhead's edition, with respect to years, Statutes and Chapters'.

Subsequent amendments and repeals are noted under each entry. Similar information is provided for Church Assembly Measures. The vol. includes a 'Chronological Table of the Acts of the Parliaments of Scotland, 1424–1707'.

Index to Local and Personal Acts. 1 vol., latest ed., 1949. This guide contains classified lists of the Local, Personal and Private Acts for 1801–1947, of Special Orders and Special Procedure Orders.

Analytical Table of Private Statutes, ed. George Bramwell, 2 vols., 1813 and 1835. In spite of the use of the term 'Statutes' in its title, this work refers to those Acts which were not 'Public'. The Acts are listed with, in some cases, long titles as well as short, from 1727 to 1834. Indexes of Estate and Inclosure Acts are appended.

CHURCH ASSEMBLY AND GENERAL SYNOD MEASURE RECORDS

In accordance with the Church of England Assembly (Powers) Act, 1919, 9 & 10 Geo. V, c. 76, Royal Assent was given in Parliament to Measures which had been passed by the Church Assembly. Since 1970 Assent has similarly been given to Measures presented to Parliament by the successor to the Church Assembly, the General Synod of the Church of England (under the Synodical Government Measure, 1969). Such Measures go through the following procedure: (1) They are considered by the Ecclesiastical Committee of the two Houses; (2) That Committee reports to the Legislative Committee of the General Synod, and then, if the Legislative Committee decides to proceed with the Measure, also to each House, on the nature, legal effect and expediency of the proposed Measure; (3) Resolutions are then agreed to (or rejected) by the Houses. The motions may not be amended in either House; (4) If both Houses resolve in favour of the Measure, the Royal Assent is given, with the formula 'La Reyne le veult', as for Public Acts.

The records produced in the passage of Measures are:

Printed Texts of the Measures, as laid before the Ecclesiastical Committee and the Houses (preserved as COMMITTEE PAPERS and also as SESSIONAL PAPERS).

Reports of the Ecclesiastical Committee, as laid before the Houses (preserved as SESSIONAL PAPERS).

Proceedings and Papers of the Ecclesiastical Committee (*see* COMMITTEE PAPERS). These are preserved for 1920–64 in files, and also in 4 vols. into which loose documents have been inserted. The main constituents are: Minutes of Proceedings of the Ecclesiastical Committee; Minutes, usually verbatim, of Conferences with the Legislative Committee of the Church Assembly; Appointments of Members; Correspondence with the Church Assembly and others; Certified copies of the Church Assembly Measures submitted by the Assembly; copies of Comments and Explanations of the Measures by the Assembly; Draft Reports of the Ecclesiastical Committee for the Houses. Amongst the papers is the 'Deposited Book' of the Prayer Book Measure, 1927.

Church Assembly and General Synod Measures. These are preserved for 1920 to date (145 docs.) and are the authentic texts of those Measures which have received the Royal Assent. They are printed in separate volumes on vellum leaves, bound with black silk tape; they are superscribed with the Royal Assent, and are signed by a Clerk. Two exact duplicates are also prepared, for deposit, respectively, in the General Synod and in the Public Record Office.

PRINTED VERSIONS. The full texts of Measures appear in the annual volumes of *Public General Acts and Measures,* and a separate volume of Measures (1920–48) was published as part of the 3rd ed. of *Statutes Revised* (1950).

USE. Certain of the Committee Proceedings and Papers are restricted for 30 years from their date of origin; the remaining records are unrestricted.

Jurisdiction exercised by Parliament dates back to the 13th century and was very frequently original jurisdiction. Subsequently, the Lords received many petitions of rights and *monstrans de droit*, and they also dealt with other cases where justice could not be obtained in the ordinary courts. Three special categories of original jurisdiction were those of Impeachment (which originated in 1376); of Crown accusation of great offenders (as in the case of Nicolas de Segrave, 1305); and of private accusation (or 'appeal') by one subject of another in a matter of great crime (as in accusations by the Lords Appellant, 1387–8). Closely allied to these categories was the trial of peers by the House, which was considered to be founded upon Magna Carta.

By the beginning of the 16th c. this range of original jurisdiction had largely fallen into abeyance, the last mediaeval impeachment, for instance, being in 1459. The Council and the new Courts of Equity heard many such cases affecting lesser subjects; Parliamentary Acts of Attainder served as substitutes for some of the other processes; and ordinary Private Acts provided remedies for many private petitions.

In the course of the 14th c. the lords in Parliament had also come to exercise a certain proportion of jurisdiction in error. In Flourdew's case (1 Hen. VII) the judges laid down the procedure to be followed in cases of 'error'. The aggrieved party had to petition the King for a writ of error and, if the petition was endorsed by the King, the Chancellor was bound to issue the writ directed to the Chief Justice of the King's Bench. The petition, the writ, and a transcript of the process and pleadings were then delivered to H.L. Error lay to the Lords, at this time, from the courts of King's Bench and Chancery (on the common law side). In 1459 it had been laid down by Chief Justice Prisot that no appeal lay to Parliament from decisions of the Chancellor in matters of equity.[1]

Jurisdiction in error largely fell into abeyance in the 16th c. but a few cases are known during the reign of Elizabeth I. The statute erecting a new Court of Exchequer Chamber in 1585, 27 Eliz. I, c. 8, for the purpose of amending the errors of King's Bench in certain specified types of action, also recognised a right of further appeal from the Exchequer Chamber to Parliament. An amending Act, the Error Act, 1588, 31 Eliz. I, c. 1, provided, moreover, that a plaintiff in error against a judgment in King's Bench might 'at his election' sue in Parliament instead of in Exchequer Chamber, but error still lay direct from the King's Bench to H.L. in all proceedings other than those specified in this and the previous Act.

The resumption of judicial powers by the Lords in 1621 arose from the Commons impeachment of Mompesson, followed by the House's attempt in Floyd's case to try a criminal case itself. This led on 26 May 1621 to the Lords judgment in the case, and on 29 May to the appointment of a Lords committee to consider petitions. To this committee were referred subsequent

[1] H.L. established its right to hear such appeals in 1675.

complaints against lower courts and also all requests for original hearings. In 1621, also, the Lords in Bourchier's case considered whether they had the right to receive appeals from the equitable jurisdiction of the Chancellor. Although in this case a committee of the Lords reported that there were no precedents for hearing such appeals, a number of petitions asking for review of decrees in Chancery were presented to the Lords in subsequent years, and in 1640 the Lords reversed a decree of the Chancellor. After the Restoration, the House asserted its right to hear appeals from Chancery. This was challenged by the Commons in the case of Shirley *v.* Fagg in 1675, but opposition eventually ceased, and the Lords retained this jurisdiction.

Note that the classification of Judicial records in this section follows that of Judicial procedure in Parliament outlined by Sir William Holdsworth in *A History of English Law*, vol. i (7th ed., 1956), c. 4.

BIBLIOGRAPHY

M. Hale, *The Jurisdiction of the Lords House of Parliament . . .*, ed. F. Hargrave (1796).

W. Holdsworth, *History of English Law*, vol. i, 7th ed. (1956).

J. Macqueen, *Appellate Jurisdiction of the House of Lords and Privy Council . . .* (1842).

Notes on the Debates in the House of Lords . . . 1621, 1625, 1628, ed. F. H. Relf (1929).

C. S. Sims, 'The moderne forme of the Parliaments of England', *American Historical Review*, vol. liii (1948), pp. 288–305 (gives Elsynge's account of 'Proceedings in Judicature', *c.* 1625).

A. S. Turberville, 'The House of Lords as a Court of Law, 1784–1837', *Law Quarterly Review*, vol. lii (1930).

ORIGINAL JURISDICTION (1621–93)

The Lords, having resumed the power to hear and determine original causes in 1621, continued to exercise this power in subsequent years, and notably in the period 1640–9. Their right to deal with original causes was successfully challenged by the Commons in 1666 over Skinner *v.* East India Company (see the records calendared in *8th Rept.*, H.M.C., app. pp. 165–74), and after this there was only a single and unsuccessful attempt to exercise original jurisdiction, in 1693.

Original cases were initiated by petition to the Lords, and on 29 May 1621 the Lords appointed the first of a series of committees 'to consider of all petitions . . . and to report . . . answers'. By 1626 such a committee was being regularly appointed at the opening of each session. It dealt with both Appeal cases and Original cases. On 26 November 1640 a second 'judicial committee' was appointed, to examine Abuses in Courts of Justice, but on 18 March 1641 all its business was transferred to the Committee for Petitions, which thereafter dealt with most original cases. A case concerning a peer, such as the libel by

Fitton *et al. v.* L. Gerard of Brandon, 1663, might be referred to the Committee for Privileges for preliminary investigation. Frequently, the Committees for Petitions seem to have determined causes without much further reference to the House, but the proper conclusion to a cause was a Report to the House and Judgment there. The absence of adequate records of the proceedings of the pre-1649 Committees makes the initial petitions (with what may frequently be ample ancillary matter) the most fruitful source of information.

(i) For Records of Proceedings on Original Causes *see*:

>   JOURNALS OF THE HOUSE, 1621 to 1693, pp. 28–32 above.
>
>   MANUSCRIPT MINUTES OF THE HOUSE, 1621 to 1693, pp. 33–6 above.
>>   Some of the Orders of the House, subsequently entered *in extenso* in the Journals and Minutes, have survived among the Main Papers.
>
>   MINUTES OF PROCEEDINGS OF COMMITTEE FOR PETITIONS, 1628, 1660–95, p. 43 above.
>>   These vols. comprise the Minutes of the Committee for Petitions: they include material other than that relating to Original causes.

Committee Order Books

1640 to 1663   3 vols.

1 vol. 'Orders on Petitions in private causes, 23 Dec. 1640 to 6 Aug. 1641' (imperfect).

2 vols. Books of Orders, 1660–3. Draft Orders and Signed Orders of the Committees may also be found for a small percentage of cases among the Main Papers.

(ii) Other Records relating to Original Causes:

Originating Petitions

1621 to 1693   350 docs.

The Address is normally to the Lords Spiritual and Temporal, but occasionally it is to the Lords Committee for Petitions. The main text usually consists of an abbreviated recital of complaint, which may be against named parties, or against more vaguely described opponents, and is followed by a Prayer for relief. The Petition is signed; it may be endorsed by the Clerk of the Parliaments with a registration number and the dates of receipt and of reading in committee, but only rarely with a note of action taken by either the committee or the House.

Answers to Petitions

1621 to 1693   40 docs.

These survive infrequently, are usually (as e.g. Walter *v.* Walter, 21 June 1641) in the form of a counter-petition, and are signed.

Ancillary Papers

1621 to 1666   200 docs.

These Papers include those handed in by Petitioners or otherwise received by the Clerk, e.g. detailed statements of complaint, interrogatories, depositions, affidavits, copies of previous orders, reports from judges or other referees.

IMPEACHMENTS

The procedure of impeachment is held to have originated in 1376 when the Commons 'impeached', i.e. accused before the Lords, Richard Lyons, a London merchant. Although subsequent proceedings were varied in nature, impeachment retained this general character of an accusation made by H.C. against a person or persons before H.L. The last mediaeval impeachment was in 1459; from then until 1621 the prosecution of alleged traitors in Parliament became largely a legislative process in which H.C. participated with H.L. in the reading, debating and passing of Bills of Attainder or of pains and penalties. Impeachment was revived in 1621 as a consequence of H.C. seeking to exercise effectively their traditional function of searching out and redressing grievances. A Commons committee, which was then appointed to search for precedents 'to show how far and for what offences the power of this House doth extend to punish delinquents against the State', reported that the Commons must join with the Lords for punishing such offences and that this was relevant to the case of Sir Giles Mompesson then pending, there 'being no offence against our particular House or any member of it, but a general grievance'. The proceedings against Bacon in the same year once more made Ministers of the Crown subject to judicial accusation by the Commons. Between 1621 and 1805–6 there were some 54 cases.

The usual procedure in impeachment, from 1621 onwards, was for H.C. to refer accusations to a committee for the drawing up of Articles of Impeachment. The Articles were then debated in the House and, if agreed, were engrossed and carried up to H.L. The accused made a formal Answer, and H.C. appointed managers to prepare evidence and conduct proceedings. The trial was usually presided over by the Lord High Steward if a peer was being impeached of high treason, otherwise by the Lord Chancellor or Lord Keeper. The H.C. attended the trial as a C.W.H.; their managers (from 1628) presented the case, they were answered by counsel for the accused, witnesses were heard and the managers exercised the right of reply. The peers then voted as to the verdict to be given, and, upon the demand of H.C., a judgment was delivered.

(i) For Records of Proceedings in Impeachments *see*:

JOURNALS OF THE HOUSE, 1621 to 1806, pp. 28–32 above.

MANUSCRIPT MINUTES OF THE HOUSE, etc. (including some committee proceedings, notes of speeches, evidence and voting at the trial), 1621 to 1806, pp. 33–6 above.

COMMITTEE MINUTE BOOKS, 1660 to 1806, p. 43 above.

COMMITTEE FOR PRIVILEGES MINUTE BOOKS, 1660 to 1806,
p. 43 above.
JOINT COMMITTEE MINUTE BOOK, 1679 to 1695, p. 57 above.

(ii) Other Records relating to Impeachments.

Articles of Impeachment

1621 to 1806   60 docs.

The earliest Articles or 'Declarations of Grievances' are written on paper
sheets filed at the head. From 1626 to 1806 the Articles are engrossed on parchment, either on a single membrane or in roll form. Drafts and notes concerning
the Articles are to be found amongst the Main Papers. The earliest Articles are
summarised in the Lords Journals, and from 1626 they are usually printed there
in extenso. For the Civil War period certain of the Articles not entered in full
in the Journals are to be found in J. Nalson, *Impartial Collection of the Great
Affairs of State* . . . (1682–3).

Answers of the Accused

1621 to 1806   60 docs.

The earliest Answers are in the form of paper drafts, but from 1626 they are
engrossed on parchment. The text is given *in extenso* in the Lords Journals.

Petitions and Orders

1621 to 1806   200 docs.

This class includes Petitions to H.L. (and, in 17th c., a few to H.C.) against
the accused, Petitions of the accused for more time, for counsel to be assigned
to them, and upon other matters. The Orders are those made by H.L. for the
accused to be brought before it, for taking the accused into custody, and for
committees to examine precedents in Impeachment trials. The Petitions and
Orders, together with draft Orders, may be found in the Main Papers. The
texts are usually given *in extenso* in the Lords Journals.

Evidential Documents

1617 to 1795   420 docs.

A considerable number of documents survives relating to the impeachment
of Mompesson and the other monopolists, e.g. 1617, Patent for granting
licences to innkeepers; 1618–9, duplicate account of receivers of fines, etc., for
licences to innkeepers; 1620, register of proceedings of commissioners under
patent for making gold and silver thread (*Calendar, 3rd Rept.*, H.M.C., app.
pp. 15–21).

For the trial of Warren Hastings many evidential documents have been
preserved, including copies of correspondence between the governors of Bengal
and Madras and the Indian princes, and 5 vols. of East India Company accounts,
1783–8.

Judgments

1621 to 1806   60 docs.

Draft and final judgments survive amongst the Main Papers. The text is given *in extenso* in the Lords Journals. Occasionally the manuscript is more detailed, e.g. the sentence against Mompesson, 1621, contains three paragraphs which are not in the Journals.

PRINTED VERSIONS are included in the various collections of 'State Trials', notably in *A Complete Collection of State Trials and Proceedings for High Treason . . .*, ed. W. Cobbett, T. B. Howell *et al.*, 42 vols. (1816–98).

TRIALS OF PEERS

During the Middle Ages the legal basis of the right of peers to be tried by peers was considered to be Magna Carta, as confirmed by Henry III. The Peeresses Act, 1442, 20 Hen. VI, c. 9, provided that the privilege should extend to peeresses but should relate solely to accusations of treason and felony. By the 15th c. it was customary for trials of peers accused of treason or felony to be presided over by the Lord High Steward, whether the peer had been indicted or had been impeached. By the beginning of the 16th c. it had become usual to try peers before a jury of selected peers sitting independently of Parliament in 'the Court of the Lord High Steward'.

During the 16th and 17th c. the Crown continued to use the Court of the Lord High Steward for the trials of peers and for other state trials. This Court was not usually convened at a time when Parliament was sitting and no records of trials held before the Court have survived in H.L.R.O. During this period the privilege of trial by peers had been safeguarded in all new Acts which related to treason and felony, such as the Sedition Act, 1661, 13 Cha. II, sess. 1, c. 1. Whether trials were in H.L. (as they normally were, if Parliament was in session) or in the Court of the Lord High Steward the process started with a true bill being found by a grand jury, and the indictment was then removed to the appropriate court by writ of *certiorari*. The first trial of a peer before the whole House for which H.L. records have survived, is that of E. Pembroke for murder, in March 1678. The Court of the Lord High Steward was still, however, being used for trials of peers, and in June 1678 L. Cornwallis was tried before it for murder, although Parliament was then sitting. In 1686 L. Delamer was tried before the Court for treason, but from this time the Court fell into abeyance.

In 1690, the House resolved that peers could be judged only in full Parliament for a capital offence. By the Treason Act, 1695, 7 & 8 Will. III, c. 3, jurisdiction in trials for treason was placed in the whole body of peers, whether Parliament was sitting or not. For such trials every peer who had the right to sit and vote, was to be summoned and was to vote. The Act did not refer to felony, but peers charged with felony were tried before the Whole House from this time onwards. The Lord High Steward continued to preside over the trials. The last peer to be tried in H.L. was L. de Clifford (for manslaughter) in 1935. The privilege of peers to be tried by the House of Lords was abolished under the Criminal Justice Act, 1948, 11 & 12 Geo. VI, c. 58.

BIBLIOGRAPHY. L. W. V. Harcourt, *His Grace the Steward and Trials by Peers* (1907).

(i) For Records of Proceedings at Trials of Peers, *see*:

JOURNALS OF THE HOUSE, 1678 to 1935, pp. 28–32 above. (An outline of the proceedings is to be found in the Journal, together with speeches of the Lord High Steward upon delivering judgment and the judgments themselves. Manuscript verbatim proceedings survive from 1901 onwards but certain of the speeches made before then at trials survive in manuscript, e.g. Lord Ferrers' speech in 1760.)

MANUSCRIPT MINUTES OF THE HOUSE, etc., 1678 to 1935, pp. 33–6 above.

COMMITTEE MINUTE BOOKS, 1678–1935, pp. 43–6 above.

(ii) Other Records relating to Trials of Peers.

Petitions

1641 to 1776   10 docs.

The petition was addressed by the peer to H.L.; it described the bringing of the indictment against the petitioner, and asked for a speedy trial before the House. After 1776 the L. Chancellor informed the House of the indictment. The texts are entered in the Journal, H.L.

Commissions Appointing the Lord High Steward

1678 to 1935   10 docs.

The Commissions are engrossed on parchment, sealed with the Great Seal, and signed by the Sovereign. The language is Latin until 1733, afterwards English. The Commissions appoint the Lord Chancellor to be Lord High Steward for the duration of the trial. The Commissions are entered in the Journal, H.L.

Recognisances of Witnesses

1678 to 1935

These Recognisances were entered into by witnesses for their attendance at the trial before H.L. The language is Latin until 1733, afterwards English.

Orders of the House

1641 to 1935   10 docs.

The Orders referred cases either to the Committee for Privileges (to 1693) or to a Select Committee (from 1697 onwards). The committees were to inspect the Journals and report on the correct form of procedure for the trial. The texts are entered in the Journal, H.L.

Miscellaneous Petitions and Orders

1641 to 1935   12 docs.

This class includes Petitions of peers asking for more time to prepare their case or to be represented by counsel, Petitions upon other matters, and Orders made by the House concerning the Petitions. The texts are usually entered in the Journal, H L.

Writs of Certiorari

1678 to 1935   10 docs.

The Writs ordered that the indictment be brought up from the lower court into Parliament. The language is Latin until 1733, afterwards English. The Writs are entered in the Journal, H.L.

Indictments and Inquisitions

1678 to 1935   10 docs.

The Indictments and Inquisitions record the circumstances of the bringing of the charge against the peer in the lower court, the nature of the charge and the finding of the grand jury on it. The Inquisitions are signed and sealed by the jurors. These documents were sent into Parliament annexed to the writ of *certiorari*. The language is Latin until 1733, afterwards English. The Indictments and Inquisitions are entered in the Journal, H.L.

See also records of the Lord Great Chamberlain, pp. 253–5 below.

List of Trials of Peers in Parliament (other than Impeachments) 1678–1935

I. *Trials for which there are substantial records*

1678   E. Pembroke for murder (*Calendar*, H.M.C. 9th Rept., app. pt. ii, p. 107).
1693   L. Mohun for murder (*Calendar*, 1692–3, pp. 294–8).
1699   E. Warwick and Holland and L. Mohun for murder (*Calendar*, 1697–9, pp. 8–9).
1746   E. Kilmarnock, E. Cromarty and L. Balmerino for treason.
1760   E. Ferrers for murder.
1765   L. Byron for murder.
1776   Duchess of Kingston for bigamy.
1841   E. Cardigan for felony.
1901   E. Russell for bigamy.
1935   L. de Clifford for manslaughter.

II. *Indictments, etc., for which there are preliminary records only*

The following peers were indicted but not brought to trial before the House. Preliminary records for these cases survive amongst the Main Papers.

1642   L. Morley for murder.
1685   E. Stamford for treason.
1697–8   L. Mohun for murder.
1848   V. Arbuthnott for felony.

PRINTED VERSIONS. From 1693 onwards the proceedings at peerage trials were always ordered by H.L. to be printed and published. From 1841 the prints are to be found amongst SESSIONAL PAPERS, H.L. Accounts of trials to 1776 are printed in *State Trials*, ed. Cobbett, Howell *et al.*

APPEAL CASES

Until 1873 appeals were received by H.L. from a varying number of courts of equity which by 1700 included the courts of Chancery, Exchequer, Exchequer Chamber, the Lord Mayor of London's Court, the Duchy Court of Lancaster, the Chancery of Durham, the Vice-Chancellor of Chester, and the Chancery of Brecon, in England and Wales; and the courts of Chancery, and Exchequer in Ireland as courts of equity.

After 1707 appeals were also received from the Court of Session, the Commission of Teinds, and the Court of Exchequer, on the equity side, in Scotland.[1] At first, Scottish appeals were received from final decrees only and it was not until 1726 that H.L. began to hear also appeals against interlocutory orders. The Court of Session Act, 1808, 48 Geo. III, c. 151, however, provided that there should be no appeals from interlocutory judgments except with the leave of the lower court or where the judges disagreed. The Irish appeals ceased to come between 1782 and 1800,[2] during that period being heard in the Irish House of Lords.

The Supreme Court of Judicature Act, 1873, 36 & 37 Vict., c. 66, abolished the appellate jurisdiction of H.L., but this provision did not become operative, and in 1876 the Appellate Jurisdiction Act, 39 & 40 Vict., c. 59, provided that English appeals thereafter should come to the House from the newly formed Court of Appeal, and should continue from those Scottish and Irish courts from which appeals had previously been received. The Act also stipulated that a quorum for hearing an appeal should include not less than three peers among the following: the Lord Chancellor, the Lords of Appeal, and such peers who held or had held high judicial office. The Administration of Justice (Appeals) Act, 1934, 24 & 25 Geo. V, c. 40, ordered that the leave of the Court of Appeal or of the House was needed before an appeal could be received by H.L. The Administration of Justice Act, 1969, provided that civil appeals could be brought direct to H.L. from the High Courts of England and Wales and of Northern Ireland (by-passing the Courts of Appeal) if the parties consented and the High Court Judge certified that certain conditions had been fulfilled.

Appeals in criminal cases to H.L. became possible under the Criminal Appeal Act, 1907, 7 Edw. VII, c. 23,[3] which abolished procedure by writ of error and allowed appeal to H.L. from decisions of the Court of Criminal Appeal on a certificate from the Attorney-General. Similar provision was made with

---

[1] The Act of Union, 1706, 6 Anne, c. 11, contained no provision to this end, but it seems to have been considered that the Parliament of Great Britain inherited the functions of the Scottish Parliament, which had included the hearing of appeals (cf. *Calendar*, 1706–8, p. xlii).

[2] The Repeal of the Act for Securing Dependency of Ireland Act, 1782, 22 Geo. III, c. 53, and the Irish Appeals Act, 1783, 23 Geo. III, c. 28, ended the hearing of appeals by the English House; the Act of Union, 1800, 39 & 40 Geo. III, c. 67, revived it.

[3] It had, however, already been possible for criminal appeals to come to H.L. if they were Scottish and were causes in which a crime had arisen out of a civil suit pending.

regard to decisions of the Court of Criminal Appeal in Northern Ireland by the Criminal Appeal (Northern Ireland) Act, 1930, 20 & 21 Geo. V, c. 45, and to decisions of the Courts Martial Court by the Courts Martial (Appeals) Act, 1951, 14 & 15 Geo. VI, c. 46. The Administration of Justice Act, 1960, 8 & 9 Eliz. II, c. 65, further allowed criminal appeals from any Divisional Court of the Queen's Bench Division as well as from the Court of Criminal Appeal, if leave were obtained of either the court below or of H.L. itself.

Procedure on appeals in H.L. evolved between 1621 and 1698, being first dealt with in S.O.s 38 and 39 of 1624 and then codified in a series of Orders and Standing Orders of the House between 1678 and 1698. It has since been modified by Resolutions of the House, by further Orders and by Statutes. The main procedural stages have continued to be as follows: an appeal originates in a Petition to the House from the Appellant against a decree of a lower court; to this the House orders the Respondent to put in an Answer. On a day appointed for hearing, counsel plead on behalf of each side. Judgment is then given in the form of an Order of the House affirming, reversing or otherwise altering the decree complained of.

In 1678 it was finally established that appeal cases could continue, if necessary, from session to session and from Parliament to Parliament. The Appellate Jurisdiction Act, 1876, made possible the hearing and determining of appeals during prorogation and dissolution (in the latter case, under authority to be given by the Sovereign under Sign Manual).

A preliminary scrutiny of Petitions of Appeal was assigned to a Lords committee in 1689, and from 1812, sessional committees for that purpose (Appeal Committees) have been appointed continuously.[1] The hearing of the appeal itself until 1948 invariably took place in the House. After 1705 the hearing was normally taken before other business; after 1715 the priority was absolute, although from 1848 an adjournment for a sitting of the Committee for Privileges was permitted. In 1948 a new practice originated by which one or more Appellate Committees might be appointed with power to hear appeals; such committees report their decisions to the House, which in every instance makes the final Judgment and Order.

LISTS. Papers concerning Appeals and Writs of Error are listed in the Manuscript Main Papers Lists (in progress), and in the Parchment Collection Lists, in H.L.R.O. Search Room.

BIBLIOGRAPHY

C. M. Denison and C. H. Scott, *Procedure and Practice relative to English, Scotch and Irish Appeals* (1879).

J. Macqueen, *Appellate Jurisdiction of the House of Lords and Privy Council . . .* (1842).

L. McRedmond, 'Irish Appeals to the House of Lords in the Eighteenth Century', *Analecta Hibernica*, no. 23 (1966).

F. B. Palmer, *Practice in the House of Lords on Appeals, Writs of Error and Claims of Peerage* (1830).

Form of Appeal, Method of Procedure and Standing Orders, House of Lords (1967).

See also *Calendar* for cases to 1714.

[1] *See* below, PROCEEDINGS OF APPEAL COMMITTEES.

(i) For Records of Proceedings in the House on Appeal Cases *see*:

> JOURNALS OF THE HOUSE, 1621 to date. These contain brief headings of proceedings at practically every stage with notes as to the nature of incidental petitions, and the full texts of Reports from Committees, Judgments and Orders of the House. *See* pp. 28–32 above.
>
> MANUSCRIPT MINUTES OF THE HOUSE, 1621 to date. Those between 1661 and 1714 give extended details of hearings and opinions of judges called in as assistants. *See* pp. 33–6 above.

(ii) For records of Proceedings in Committee on Appeal Cases *see*:

> MINUTES OF THE COMMITTEE FOR PETITIONS, 1621 to 1695, p. 43 above.
>
> MINUTES OF COMMITTEES, 1661 to 1837, pp. 43–4 above.
>
> MINUTES OF COMMITTEES ON UNOPPOSED BILLS AND APPEALS, 1837 to 1848, pp. 44–5 above.

Proceedings of Appeal Committees

1849 to date   65 vols.

Specific petitions in appeal cases were on occasion from 1689 referred to a Select Committee, especially during the period 1801–12. In 1812 the first Sessional Committee was appointed 'to consider of the Causes in which Prints of the Appellants' and Respondents' Cases now depending in the House . . . have not been delivered . . .'. Similar committees have since been appointed annually. The present terms of reference are to consider 'such Petitions as may be referred to them and other matters relating to Causes depending in this House, and to Causes formerly depending in this House; and all other matters relating thereto'. From 1849 the new series of Appeal Committee Books contain the complete proceedings of the Committee including verbatim Evidence. From 1900 to date the draft Reports of the Appeal Committees have been preserved in an ancillary series of 8 vols. The Judicial Office also preserves a bound set of Memoranda from the Office to the Committee for 1916 to date, in 9 vols.

Proceedings of Appellate Committees

1948 to date   5 vols.

Since 1948, by sessional resolution, the House has appointed an Appellate Committee or Committees to hear Appeals. The majority of Appeals are now heard not in the House, but in committee. A Report is made to the House, and Judgment and Opinions then read there. The Minutes of Proceedings in Appellate Committee are in the main formal, consisting of lists of lords present; counsel acting; order and time of speeches; with notes on important procedural points. There are Indexes of cases and points of procedure, and a list of hearings. Except in connection with procedural matters no record is made of words spoken (*see* the *Law Reports* for such material).

(iii) Other Records relating to Appeal Cases:

Petitions

1621 to date   20,000 docs.

See plate 8

Petitions contain the address to the Lords Spiritual and Temporal in Parliament assembled; the statement of the names of complainants; their description and abode; the recital of all proceedings in courts below; the statement of Appeal; the Prayers for relief and for the Respondents to be ordered to answer. Before 1698 the Petitions were signed by Petitioners; then S.O. 89 confirmed the rule that all appeals were to be signed by two counsel. The Petitions are on vellum membranes, 17th–19th c.; thereafter in printed vellum books.

PRINTED VERSIONS. The texts are summarised in varying degrees of detail in the *Calendar* and in the *Law Reports*. They are noted in the Journal.

Respondents' Answers

1624 to date   20,000 docs.

See plate 8

These docs. are largely formal, comprising a general negation of the Petitioner's Appeal, followed by a submission that the decree complained of be affirmed, and the Appeal dismissed. The Answers are on vellum membranes, generally annexed to the Originating Petitions 17th–19th c.; thereafter, in printed vellum books.

PRINTED VERSIONS. The texts may be noted in the *Calendar*, the *Law Reports* and the Journal.

Printed Cases

1702 to date   4,812 vols.

Printed texts of the Originating Petition, the Answer of the Respondent and related material may be found amongst the Main Papers, H.L., from 1660 onwards. Collected and continuous series of Cases survive in H.L.R.O. as follows:

Two separate but overlapping series were formed in the early 19th c.: (i) 109 vols. entitled 'Appeal Cases', 1702–1840; (ii) 1,100 vols. entitled 'Appeal Cases and Writs of Error', 1702 and continued to date.

In addition there are two further series: (i) of collected and bound prints, in 63 vols., for 1848–57; (ii) of individual printed Cases in 3,540 vols. for 1879 to date. Other copies of Cases may be found in private possession, in the British Museum, and in other Public Libraries.

S.O. 89 of 1698 ordered that prints of the Cases of Appellants and Respondents should be signed by counsel. The earlier Cases include the points of Appeal and those proofs which had been offered in the courts below, together with documentary references on which arguments were to be offered. Verbatim transcripts of proceedings in lower courts were included from the mid-19th c. By S.O. 194 of 1813 the proofs and documents were ordered to be printed as Appendices to the Cases. Sometimes a joint or 'mutual' Appendix has been issued. Most of the 17th and 18th c. Cases have Judgments endorsed in MS. It has become customary in the 20th c. to bind with the Cases some or all of the following related documents, the nature of which is explained elsewhere in this section: Originating Petition; Opinions of Lords; Judgment of House.

Ancillary Appeal Case Records

A number of subsidiary classes of record have been preserved intermittently in relation to the progress of an Appeal through the House. These may be grouped most conveniently in ten series as follows:

(i) Original Orders of the House

1624 to date

These Orders may be for service of notice on Respondents; for peremptory Answer; for hearing of the cause; for the hearing *ex parte*; or in reply to the incidental Petitions noted below. They are entered in the BOOKS OF ORDERS (*see* below) or the Journals.

(ii) Books of Orders and Judgments

1640 to 1693   21 vols.

The books contain texts of Judgments and also of certain Orders made by the House incidental to hearings, such as those for attachment of Defendants; for Witnesses to attend; for Petitions to be heard, or to be referred to the Committee for Petitions. Much of this material is not contained in the Journals, or is there entered more briefly. The vols. contain contemporary indexes. *See* also p. 171.

(iii) Affidavits of Service of Notice on Respondents

1714 to date

These may be individual documents, or the affidavits may be endorsed on the Petitions of Appeal. They are signed by the solicitors acting for the Appellant.

(iv) Registers of Orders of Service

1877 to date (omitting 1905–8)   7 vols.

(v) Original Recognisances

1680 to date

These are the records of acknowledgments and conditions of recognisances. They are signed and sealed by the Appellants, and are witnessed before Commissioners of Oaths or Scottish Justices of the Peace. The series has been preserved intermittently from 1680, but continuously from 1920.

(vi) **Recognisance Books**

1680 to 1761 (series 1)   6 vols.

1852 to date (series 2)   6 vols.

These vols. comprise registers of Recognisances entered into. In series 1, vol. 1 includes the Order of 20 Nov. 1680 concerning Recognisances, and vol. 6 includes Forms of Recognisance for payment of costs, appearance at the Bar, and keeping the peace, an original Order of Estreat of Recognisance, 1730, and Receipts, 1730 and 1735.

(vii) **Incidental Petitions**

1624 to date

These docs. include Petitions by the Appellants or Respondents for any of the following purposes: to amend Appeal; to amend Answer; to object to an irregular Appeal; for enlargement of time; to rectify improper matter; to revive Appeal; for an early hearing; that the judges be summoned to attend; to sue *in forma pauperis* (together with Affidavit of poor person); to withdraw Appeal. They are in prescribed form (for which *see* Macqueen, *op. cit.*), and are signed by the Petitioner. They are entered, and their content summarised, in the Journals.

(viii) **Transcripts and other Papers from the Lower Courts**

1624 to 18th c.

Relatively few papers of this type survive, although in the 17th c. memoranda of proceedings, terms of agreements, vols. of evidence, copies of statements, etc. were deposited, and there are occasional deposits of this type in the 18th c. Such material of pre-1714 date is listed in the *Calendar*.

(ix) **Registers of Appearances**

1877 to date   7 vols.

The Registers are signed by Agents of Respondents who thus signify their intention of lodging Cases.

(x) **Registers of Proceedings**

1826 to date   14 vols.

The Registers contain a chronological series of entries of all stages in the hearing of Appeal Cases and Cases in Error.

See also the Judicial Office Papers noted amongst the PARLIAMENT OFFICE PAPERS, below, pp. 188–9.

Registers of Judgments

(i) 1839 to date   271 vols.

These vols. record the Opinions of those peers who spoke at the conclusion of each hearing, together with the Judgment of the House in the cause. Until 1922 they are in manuscript, thereafter in typescript.

(ii) 1922 to date   36 vols.

These comprise two separate series of prints of Judgments, and of Opinions, bound together in chronological order. They are entitled 'Judgments and Opinions'.

(iii) 1760 to 1844   6 vols.

These manuscript vols. contain the Journal entry of the Judgment stage only, i.e. they do not contain the Opinions recorded in series (i) and (ii).

(iv) 1850 to 1868   8 vols.

These vols. are similar to (iii), but are printed, having been formed from a collection of separate prints.

For further material concerning Appeal Cases see PARLIAMENT OFFICE PAPERS, *below, pp.* 185, 186, 188–9.

PRINTED VERSIONS. Appeal Case docs. to 1714 may be entered in the *Calendar*. Hearings are recorded for certain cases in J. Brown and T. E. Tomlins, *Reports of Cases upon Appeals and Writs of Error determined in the High Court of Parliament*, 2nd ed., 8 vols. (1803) (for the period 1702–1800); and these together with other printed reports are collected in *English Reports*, vols. i–xi (1901), with index (1932), for the period 1694–1864. Since 1865 hearings have been reported in *The Law Reports in all the Courts* (1866, in progress).

CASES IN ERROR

Writs of Error lay to H.L. in England from all judgments of the Exchequer Chamber; from all judgments of King's Bench that were not intermediately reviewable by Exchequer Chamber; from all judgments of the common law or petty bag side of Chancery; and from all judgments of the Commissioners of Error appointed to review the common law proceedings of the London municipal jurisdictions.

In Ireland, writs of error lay from the court of King's Bench either to the King's Bench in England or to the Irish House of Lords, but from there to the English H.L. until the Acts of 1782 and 1783 brought the hearing of Irish Appeals and Writs at Westminster to an end (*see* p. 114 above). The Act of Union with Ireland, 1800, 39 & 40 Geo. III, c. 67, however, provided that all Irish Writs of Error previously received by either Parliament should thereafter come to the Parliament of the United Kingdom. The Supreme Court of Judicature (Ireland) Act, 1877, 40 & 41 Vict., c. 57, transferred all jurisdiction concerning Irish Writs of Error in criminal cases on appeal from the Queen's Bench Division to the Irish Court of Appeal.

By the Exchequer Court Act, 1707, 6 Anne, c. 53, a writ of error was allowed from all judgments on the common law side of the Court of Exchequer in Scotland.

All Writs of Error in causes other than criminal to H.L. were ended as a result of the Common Law Procedure Act, 1852, 15 & 16 Vict., c. 76, but they were still allowed to be brought in criminal causes. This residual jurisdiction in error was ended by the Criminal Appeal Act of 1907, 7 Edw. VII, c. 23.

The general procedure in cases in error was based on a Writ of Error sued out by the Plaintiff in Error in order to remove the judgment to H.L. The court below prepared a Transcript of Record and delivered it to H.L. together with the original Record (subsequently returned) and the Writ itself. The Plaintiff then lodged an Assignment of Errors, stating that the Judgment was erroneous. The Defendant in Error put in his reply or Joinder in Error and prayed the Judgment be affirmed. The House appointed a day for hearing. Printed Cases were usually prepared, signed by counsel, exchanged and delivered into the House. Counsel on the day appointed were heard, and the House gave its Judgment, which was then remitted to the court below. Many broader aspects of procedure were identical with those for Appeal Cases, e.g. cases could continue from session to session (*see* pp. 114–15 above).

PRINTED VERSIONS, as for APPEALS (p. 120 above).

(i) For Proceedings in the House and in Committee, *see* above, APPEAL RECORDS, p. 116.

(ii) Records of Cases in Error.

Originating Petitions

1621 to 1624   10 docs.

Petitions were addressed to the Sovereign by the Plaintiff in Error, and comprised the names of the parties to the case, a brief account of proceedings in the lower courts, an allegation of errors of an unspecified nature in these proceedings, and a prayer that the Record be ordered to be brought into Parliament and the errors corrected by the advice and assent of the lords. The Petitions may bear the Sign Manual of the Sovereign as authority for the issuing of a Writ of Error to the lower court. The Petitions are on parchment or paper membranes of varying size; the language is English. The texts of Originating Petitions may be given in the Journal from 1566 onwards. From 1640 it became the practice to issue the Writ not on a Petition, but on a Warrant from the Attorney General.

Writs of Error

See plate 9

1621 to 1857   2,000 docs.

The Writs were addressed to the Chief Justice of the court in which the error was alleged to have been made. In the Writs the names of the parties to the case and the nature of it were specified. The Chief Justice was ordered by them to bring the records and processes into Parliament either without delay, or on a specified day, so that what might be necessary should be done. The Writs were endorsed with notes to the effect that the Chief Justice had brought them up with the Record into Parliament and had left transcripts of the Record with the Clerk of the Parliaments. The endorsements were signed by the Chief Justice. The Writs are on parchment membranes of usual writ size; the language is Latin to 1733, thereafter English.

Note that this and the succeeding classes of records noted below were not continued, or were only partially continued, for criminal cases *post* 1852.

Transcripts of Record

1621 to 1860   2,000 docs.

See plate 9

These were transcripts of the entries on the Plea Roll of the lower court of the proceedings in which error was alleged to have occurred. Each Transcript was headed with the date, term and roll number of the Plea Roll. If the case had previously come to the King's Bench or Court of Exchequer Chamber from an inferior court the proceedings of that Court were also recorded in the Transcript. The Transcripts are on parchment membranes, sewn together in Chancery style, but 19th c. Transcripts may be sewn at the head in Exchequer style. The language is Latin until 1733, thereafter English.

Transcripts of Proceedings

1624 to 1852   2,000 docs.

These Transcripts comprised the Plea Roll entries (as above) but might also include copies of the Writ of Error, Assignment of Errors, Proceedings in H.L. and Judgment. In a few instances, both a parchment and a paper Transcript survive, but usually a paper Transcript exists for cases carried to a judgment in H.L., and a parchment Transcript for those cases which lapsed. This distinction, however, is not invariable. The membranes of the Transcripts are attached at the head in Exchequer style.

Assignments of Errors

1642 to 1854   2,000 docs.

By an Order of H.L., 13 December 1661, Plaintiffs were to assign their errors within eight days of the bringing in of the Writ and Record. The Assignment might be either general or special, i.e. it might allege errors in general terms or specify particular errors on the face of the Record. When it became the practice to lodge printed Cases setting out the errors intended to be argued, it was less necessary to specify those errors in detail in the Assignment. The Assignment is usually subscribed by counsel and is on parchment or paper. The language is Latin until 1733, thereafter English.

Joinders in Error

1670 to 1852

The original method of requiring the Defendant in Error to appear and join issue in Parliament was by Writ of *scire facias* awarded upon assignment of errors. The Writ was directed to the Sheriff and required him to give notice to the Defendant *ad audiendum errores*. This procedure was abandoned after 1673. Thenceforward the Defendant usually lodged his Joinder in Error voluntarily, after errors had been assigned. If a Joinder was not lodged, the Plaintiff could petition the House to order the Defendant to plead. If he did not, the Judgment could be reversed, or the case set down *ex parte*. The Joinder in Error is a formal document in which the Defendant states that there is no error in the Judgment and asks that it be confirmed. It is on parchment or paper.

Printed Cases

1702 to 1899   487 vols.

The bound vols. consist of two separate, but overlapping sets of individual prints which appear to have been formed in the early 19th c.: (i) 'Writs of Error', 1713–1827, 5 vols.; (ii) 'Appeal Cases and Writs of Error', 1702–1899, 482 vols. (see pp. 117–18 for a description of this series).

The practice of the House did not insist on the lodging of printed cases on every Writ of Error. When the question raised was short and clear, and when the Plaintiff seemed disposed to seek delay, the House would hear the cause immediately and dispense with Printed Cases. Generally, however, in accordance with S.O. 117 of 1724, Printed Cases were to be deposited in the Parliament Office by both parties at least two days before the hearing of the cause. By S.O. 177 of 1811 it was ordered that the Plaintiff and Defendant should lay prints of their cases on the Table, or deliver them to the Clerk of the Parliaments, within a fortnight after the day appointed for the assignment of errors. By S.O. 89 of 1698 prints were to be signed by counsel before being delivered to the House.

Usually the case consists of a copy or abridgment of the record of proceedings in the lower courts and a series of 'reasons' for reversing (or for affirming) the Judgment complained of. By S.O. 181 of 1813 the proofs taken in the courts below which were to be relied on in the hearing of the cause, and the references to the documents in which they might be found, were to be reprinted, as appendices to the Case. Most of the 17th and 18th c. and some of the 19th c. cases have the Judgment endorsed on them in MS.

Ancillary Records

(i) Original Orders of the House

1621 to 1877

These are the Orders concerning Cases in Error which are mostly entered in the Books of Orders and the Journals.

(ii) Incidental Petitions

1621 to 1876

This class includes petitions for leave to lodge cases, for Writs of *scire facias*, etc.

(iii) Book of Receipts of Rolls

1859 to 1877   1 vol.

The vol. comprises receipts signed by clerks of the various courts for the return of original Judgment Rolls from the Parliament Office.

For further material concerning Cases in Error see PARLIAMENT OFFICE PAPERS *below, pp. 185, 186, 188–9.*

CASES OF PRIVILEGE

Privilege of the peerage seems to have originated in the feudal customary privilege of barons. The first distinct statement by H.L. itself of the character and extent of specific privileges was during the years 1624–8. The privilege of a peer's freedom from arrest was limited to matters other than treason, felony or refusal to give security for the peace (S.O. 48–9), but was formulated to include the protection of menial servants of the peers' families and those employed on their estates. The rights of privilege extended from the date of the Writs of Summons sent to the peers and continued 20 days before and after each session (S.O. 41). Further recognition for the privilege of freedom from arrest was given by the Privilege of Parliament Acts, 1700, 12 & 13 Will. III, c. 3 and 1703, 2 & 3 Anne, c. 12. The protection of the goods of privileged persons had been included in the privileges under S.O. 54. The number of cases arising and the tendency of peers to extend protections to others than peers' servants caused H.L. to order, at the end of the 17th c., that privilege be denied to minor peers, noblewomen (except peeresses in their own right and the wives of peers), royal servants, attorneys and solicitors (S.O. 79–80 and 86), but in 1707 it was ordered by H.L. that privilege extended to eldest sons of peers (S.O. 111). In 1704 the two Houses agreed that no additional privilege could thereafter be created. In 1712 H.L. forbade the giving of written protections to others by peers (S.O. 67 on Roll C), but protections did not end until servants' privilege of exemption from arrest in a civil suit was omitted from the Parliamentary Privilege Act, 1770, 10 Geo. III, c. 50.

The protection of the order, freedom and dignity of the House of Lords as a whole was largely dealt with on a customary basis, except that in 1699 H.L. resolved that printing of proceedings without leave of the House constituted a breach of privilege (S.O. 92), and from 1722 to 1845 it was even deemed a breach to print works and speeches of peers after their death without permission of the heirs, etc. (S.O. 113). Actions which could be construed as contempt of H.L. included misconduct by strangers or witnesses in the presence of the House or its committees, disobedience to the rules or orders of the House, abuse of the right to petition, conspiracy to deceive the House or its Committees, and speeches or writings reflecting on the character or proceedings of the House.

Since 1853 few cases of privilege have been heard by the Lords. Between 1660 and 1853 some 700 cases were dealt with; these include: (1) Privilege for estates of peers; (2) Privilege for peers and peeresses personally; (3) Privilege for servants; (4) Privilege for persons to attend the House; (5) Privilege for staying trials; (6) Privilege for persons executing the orders of the House; (7) Contempt of the House itself and its proceedings.

The procedure was usually simple. The peer or other person aggrieved petitioned the House, or attempted by letter, information or deposition to make out a prima facie case. The House, having considered this, might make any necessary Orders to bring those concerned to the Bar of the House or to obtain information, and then either heard the cause itself or, in a minority of cases, referred it to the Committee for Privileges (first set up in 1621). The case was concluded by a resolution of the House and an Order made upon it, involving, if necessary, the infliction of the punishment of reprimand, of fining or of imprisonment.

BIBLIOGRAPHY

Statements of the Law of Privilege appear in the various editions of Erskine May's *Treatise*.
See also the Report of Precedents, 25 Nov. 1724, *Lords Journal*, vol. xxii, pp. 353–5.

(i) For Records of Proceedings in Cases of Privilege, *see*:

> JOURNALS OF THE HOUSE 1510 to date. These contain very full summaries of petitions and, often, of incidental papers, together with the texts of Orders made during the hearing, of the final Order, and the record of the final reprimand or other punishment. *See* pp. 28–32 above.

> MANUSCRIPT MINUTES OF THE HOUSE, etc. 1610 to date. These, especially for 1661–1714, contain a full summary of proceedings, often with verbatim evidence. *See* pp. 33–6 above.

Committee for Privileges Minute Books

1661 to 1885   46 vols.

This committee deals principally with general questions of precedence in the House, and with peerage claims, but other privilege cases may be referred to it. The Minutes may include verbatim evidence, and usually have a full summary of proceedings (cf. the Case of E. Torrington (Privilege), as printed in *Calendar*, 1710–12, pp. 228–30). For records of its proceedings since 1885, *see* Reports, Minutes of Proceedings, etc., bound in vols. of SESSIONAL PAPERS.

(ii) Other Records relating to Cases of Privilege.

Petitions

1601 to date   500 docs.

Cases of privilege might originate in the Petition of an aggrieved peer or other person. Such petitions are in normal petitioning form, signed by the aggrieved person; but they are sometimes replaced by letters or statements of information from witnesses or others concerning an alleged contempt.

Registers of Protections

1690 to 1697   5 vols.

These registers, containing lists of protections granted by peers to others, were kept by the Clerk of the Parliaments. The dates when protections were vacated may be given.

Ancillary Privilege Papers

1610 to date   900 docs.

The incidental papers are almost entirely those antecedent to the hearing: WRITS OF HABEAS CORPUS to those imprisoning petitioners; RETURNS

OF SHERIFFS or BAILIFFS to the Writs; the originals or copies of the PEERS'
PROTECTIONS; texts of the LIBELS or unauthorised PUBLICATIONS,
or similar evidence of contempt; CERTIFICATES of Privilege; DEPOSI-
TIONS concerning the evidence; PETITIONS of defendants and others
concerned in the case; and (subsequent to judgment) PETITIONS of those
sentenced for liberty, etc. From *c.* 1714 onwards there are fewer incidental
papers, those surviving being almost entirely supplementary petitions. For
examples of the earlier papers see those printed *in extenso* in *Calendar*, vol. xi.

SESSIONAL PAPERS, HOUSE OF LORDS

From the 17th c. onwards all papers arising in H. L. or used by it[1] have been preserved session by session in chronological sequence within the Palace of Westminster. This series of sessional papers consists of the following 9 principal categories:

1. Returns
2. Command Papers
3. Act Papers
4. Papers laid pursuant to subsidiary legislation

   (*Note* that papers in the categories 1–4 were all 'Ordered to lie on the Table' as described on pp. 130–1 below.)

5. Petitions, *see* pp. 172–3.
6. Private Bill Papers, *see* pp. 83–92
7. Judicial Papers, *see* pp. 108–126
8. Public Bill Papers, *see* pp. 65–8

(*Categories 1–8, stored as* 'Main Papers, H.L.')

9. This category consists of documents of large or awkward format, the greater number of which are stored separately in the 'Parchment Collection', e.g. ROYAL COMMISSIONS, *see* pp. 175–6; and WRITS OF SUMMONS, *see* pp. 179–80.

Categories 1–4 of Sessional Papers are described in this introductory section; for the remaining categories 5–9 the reader is referred to the pages of this *Guide* shown in the table above.

Returns

These papers are so called because they are 'returned' to the House in answer either to an Order of the House or to an Address to the Sovereign asking for papers. Apart from the record of the trial of Mary, Queen of Scots, which seems to have been made for the use of the House in 1588, the earliest Returns noted in the Journals are those for 1626 onwards, which were provided mainly for the information of committees of the House. From 1641 H.L. began to request or require that papers on various matters should be laid before them, and thereafter the sequence of Returns to the House is continuous. The Sovereign was prominent amongst the recipients of requests for papers from 1678 onwards. These requests were in the form of 'Humble Addresses', and in the 18th c. and later they normally related to subjects that were the concern of a Secretary of State. Matters dealt with by other Ministers or by bodies outside the Government were the subject of Orders. The Order took the form 'Ordered, that there be laid before the House papers relating to . . .', and it was delivered

[1] I.e. excluding records of proceedings such as Journals and Minutes. For similar papers presented in H.C., *see* SESSIONAL PAPERS, H.C., pp. 232–6 below.

to the officer or authority concerned. The practice of ordering papers direct from persons or bodies outside the Government became, in the 19th c., increasingly rare. The normal practice in its full development was for bodies outside the Government to be required to produce their papers to the Minister concerned, who then laid them before Parliament.

In the early and middle part of the 19th c. both Houses made numerous Orders and Addresses for Papers containing statistics and information on the widest range of subjects, and these series subsequently became established in two sequences as either Command Papers (*see* below) or Act Papers (*see* pp. 128–30). This had the result of diminishing the number of Returns to Orders and Addresses. In H.L. the 'Motion for Papers' almost entirely lost its original function in the second half of the 19th c. and became instead a means of initiating a general debate on which no vote was taken, the motion normally being withdrawn at its conclusion. Since 1945 there have only been 11 Motions for Papers which have not been withdrawn, and which have therefore led to the making of Returns to the House. In 1956 the differentiation between Orders and Addresses was abandoned.

Command Papers

Papers have been presented to H.L. 'by command' of the Sovereign from the 17th c., the first paper so recorded being of 1625, and the first paper that survives today in H.L.R.O. being of 1641. Increasing quantities of papers concerning diplomatic, military and commercial affairs were received during the 18th c. by H.L. (*see* the classified subject list, below). 'Presentation' of a paper was originally by a Member of the House rising in his place and producing it in the House; it was then ordered to lie on the Table, where it was available for perusal by Members. The actual laying of the paper on the Table of the House probably ceased in the first quarter of the 19th c. and the number of papers lying on the Table for some years before that must have been restricted by the space available and by other practical considerations.

Command Papers, which were regularly printed by official printers from 1833[1], were first numbered continuously from 1–4,222 (although these numbers did not appear on the papers until 1839), then in four consecutive series: C.1–C.9,550 (1870–99), Cd.1–Cd.9,239 (1900–18), Cmd.1–Cmd.9,889 (1919–56), Cmnd. 1 *seq.* thereafter. It should be added that during the whole of this time it has been possible for a paper to be presented to Parliament by command without being printed; but the number of such unprinted Command Papers is small.

Command Papers are always 'Government' Papers. They either expound Government policy (in which case they tend to be known as 'White Papers') or give information in the possession of the Government. Much of this information is of a well-established character; for example nearly all treaties agreed to by this country are made public in the 'Treaty Series' which are Command Papers.

Act Papers

This class of Papers, dating from the 17th c., comprises those required

---

[1] Command papers had been printed from the early 18th c. but MS. versions were presented to Parliament in that c.

by Act of Parliament to be laid before each House (or in the case of Papers relating to revenue matters, before H.C. only).

From about 1669 Acts setting up bodies of Commissioners directed that the Accounts or Reports of the Commissioners should be laid before the two Houses. This practice became more frequent in the 18th c. when such bodies of Commissioners were set up with increasing frequency by Acts relating to bridges, turnpike roads, etc. A short series of Papers laid in 1717 under the Dagenham Breach Act is preserved in H.L.R.O., and thereafter until *c.* 1850 the greater number of Act Papers concerns private undertakings of a public nature, such as the City of London Orphans Fund, Richmond Bridge and the streets of Westminster. For the most part such Act Papers were not ordered to be printed, but a substantial number of originals survives in H.L.R.O. among the Main Papers. From *c.* 1850 a considerable (and now the greater) number of Act Papers has been ordered to be laid by Ministers, and concerns public matters.

Act Papers can usefully be described as of three kinds:

(a) *Delegated Legislation*. This expression indicates Orders in Council, Regulations and Ministerial Orders, Licences, Schemes, Directions, etc., made under the authority of Act of Parliament. They originated in the early 16th c., but it was not until mid-19th c. that Parliament found it necessary, owing to the increasing complexity of the matters with which Acts of Parliament dealt, to delegate much of its legislative power to Ministers or other official bodies. Most, but not all such delegated legislation is required by its parent Act to be laid before Parliament; and of the part which is so laid a substantial proportion (though not all) is subject to some form of Parliamentary control.

Generally speaking, nearly all delegated legislation is subject to the Statutory Instruments Act, 1946, 9 & 10 Geo. VI, c. 36, and since 1948 has been issued in the form of 'Statutory Instruments'. Of these, the least important are not required to be laid before Parliament. The remainder fall into three categories. Some Statutory Instruments are laid before Parliament simply for information, and the parent Act makes no provision for Parliamentary control. The second type comprises those subject to Parliamentary control by 'Negative Resolution', as provided for by the parent Act and by sections 5 and 6 of the Statutory Instruments Act. Instruments subject to this procedure can be 'prayed against' in either House for a period of 40 days of active Parliamentary time after their laying. The third type of Instrument requires affirmative resolutions of both Houses (or in the case of revenue instruments, of the H.C. only) before it can come into force or continue in force for more than a short period after its making. During the present century an average of some 2,000 instruments of delegated legislation has been issued annually. Of these, about half are laid before Parliament and are to be found among the Main Papers. Since 1890 there has been provision for the printing and publication of most delegated legislation (*see* p. 132 below).

(b) *Government Reports and Accounts*. Acts of Parliament which confer powers and duties upon a Minister of the Crown commonly require that he shall lay before Parliament copies of Accounts and Reports showing the progress of his activities. He may also be required to lay Papers giving details of decisions he takes in his discretion (e.g. the names and salaries of the members of various boards he may have the duty to appoint). Many Accounts and Reports are ordered to be printed by H.C., and consequently find their place

in the series of the SESSIONAL PAPERS, H.C., notably all Accounts audited
by the Controller and Auditor General and subsequently laid before Parliament.
The rest of these Reports and Accounts may have their own numbering system
(e.g. recent Census Reports of the Registrar General, and the papers of the Law
Commission), but otherwise they are unnumbered and are nowhere listed except
under the heading 'Accounts and Papers' in the index to the Commons Journal.
In the Lords Journals they are indexed individually. The greater number are
printed and published by H.M. Stationery Office; but a few, e.g. those dealing
with matters of relatively slight importance or those of considerable bulk, may
still be unprinted.

(c) *Other Reports and Accounts.* Many semi-official bodies, such as nationalised
corporations and Dock and Harbour Boards, are required by their parent Acts
to submit Accounts and Reports of their activities annually to a Minister, who
must lay them before each House of Parliament. In certain cases these Reports
are ordered to be printed by H.C.; in other cases they are printed by H.M.
Stationery Office, but not to the order of H.C.; and in some instances they are
printed privately by the body concerned. A small number each year remains
unprinted. The only comprehensive list of these Accounts and Reports is to be
found, as with the Government Accounts and Reports, in the 'Accounts and
Papers' section of the Index to the Commons Journal.

In total, the Government and other Accounts and Reports probably average
about 650 annually, about half of them being printed to the order of H.C., and
so being included in SESSIONAL PAPERS, H.C. Very few are included in
the Sessional Papers, H.L., except for the Lord Chancellor's memoranda under
the Consolidation of Enactments (Procedure) Act, 1949, 12 & 13 Geo. VI, c. 33
and occasional papers such as the Report of the Tribunal on the Aberfan
Disaster in 1966, which was ordered to be printed by both Houses.

Papers Laid Pursuant to Subsidiary Legislation

Church Assembly Measures (*see* pp. 104–5) occasionally provide for delegated legislation to be laid before Parliament. Such instruments of delegated
legislation are virtually analogous to Statutory Instruments (*see* above, p.
129). Orders, Accounts and Reports (for the most part relating to Armed
Forces Pensions) may similarly be laid before the House pursuant to Royal
Warrant. Finally, a few Reports and Accounts are laid before the House pursuant to the requirements of Statutory Instruments, and delegated legislation
may be made under powers conferred by Statutory Instrument (though such
'grand-children' of statutes have been condemned by Select Committees).

The Procedure of laying before the House is described in detail in 18th and early
19th c. Journals, e.g. H.L. Journal, 18 June 1824:
> 'The House being informed, "That Mr Wooller, from the Office of Woods
> and Forests, attended;" He was called in; and delivered at the Bar, pursuant
> to the Directions of an Act of Parliament, "First Report of the Commis-
> sioners for the further Improvement of the Road from London to Holy-
> head." And then he withdrew'.

The laying of papers before Parliament is by an official or other person who is
not a Member of the House; the process is therefore carried out at the Bar of
the House. On the other hand, a Paper is 'presented' within the House, by a

Member of the House. The Order 'to lie on the Table' means that the Paper is to be held available in the House for perusal by Members, and ultimately Papers ordered to lie on the Table are preserved, with the other records of the House, in H.L.R.O.

THE PRINTING OF LORDS PAPERS

The earliest record of the printing of Parliamentary papers is the order of the Commons on 5 May 1641 that the Protestation (*see* p. 154) be printed. Orders of H.L. might also be printed from 1641, and on 20 April 1660 the Lords ordered a joint resolution on Thanksgiving to be printed.[1] Printing for both Houses became quite frequent in the later 17th c. The Commons *Votes and Proceedings* began to be issued regularly in 1680 and from 1696 the Lords consistently ordered the printing of communications between them and the Crown. On 23 June 1701, proceedings concerning the impeachment of certain lords were ordered to be printed by H.L. but a similar resolution concerning the printing of Bills in the following year produced a protest from L. Dartmouth and others that such printing and publication (that is, of Bills) were 'highly derogatory to the honour and dignity of the House of Lords', since 'it is an appealing to the people'. The general principle had been established, however, and from 1701 onwards prints may be discovered of proceedings, reports, bills and other papers relating to H.L., although regular and officially printed Minutes of Proceedings, similar to those ordered for the Commons in 1680, do not appear until 1825. Public Bills began to be printed by H.L. as a normal procedure in about 1730.

The list of the Lords Orders to Print for 1660 to 1800 contains about 1,200 titles including those of Resolutions, Orders, Addresses, Standing Orders, Reports of Committees, Proceedings in Trials of Peers and Impeachments, Bills, Accounts and other Papers. Of this total number of prints ordered, H.L. Library since the early 19 c. has held a set of 32 reports, 82 accounts and 144 other papers, of which 44 are duplicates. These were arranged in 31 vols, and dated between 1788 and 1800. In 1970, with the help of the Librarian of the Board of Trade and the authorities of certain other departments, this set was combined with originals or copies of prints from the Board of Trade, the Treasury, the Home Office, the British Museum, etc. The resulting set for 1788 to 1800, which is almost complete from 1790 (except for about 25 bills missing out of a total of 400) is preserved in H.L. Library and is available for the use of students in H.L.R.O.[2] In addition H.L. Library holds a few early printed papers from 1703.

In 1801 the regularly preserved and numbered sets of printed Lords papers commence. Each print was, from 1804, assigned a number in chronological order as a Sessional Paper, and from 1833 onwards printed Command Papers have also been consecutively numbered—but in a separate series, and without regard to session. In the bound sets the individual prints are arranged in series of Bills; Reports of Committees and Commissions; and Accounts and Papers.

For the period 1801 to 1921, the general picture in H.L. is of an ever-increasing

---

[1] See the typescript List of 'Orders to Print, H.L., 1660–1800' in H.L.R.O.

[2] Mr. F. W. Torrington, who assembled the new set, is in course of preparing a similar set of originals or copies of H.L. Sessional Papers from 1660 onwards.

resort to printing and publication. By about 1818 nearly all Command Papers were printed, Reports of Committees and Commissions were frequently printed, but often without the annexed evidence. Act Papers and Petitions were rarely printed. In 1854 the Clerk of the Parliaments stated that Command Papers were usually presented printed, that papers laid by Order of the House were usually printed as a matter of course, and that Act papers were not often delivered printed, but that about a quarter of them were ordered to be printed.

Although in the present century the percentage of Papers printed and therefore included in Sessional Papers has increased considerably, very many Act Papers, some Evidence annexed to Reports, and most Petitions, have remained unprinted, and therefore survive only in the MS. copy preserved in H.L.R.O. When a paper has been printed, a single copy has been supplied for ultimate preservation as the official record copy in H.L.R.O.

It should be noted that full sets of printed H.L. SESSIONAL PAPERS are rare—probably only five sets were issued to libraries and other institutions in the early 19th c. No greater number of full sets of H.C. SESSIONAL PAPERS was issued at that time, but H.C. sets starting at a later date are more numerous, and to a considerable extent the H.L. vols reproduce the material in H.C. SESSIONAL PAPERS, including e.g. the printed Command Papers up to 1900. (The only papers now appearing identically in each are the reports of Joint Committees of both Houses.) Students are advised to consult both the H.L. and the H.C. SESSIONAL PAPERS to avoid overlooking relevant material.

The Printing of Delegated Legislation

Delegated Legislation has been printed and published since 1890 in annual vols. These were entitled *Annual Volumes of Statutory Rules and Orders* until 1949, since when they have been known as *Annual Volumes of Statutory Instruments*. From 1890 until 1952 orders of a local, personal or temporary character were excluded; since then summaries of the provisions of Statutory Instruments relating to local matters have been included.

LISTS AND INDEXES

1. *Sessional Papers, 1510–1714*

The Lords Journals mention virtually all Lords papers, printed and manuscript (*see* pp. 28–32 above). Those papers now preserved in H.L.R.O. are calendared, sometimes *in extenso*, in the relevant vols. of the *Calendar*.

2. *Sessional Papers, 1714–1800*

In this period, papers may be traced in the appropriate Lords Journal, and in the MS. lists of Main Papers and of the Parchment Collection, which are available in H.L.R.O. These lists are arranged in chronological order according to the date on which the papers were laid or presented.

3. *Sessional Papers, 1801–date*

Papers may be traced in the Lords Journal under the dates of laying or presentation. The copies of the Journals available in H.L.R.O. Search Room are marked to indicate which papers have been preserved, and MS. lists of Main

Papers and the Parchment Collection in chronological order are also available in H.L.R.O.

A complete guide to Lords Sessional Papers ordered to be printed from 1801 onwards is to be found in the following indexes of printed Sessional Papers:

(i) For the period 1801–85, the 3 vols. of the *General Index to the Sessional Papers printed by Order of the House of Lords or presented by Royal Command* comprise a simple cumulative subject index, arranged alphabetically. They contain a few references to papers unprinted or not officially published.

(ii) For the period 1886–1920 there are separate *Tables and Indexes* to *The Sessional Papers printed by Order of the House of Lords or presented by Royal Command* for each session. These contain (a) general tables of contents showing the arrangement of the papers; (b) tables of papers ordered by H.L., arranged numerically, showing the date of the order of printing, general subject and nature of each paper; (c) tables of Command Papers, giving similar details; (d) alphabetical indexes to the titles of all papers. The Tables up to 1914 also include (e) tables of the titles of all Acts passed, in chronological and alphabetical order; (f) tables showing the effect of the session's legislation; (g) addenda to the general index of local and private Acts. These Tables are themselves numbered amongst the Sessional Papers of their year, though for convenience, sets covering periods of up to 10 years have been bound together in H.L.R.O. and H.L. Library. From 1901 onwards, few if any specially paginated bound sets of Sessional Papers were prepared; the bound set in H.L. Library is of separate pieces not always continuously paginated.

(iii) For the period 1921 to date, sessional indexes have not been issued as separate vols. General tables of contents have been prefixed to the vols. of Sessional Papers for each year.

4. *Statutory Instruments, etc., 1671–date*

Statutory Instruments may be traced in the *Tables of Government Orders* (current ed., 1968) which provides a 'list of general legislative instruments made under the Royal Prerogative and under statutory authority respectively', 1671 to date. It records all revocations to date of the instruments, together with amendments, modifications, etc. *The Index of Statutory Rules and Orders and Statutory Instruments . . . showing the Powers under which they were made*, arranged alphabetically by subject matter, notes instruments in force. The 1st ed. was published in 1891; from 1951 the title was changed to *Guide to Government Orders*, and in 1965 to *Index to Government Orders* (H.M.S.O.). In addition, H.M.S.O. publishes monthly and annually *Lists of Statutory Instruments*.

5. *Her Majesty's Stationery Office Publications, 1837–date*

Lords and Commons Sessional Papers, together with other publications relating to Parliament and issued by H.M. Stationery Office, have been listed in the H.M.S.O. *Annual Lists of Publications* since 1837. These lists have also been consolidated into quinquennial indexes from 1936–40. The current annual list, now called the *Catalogue of Government Publications*, comprises:

   i. Papers and Bills, H.L.
  ii. Parliamentary Debates (Hansard), H.L.
 iii. Papers, H.C.
  iv. Parliamentary Debates (Hansard), H.C.
   v. Bills, H.C.
  vi. Command Papers
 vii. Public General Acts
viii. Local Acts
  ix. Church Assembly Measures

These *Catalogues* are fully indexed. H.M.S.O. also publish daily and monthly catalogues. Any enquiry concerning these should be addressed to H.M.S.O. (P.10), Atlantic House, Holborn Viaduct, London EC1.

BIBLIOGRAPHY (H.L. AND H.C.)

H. H. Bellot, 'Parliamentary Printing, 1660–1837', *Bulletin of the Institute of Historical Research*, vol. xi (1933–4), pp. 85–98.

H. H. Bellot, 'British Parliamentary Papers: Catalogues and Indexes', *Bulletin of the Institute of Historical Research*, vol. xi (1933–4), pp. 24–30.

P. and G. Ford, *A Guide to Parliamentary Papers*. 2nd ed. (1956).

P. and G. Ford, *Select List of British Parliamentary Papers, 1833–1899* (1953).

P. and G. Ford, *A Breviate of Parliamentary Papers, 1900–1916* (1957).

P. and G. Ford, *A Breviate of Parliamentary Papers, 1917–1939* (1951).

P. and G. Ford, *A Breviate of Parliamentary Papers, 1940–1954* (1961).

General Index to the Bills, Reports and Papers . . . of the House of Commons, 1900 to 1948–9 (1960). Introduction.

Hansard's Catalogue and Breviate of Parliamentary Papers, 1696–1834. Reprinted in facsimile with an introduction by P. and G. Ford (1953).

L. W. Hanson, *Contemporary Printed Sources for British and Irish Economic History, 1701–1750* (1963).

H. V. Jones, *Catalogue of Parliamentary Papers, 1801–1900*, with supplements *1901–10* and *1911–20*, 4 vols. (1904–22).

S. Lambert, 'Guides to Parliamentary Printing, 1696–1834', *Bulletin of the Institute of Historical Research*, vol. xxxviii (1965), pp. 111–17.

S. Lambert, 'The Presentation of Parliamentary Papers by the Foreign Office', *Bulletin of the Institute of Historical Research*, vol. xxiii (1950), pp. 76–83.

S. Lambert, 'Printing for the House of Commons in the Eighteenth Century', *The Library*, 5th ser., vol. xxiii (1968), pp. 25–46.

S. Lambert, *List of House of Commons Sessional Papers, 1701–1750* (1968).

K. A. C. Parsons, *A Checklist of British Parliamentary Papers (Bound Set), 1801–1950* (1958).

W. R. Powell, *Local History from Blue Books*, Historical Association Pamphlet no. 64 (1962).

Report of the Select Committee of the House of Lords on the Subject of Printing Papers for the House, H. L. 1854 (119), vol. xxi.

H. Temperley and L. M. Penson, *A Century of Diplomatic Blue Books, 1814–1914* (1938).

R. Vogel, *A Breviate of British Diplomatic Blue Books, 1919–1939* (1963).

See also the following general guides to British manuscripts each of which contains sections or lists relating to the Sessional Papers and other documents preserved in H.L.R.O.

America

C. M. A. Andrews and F. G. Davenport, *Guide to the Manuscript Materials for the History of the United States to 1783, in the British Museum, in Minor London Archives, and in the Libraries of Oxford and Cambridge* (1908).

C. O. Paullin and F. L. Paxson, *Guide to the Materials in London Archives for the History of the United States since 1783* (1914).

B. R. Crick and M. Alman, *Guide to Manuscripts relating to America in Great Britain and Ireland* (1961).

Asia

M. D. Wainwright and N. Matthews, *Guide to Western Manuscripts and Documents in the British Isles relating to South and South East Asia* (1965).

Ireland

B. Dietz, 'Survey of Manuscripts of Irish Interest for the period 1715–1850 in the House of Lords Record Office'; and L. McRedmond, 'Irish Appeals to the House of Lords in the Eighteenth Century', *Analecta Hibernica*, no. 23 (1966).

The West Indies

L. J. Ragatz, *A Check List of House of Lords Sessional Papers Relating to the British West Indies and to the West Indian Slave Trade and Slavery, 1763–1834* (1932).

SESSIONAL PAPERS, H.L. (1641–1800)

Subject classification: main headings

Accounts, Public	*page* 136
Army	138
Carlisle to Newcastle Military Road	139
City of London	139
Colonies	140
Crown Estates	141
Customs and Trade	142
Dagenham Breach	149
East India	149
Ecclesiastical	149
Forfeited Estates	150
Greenwich Hospital	150

Ireland	151
Kensington, Chelsea and Fulham Roads	151
Lieutenancy Commissions	151
Mercers' Company	151
Miscellaneous	151
Navy	152
Poor	153
Post Office	153
Protestation Returns	154
Public Offices	155
Richmond Bridge	155
Scotland	155
Treaties, etc.	157
Westminster Bridge	158
Westminster Paving	158

In the following lists brief headings are given for all series of Returns, Act Papers and other Papers, manuscript or printed, which survive for dates up to and including 31 December 1800. Minor individual non-recurring deposits are normally not included, but may be traced in the appropriate volumes of the *Calendar*, or in the *Lords Journals* (documents dating before 1 August 1714 have been listed, and sometimes transcribed at length, in the *Calendar*). The grouping of subjects under general headings below is for convenience only and does not necessarily indicate *provenance*. In particular, the categories of 'Colonies', and of 'Customs and Trade' overlap and reference must, in cases of doubt, be made to both.

Unless otherwise indicated, the dates given are those of presentation to the House. When the dates of the material dealt with in the Papers differ significantly from that of presentation, they are given, in brackets, immediately after the date of presentation.[1] The name of the originating department appears, in italics, after the title of the series, unless the title itself sufficiently indicates the department. The number of documents in the series is indicated only if it is more than two, and if it is not implied in the remainder of the entry.

ACCOUNTS, PUBLIC

ANNUITIES. *Exchequer*. Annual accounts of money paid into the Exchequer under the National Debt Act, 1789, 29 Geo. III, c. 37; 1790–5, 5 docs.

CIVIL LISTS. *Treasury*. Accounts (various) of receipts, payments, sums due, debts, etc. for the Civil Government and maintenance of the Royal Household and Family, 1729, 3 docs.; 1769; 1770 (1752–69), 18 docs.; 1777 (1769–77), 8 docs.; Plan for relieving the Civil List, 1782; 1783, 3 docs.; 1784, 20 docs.; 1786 (1781–6), 4 docs.

COMMISSIONERS OF ACCOUNTS, appointed under the Public Accounts Act, 1667, 19 & 20 Cha. II, c. 1, and subsequent Acts. Reports, 1669; 1702; 1704; 1711; 1713; 1714; 1781; 1785 (1780–5), 13 docs. State of

---

[1] It may be assumed that when no such dates are given in brackets for annual accounts, the accounts cover the appropriate financial year fully concluded before the date of presentation.

supplies of money for the Navy, etc., 1693 (1688–93), 4 docs. Statements of Incomes and Issues of Public Revenue, etc., 1691 (1688–91); 1692; 1693; 1695 (1693–4); 1696 (1694–5); 1703 (1700–3); 1704 (1702–3), 35 docs.; 1712 (1710–11); 1713 (1709–10, 1711–12); 1714 (1703–4, 1712–13), 3 docs.

COMMISSIONERS OF ACCOUNTS DUE TO THE ARMY, appointed under the Debts due to the Army Act, 1698, 11 Will. III, c. 8 and subsequent Acts. Reports and Accounts, 1705 (1689 *seq.*), 3 docs.; 1713; 1716; 1717; 1722.

COMMISSIONERS OF THE EQUIVALENT, appointed under the Act of Union with Scotland, 1706, 6 Anne, c. 11. Reports and Accounts, 1709; 1711; 1714; 1717; 1719; Memorial (Customs and Excise), 1719.

COMMISSIONERS OF LAND REVENUE appointed to enquire into the state of the woods, forest and land revenues of the Crown under the Crown Land Revenues Act, 1786, 26 Geo. III, c. 87. Reports, 1790 (4 Reports); 1793 (4 Reports). Cf. also 1st Report of the Surveyor of the Land Revenue, 1798.

COMMISSIONERS FOR THE REDUCTION OF THE NATIONAL DEBT, appointed under National Debt Reduction Act, 1786, 26 Geo. III, c. 31. Accounts, 1787–1800, 13 docs. Cf. also Returns from the Bank of England of receipts and expenditure by the Commissioners, 1790–1800, 9 docs.

NATIONAL (PUBLIC) DEBT. *Exchequer.* State of the Public (from 1724–5, National) Debt, 1723–64, annual returns, 36 docs. (cf. also Estimate, 1721). Account of the National Debt, 1778 (1770–77), 8 docs.

NAVY ACCOUNTS (MISC.)

Navy Office. Accounts of Expenses, 1735. Estimate of debt, 1797.

Commissioners of the Navy. Estimates of Debt, etc., 1722; 1723 (1711–22); 1733; 1734 (1720–33) 14 docs.; 1747; 1748; 1758, with Account of Seamen and Marines employed; 1761; 1789.

Admiralty Office. Ordinary and extraordinary Estimates, 1778 (1771–8), 17 vols.

PARLIAMENTARY GRANTS. *Treasury.* Accounts of Parliamentary grants, remains and deficiencies, etc., 1704 (1702–4). Accounts of Supplies voted, 1714 (1710–12).

PENSIONS. *Treasury.* Annual Lists of Pensions granted under Civil List and Secret Service Money Act, 1782, 22 Geo. III, c. 82, 1785–9, 7 docs.

PUBLIC DEBT. *Treasury.* Estimate of Debt unprovided for by Parliament, 1721. Accounts laid under Customs and Excise Act, 1787, 27 Geo. III, c. 13, relating to the total produce of Duties of Custom, Excise, Stamps and Incidents, and to charges to meet loans under the Act, 1790, 9 docs.; 1792, 24 docs.; 1794, 7 docs.; 1795, 15 docs.; 1800.

PUBLIC INCOME AND EXPENDITURE. Accounts laid, 1789 (1786–9) by *Exchequer, Treasury, Hackney Coach Office, Post Office, Salt Office, First Fruits, Commissioners of Customs* and *Tax Office*, 56 docs.

TAXES AND CONSOLIDATED FUND. *Treasury.* Accounts of net produce of Taxes, and of Income of and Charges on Consolidated Fund; 1796, 11 docs.; 1797, 6 docs.

ARMY[1]

AMERICAN WAR OF INDEPENDENCE PAPERS
Secretary of State. Papers concerning raising of regiments, 1777–8, and state of forces under General Howe, 1778, 21 docs. Papers concerning the campaign of Saratoga, 1778, 61 docs.
Admiralty Office. The Army under E. Cornwallis, 1782, 307 docs. *See* also under *COLONIES*, AMERICAN PAPERS.

ARTILLERY, ROYAL
Ordnance Office. Return, 1778.
Home Office. Account of men received from Militia, 1796.

BARRACKS
Home Office. Accounts for erection of barracks, 1796 (1792–5).
Lord Chancellor. Accounts of numbers, superintendence, etc., of new barracks, 1796, 6 docs.

COMMISSIONERS OF ACCOUNTS DUE TO THE ARMY. *See ACCOUNTS, PUBLIC*

COURTS MARTIAL
Judge Advocate General. Account of General Courts Martial (Great Britain, Gibraltar, N. America and W. Indies), 1778, (1774–8), 3 docs.
Secretary of State. Returns (Ireland), 1778 (1774–8), 20 docs.

ESTABLISHMENT (1) Lists of Officers
Master General of the Ordnance. List of General Officers, etc., 1695; 1741 (1739); 1742.
Secretary at War. List of Officers displaced and their successors, 1718 (1714–18). Lists of half-pay Officers, 1718; 1721 (1715–21), 7 docs.; 1729. Cf. also Accounts of Warrants (half-pay Officers), 1725. Accounts of Army Vacancies, 1721. Lists of Officers, 1729; 1763. List of Promotions of Officers, 1730; 1732; 1733; 1734; 1736; 1737; 1739.

ESTABLISHMENT (2) Miscellaneous
Secretary at War. Constitution and number of Regiments, 1718 (1715–17), 7 docs. Augmentation of Army, 1723. List and Quarters of Forces, 1735.
Secretary of State. Establishment in Great Britain and Ireland, 1719. Return of Men Impressed, 1779 (1778).

ESTIMATES
Secretary at War. Returns of Estimates of the charges of the Army, 1741, 4 docs.; 1743, 7 docs.; 1763, 7 docs.
War Office. Returns of Estimates of charge of troops in Hanover, 1744.

EXTRAORDINARY SERVICES (MILITARY)
Secretary of State. Accounts of payments and receipts, 1779 (1775–9), 7 docs.
Pay Office. Accounts of Expenses (1795–6) and distribution of sum granted, 1797.

MILITIA
Council Office. Return respecting Militia Pay Act, 1757, 31 Geo. II, c. 30, 1758.

---

[1] Papers relating to the Army emanating from the Treasury or the Exchequer are noted under the general heading ACCOUNTS; all other financial papers are given in this section.

Secretary of State. Returns respecting Volunteer Companies, 1780, 15 docs.; Officers, 1780, 38 docs.; Qualifications, 1779, 44 docs.; 1791, 35 docs.; 1793, 25 docs.; 1794, 29 docs.; 1796, 24 docs.; 1797, 24 docs.; 1798, 32 docs.; 1799, 36 docs.; 1800, 21 docs.; Men enlisted in room of those transferred, 1796; Supplementary List, 1798; Offers of service in Ireland, 1798, 11 docs.

ORDNANCE

Officers of the Ordnance, State of the Ordnance, 1692. Papers relating to vessels and prizes taken by the Americans, 1778 (1775–8), 18 docs.; defence of Dominica, 1778, 1779.

Board of Ordnance and others. Returns concerning numbers of persons in transport service, 1795, 4 docs. Accounts of Transport service, 1796, 6 docs.; of Ordnance unprovided services, 1796; of Ordnance, 1797.

RULES AND ARTICLES OF WAR. *Secretary at War,* 1718, 1723, 1724, 1727, 1729, 1730, 1731, 1733, 1734, 1737, 1738, 1739, 1740, 1749.

SPANISH WAR

Lord Privy Seal. Papers concerning the war in Spain, 1705, 4 docs.

Secretary of State. The like, 1707, (1705–7), 123 docs.; 1711 (1706–11), 44 docs. *See* also *TREATIES, ETC.,* below.

CARLISLE TO NEWCASTLE MILITARY ROAD

Commissioners and Trustees of the Carlisle to Newcastle Military Road appointed under the Carlisle and Newcastle Road Act, 1750, 24 Geo. II, c. 25. Contracts, 1753; Accounts, 1753; 1755; 1756; 1757; 1758; 1759.

CITY OF LONDON[1]

Note that the following accounts are almost all annual accounts, delivered by the Chamberlain of the City of London.

BISHOPSGATE INTO BARBICAN STREET. Accounts, 1781 (1778–80) for making a street from Bishopsgate into Barbican, under the London Streets Act, 1778, 18 Geo. III, c. 71.

BLACKFRIARS BRIDGE. Accounts of money received and paid for building Blackfriars Bridge, under the Blackfriars Bridge Act, 1756, 29 Geo. II, c. 86; 1761–85 (from 1759), 22 docs.; in connection with tolls on the Bridge, under the Thames Embankment Act, 1766, 7 Geo. III, c. 37, 1772–8 (from 1770), 7 docs.; for repairing, lighting, watching and cleansing the Bridge, under the Blackfriars Bridge (Sunday Tolls) Act, 1786, 26 Geo. III, c. 37, 1785–1800 (from 1783), 14 docs.

LONDON BRIDGE. Accounts of money received and paid under the London Bridge Act, 1756, 29 Geo. II, c. 40, 1757–65, 7 docs.; of tolls, 1772–8 (from 1770), 7 docs.

[1] Cf. the relevant sections in P. E. Jones and R. Smith, *Guide to the Records in the Corporation of London Records Office and the Guildhall Library Muniment Room* (1951) for further details of the funds and their records.

MOORFIELDS INTO BISHOPSGATE STREET. Accounts for making a
street from Moorfields into Bishopsgate Street, under the London Streets
Act, 1778, 18 Geo. III, c. 71, 1782–1800 (from 1780), 17 docs.

NEW BRIDGE STREET, BLACKFRIARS SEWER. Accounts for repairing the common sewer in New Bridge Street, under the Blackfriars
Sewer Act, 1795, 35 Geo. III, c. 131, 1797–1800, 4 docs.

NEWGATE GAOL. Accounts for rebuilding Newgate Gaol under the
Thames Embankment Act, 1766, 7 Geo. III, c. 37, 1768–85, 15 docs.,
including Account of £10,000 grant, 1781.

ORPHANS' FUND. The fund was established under the Orphans, London,
Act, 1694, 5 & 6 Will. & Mary, c. 10; under the Orphans, London, Act,
1747, 21 Geo. II, c. 29, the Chamberlain was to lay before Parliament
Accounts of the surplus of the fund and the debt undischarged. Accounts,
1757–1800, 37 docs.

PAVING AND CLEANSING. Accounts for paving and cleansing the City
of London, under the London Paving and Lighting Act, 1766, 6 Geo. III,
c. 26, and the City of London Sewerage Act, 1771, 11 Geo. III, c. 29, 1767–
72, 7 docs.; 1784 (from 1782).

ROYAL EXCHANGE. Accounts for rebuilding the Royal Exchange, under
the Thames Embankment Act, 1766, 7 Geo. III, c. 37, 1768–78, 8 docs.

TEMPLE BAR. Accounts for widening the entrance into the City near
Temple Bar, and for making a street at Snow Hill, under the Temple Bar,
etc., Act, 1795, 35 Geo. III, c. 126, 1797–1800, 4 docs.

THAMES EMBANKMENT. Accounts for embanking part of the north
side of the River Thames, under the Thames Embankment Act, 1766, 7
Geo. III, c. 37, 1768–85, 14 docs.

THAMES NAVIGATION. Accounts for completing the navigation of the
Thames, under the Thames Navigation Act, 1776, 17 Geo. III, c. 18, 1777–
1800, 23 docs.

VAULTS, DRAINS AND SEWERS. Accounts for enlarging, amending
and cleansing vaults, drains and sewers within the City of London, under
the City of London Sewerage Act, 1771, 11 Geo. III, c. 29, 1775–1800
(from 1771), 22 docs.

COLONIES

AMERICAN PAPERS

An extensive list of materials for American history in H.L.R.O. appears
in C. M. Andrews and F. G. Davenport, *Guide to the Manuscript Materials
for the History of the United States to 1783* . . . (1908), pp. 189–272, and in
C. O. Paullin and F. L. Paxson, *Guide to the Materials in London Archives
for the History of the United States since 1783* (1914), pp. 326–60,[1] supplemented by the additional lists and information in B. R. Crick and M.
Alman, *Guide to Manuscripts relating to America in Great Britain and*

[1] It should be observed, however, that these two reference lists include many documents
presented to the House and registered in the *Journals*, but not now surviving amongst the
records.

Ireland (1961), pp. 226–36. The entries in the list below do not include purely formal documents deposited by the Departments named.

Admiralty. Courts of Vice-Admiralty; appointment of Judges for North America, 1766 (1763–4), 11 docs. American Disturbances, 1770, 9 docs. Papers relating to American vessels taken by English ships, 1778 (1775–8), 17 docs.

Board of Trade and Plantations. Copies of charters and grants to Massachusett's Bay, etc. 1734 (1632–1691), 5 docs. Province of South Carolina, 1739 (1722–38), 4 docs. Encroachments by the French in North America, 1756 (1749–55), 149 docs.

Secretary of State. Papers concerning the following subjects (listed here in chronological order): Spanish Depredations and Georgia, etc., 1739 (1736–8), 25 docs. Encroachments by the French in North America, 1756, (1749–55), 210 docs. Stamp Act Papers: Civil and Military papers, 1766, 5 docs.; Riots in America, 1766, 218 docs.; Letters from Governors, 1767, 7 docs. Assembly Proceedings, New Jersey and House of Representative Proceedings, Massachusetts Bay, 1767. Voidance of Acts of Assemblies (precedents for Orders in Council), 1767, 15 docs. Georgia Papers, 1767, 3 docs. Falkland Island Papers, 1771, 45 docs. Commissioners for Restoring Peace in America, 1778, 25 docs. Accounts of men lost and disabled, and monthly returns of troops in North America, 1778 (1774–7), 8 docs. Embarkation of troops returns, 1778 (1774–7), 42 docs. General Burgoyne's Expedition, 1778, 37 docs. New raised Corps, Lists of Officers, 1778, 3 docs. Papers published at New York by King's Commissioners, 1778. American Trade, Orders in Council, 1783, 7 docs.

Secretary of State for American Colonies. Papers concerning the following subjects (listed here in chronological order): Letters and a Diary concerning Boston, 1768, 9 docs. Governors' and Generals' Letters and Minutes of Council, 1768, 60 docs.; 1769, 16 docs. American Disturbances, 1770, 19 docs., 1774, 142 docs. Free Ports in Jamaica, 1774, 12 docs. Nova Scotia, etc., Instructions to Governors, 1774 (1768–73). Boston Disturbances, 1774, 7 docs. Quebec, 1774 (1768–74), 23 docs. American Disturbances, 1775, 51 docs. Meetings of Deputies, Annapolis, 1775. Purchase of Spanish and Portuguese coins for Army, 1780 (delivered by 'Mr. Neale').

Secretary of State for Home Department. Grants to Edmund Burke, West Indies 4½% duties, 1795 (1784–95).

Treasury. Papers relating to Stamps, Trade, Annual expense; Courts of Vice-Admiralty, 1766, 39 docs.

NOVA SCOTIA

Secretary of State and Board of Trade. Copies of letters, Council records, estimates of expenses etc., 1753 (1749–52), 143 docs.

CROWN ESTATES

Commissioners of Woods, Forests and Land Revenues of the Crown. Schedule of estates held by lease from the Crown, 1787. Reports of Commissioners (incomplete), 1787–93, 10 vols.

CUSTOMS AND TRADE

Customs and Trade Papers are listed below under the four general sub-headings of (1) COMPANIES, (2) COMMODITIES, (3) COUNTRIES, and (4) GENERAL ACCOUNTS, in accordance with the general title given them in the House, but this classification is not exclusive, and individual accounts relating to a specific commodity may, for instance, be found amongst the General Accounts (e.g. Accounts of Prohibited Goods).

(1) COMPANIES

EAST INDIA COMPANY

Accounts and Estimates, 1767 (1743–67), 10 docs.; 1768 (1767), 6 docs.; 1768 (1767–8), 2 docs.; 1783 (1771–81), 14 docs.; 1786 (1784– 6), 12 docs.; 1789 (1787–9), 23 docs.; 1790, 6 docs.; 1791, 6 docs.; 1792, 6 docs.; 1794 (1791–4), 26 docs.; 1795 (1793–5), 6 docs.; 1796 (1794–6), 24 docs.; 1797 (1795–7), 24 docs.; 1798 (1797–8), 1 doc.; 1800, (a) (1797–1800), 23 docs., (b) (1798–1800), 22 docs.

Miscellaneous Papers, including Extracts and Letters from Fort William, 1767, 10 docs.; Propositions and Resolution of Court of Directors, accounts, 1767, 6 docs.; Copies of charters, 1767; Papers relating to Treaties and Territorial acquisitions, 1769 (1756–69), 11 docs.; Letters to and from the Board of the Company relating to India during the War of American Independence 1783 (1775–83), 4 vols.; List of offices, 1785; Papers relating to Military Establishments, 1788, (a) (1783–8), 16 docs., (b) 10 docs. (1785–7); Accounts of sales, debts, and estimates of receipts and payments, 1788 (1787–90), 6 docs.; Value of goods and exports, 1793 (1790–3); Account of persons employed on the river Thames, 1795; Proceedings respecting an annuity to Warren Hastings, 1796, 3 docs.

EAST INDIA COMPANY (SCOTLAND)

Papers delivered from the *Royal African Company*, the *East India Company*, the *Commissioners of Customs, Jamaica and other Merchants*, relating to the Scotch Act for a Company trading to Africa and the Indies, 1695–6, 38 docs.

ROYAL AFRICAN COMPANY

Admiralty Office. Reports, etc., on the state and condition of forts and settlements of the Company, 1752, 4 docs.; 1755; 1764 (1758–63), 30 docs.; 1765 (1763–4), 4 docs.; 1766–8, 1771–7, 1783, 1784, 1786, 1789, 1790 (a) and (b), 1791, 1793, 1795, annual reports containing various numbers of docs. *See* also SLAVE TRADE.

COMPANY OF MERCHANTS TRADING TO AFRICA

Accounts of Merchants' Committee, 1752, 2 docs.

Sierra Leone Company

Accounts of capital subscribed, profits and expenditure, etc., 1799 (1795–8), 5 docs.

South Sea Company

Copies of Minutes: General Court, 1721 (1719–20); 1733 (1728); Court of Directors, General Court, Committee of the Assiento, with orders, letters, etc., 1714 (1713–14), 1 vol.; Committee to treat with the Bank of England, 1721 (1719–20); Committee of Correspondence, 1721 (1719–20); Committee of Buying, 1721 (1719–20); Committee of Treasury, 1721 (1720); Committee of Secrecy, 1st Report, 1721.
Accounts: Ledgers of Loan, 1721 (1720); Stock, 1721; Defaulters, 1721; Money owed by Company, 1721 (1719–21); with Bank of England, 1721 (1719–20); Debts 1721 (1719–21). Commissions for taking subscriptions, 1721 (1711–20). Books of Subscriptions, 1721 (1720), 7 vols. Inventories of Estates, 1721, 31 docs. Directions from the Treasury, 1721. Reports of Trustees for raising money by the sale of Estates, 1722–28 (annual), 8 docs.; Accounts of Trustees, 1733. Report of Committee to inspect South Sea Company accounts, 1733. *See* also the TICKELL PAPERS.

(2) COMMODITIES

Note. See also the following Sections (3) and (4).

Brandy, etc.

Commissioners of Customs. Returns concerning import of brandy, 1732 (1712–32), 3 docs.; imports through Dunkirk, 1732 (1725–32), 3 docs.; spirituous liquors, 1743, 7 docs.

Brass

Commissioners of Customs. Account of brass for export, 1783 (1700–83).

Bullion

Commissioners of Customs. Return of foreign coin and bullion, 1719 (1710–18). (Cf. also, Account of bullion for export, 1714–18, Committee papers, 1718).
Bank of England. Account of bullion from North America and West Indies, 1766.

Candles. *See* Tallow and Candles.

Coal

Commissioners of Customs. Account of coals exported to France, Holland and Germany, 1787 (1761–86).

COFFEE. *See* TEA AND COFFEE.

CORN AND WHEAT

> *Commissioners of Customs.* Return of corn and grain exported under Exportation Act, 1698, 10 Will. III, c. 3, 1700. Account of import of foreign wheat, 1800. Return of Corn etc. exported, 1741. Account of Corn Exports, 1765 (1754–64).
> *Board of Trade.* Proceedings relative to stock of grain, etc., 1795, 14 docs.
> *Home Department.* Orders in Council concerning export of wheat, etc., 1796, 2 docs.; 1797, 6 docs.; 1800, 2 docs. Cf. also Report from H.L. Committee on imports of corn and flour, 1797 (1793–6).
> *Secretary of State for Foreign Affairs.* Orders in Council and Account of average prices of corn and grain, 1790, 8 docs.; Representation concerning Corn Laws of Committee of Council, 1790; Accounts concerning trade in wheat, 1800 (1697–1800), 9 docs.

COTTON WOOL

> *Commissioners of Customs.* Account of imports, 1796 (1792–3).

FISH

> Mr. Brooke Watson's Report on State of exports to North America and of N. American fisheries, 1775 (1764).

HEMP AND FLAX

> *Home Department.* Accounts of growth, and of bounties (cf. Growth of Hemp and Flax Act, 1781, 21 Geo. III, c. 58), 1786.
> *Treasury.* Similar annual accounts (cf. Hemp and Flax Act, 1786, 26 Geo. III, c. 43), 1787–95, 16 docs.

IRON

> *Commissioners of the Navy.* Reports on Iron imported from the Plantations, 1750. Accounts of quantities of Iron imported from America, 1750 (1710–49), and of quantities of Bar Iron exported to America, 1750 (1746–9).

PEPPER

> *Commissioners of Customs.* Accounts of Malagreeta Pepper imported from Africa, 1799 (1794–8).

POTATOES AND SALTED PROVISIONS

> *Foreign Secretary.* Accounts of imports, 1800, 9 docs.

RICE. *See* SUGAR AND RUM.

Rum. *See* Sugar and Rum.

Salt

>   *Commissioners of Salt Duties.* Returns relating to Duties, 1730 (1727–30); 1732 (1723–30), 4 docs.
>   *Exchequer.* Returns relating to Duties (Scotland), 1732 (1713–31).
>   *Secretary of State.* Returns relating to Foul Salt Duty, 1781, 4 docs.

Salted Provisions. *See* Potatoes and Salted Provisions.

Ships

>   *Commissioners of Customs.* Accounts of ships licensed to carry goods, 1766, 5 docs. Account of ships cleared out of British Colonies, 1766. Account of ships arrived in Scotland from British Colonies, 1766.

Silk

>   *Commissioners of Customs.* Return of exports of manufactured silk, 1741 (1720–40).

Slave Trade

>   *Foreign Secretary.* Africa Papers concerning Slave Trade, 1789 (1759–89), 20 docs. Report of Committee of General Assembly, Barbadoes, etc., 1790, 6 docs. Accounts of Voyages in 1792, 25 docs.
>   *Lords of Committee of Council for Trade and Plantations.* Report on Slave Trade, 1789.
>   *Commissioners of Customs.* African and West Indies Trade accounts, including Slaves, 1793 (1700–88), 16 docs. Accounts of vessels and numbers of slaves, 1794 (1789–94), 3 docs. Slave Trade Ships Journals and Mortality Lists, etc., extracts, [1794] (1792–3), 51 docs.; 1796 (1794–6); 1799 (1791–7); 1800 (1791–7). Slave Ships arriving in West Indies, 1799 (1791–8) 6 docs. Slave Trade Accounts, 1799 (1789–98), 3 docs. Number of Slaves exported from Africa, 1799 (1791–7); imported into West Indies, 1794 (1789–93), 1799 (1793–9).
>   *Home Secretary.* Correspondence with West India Governors, etc., 1799 (1797–9), 22 docs.

Sugar and Rum

>   *Board of Trade.* Representations relating to Sugar, Tobacco and Rice, 1730 (1724); to Rice, 1730 (1721).
>   *Commissioners of Customs.* Returns of Sugar Imports and Exports, 1732 (1710–30), 5 docs.; of Rum Imports, 1732 (1720–30); of Sugar Trade with Plantations, 1731 (1718–31); of Sugar Trade, 1739 (1708–37); of Rum Trade, 1739 (1727–37); of Rum and Sugar Imports to North America, 1739 (1727–37), 4 docs.; of prices of Sugar and Rum, 1739 (1709–39).
>   *Excise Office.* Account of Rum Duties, 1791 (1789–91).

TALLOW AND CANDLES

> *Commissioners of Customs.* Accounts of trade and duties, 1759 (1751–8), 4 docs.

TEA AND COFFEE

> *Commissioners of Customs.* Return of Tea and Coffee imports and duties, 1733 (1724–31).

TOBACCO

> *Commissioners of Customs.* Account of Tobacco imports and exports, Scotland, 1733 (1721–31); 1775 (1769–74); of Tobacco import duties, Scotland, 1733 (1721–31), England, 1775 (1769–74); Account of Imports, Exports and Home trade in Tobacco, 1789 (1774–89); 1790 (1774–90), 6 docs.

WHEAT. *See* CORN AND WHEAT.

WINE

> *Commissioners of Customs.* Account of imports and exports, 1786 (1735–85), 3 docs.
> *Commissioners of Excise.* Wine Accounts, 1787, 3 docs.

WOOL

> *Commissioners of Customs.* Wool Accounts, 1800 (1791–1800), 3 docs.

WOOLLENS

> *Secretary of State for the American Colonies.* Woollen goods exported, 1779 (1758–71, 1776–8).
> *Commissioners of Customs.* State of Exports, 1787 (1704–61), 3 docs.

(3) COUNTRIES

For the Assiento *see* SPAIN (below).

AFRICA

> *Board of Trade.* Representation etc., for improving Trade to Africa, 1750, 8 docs.
> *Commissioners of Customs.* Returns of Trade with Africa, 1775 (1739–73), 3 docs.
> *Commissioners for losses in African Trade.* Report concerning losses, 1790.
> *Admiralty.* Report on Cape Coast Castle, 1795, 2 docs.

AMERICA

> *Commissioners for Trade and Plantations.* Account of Trade (1701–2) and Papers relating to irregularities in Pennsylvania etc., 1702, 27 docs. Representations concerning Duty on Timber and Naval Stores, etc., 1730, 25 docs.; laws and manufactures in America affecting trade of this Kingdom, 1734; trade and security of the colonies, 1735, 18 docs.; Chief Sachem's Conference Paper and Massachusetts House of Representatives Journal, 1733. Bills of credit (a) in South Carolina, 1740 (1700–40); (b) in New York etc., with other papers, 1740 (1700–40), 14 docs. Paper Currency in Virginia, etc., 1741 (1700–40), 5 docs. Expense of establishments in America, 1766.
>
> *Commissioners of Customs.* Customs returns relating to Trade with Carolina, etc., 1730 (1704–24), 11 docs. Accounts of exports, to West Indies and America, 1731 (1714–26), 6 docs.; to North America, 1776, 2 vols. Accounts of Trade with North American colonies, 1764 (1739–64), 2 docs.; 1774; 1775 (including West Indies); 1776, 28 docs.
>
> *Admiralty.* Return of licences for export of provisions, 1776, 3 docs. Account of ships employed in North America, 1778 (1774–8), 4 docs.

FLANDERS

> Accounts of exports and imports between England and Flanders, 1780 (1772–9).

FRANCE

> *Commissioners of Customs.* Account of British and Foreign produce exported to France, 1787 (1714–87), 4 docs.

GERMANY

> *Commissioners of Customs.* Accounts of Exports to Germany and Holland, 1767 (1758–66), 3 docs.

HOLLAND. *See* previous entry.

IRELAND

> *Commissioners for Trade and Plantations.* Representation concerning the running of Wool from England to Ireland, 1731. Accounts of Imports and Exports, 1779, 1785 (1772–84), 11 docs.
>
> *Secretary of State.* Accounts relating to Ireland, 1779, concerning (a) trade between Scotland and Ireland (1764–79); re-export of hemp from Britain to Ireland (1746–77); imports of beef, tallow, pork and linen cloth from Ireland (1768–78); export of cotton wool to Ireland (1751–79), and of raw sugars to Ireland (1750–78), 15 docs.; (b) concerning trade in beef, pork, linen cloth, cotton wool, and sugar (1740–79), 18 docs.
>
> *Commissioners of Customs.* Accounts of trade with Ireland, 1799 (1789–99), 4 docs.

PORTUGAL
> *Commissioners of Customs.* Accounts of Imports and Exports, 1787 (a) (1772, 1773, 1785), 3 docs.; (b) (1703–87), 6 docs.; (c) (1704–61), 3 docs.

RUSSIA

> *Commissioners of Customs.* Account of trade with Russia, 1750 (1743–50).

SCOTLAND

> *Commissioners for Trade and Plantations.* Accounts of bounties on export of fish, beef and pork in Scotland, 1732 (1713–30).
> *Commissioners of Customs (Scotland).* Accounts of Corn and Grain exported from Scotland, 1741; 1757; 1758; 1765 (1754–64); 1766; 1770; 1771; 1772; 1773. Account of exports and imports between Scotland and America, 1775 (1739–75).

SPAIN

> *See* also (1) COMPANIES, SOUTH SEA COMPANY.
> *Commissioners for Trade and Plantations* and the *Admiralty.* Papers relating to Spanish trade and the Assiento, 1714 (1713–14). 41 docs.

TURKEY

> *Commissioners of Customs.* Account of trade with Turkey, 1744 (1720–43).

WEST INDIES

> *Secretary of State.* Papers concerning the embargo at Jamaica, 1730, 11 docs.
> *Commissioners for Trade and Plantations.* Acts concerning Import duties passed in Barbadoes, etc., 1732 (1715), 2 docs.
> *Commissioners of Customs.* Accounts of Imports and Exports, West Indies, 1774 (1769–74), 4 docs.; of Exports to Jamaica, 1774 (1748–73), 2 docs. Accounts of Imports and Exports, 1799 (1797–8).
> *See* also Accounts of Exports to West Indies, 1788 (1782–8).

(4) GENERAL ACCOUNTS

> *Commissioners of Customs.* Annual Returns (1) of Naval stores imported into England by merchants trading to Russia (cf. Russia Company (Membership) Act, 1698, 10 Will. III, c. 6) and (2) of Prohibited Goods imported by the Old East India Company, the United East India Company, the Company of Merchants trading to the East Indies, and the New East India Company [for the appropriate dates, cf. East India Company Act, 1697, 9 Will. III, c. 44; Duties on East India

Goods Act, 1707, 6 Anne, c. 37; and the East India Company Act, 1711, 10 Anne, c. 35], 1702 (1699–1701; Naval Stores only); 1709–1800, 8 to 10 docs. deposited annually. Returns of Exports and Imports, 1696 (1692–5), 12 vols. Abstract of Imports and Exports, 1702 (1696–9), 4 docs.; 1796 (1785–95); 1797 (1790–6). Accounts and Papers relating to trade, 1713, (a) (1699), 5 docs.; (b) (1622–86), 10 docs.; (c) (1668–76), 6 docs. Account of the Produce of the Customs, 1721 (1714–20). Returns of receipts for imports from Ostend and Dunkirk, etc., 1741 (1736–40), 7 docs. Returns of ships clearing the port of Hull, 1800 (1794–1800).

Commissioners of Excise. Account of Excise (1727–8), Drawbacks on Naval stores from America, etc., 1729. Accounts of Duties on Home made Spirits, 1732 (1722–31). Account of Duties on Leather, 1750 (1732–8). Account of Coach Duty, 1752 (1747–51). Account of Silver Plate Duty, 1766 (1756–65); 1767 (1755–66); 1776 (a) (1763–75); (b) (1755–63); Lists of persons avoiding Plate Duty, 1768, 1777. Account of Men and Vessels employed by the Excise, 1795.

Commissioners for Trade and Plantations. State of Trade in 1697, 1713. Reports of Commissioners, 1702, 1703, 1704, 1721 (a) Wool running to foreign parts; (b) Prohibition of Calicoes.

Treasury. Accounts of total produce of Duties of Customs, Excise and Stamps, 1787, 6 docs.; 1790, 7 docs.; 1795 (a) (1793–4), 5 docs.; (b) (1794–5), 6 docs.; 1796, 6 docs.; 1797, 6 docs.; 1798, 6 docs.; 1800, 5 docs. Statement of Countervailing Duties, 1800.

Tax Office. Account of House Duty, 1779.

DAGENHAM BREACH

Accounts and Papers laid by the Trustees for repairing the breach in the River Thames at Havering and Dagenham under Dagenham Breach Act, 1713, 13 Anne, c. 20, 1717; 1718; 1719 (1714–19); 1720; 1721; 1722; 1724.

EAST INDIA

Papers relating to East India Trade are listed under CUSTOMS AND TRADE. Those noted here relate more generally to administration.

East India Company. Papers relating to India Government, 1783 (1772–83) 13 docs.; Offices, Places and Employments, 1786; War, 1791 (1784–91) 13 docs. Management of Carnatic and Tanjore by Government of Madras, 1791, 116 docs.; Hostilities with Tippo Sahib, 1799, 32 docs.

ECCLESIASTICAL

Commissioners for Building Churches appointed under New Churches in London and Westminster Act, 1710, 9 Anne, c. 17; amended by Churches in London and Westminster Act, 1711, 10 Anne, c. 20. Report, 1711; with Accounts, 1715, 3 docs.

DIRECTORY FOR THE PUBLIC WORSHIP OF GOD
  Original text as read in H.L., 1645.
DURYE PAPERS
  Letters and Memoranda relating to John Durye's mission to the continent
  to effect a reconciliation between Lutherans and Calvinists, including
  correspondence with Archbishop Laud, 1631–40, 88 docs.
PAPISTS LISTS
  Secretary of State. Lists of Commissioned Officers in Army and Navy,
    Deputy Lieutenants and Justices of the Peace, who are Papists, 1680,
    60 docs. Lists of Papists in the several counties, 1680, 69 docs.[1] Return
    of Papists in the several dioceses, 1767, 26 bundles; 1781, 27 docs.
  Lord Steward. Returns by Deputy Lieutenants of counties, 1706, 30 docs.
  Archbishop of Canterbury, etc. Returns of Papists in the various dioceses
    (incomplete), 1706, 13 docs.
  See also *FORFEITED ESTATES.*
PARISH REGISTERS
  Bishops' Transcripts of registers of Baptisms, marriages and burials at
  various dates, 1560–1643, for 203 parishes, co. Kent.
VISITATION PAPERS
  Archbishop Abbot. Visitation Articles, Answers, etc. for Salisbury Cathe-
    dral, 1613; for Chichester Cathedral, 1615.
  Archbishop Laud. Visitation Articles, Answers, Orders, etc. for the
    following Cathedrals etc.: Canterbury, Salisbury, Exeter, Wells,
    Bristol, Rochester, Winchester, St. Paul's, Lichfield, Gloucester,
    Norwich, Peterborough and Worcester; and Eton College, 1634–6.

FORFEITED ESTATES

  Commissioners appointed by the Forfeited Estates Act, 1715, 1 Geo. I, sess. 2,
    c. 50. Reports, etc., relating to England and Ireland, 1717; 1718, 1719
    (including 2 registers); 1720; 1721; 1724 (2 reports). Reports, etc., relating
    to Scotland, 1717 (with abstract of claims); 1718; 1719; 1720; 1721; 1723;
    1724; 1725; 1727.
  Commissioners for Forfeited Estates in Ireland. Reports, etc., laid by the Com-
    missioners and Trustees appointed respectively by the Act granting a sum
    to disband the army, etc., 1698, 10 Will. III, c. 9, and the Act for the Sale
    of Forfeited Estates in Ireland, 1698, 11 Will. III, c. 2, 1699, 14 docs.;
    1701; 1702 (1699–1702), 10 docs.; 1703, 4 docs.
  Treasury. Reports laid by Commissioners appointed by the Forfeited Estates
    in Scotland Act, 1751, 25 Geo. II, c. 41, 1756; 1757; 1758; 1759; 1760;
    1762; 1763; 1765 (1761); 1772; 1773.

GREENWICH HOSPITAL

  Admiralty. Papers laid before the House relating to the following subjects.
    Copies of Commissions, 1779 (1695, 1703, 1715, 1727) 4 docs.; List of

---

[1] These are Committee Papers, *see Calendar*, 1678–88, pp. 225–237.

Officers, Servants, etc., with Warrants of appointments of Lieutenant-Governors, 1779 (1704–78), 13 docs.; Lieutenant Stutteville, 1779 (1771), 3 docs.; Captain Baillie, 1779 (a) 2 docs.; (b) 2 docs.; Prize Money forfeited to the Hospital, 1779; Abuses and neglects in the Hospital, 1779 (1777–8), 3 docs.; Coals and Candles, 1779 (1775–8), 4 docs.; Commission of 1763, Charter of 1775, Lists of Officers, Servants, etc. and other papers, 1779 (1763–78), 30 docs.; Evidence for Enquiry into Management, 1779, 3 vols.

Commissioners of Greenwich Hospital. Reports of Proceedings of Commissions with Accounts, 1736, 6 docs.; 1740–77, annually with a few gaps. Derwentwater Estate Accounts, 1738, 19 docs.; 1739.

IRELAND

Secretary of State. Papers and letters intercepted on their way from Ireland, Committee of Privy Council Proceedings, etc., 1689, 34 docs. *See* also under *CUSTOMS AND TRADE* and *FORFEITED ESTATES*.

KENSINGTON, CHELSEA AND FULHAM ROADS

Accounts laid by the Trustees appointed by the Kensington, Chelsea and Fulham roads (tolls) Act, 1725, 12 Geo. I, c. 37, 1732 (1726–32); 1739 (1726–39).

LIEUTENANCY COMMISSIONS

Original Commissions of Lieutenancy, 1642 (1625–41), 17 docs.

MERCERS' COMPANY

Annual Accounts presented by Mercers' Company pursuant to the Mercers, London, Act, 1748, 21 Geo. II, c. 32 (amended by London and Mercers Company Act, 1750, 24 Geo. II, c. 14 and Mercers Company, London, Act, 1751, 25 Geo. II, c. 7), 1753–1800.

MISCELLANEOUS

CORONATIONS
Papers concerning the ceremonial at Coronations (1727, 1761), 1797, 9 docs.
COVENANT LISTS
Lists of inhabitants of 15 villages, co. Norfolk, who have taken the Covenant, 1644, 15 docs.
DEATH WARRANTS (CIVIL WAR)
Original warrants from High Courts of Justice for the Trying and Judging, respectively, of King Charles I; James, Earl of Cambridge (Duke of Hamilton); Henry, Earl of Holland; and Arthur, Lord Capell, 1649, 4

docs. Cf. *The Death Warrant of King Charles I* (Historic Parliamentary Documents Reproduction No. 7, 1960) which includes an illustration, transcript and descriptive notes.

DECLARATION OF RIGHTS, 1689. *See* plate 11.

DISTILLERS' COMPANY

Ordinances of the Company, examined and approved in accordance with Ordinances of Corporations Act, 1503, 19 Hen. VII, c. 7, 1639, 1 doc.

HOLLES AND WHITELOCK PAPERS

Examinations, Informations and Answers relating to the charge that Mr. Holles and Mr. Whitelock had correspondence with the King at Oxford, 1645, 33 docs.

THE KING'S GOODS

Returns by persons who had become possessed of King Charles I's goods, with letters, draft orders, etc., 1660, 51 docs.

NASEBY PAPERS

The papers taken in King Charles I's Cabinet of Papers at the Battle of Naseby, 1645 (1641–5), 46 docs.

PEERAGE

Original MS. of John Selden's *Privileges of the Baronage*, and associated papers, 1621.

PRISONERS

Lord Chancellor. List of Prisoners in the Fleet Prison, 1729.

REGICIDE PAPERS

Notes of proceedings, petitions and depositions relating to those attainted of high treason for the murder of Charles I, 1660–2, 24 docs.

NAVY

Admiralty. Papers laid before the House relating to the following subjects: Naval Miscarriages, 1692, 19 docs.; Various subjects, including 2 papers from the Turkey Company, 1694, 13 deposits; Naval Expeditions, Admiralty Orders, etc., 1695, 20 docs.; Merchants' Losses at Sea, 1696, 47 docs.; State of the Fleet, Loss of Ships from Ireland and Refusal of Letters of Mart, etc., 1697, 40 docs.; Account of Ships, 1701, 7 docs.; Ships and their Complements, Instructions to Admirals, etc., 1704, 95 docs.; Expenses and Debts of Navy, 1704 (1697–1704), 22 docs.; Convoys, 1707, 200 docs.; Cruisers and Convoys, 1710, 1711, 1713; State of Repair, 1714; Instructions to Vice-Admiral Hosier, 1729 (1725–7), 7 docs.; Ships of Royal Navy sent to America and West Indies for defence, 1734 (1720–34); Losses sustained by Spanish depredations, 1739, 143 docs.; Account of Spanish ships taken in 1718, etc., 1739; List of Admirals of the Fleet, 1741; Returns concerning Ships, 1742 (1739–41); Orders, correspondence with Sir J. Norris, 1742 (1740–1); Ships built since 1739, 1741; Weekly accounts of squadron under Rear Admiral Haddock, 1741 (1740–1); Convoys, etc., 1742 (1739–42), 172 docs.; Paying off Ships, etc., 1758 (1755–8); Regulations for His Majesty's Service at Sea, etc., 1758, 4 docs.; Payment of Wages, etc., 1758, 1735, 1751, 8 docs.; Condition of Ships, 1777, 29 docs.; Seamen and Marines in Royal Navy, Victualling and transport accounts, 1777 (1775–7);

Victualling accounts, 1778 (1775–7), 4 docs.; Marine Forces at home, 1777, 29 docs.; Ships under line of battle, 1778 (1775–7); Merchantmen proceeding without convoy, 1778 (1776–7), 12 docs.; Repair with foreign oak-timber, 1778 (1770–7), 4 docs.; Purchase of ships, 1778 (1776–8); State of ships in America, 1778; Letter from Members of Court Martial of Admiral Byng, 1779 (1757); Court Martial of Admiral Keppel, 1779, 44 docs.; Instructions to Admiral Byron, 1779; Ships destroyed and in commission, 1779 (1751–9, 1771–9); Admiralty perquisites, 1779 (1774–9); Return of men raised under the Recruiting Act, 1778, 18 Geo. III, c. 53, 1779, 12 docs.; Instructions given to Captain Montery, 1780, 5 docs.; Damaged dry stores, 1781 (1778–81); Movements of Spanish and French fleets, 1782 (1779–81), 58 docs.; the Army under E. Cornwallis, 1782, 307 docs.; Ships in Commission, 1783, 5 docs.; same, 1792 (1790–1), 3 docs.; Protected Persons, 1795 (1793–5), 8 docs.; Numbers of seamen raised, 1796, 5 docs.; State of ships under Admiral Curtis, 1797, 3 docs.

Commissioners of the Navy. Account of quantity of naval stores remaining in yards, 1734 (1721, 1727, 1733).

Commissioners for Portsmouth and Other Docks. Copy of Judgments and Decrees, 1759, 1 vol.

Commissioners of Trade and Plantations. Return relating to Naval Stores, 1711.

Comptroller of the Navy. Account of Deserters, 1758 (1755–7).

Lord Chancellor. Return of Navy Exchequer Bills, 1796, 6 docs.

Office for Sick and Wounded Seamen. Returns for bounty to prisoners during War of Spanish Succession, 1742.

Secretary of State. Papers laid before the House relating to: Expeditions to Cadiz and Vigo, 1702, 24 docs.; Instructions to Admirals in the West Indies and the Mediterranean, 1729 (1726–8), 296 docs.; Admiral Vernon's Letters from Jamaica, etc., 1741 (1739–40), 31 docs.; Admiral Haddock's and Admiral Ogle's Letters, 1741, 8 docs.; 1742 (1739–41), 320 docs.; Rum Contracts, 1778 (1776–7), 20 docs.; Toulon Fleet, 1778.

Secretary of State for Foreign Affairs. Sums granted by Parliament (Navy and Victualling Bills), 1796, 3 docs.

Victualling Office. Account of expense of freight of store ships carrying provisions to North America, 1778 (1775–8), 4 docs. Victualling Accounts, 1778 (1770–7), 8 docs. Accounts of contracts for Salt, 1732 (1729–31). Account for victualling the Navy with beef, 1766 (1745–66).

POOR

Returns by counties made by Justices of the Peace relating to the state of the Poor pursuant to the Poor Act, 1776, 16 Geo. III, c. 40, 44 docs.

POST OFFICE

Postmaster General. Accounts, 1729 (1727–8), 1732, Scotland only (1716–31), 1764 (1715–63).

PROTESTATION RETURNS

See plate 10

Certificates or returns of the names of those persons who made the protestation 'to maintain the true Reformed Protestant Religion' in accordance
with a letter of instructions from the Speaker of the House of Commons,
dated 19 Jan. 1642.[1] The surviving returns relate to the following areas
(but in some instances the returns relate only to part of the area in
question or comprise solely certificates of local officials concerning the
protestation). *Berks*: Abingdon, Newbury and Reading Divisions; *Bucks*:
Buckingham and Cotteslow Hundreds; *Cambridge University*; *Chester*:
City;[2] *Cornwall*: East, Kerrier, Penwith, Lesnewth, Powder, Pyder,
Stratton, Trigg and West Hundreds; *Cumberland*: Allerdale-above-
Derwent, Allerdale-below-Derwent, Cumberland, Eskdale, Leath Wards;
Denbigh; *Devon*: Bampton, Halberton, Hayridge, Hemyoek, Tiverton,
Black Torrington, Shebbear, Hartland, Winckleigh, Braunton, Budleigh
West, Cliston, Colyton, Crediton, Coleridge (North), Coleridge (South),
Stanborough (North), Stanborough (South), Ermington, Plympton,
Exminster, Fremington, Haytor, Teignbridge, Wonford, Lifton, Robor-
ough, Sherwill, Tavistock, North Tawton, South Molton, Witheridge,
Hundreds; *Dorset*: Bindon Liberty, Coomb's Ditch, Corfe Castle, Hasilor,
Hundredsbarrow Hundreds, Owermoigne Liberty, Pimperne, Row-
barrow, Rushmore, Winfrith, Sherborne, Yetminster Hundreds, Halstock,
Ryme Intrinsica Liberties, Buckland [Newton], Whiteway Hundreds,
Piddletrenthide, Alton Pancras Liberties, Cerne, Totcombe, and Modbury
Hundreds, Sydling Liberty, Sturminster Newton Castle, Brownshall,
Redland Hundreds, Stower Provost Liberty, Beaminster Hundred,
Broadwinsor Liberty, Poorstock Hundred, Frampton, Lothers and
Bothenhampton Liberties, Whitchurch Canonicorum, Godderthorne,
Eggerton, Cogdean, Monckton-up-Wimborne, Loosebarrow, Knowlton
Hundreds, Gillingham Liberty, Badbury, Cranbourne, Wimborne St.
Giles, Sixpenny Handley Hundreds, Alcester Liberty, Culliford Tree
Hundred, Sutton Poyntz, Wyke Regis Liberties, Isle of Portland, George,
Puddleton, Tollerford, Ugscombe, Bere Regis Hundreds; *Durham*:
Chester, Darlington, Easington, Stockton Wards; *Essex*: Hinckford
Hundred; *Hants*: Southampton; *Hertford*: Cashio Hundred; *Huntingdon*:
Hurstingstone, Leightonstone, Normancross, Toseland Hundreds; *Kent*:
Bewsborough, Bleangate, Bridge and Petham, Cornilo, Downhamford,
Eastry, Kinghamford, Preston, Ringslow or Thanet, Westgate, Whit-
stable, Wingham Hundreds, Romney Marsh Liberty, Axton, Codsheath,
Somerden, Westerham Hundreds; *Lancaster*: Amounderness, Blackburn,
Leyland, Salford, West Derby Hundreds; *Lincoln*: Elloe, Kirton Wapen-
takes, Skirbeck Hundred, Winnibriggs and Threo, Beltisloe, Ness,
Aveland, Loveden Wapentakes, Lincoln Liberty, Lawress, Aslacoe,
Bradley Haverstoe Wapentakes, Louth Eske Hundred, Ludborough
Wapentake, Calceworth, Hill Hundreds, Manley, Corringham, Walsh-
croft, Well, Yarborough Wapentakes; *Middlesex*: Edmonton, Elthorne,

---

[1] It is not clear whether the surviving returns came by design or accident to be preserved
amongst the Lords Papers; in intention they were Commons Papers.
[2] Cheshire returns are in British Museum, Harleian MS. 2107.

Gore, Isleworth Hundreds, Ossulston Division, Spelthorne Hundred; *Northumberland*: Morpeth Ward; *Nottingham*: Bassetlaw, Bingham Wapentakes, Broxtow, Newark, Rushcliffe, Thurgarton Hundreds; *Oxford*: Bampton, Banbury, Binfield, Bloxham, Chadlington, Langtree, Wootton Hundreds, Oxford University; *Salop*: Stottesden Hundred, Wenlock Liberty; *Somerset*: Abdick and Bulston, Bemstone, Carhampton, Crewkerne, Glaston Twelve Hides, Kingsbury and Crewkerne, Kingsbury (Eastern Division), Kingsbury (Western Division), Milverton, North Curry, North Petherton, South Petherton, Taunton Dean, Wells Forum, Whitstone, Williton Fremanors Hundreds; *Stafford*: Offlow (North Division), Offlow (South Division), Pirehill (North Division), Pirehill (South Division) Hundreds; *Surrey*: Reigate, Tandridge (First Division), Tandridge (Second Division); *Sussex*: Avisford, Bury, Poling, Rotherbridge, West Easwrith, Brightford, Burbeach, East Easwrith, Fishergate, West Grinstead, Patching, Singlecross, Steyning, Tarring, Tipnoak, Windham and Ewhurst, Aldwick, Bosham, Box and Stockbridge, Dumpford, Easebourn, Manhood, Westbourne and Singleton Hundreds; *Warwick*: Coventry City and County, Knightlow Hundred; *Westmorland*: East Ward, West Ward; *Wilts*: Aldersbury, Amesbury, Branch and Dole, Cawden and Cadworth, Chalk, Downton, Elstub and Everley, Frustfield, Underditch Hundreds; *Worcester*: City; *York*: Allertonshire Division, Agbrigg, Morley, Claro, Osgoldercross Wapentakes.

The Protestation of the Lords is preserved separately on a vellum roll, amongst the Original Acts (17 Cha. I, no. 36). For a complete list of Parishes etc. see *Calendar*, 1642–3, 120–34. It is possible that certain returns not preserved in H.L.R.O. may be found copied into the appropriate local parish registers (W. E. Tate, *The Parish Chest*, 3rd ed. (1969), pp. 71–2).

PUBLIC OFFICES

Secretary of State for Home Department. Reports on Public Offices: Secretaries of State, Treasury, Admiralty, Treasurer of Navy, Commissioners of Navy, Dock Yards, Office for sick and wounded seamen, Victualling office, Naval and Victualling departments in foreign or distant parts, Post Office, 1795 (1786–8), 10 vols.

RICHMOND BRIDGE

Commissioners for building Richmond Bridge appointed under the Richmond Bridge Act, 1773, 13 Geo. III, c. 83, Cash accounts, 1775–1800, 22 docs.

SCOTLAND

ARMS

Master General of the Ordnance. Account of Arms received into store at Edinburgh and Fort William, 1732.

Secretary of State. Accounts of Arms delivered up by Highland clans, 1732 (1725).

COMMISSIONS OF PEACE

Clerk of the Crown. Copies of several Commissions for the Shires, 1732, 13 docs.

CONSPIRACY IN SCOTLAND

Secretary of State. Petitions, memorials etc., relating to the conspiracy in Scotland, 1704, 16 docs.

FORCES

Secretary of State. Abstract of forces, stores and revenues with list of Justices of the Peace, 1709, 5 docs.

'THE INCIDENT'

Depositions etc. relating to the reported design during Charles I's second visit to Scotland, 1641, 36 docs.   .

INVASION OF SCOTLAND

Advices and other letters concerning a projected French invasion, 1708, 4 docs.; 1709, 467 docs.

NORTHERN LIGHTHOUSES

Commissioners of Customs (Scotland). Accounts presented under the Erection of Lighthouses Act, 1786, 26 Geo. III, c. 101, 1789, 1790, 1792, 1793, 1794, 1795, 1797 (1795–6), 1800.

PLATE

Commissioners for Excise in Scotland. List of persons not making due entry of plate, 1776.

PORTEOUS RIOTS AT EDINBURGH

Examinations, correspondence etc. relating to the Porteous Riots at Edinburgh, 1737 (1735–7), 11 docs.

SCHOOLS

Treasury. Return of money expended on schools arising from sales of Forfeited Estates, 1732.

UNION BETWEEN SCOTLAND AND ENGLAND

Lord Steward. Papers relating to Union, 1705, 5 docs.
Secretary of State. Articles of Union agreed 22 July 1706; copies of Scottish Acts of Ratification and of Election of Representative Peers; Minutes of Proceedings of Commissioners, 1706, 4 docs.

WHALE FISHERIES

Commissions of Customs (Scotland). Annual accounts of Scottish ships employed in Whale fishing (cf. Whale Fishery Act, 1755, 28 Geo. II, c. 20), 1757–97, 33 docs.

See also under *ACCOUNTS PUBLIC, CUSTOMS AND TRADE,* and *FORFEITED ESTATES.*

TREATIES, ETC.

(1) TREATIES AND CONVENTIONS

The following series of papers comprises the deposited texts of Treaties and Conventions and of drafts preparatory to them, together with in many instances, proceedings, correspondence and other materials. Classification is by country, etc., concerned, but it should be noted that the treaties may not in every case be with Great Britain. A two date entry with an intervening comma indicates two deposits only; a two date entry joined by a hyphen, a series of deposits between and including the two dates given. It should be noted that the dates relate to the years of deposit in the House of Lords and not to the years in which the treaties were concluded. Thus the first deposit concerning France, in 1701, includes the text of a treaty of 1697. In every case full titles of the papers laid appear in the *Lords Journals.*

Secretary of State; (from 1782) *Secretary of State for Foreign Affairs*[1]

BADEN, 1794
BAVARIA, 1747–1800
BOHEMIA, 1747
BRANDENBURG–ANSPACH, 1777
BRUNSWICK, 1760, 1776
BRUNSWICK-LUNEBURG-WOLFENBUTTEL, 1728
DENMARK, 1701–41
EAST INDIA COMPANY, 1791
EMPIRE, HOLY ROMAN, 1701–1800
FRANCE, 1701–1800
GENOA, 1749
HANOVER, 1741
HESSE-CASSEL, 1703–94
HESSE-DARMSTADT, 1794, 1797
HOLSTEIN, 1703
HOLSTEIN-GOTTORP, 1703
HUNGARY, 1742–9
INDIAN PRINCES, 1784–91
LUNEBURG, 1702, 1703
MAINZ, 1745
MODENA, 1749
MUNSTER, 1703, 1745

[1] Certain papers of 1701, however, were laid, respectively, by the *Lord Chamberlain* and the *Earl of Marlborough.*

NAPLES, 1793, 1799
OTTOMAN PORTE, 1792
PALATINATE, 1703
POLAND, 1745
PORTUGAL, 1703, 1794
PRUSSIA, 1705–95
RUSSIA, 1741–99
SARDINIA, 1718–93
SAXE-GOTHA, 1703
SPAIN, 1712–94
STATES-GENERAL (HOLLAND OR THE NETHERLANDS), 1701–1800
SWEDEN, 1701, 1721
TREVES, 1702
TWO SICILIES, 1794
UNITED STATES OF AMERICA, 1778–96
WALDECK, 1776

(2) PAPERS CONCERNING FOREIGN RELATIONS

Secretary of State; (from 1782) *Secretary of State for Foreign Affairs.* Papers laid before the House relating to Demolition of Dunkirk, 1714, 24 docs.; Depredations of the Spanish, 1735 (1730–5), 120 docs.; 1738 (1729–38), 57 docs. Actions of French shipping, 1742 (1739–41), 106 docs.; Intended Invasion by the Pretender, 1744, 8 docs.; French Regulation of prizes of neutral ships, 1745; the rupture with Spain, 1762, 31 docs.; French proposals concerning prisoners of war, 1765 (1755–62), 4 docs.; Spanish rescript, 1780, 13 docs.; relations with Holland, 1781 (1778–80), 9 docs.; the Imperial Loan, 1797, 3 docs.; Expedition of the enemy to the coast of Ireland, 1797, 40 docs.

Duke of Roxburgh. Correspondence concerning a rebellion supported by a force from Sweden, 1717, 1 vol.

WESTMINSTER BRIDGE

Commissioners for Westminster Bridge appointed under the Westminster Bridge Act, 1735, 9 Geo. II, c. 29, and subsequent Westminster Bridge Acts. Accounts, 1738–92, 44 vols., also separate accounts and proceedings, 1770; 1772; 1774 (1772–4); 1774; 1775; 1797 (1795–7); 1798; 1799; 1800. Proceedings of the Commissioners, 1738–91, 44 vols. Books of Contracts, 1738–50, 12 vols.

WESTMINSTER PAVING

Commissioners for Paving Westminster Streets appointed under the London Streets Act, 1762, 2 Geo. III, c. 21 and subsequent Streets Acts. Proceedings of Commissioners and (from 1765) Contracts, 1762–80, 16 vols. Treasurer's Accounts, 1762–7, 5 vols.; also separate docs. for 1767, 1770, 1772, 1773, 1778, 1781.

WOODS AND FORESTS, *see* CROWN ESTATES

Sessional Papers, H.L.

1801 to date   6,928 vols. (printed papers), and unprinted

From 1801 onwards the Lords Sessional Papers are so numerous and varied that it is not possible to give a brief classified list. After 1801 it became increasingly common for the papers to be printed, and these papers have been comprehensively indexed, as described on pp. 132–3 above.

Papers presented or laid on the Table, whether printed or MS., but not subsequently ordered to be printed by H.L., may be traced through the relevant entries in the Lords Journals, and are currently being listed amongst the entries in the MS. lists of Main Papers, H.L. available in H.L.R.O. Search Room.

RECORDS OF PEERAGE CLAIMS

In ordinary claims, where the descent is clear, applications by peers for a Writ of Summons are made to the L. Chancellor; but where a serious doubt exists, claims to the receipt of a Writ of Summons or for the calling of a peerage out of abeyance are made to the Crown. Until the 17th c. they might then be referred to any one of a number of authorities for decision, to H.L., to the Council, to the Council and judges, or to the Earl Marshal, but by the end of the 17th c. it had become usual to refer every such claim to H.L. unless no doubt existed about the appropriate answer to be returned to the claimant. In addition to this subordinate jurisdiction over peerage claims, the House has from time to time exercised an immediate domestic jurisdiction over its own membership (which has in effect determined peerage claims) or has decided on the effect or validity of the creation of new peerages by the Crown.

The Parliamentary procedure followed in the first claim for which records survive at Westminster, that of De La Warr in 1597, became customary. It is in three stages: the House refers the petition of claim to a committee (from 1621, that for Privileges); the committee meets, hears and inspects evidence, and reports back to the House; the House comes to a resolution on the case, which is submitted to the Crown. In order to assist the committee in its work, reports by the Attorney-General or by the Lord Advocate on the claim already made to the Crown are considered, as also, on occasion, reports made to the House by the judges, the Earl Marshal, or other authorities. There was a marked increase in the number of claims (most of them Scottish) after 1760; and controversy concerning the Willoughby of Parham case led to S.O. 129 of 1767 (repealed in 1802) ordering Garter to deliver at the Table a pedigree of each newly admitted peer, whether by creation or descent. The documents resulting from this Order were intended to assist the House in the determining of claims and are noted below. The Marmion Claim in 1815 caused the House to appoint a committee to search records for precedents concerning the Dignity of a Peer, and the materials then accumulated and printed afford information concerning both the peerage and the history of Parliament (*see* p. 188), although they led to no general alteration in procedure. The special class of claims concerning peerages in abeyance was considered by a H.L. Select Committee, 1925–7, and resulted in a much stricter treatment of such claims.

When ordinary applications for a Writ of Summons are made to the Lord Chancellor a writ is normally issued after facts of succession, etc. have been established. In cases where the Lord Chancellor is unable to satisfy himself of the facts alleged, the claimant to a peerage may then begin a formal peerage claim as described in the previous paragraph. The Lord Chancellor's reports to the House are noted in the Journals and included at length in the *Debates*.

See also HISTORICAL COLLECTIONS H.L.R.O. (COMPLETE PEERAGE TRUST PAPERS).

BIBLIOGRAPHY

Burke's Peerage, Baronetage and Knightage.

R. P. Cave, 'Peerages and Dignities' in *Encyclopaedia of Court Forms and Precedents* (1949).

G. E. C[okayne], *The Complete Peerage* (1910–59). *See* also the records of the Complete Peerage Trust described below, p. 274.

Debrett's Peerage, Baronetage, Knightage and Companionage.

Sir James Fergusson, *The Sixteen Peers of Scotland* (1960).

E. Halsbury, *The Laws of England*, 3rd. ed., vol. 29 (1960).

W. Holdsworth, *History of English Law*, vol. xiv (1964), pp. 141–7.

F. B. Palmer, *Peerage Law in England* (1907).

L. O. Pike, *Constitutional History of the House of Lords* (1894).

J. Riddell, *Inquiry into the Law and Practice of Scottish Peerages* (1842).

Reports on the Dignity of a Peer, H. L. 1829 (117–20, 222), cclii–vi (new series reprinted).

J. C. Sainty, *A List of Representative Peers for Scotland, 1707 to 1963, and for Ireland, 1800 to 1961* (H.L.R.O. Memorandum no. 39, 1968).

See also BIBLIOGRAPHY for Peerage Creations, above, pp. 22–3.

(i) For Records of Proceedings on Peerage Claims, *see*:

JOURNALS OF THE HOUSE, 1510 to date, pp. 28–32 above.

MINUTES OF THE HOUSE, 1610 to date, pp. 33–6 above.

COMMITTEE FOR PRIVILEGES MINUTE BOOKS, 1661 to 1885.

These Minutes provide the only systematic and complete record of proceedings in committees on peerage claims. They are not verbatim, until, in the 19th c., full Minutes of Proceedings were ordered to be presented to the House. The later vols. of Committee for Privileges Minute Books consist largely of such printed Minutes bound as a series. (In the 20th c. the prints have been entitled indifferently *Speeches delivered by Counsel* and *Proceedings and Minutes of Evidence*.) Prints relating to claims 1885 to date have not been added to the class of Minutes but exist separately as SESSIONAL PAPERS. *See* also p. 43 above for a full description of the Minute Books.

Minute Entry Registers (Judicial Office)

1607 to date   4 vols.

Registers of the brief entries of relevant proceedings from the Journal or printed Minutes. This series serves as a complete guide to the work of the Committee for Privileges.

Manuscript Evidence Volumes

1791 to date   152 vols.

The vols. contain original transcripts of the speeches of counsel before the

Committee and of cross-examination of witnesses. They are preserved separately in the series of Main Papers, and in the boxes of MS. Peerage Papers.

Manuscript Speeches

1826 to 1908   35 vols.

Verbatim reports of sittings of the Committee relating to Peerage Claims. The reports are not complete in that, in various places, references are provided to the relevant volumes of PRINTED EVIDENCE (*see* below), which is not then transcribed. The vols. are arranged alphabetically under peerages, and were bound *c.* 1908.

Baronies by Writ Proceedings

1836 to 1912   3 vols.

Verbatim proceedings of the Committee on claims to Baronies by Writ, similar in character to the foregoing series. The volumes were formed *c.* 1912 from typescript copies of earlier shorthand notes, MS. or printed copies, etc.

Printed Evidence

1794 to 1858   16 vols.

A series of separate prints bound in brown cloth. The series supplements the MANUSCRIPT SPEECHES (*see* above) by giving verbatim proceedings relating to the evidence produced for the claims. The vols. usually include transcripts of the documentary evidence, either as part of the proceedings when it was read in committees, or collected in an appendix. The documentary evidence comprises wills, pedigrees, coats of arms, and extracts from the most varied classes of public and private documents.

1806 to 1928   11 vols.

A second series of separate prints similar to the foregoing but varying slightly in its composition.

1794 to 1863   22 vols.

A third series of separate prints of Evidence and of Cases (*see* also below) previously in the keeping of the Middle Temple Library.

Note that the *Law Reports of England* normally contain abbreviated reports of proceedings and judgments in claim.

(ii) Other Records relating to Peerage Claims:

Petitions of Claim

1597 to date   250 docs.

The Petitions are addressed to the Crown, are signed by the claimant, and are undated. They contain the statement of claim, sometimes set out at length. The Petitions are subscribed or endorsed by the Secretary of State with the reference to H.L. They are subsequently endorsed with a statement of proceedings on them in the House. The Petition itself is entered in the Journal and its text may be transcribed or summarized there. The first surviving Petition (De La Warr, 1597) has always been preserved amongst the Acts of Parliament, as noted in the Journal. The remainder are with the Main Papers.

Attorney-General's Reports

1718 to date   200 docs.

The Reports are addressed to the Crown, are signed by the Attorney-General, and dated. They include a full analysis of the proofs advanced in the Petition of Claim and conclude with advice as to whether the claim has been made out and whether the petition should be referred to the House. The Reports are endorsed with a statement of proceedings in H.L. They are kept amongst the Main Papers.

Printed Cases (Separate Prints)

1734 to date   440 docs.

The Cases vary in length from 4 to 200 pp. They include a full statement of the proofs relied on by the claimant, and much relevant documentary evidence, including pedigrees. Appendices may include prints of the petition of claim, the Attorney-General's Report and evidential documents. Supplementary Cases of a similar character may be presented in the course of the hearing. They are kept with the Main Papers.

Printed Cases (Bound)

Series 1. 1794 to 1929   54 vols.

This series of blue bound volumes includes Cases, Additional Cases, Lists of Further Proofs and miscellaneous printed papers submitted by the Claimants. It is arranged alphabetically by peerages and was originally formed c. 1907.

Series 2. 1794 to 1928   11 vols.

An incomplete set of Cases, etc., bound in red, and arranged in 1928.

Series 3. 1720 to 1885   11 vols.

This series is preserved in H.L. Library and comprises 3 sets: 1720–1853 (5 vols.); 1854–75 (5 vols.); 1876–85 (1 vol.). It is similar to Series 1 (above). Vol. 1 of the first set contains a unique sequence of Cases for 1720–99, formed in the Parliament Office during the 18th c., in which each Case has the Clerk's endorsement as to the final outcome of the claim. These Cases, together with other peerage works in the Library and material in the Minutes of the Committee for Privileges, are fully indexed in H.L. Library Card Index of Peerage Claims.

Peers' Pedigrees

1767 to 1802   186 docs. bound in 4 vols.

See plate 12.

The pedigrees are those laid by each newly admitted peer in accordance with

12—R.O.P.

the S.O. of 11 May 1767. The S.O. was repealed in 1802. The pedigrees are inscribed on vellum and consist of genealogical trees for from two to eight preceding generations. Collateral descents and brief biographies are included. The pedigrees are subscribed and certified by the peers. They are illuminated with the coats of arms of the peers.

Peers' Pedigrees (Uncertified)

c. 1770 to 1784   15 docs.

A file of similar pedigrees, without certification.

Pedigree Proofs

1767 to 1802   800 docs.

Files of papers delivered at the Bar to the Committee for Privileges by Heralds upon oath. The papers comprise much of the evidence upon which the pedigrees (*see* entry above) were based. The principal constituents are attested copies of Parish Registers and monumental inscriptions. There are files for most peers newly introduced during the period covered. *See* also Evidential Papers below.
List. A typescript list is available in H.L.R.O.

Original Petitions, Reports, and Orders

1663 to date.   900 docs.

The following documents are preserved amongst the Main Papers:
1. c. 400 Petitions presented to H.L. (1663 to date) during claims, from the claimant relating to the further progress of the hearing, from opponents to the claim, and from other interested parties; they are undated but signed and endorsed with procedural annotation.
2. c. 100 original Reports of the Committee for Privileges (1767 to date).
3. c. 400 Orders and Resolutions of the House (1674 to date). The Reports and Orders were subsequently entered in the Journals.

Evidential Papers

1708 to date   450 docs.

This evidence, in varying format, was submitted by claimants, and included pedigrees on paper or parchment, affidavits, letters, original patents, copies of evidential records, and also the Tracy Peerage Tombstones (1845). Amongst the original Patents preserved are *Banbury* (1626), *Kiltarton* (1810), *O'Brien of Kilfenora* (1900) and *Stuart of Decies* (1839). The Patent of *E. Berkeley* (1679) is preserved in the Main Papers.

Other Peerage Papers

1628 to date   100 docs.

A small sub-class, largely dating from the 17th c., and including claimants' Replications, Questions to Judges, Judges' Opinions.

RECORDS CONCERNING REPRESENTATIVE PEERS FOR SCOTLAND

In accordance with the provisions of the Union with Scotland Act, 1706, 6 Anne. c. 11 and the Scottish Representative Peers Act, 1707, 6 Anne, c. 78, the Scottish Peers elected for each Parliament 16 representatives from amongst themselves. When one of the Representative Peers died or became legally incapable, another was elected in his place. On 12 February 1708 an 'authentic' list of the Scottish peerage was enrolled (*see* 'The Long Roll' below), to which other names were added by Order of the House when claims were established. The Representative Peers (Scotland) Act, 1847, 10 & 11 Vict., c. 52 provided that no title standing in that roll, in right of which no vote had been given since 1800, should be called over at an election without an Order by the House, and the Representative Peers (Scotland) Act, 1851, 14 & 15 Vict., c. 87 provided that where votes had not been received or counted for 50 years titles should not be called if the House so ordered. The Peerage Act, 1963, c. 48, gave all holders of a Scottish peerage the right to receive a Writ of Summons to H.L., and the legislation relating to Representative Peers thereby ceased to have effect.

The electoral procedure required the peers of Scotland to assemble, attended by the Lord Clerk Register or two of the Clerks of Session. At the election each peer present made out and signed a List of 16 peers of his choice. To these were added Lists sent in by absent peers. The final list of 16 peers chosen was certified by the Clerk Register or Clerks of Session to the Clerk of the Privy Council of Scotland, and this certificate was forwarded to H.L. S.O. 112 of 27 November 1710 ordered that this Return was to be read at the beginning of every Parliament.

Claims to vote at the elections which were not accepted there, i.e. which did not seem to be of a peer whose title was on the Union Roll, were decided by H.L. in somewhat similar manner to claims to English, British, or United Kingdom peerages. The claimant's Petition was submitted to the House, which then normally referred it to the Committee for Privileges.

Petitions concerning the proceedings at any election, alleging a breach of privilege or a refusal to accept a peer's vote, were likewise made to the House and referred to its Committee for Privileges. The final Resolution of the House concerning the election of Representative Peers might declare that a certain individual had or had not the right to vote, or was or was not rightly elected; the House on occasion ordered the Return of Election to be produced for amendment.

Between 1709 and 1964 many questions dealing with the Scottish Peerage were brought before the House and referred either to the Committee for Privileges or to a Select Committee, the latest in that series being the consideration in 1964 of matters connected with the issue of Writs of Summons to all peers of Scotland. The collected Indexes to the Lords Journals provide the most convenient form of reference to these proceedings.

(i) For Records of Proceedings concerning Scottish Elections and Claims, *see*:

JOURNALS OF THE HOUSE, 1707 to 1964, pp. 28–32 above.

MINUTES OF THE HOUSE, 1707 to 1964, pp. 33–6 above.

MINUTES OF THE COMMITTEE FOR PRIVILEGES, 1707 to 1964, p. 43 above.

Evidence

1850 to 1877   5 docs.

Minutes of Evidence given in the Committee for Privileges and ordered to
be printed by the House. The separate prints were assembled *c.* 1906 in 3 vols.
together with a far greater number of prints of Evidence of Irish Claims. A
similar set of prints is preserved in H.L. Library.

(ii) Other Records relating to Scottish Elections and Claims:

The Long Roll or Union Roll

1708   1 doc.

The 'Authentic List of the Peerage of the North part of Great Britain called
Scotland as it stood 1st May 1707'. *Note* that subsequent copies of this Roll,
revised in accordance with the House's decisions on Claims to Vote, are preserved amongst SESSIONAL PAPERS.

Certificates of Election

1707 to 1963   138 docs.

Returns delivered to the House by the Clerk of the Crown of the names
of peers chosen as Representative Peers for Scotland, including returns made as
vacancies occurred between General Elections. From 1869 onwards the Returns
were also ordered to be printed by the House.

Minutes of Proceedings at Elections

1761 to 1963   100 docs.

Minutes survive irregularly in manuscript, until the House, in 1869, began
to order them to be printed. In 1832 a collected series of 'authentic copies' of
election proceedings, 1822–32, was delivered to the House. Annexed to the
Minutes, from 1851 onwards, were returns of titles called at elections in right
of which no votes had been cast for 50 years (under the Representative Peers
(Scotland) Act, 1851, 14 & 15 Vict., c. 87). A complete list of elections to
1959 is given by J. Fergusson, *The Sixteen Peers of Scotland* (1960).

Petitions concerning Elections

1708 to 1880   100 docs.

The Petitions concern, e.g. the rights of participants to vote, the correctness
of the return, the occurrence of technical illegalities. The Petitions are addressed
to H.L. Petitions were referred to the Committee for Privileges, or, upon occasion, to Select Committees. Upon Report, the House came to a Resolution,
which might lead to the amending of the Return.

Petitions of Claim to Vote

1723 to 1877   30 docs.

The Petitions are addressed to the House, are signed by the claimant, and
are undated. Each contains a statement of claim, with supporting reasons, and

is endorsed with a statement of proceedings on it in the House. The Petition itself is entered in the Journal and its text may be transcribed or summarised there.

Case

1877   1 doc.

A full statement of Claim in the case of E. Loudoun *et al.* (1877) is included in the bound vol. of Irish Cases (*see* p. 168).

Additional Papers

1828 to 1877   20 docs.

The series preserved amongst the Main Papers includes incidental Petitions, Evidential material in support of the claim, Reports of the Committee for Privileges, Orders and Resolutions of the House.

RECORDS CONCERNING REPRESENTATIVE PEERS FOR IRELAND

In accordance with the Union with Ireland Act, 1800, 39 & 40 Geo. III, c. 67, 4 Lords Spiritual, in rotation, and 28 Lords Temporal, elected for life, sat in the United Kingdom House of Lords. The bishops were withdrawn after 1 January 1871 on the disestablishment of the Irish Church (Irish Church Act, 1869, 32 & 33 Vict., c. 42). The Lords Temporal were elected by the peers of Ireland, who delivered in to the Clerk of the Crown in Ireland or his deputy, Lists of their choice, from which the Clerk made a Return of the peers elected to H.L. Elections took place on the death or forfeiture of a previously elected Representative Peer. As a result of the Irish Free State (Agreement) Act, 1922, 12 & 13 Geo. V, c. 4, elections of Representative Peers ceased. A Petition of Irish Peers that the House should provide means for the representation of the Peers of Ireland by 28 peers in H.L., presented to the House in 1965, after being considered by the Committee for Privileges, was rejected.

Claims to vote at elections of peers were submitted to H.L. S.O. 160 of 2 April 1802 provided that the claim should be made in a Petition to the House, stating the derivation of the peerage claimed. The practice of the House until 1857 was to refer the Petition directly to the Committee for Privileges; after 1857 the procedure was similar to that on ordinary applications for a Writ of Summons (*see* PEERAGE CLAIMS). In 1969 the House, by revising its S.O. 68, ceased to receive claims of rights to vote but continued to accept claims 'to any peerage of Ireland'.

Claims as coheirs to an Irish peerage in abeyance were also to be submitted to the House, under the S.O.s 162–3, but, in addition, they needed the commendation of the Crown, before being referred to the Committee for Privileges.

(i) For Records of Proceedings concerning Irish Elections and Claims, *see*:

JOURNALS OF THE HOUSE, 1800 to 1961, pp. 28–32 above.

MINUTES OF THE HOUSE, 1800 to 1961, pp. 33–6 above.

MINUTES OF THE COMMITTEE FOR PRIVILEGES, 1800 to 1961, p. 43 above.

Register of Claims

1800 to 1916   1 vol.

Entries are alphabetical under headings of Peerage, Date of Claims, Claimant, Result.

Evidence

1812 to 1906   7 vols.

The vols. contain bound verbatim Evidence given before the Committee for Privileges in 81 claims to vote. They comprise two overlapping series: (a) manuscript evidence, 4 vols; (b) printed evidence, 3 vols.

(ii) Other Records relating to Irish Elections and Claims:

Election Returns

1801 to 1919   131 files

The Certificate consisted in 1801 of the full list of 28 Lords Temporal chosen to represent the Peers of Ireland, thereafter of the name of the peer chosen to replace a specific Representative Peer. The Certificate was signed by the Clerk of the Crown in Ireland or his Deputy, and was endorsed by the Clerk of the Parliaments with the date and manner of delivery at the Table. Annexed to the Certificate was a file of Writs, sent by the Clerk of the Crown to each Irish Peer, and of the Returns signed and sealed by each peer, which were returned to the Clerk of the Crown, and on the basis of which the Clerk had made out his Certificate of Election.

Petitions of Claim

1802 to date   700 docs.

The Petitions are addressed to H.L. They summarise the evidence for the Petitioner holding a named Irish peerage, and claim the right to vote; they are signed, but not dated, and are endorsed with the date of presentation etc. Certain Petitions were also printed, and these may be included in CASES (*see* below). The Petitions are entered in the Journals.

Cases

1826 to 1905   1 vol.

This vol. contains Cases setting out proofs, documentary evidence, etc. for 13 claims to vote. It was assembled *c.* 1906. There is a similar volume in H.L. Library.

Statements of Proof

1822 to 1841   3 docs.

MS. Statements of Proof are preserved for the Athlone (1841), Ely (1822) and Listowel (1837) claims.

Additional Papers

1802 to 1964

The papers include incidental Petitions, Reports from the Lord Chancellor, Orders and Resolutions of the House.

The following section comprises those small classes of H.L. records which have not been described above. The classes are arranged in alphabetical order.

Accession Declarations

1936, 1952   2 docs.

Every Monarch must make a declaration that he or she is a faithful Protestant, etc., either at a sitting of Parliament or at the coronation, whichever first happens (cf. Bill of Rights, 1688, 1 Will. & Mary, sess. 2, c. 2; Coronation Oath Act, 1688, 1 Will. & Mary, c. 6; Act of Settlement, 1700, 12 & 13 Will. III, c. 2; Accession Declaration Act, 1910, 10 Edw. VII & 1 Geo. V, c. 29). The Declarations consist of the text printed on vellum and the sign manual; they are those made in H.L. respectively by King Edward VIII and by Queen Elizabeth II.

Clerk of the Parliaments Rolls

1825 to date   145 docs.

Marshalled lists of Lords Temporal were laid by Garter from 1621 onward (see GARTER'S ROLLS). In 1825, and then regularly from 1827 onwards, lists or Rolls of Lords Spiritual and Temporal were separately prepared by the Clerk of the Parliaments for each session and were printed by order of the House. In these Rolls, the titles of all Lords Spiritual and Temporal are given, but by contrast with Garter's Rolls, (i) the surnames of peers are not given, (ii) the Christian names of peers who have not received Writs of Summons are given in addition to their titles (except for 1945–50), and (iii) Scottish and Irish titles are included, where appropriate, in brackets after the titles by virtue of which the peers sit. The Rolls are numbered as Sessional Papers. Since the discontinuance of Garter's Roll in 1966, single record copies of each sessional Clerk's Roll have been specially printed, illuminated with the Royal Arms, and bound in vellum.

Garter's Rolls

1621, 1628, 1661 to 1964   311 docs.

Garter King of Arms is the officer traditionally concerned with the precedence of peers, although his authority ultimately derives from that of the Earl Marshal. In 1514 he was requested to display records to the House relating to the precedence of earls[1] and in 1597 he was ordered to attend to ensure that the names of peers were properly marshalled in the Journal. From at least 1621 lists of Lords Temporal were laid on the Table of the House, at

---

[1] See also the Processional Roll of Peers of 1512 (Trinity College, Cambridge, MS. 0.3.59) reproduced by Wagner and Sainty, as in BIBLIOGRAPHY below.

first probably for each Parliament, from 1678 until 1962 for each session, and again for 1964. In 1966 the laying of Garter's Rolls ended, matters of peers' precedence being thenceforward normally resolved by reference to the CLERK OF THE PARLIAMENTS ROLLS.

The lists vary slightly in their contents, but normally give Christian and family names of peers as well as titles, and indicate tenure of the great offices of state. Christian names may be omitted for peers who have not proved their succession and have not therefore been summoned, for minors, and for any others who for a specific reason had been deprived temporarily of a Writ of Summons. The Garter's Roll for 1621 includes Lords Spiritual. From 1628 to 1964 the rolls are of vellum; from 1780 they are handsomely embellished with the Royal Arms and other illuminations. The rolls for 1678–85 were prepared by Sir William Dugdale. Those for 1765–92 were also copied by the Clerk of the Parliaments into a vol. entitled 'Lords Temporal as delivered by Garter' which in fact also included sessional lists of Lords Spiritual. In 1801 a register was compiled of 'Peers of England', in alphabetical order, for 1550–1801, which is preserved in the Parchment Collection.

BIBLIOGRAPHY. A. Wagner and J. C. Sainty, 'The Origin of the Introduction of Peers in the House of Lords', *Archaeologia*, vol. 101, (1967), pp. 119–50.

Orders and Ordinances, Books of

1640 to 1695   30 vols.

During the 17th c. Orders and certain other classes of entries in the Journals of the House were also registered in several separate and overlapping series of vols. The practice probably started in the reign of James I, but the first surviving vols. date from 1640. Between 1642 and 1649 these supplementary registers in addition included the texts of Ordinances, and from 1642 to 1693 a parallel series included the texts of Judgments in Appeal Cases and Cases in Error. The entries of Orders and Judgments normally correspond with those in the Journals, but there are variations in wording, with occasional deletions, amendments and marginalia; and certain Orders, etc., may be in the Order Books but not in the Journals, and *vice versa*. It is therefore desirable to examine both sources. The texts of the Ordinances are as passed in both Houses; certain of the Ordinances are represented by copies of the officially printed text bound into the vols. Draft copies of separate Orders and Ordinances are preserved in SESSIONAL PAPERS.

The series of vols. are arranged as follows:

    BOOKS OF ORDINANCES, (both Houses), 1640 to 1649, 8 vols.

    BOOK OF ORDERS AND WARRANTS, H.L., 1640 to 1641, 1 vol.

    BOOKS OF ORDERS AND JUDGMENTS, H.L., 1642 to 1693, 21 vols.

BIBLIOGRAPHY. C. H. Firth and R. S. Rait, *Acts and Ordinances of the Interregnum, 1642–1660* (1911).

Petitions

1531 to date   3,200 docs.

Petitions to H.L. may be roughly divided into four main categories: (1) legislative, i.e. seeking permission to introduce a specific Bill, or intended to help or hinder the passage of a Bill already introduced; (2) judicial, i.e. arising from a supposed miscarriage of justice in a court of law and asking for a hearing in the Lords or for an alteration in an appeal process already under way; (3) administrative, i.e. arising from the needs or grievance of a private individual or group of individuals, and calling for administrative intervention; and (4) 'public policy' petitions, i.e. those by an individual, corporation, or group calling attention to a general matter of policy, or seeking legislation in general terms. On occasion the types may overlap, notably categories (1) and (4); and (2) and (3). Petitions in categories (1) and (2) are dealt with elsewhere (*see* BILL RECORDS and JUDICIAL RECORDS). The present class comprises the 'administrative' and 'public policy' petitions, categories (3) and (4).

Few petitions survive before 1621; from 1621 until 1649 the House received a large quantity of petitions from the public at large, and devised a special procedure for dealing with them. All petitions were sent to a 'Committee of Petitions' which reported to the House what answers should be made. (Receivers and Triers of Petitions, although appointed until 1886, no longer exercised their office.) Some of the original petitions were endorsed with a note of action taken on them, and a varying proportion were entered in the Journal. The series was resumed in 1660, but the Tumultuous Petitioning Act, 1661, 13 Cha. II, sess. 1, c. 5, which required the consent of Justices of the Peace or others for the petitioning of Parliament, led to a drastic reduction in the numbers of petitions. From the later 17th c. and early 18th c., however, petitions were received for such miscellaneous purposes as recovery of debts, obtaining a passport, or objecting to the consequences of a commercial treaty with France.

The modern system of petitioning originated in 1779, when committees began to be established in various parts of the country in order to encourage reform by holding public meetings and drawing up petitions to Parliament. During the following century public petitions, drawn in this way, came to both Houses in increasing quantities and almost completely supplanted the petition of private grievances, except in the special instance of petitions from officials of the House and others closely connected with it concerning their establishment, remuneration, etc. In the session of 1820 there were some 122 petitions to H.L., in that of 1837 there were about 5,000. In all, some 20,000 petitions were presented concerning the Roman Catholic Emancipation Act, and some 5,000 petitions preceded the repeal of the Corporation and Test Acts in 1828. The use by the public of this method of influencing Parliament continued into the middle of the 19th c.; on a single day, in 1850, for example 451 separate petitions were presented to the Lords concerning education.

The procedure of H.L. in this second period of petitioning was summarised by Erskine May, thus: 'It was ordered by the lords, 30 May 1685, "That any lord who presents a petition, shall open it before it be read." At the same time the lord may comment upon the petition, and upon the general matters to which it refers; and there is no rule or order of the house that limits the duration of the debate on receiving a petition. When the petition has been laid upon the table, an entry of that fact is made in the lords' minutes, and appears afterwards in the Journals, with the prayer of the petition, amidst the other proceedings of the house; but the nature of its contents is rarely to be collected from the entry and in very few cases indeed have the petitions been printed at length in the Journals, unless they related to proceedings partaking of a judicial character'. Since 1868 any peer presenting a petition enters his name on it. In 1969 it was ordered that no petition, other than a petition relating to judicial or private business, shall be received [by H.L.] unless it is presented by a lord and bears his signature.

The fact of presentation can usually be ascertained from the Journals. The original petition very frequently was destroyed, but throughout the period a certain number of originals was preserved (although unsystematically) amongst the Main Papers. A substantial series is separately classified and listed for 1875–1910. Since 1950 all petitions to either House have been preserved. If an original has not been preserved nor the text printed in the Lords Journals, the Commons may have received a similar petition, and information concerning its purport may survive in the PETITIONS RECORDS, H.C. For the session 1867–8 only, H.L. appointed a Select Committee to consider Petitions (as had been done in H.C. since 1833) and their Reports in H.L. Sessional Papers (1867–8, vol. xxx) list all Petitions and give summaries or complete texts in Appendices. Since the last century the number of petitions presented to the Lords has dropped sharply. In the decade 1904–13 there were three, whilst in the decade 1943–53 only a single public petition was presented, and that concerned the constitution of the House itself. Debate may arise upon a petition, and a Committee or Joint Committee may be appointed to consider it, but the normal Journal entry now records that a petition, having been 'presented, was read and Ordered to lie on the Table'.

Procedure of the House of Lords

c. 1850 to 1935   6 vols.

The vols. in this class comprise precedents extracted from the Minutes of the House classified under procedural headings, e.g. 'Addresses to the Crown', 'Adjourned Debates', 'Appeals', etc. They were compiled within the Parliament Office and printed mainly for the use of its staff. For more general guides to procedure *see* STANDING ORDERS, STANDING ORDERS (COMPANIONS), and HISTORICAL COLLECTIONS, H.L.R.O.

PROTESTS

Peers may record their dissent on any matter dealt with in the House by 'entering a protest'. The protest is a statement of opinion, and may be accompanied by an exposition of the reasons for it. It is signed by the original protestant and by other peers who concur. S.O. 57 of 5 March 1642 ordered that the protest should be entered in the 'Clerks Book' the next sitting day, and this rule continues in force. When the Journal ceased in 1830 to be kept in manuscript, a separate manuscript Book was made available for protests. Usage restricts protests to those peers who were present during the debate on the motion to which they dissent. Protests can be ordered to be expunged by the House. The first occasion on which dissentients are named in the Journals was in 1549; long and formal protests originated in 1641. Protests have had less significance since Division Lists began to be published in 1857.

Original Protest Books

1831 to date   33 vols.

Most of the first 31 vols. are for a single session each, one vol. is for the session 1866–77 inc., and the vol. beginning in 1878 is still in use. The text of the protest is frequently accompanied by relevant extracts from the Journals concerning the business protested against.

Protest Register

1641 to 1779   1 vol.

A vol. compiled *c.* 1779 in the Parliament Office, and labelled 'Lords Protests Vol. I'. The register is a complete copy of Journal entries for the period in question.

See also HISTORICAL COLLECTIONS, H.L.R.O., MISC.

PRINTED VERSIONS. Protests in a single session were occasionally printed before 1737; a number of collections appeared between then and 1797, notably *A genuine and complete collection of all the protests*, 2 vols., 1748.

See also *A complete collection of the protests of the Lords with historical introduction.*
   [1624–1874]. Edited from the Journals of the Lords by J. E. T. Rogrs, 3 vols. 1875. (There are omissions, including all protests without reasons given.)

PROXY RECORDS

Absent peers were able to vote by proxy until this right was in effect abolished in 1868 by the present S.O. 54. The privilege was regulated by S.O.s 45–7 of 1626 which provided that no lord should receive more than 2 proxies; and that Spiritual Lords' proxies should be made to Spiritual Lords, and Temporal to Temporal. S.O. 75 of 1689 prevented proxies being used in giving judgment in appeals and cases in error and S.O. 88 of 1697 prevented all judicial use of them even when procedure was by Bill. No proxy could be used in a Committee of the Whole House. The usual practice was for lords to hold proxies from lords of the same political opinions, a fact of importance in determining the history of political parties and opinions, but on rare occasions a lord might hold a proxy for a lord on the opposite side. Proxies needed to be renewed on the death of the Sovereign. The S.O. of 31 March 1868 ended the practice of voting by proxy and required two days' notice for any motion to suspend the order. No attempt to revert to the use of proxies has since been made.

Proxies for 35 and 37 Hen. VIII are included in Lords MS. Journals; an undated proxy for the Abbot of Shrewsbury is pasted in the MS. Journal for 28 Hen. VIII; the MS. Journal for 34 Hen. VIII contains rough notes concerning proxies, and that for 37 Hen. VIII a note concerning the Bishop of Norwich's proxy; subsequent proxies may also be found in the Journals, with a full record for many sessions up to 1628.

BIBLIOGRAPHY

V. F. Snow, 'Proctorial representation and conciliar management during the reign of Henry VIII', *Historical Journal*, vol. ix (1966).

H. Miller, 'Attendance in the House of Lords during the reign of Henry VIII', *Historical Journal*, vol. x (1967).

Proxy Books

1625 to 1864   146 vols.

The normal form of entry in the Proxy Books is that a named peer is said to have the proxy of one or two other named peers. The date is given. If a proxy is vacated the entry is deleted and a marginal date entered for the vacation, with a note if the vacation is 'per presentiam' of the hitherto absent peer, or 'per revocationem', 'per litteras', 'per mandatum', or 'per mortem'.

Proxy Deeds

1790 to 1864   900 docs.

The proxy deeds are printed forms with blanks in which the names of the peers giving and receiving the proxy and the date are entered. The deeds are signed and sealed by the peer granting the proxy, and are usually endorsed by the Clerk with the name of both parties. In many of the later proxies, the blanks in the form have not been filled up.[1] Included in the bundles are occasional memoranda by the Clerks concerning the proxies on a given day, etc. See HISTORICAL COLLECTIONS, H.L.R.O. for other proxy deeds, 1767–1816. See also the class of Parliamentary Proxies in the Public Record Office (S.C. 10) for 52 files of 'Letters from Spiritual peers desiring to be excused attendance in Parliament on the ground of infirmity, etc., and appointing proctors to represent them'. In the last file there are some proxies by lay peers, *temp.* Hen. III–Hen. VIII (*Guide to . . . P.R.O.*, vol. i, p. 192).

Royal Commissions (Letters Patent)

1542 to date   2,925 docs.

Functions originally or normally performed within Parliament by the Sovereign may be done on his or her behalf by Commissioners appointed by Letters Patent under the Great Seal. The full text of the Patent is inscribed in the Journal and the original documents are appropriately endorsed and preserved by the Clerk of the Parliaments.

[1] An original brass engraving plate for Proxy Deeds is preserved in the Parliament Office Papers (P.O. 268).

The documents consisted invariably of one or more membranes of parchment with the Great Seal pendent and the Sign Manual superscribed until, in 1900, the present format of printed pages with a Great Seal impressed *en placard* and the Sign Manual superscribed was adopted.

The following classes of Patents of Commission survive:

To Appoint a Speaker of the House of Lords, from 1566.

To Appoint a Lord High Steward, 1678–1935.

To Hold Parliament, from 1586.

To Pass Bills (For Royal Assent), from 1542. (Assent by this means was originally validated by the Commission Act, 1541, 33 Hen. VIII, c. 21.)

To Prorogue Parliament, from 1542. Until the later 18th c. Parliament was normally prorogued by the Sovereign in person and Commissions for prorogation are rare until then. Since 1854 all prorogations have been by Commission.

> The term 'prorogation' was also applied to the procedure described in the S.O. 7 of 1715: 'After the issuing the Writ of Summons, if the Parliament be prorogued to any further Day than was appointed for the Meeting thereof by the Writ of Summons, it is done by Writ which is directed to both the Houses ... But when the Parliament is prorogued at any Time after the first Meeting thereof, such prorogation is not to be by Writ but by Commission'. Prorogation Writs were inscribed with the sign manual, and issued from Chancery; they were discontinued in 1761.

To Dissolve Parliament, from 1558. Dissolution could be performed by the Sovereign in person; the last personal dissolutions were in 1681 and 1813. The normal practice from 1681 onwards was first to prorogue Parliament, and then to dissolve it by proclamation.

To Adjourn Parliament, from 1621.

To Command or to Approve the Election of a Speaker of the House of Commons, from 1581.

BIBLIOGRAPHY

R. W. Perceval, 'Henry VIII and the Origin of Royal Assent by Commission', *Parliamentary Affairs,* vol. iii (1949–50), pp. 307–15.

[Anon], 'The Royal Assent', *The Table,* vol. xxiv (1955), pp. 45–50.

C. E. Fryer, 'The Royal Veto under Charles II', *English Historical Review,* vol. xxxii (1917), pp. 103–11.

Royal Assent by Notification (Letters Patent)

1967 to date

By the Royal Assent Act, 1967, c. 23, it was provided that an Act of Parliament is duly enacted either by the customary method of Royal Commission (*see* ROYAL COMMISSIONS (LETTERS PATENT)), by the Sovereign in person, or by the notification to each House of Parliament (sitting separately) by the Speaker of that House of the Assent. The Letters Patent authorising assent by the last named method are preserved as a separate class.

STANDING ORDERS

The Standing Orders (S.O.s) of the House of Lords originated as a series of 'Remembrances for order and decency to be kept in the upper House of Parliament' which were enrolled in 1621. Subsequently, new Orders were added by the House, to produce, by the early 18th c., a code of procedure. The House on occasion converts a Sessional Order into a 'Standing Order' after a lapse of time.

From c. 1661 individual S.O.s which concerned the public were published in separate sheets; in 1707 H.L. ordered all Private Bill and Judicial Orders to be printed and published[1]; and subsequently occasional unofficial collections were published.[2] In 1818 the first general collection of S.O.s was made and from 1826-7 such collections often appeared in the printed series of *Sessional Papers*. The first official complete collection appeared in 1825, and since then, others have appeared from time to time. The current editions are: *The Standing Orders of the House of Lords relating to Public Business* (1969) and *Standing Orders of the House of Lords relative to Private Bills, Provisional Order Confirmation Bills, Special Procedure Orders and Special Orders, with Appendices and Index* (1961).

Each S.O. was normally entered in the Journal as it was accepted by the House, thus appearing under the appropriate day's headings in the Journal. It is not, however, always possible to determine the exact text of a S.O. from the Journal, as entries sometimes merely specify amendments in wording to previous S.O.s, referring to the engrossed rolls of S.O.s. Nowhere in the Journals is a complete roll or book of standing orders set out *in extenso*. Students are therefore advised to consult Rolls A and B as printed in the *Calendar*, 1712–1714, pp. 1–27 for Standing Orders, 1621–1712; the rolls or typescript in H.L.R.O. for Standing Orders, 1712–1848; and for later Standing Orders, either the sectional collections in *Sessional Papers* or the complete texts published in 1844, 1849 and subsequently.

Standing Orders

1621 to date   100 docs.

This class comprises the following items:

Draft S.O.s, 1621.[3]

Parchment Roll A, originally engrossed 1624, containing S.O.s 1621–64.

Parchment Roll B, originally engrossed 1664, containing S.O.s 1621–1712.

Parchment Roll C, originally engrossed 1715, containing S.O.s 1621–1848. (Typescript available in H.L.R.O.)

Parchment Roll D, originally engrossed 1715, containing S.O.s 1621–1809. This virtually duplicates S.O.s 1–176 of the 237 S.O.s in Roll C. Amended to c. 1813 (to be printed in *Calendar*, vol. xii).

---

[1] Sheets of such prints are included in various Committee Appointment Books from 1762.
[2] E.g. the 'accurate copy' of the S.O.s of H.L. included in J. Debrett, *Parliamentary Papers*, 3 vols. (1797). This collection also included the 'Rules and Standing Orders of the House of Commons', King's Speeches, 1660–1796, and Lords Protests, 1242–1796.
[3] Annexed to a draft committee report of 26 Feb. 1624 relating to the S.O. revision of that year, amongst the Main Papers.

Parchment Roll E, originally engrossed 1848, containing S.O.s 216–28, 1848–9. (Printed *in extenso* in *L.J.*, lxxx, 848–57.)

Standing Orders of the House of Lords (1825) and subsequent printed editions, 1844–date, 90 vols[1].

Chief Clerk's Book of S.O.s printed on vellum, 1849, amended to 1874 (a copy of the S.O.s printed in H.L. Sessional Papers, 1849, vol. xlvii).

Other Parliament Office copies include:

Draft S.O.s printed 1818, with undated MS. corrections.

Printed booklets entitled *Forms of Appeal, Method of Procedure, and Standing Orders* have been issued by the Judicial Office, H.L., at irregular intervals for the guidance of those participating in the judicial work of the House. The latest ed. is of 1970.

BIBLIOGRAPHY. *Calendar, 1712–14*, pp. xxxix–xlvi.

Standing Orders (Companions)

1862 to date   11 vols.

These vols. summarise S.O.s for the use of peers and officials. From 1862 to 1909 the vols. were circulated privately; from 1909 onwards they have been laid on the Table.

Subsidies of the Clergy

1543 to 1628   29 docs.

The system of taxation in the 16th c. included grants by the proctors or representatives of the clergy in Convocation on behalf of the Church, which, from 1540 onwards, were confirmed by Act of Parliament. This method of grant continued in the early 17th c. and was terminated, apparently without any formal act, by agreement between L. Chancellor Clarendon and Archbishop Sheldon of Canterbury, in 1664.

From 1543 many of the original grants, or 'subsidy books', from the Convocations of Canterbury and York survive, though they take various forms. Prior to 1610, original subsidy Acts, separate from the subsidy books, were drawn up. From 1610 onwards the instrument granting the subsidy from the Convocation of Canterbury was converted into a parliamentary Bill by adding a preamble at the head and clauses at the foot which confirmed the Canterbury subsidy and applied the act to the province of York. Normally, the York and Canterbury subsidies were granted by instruments consisting of one or more parchment skins attested by a notary public and bearing a pendent seal, which after 1571 frequently bear the signatures of the Archbishop. Five of the York subsidy bills were made up into small parchment books. The 'subsidy books' in H.L.R.O. are listed in the *Calendar, Addenda, 1514 to 1714*, and the texts of all the subsidy Bills which received the Royal Assent are printed in *Statutes of the Realm*.

---

[1] Since 1860 sections relating to public business, private bills, and appeals have generally been treated separately.

Test Rolls

1675 to date   138 docs.

Special oaths of allegiance were on occasion in the middle ages exacted from peers in Parliament, certain of which are noted in the Rolls of Parliament. The first oath of allegiance recorded in the Journals is that entered on 31 March 1534. The Oath of Allegiance Act, 1609, 7 Ja. I, c. 6, required all peers to take an oath of allegiance which included a renunciation of the Pope, and, although this was in essence an extra-parliamentary declaration, in 1626 S.O. 43 ordered that the oath be taken once in every Parliament. The Popish Recusants Act, 1672, 25 Cha. II, c. 2, required peers who were office-holders to take the oaths of supremacy and allegiance and to subscribe a declaration against transubstantiation. The Parliament Act, 1678, 30 Cha. II, sess. 2, c. 1, forbade peers to sit or vote until both oaths had been taken and a new declaration made in each Parliament. The Parliament Act, 1688, 1 Will. & Mary, sess. 1, c. 1, substituted new oaths of allegiance and supremacy, and subsequent amendments were made by the Act of Succession, 1701, 13 & 14 Will. III, c. 6. A special oath was provided for Roman Catholic peers by the Roman Catholic Relief Act, 1829, 10 Geo. IV, c. 7. The Oaths of Allegiance Act, 1858, 21 & 22 Vict., c. 48, substituted a single oath for three previously taken, to be taken by all but Roman Catholics and Quakers, and the Parliamentary Oaths Act, 1866, 29 & 30 Vict., c. 19, established one uniform oath for all. This attained its present day form in the Promissory Oaths Act, 1868, 31 & 32 Vict., c. 72. The Oaths Act, 1888, 51 & 52 Vict., c. 46 permitted affirmation as an alternative to the oath. The rolls contain a preamble, the form or forms of declaration, and the signatures of peers who took the oaths. The rolls now numbered 96 to 110 inclusive are Roman Catholic Rolls, 1829–66.

BIBLIOGRAPHY. R. W. Perceval and P. D. G. Hayter, 'The Oath of Allegiance', *The Table*, vol. xxxiii (1964), pp. 85–90.

Votes of Thanks

1858 to 1919   108 docs.

The Votes are texts of Resolutions and Orders of the House printed large on vellum, illuminated in gold, and bound in red leather. Each Vote is signed by the Clerk of the Parliaments. Included in the class are also 73 blanks or duplicates, unsigned. The texts of the Resolutions and Orders are printed *in extenso* in the Journals.

Writs of Summons

1559 to date   19,000 docs.

Lords Spiritual and Temporal are summoned to Parliament by Writs of Summons, sealed with the Great Seal and issued by the Clerk of the Crown on the direction of the L. Chancellor. Lords are commanded 'upon the faith and allegiance upon which you are bound to Us that ... you be personally present ... with Us and the Prelates and Peers ... to treat and give your counsel'. The Judges, two Law Officers, and others, are also summoned to Parliament, by Writs of Assistance, which command them, without mentioning faith and allegiance, to 'be present with Us and the rest of our council to treat and give your counsel upon the affairs aforesaid'. (See p. 22.) The Law Officers are now invariably members of H.C. and therefore do not attend on their Writs of Assistance, but an appropriate number of the Judges sit on the woolsacks at the Opening of Parliament in response to their Writs.

New Writs are issued for each Parliament, and the Lords, on attending for the first time in each Parliament to take the oath, hand in or 'return' their Writs, which are preserved among the records of the House. But since the recipients of Writs of Assistance now never attend an ordinary sitting of the House, none of their Writs has been preserved in H.L.R.O. since *c.* 1900. The Writ and the Letters Patent of a peer of a new creation who is being introduced are read and entered verbatim in the Journals; they are then given to the new peer.

Until 1917 the Writs were of parchment; since then they have been of paper. Until 1958 the Writs were kept by Crown Office officials in or near the Prince's Chamber available for peers to pick up as they went in to take the oath. Each Writ was 'plied', that is folded up into a small bundle about 3 by $1\frac{1}{2}$ inches, which was tied with ribbon. From this bundle protruded the 'fly', a strip about $1\frac{1}{2}$ inches wide and 7 or 8 inches long which was connected to the bundle by a much narrower joining strip; the 'fly' was made by making a cut almost but not quite the whole way along the bottom of the Writ; it contained the name of the Lord summoned, with the words 'A Writ of Summons to Parliament'.

All surviving pre-1715 Writs are listed in the Calendar, but both before and after 1715 the series, if compared with the lists of peers present in the Journals, is incomplete. Writs of Summons and of Assistance were enrolled on the Close Rolls until 1541, and thereafter on the 'Parliament Pawns' (Petty Bag Office), and surviving enrolments are preserved in the Public Record Office.

BIBLIOGRAPHY

Report by the Select Committee on the powers of the House in relation to the attendance of its Members, H.L. (1955–6), vii.

PARLIAMENT OFFICE PAPERS

THE PARLIAMENT OFFICE

In the middle ages a number of Chancery Masters and clerks attended upon each Parliament, some having been summoned by Writs of Assistance. One clerk had the specific title of 'clerk del Parlement', or 'clericus parliamenti', the implication being that he was clerk of the Parliament then sitting but was not regarded as holding a continuing office between Parliaments. In 1447 the clerks began to receive appointment by Letters Patent, and the grant was usually for life. In the early 16th c. the title of 'Clerk of the Parliaments' is used, perhaps as an indication that the office was now considered a continuing one.[1] The Clerk of the Parliaments dealt with the business of Parliament as a whole and with that of the Upper House sitting separately; the Under-clerk was responsible for the service of the Lower House, and acquired the alternative title of Clerk of the House of Commons, together with a separate staff and independent status (*see* pp. 243–4 below).

The Clerk of the Parliaments and his assistants in the Upper House form the department now known as 'the Parliament Office'. Originally, the office was part of Chancery, but it hived off to form a separate department *c.* 1509.[2] In 1497 the Clerk began to preserve the original Acts in his own office instead of transferring them with the enrolments to Chancery, and his successors in the 16th c. extended this practice, until by Elizabeth I's reign, nothing was so transferred except the Parliament Rolls—in spite of an attempt by Chancery in 1567 to recover the entire mass of records which had by then accumulated in the Parliament Office. The staff ceased to have any connection with Chancery; the expedient of making the Parliamentary Clerks Masters in Chancery on appointment was not adopted after John Taylor's clerkship (1509–23), and the Parliament Office staff, under barristers such as Bowyer, Elsynge and Browne, had a closer connection with the Inns of Court than with Chancery.

Although the Clerk of the Parliaments had probably always had assistance at the Table of the House of Lords, the names of assistant clerks do not appear until the time of Sir Thomas Smith (Clerk 1597–1609) who employed Owen Reynolds as 'Under-clerk'. This office then seems to have continued under the title of 'deputy Clerk' (e.g. in 1635).

After 1660 various subordinate officers were named with specific titles, notably the Clerk Assistant and the Reading Clerk, who with the Clerk of the Parliaments, sat at the Table of the House. In addition there were Committee Clerks, a Clerk of Ingrossments, a Clerk of the Journals and various writers or copying clerks.

By the middle of the 19th c. the establishment comprised, as well as three Clerks at the Table, a Clerk of the Journals and a Chief Clerk, with seven other

---

[1] Occasional mention, however, is still found in the Rolls of Parliament and in the Lords Journal of 'le clerk del Parlement'.
[2] *See* Introduction, p. 3.

first class clerks, seven second class, and fourteen third class clerks, a copyist and a summoning officer. Duties were re-allocated from time to time, and the increase of work in the 19th c. led to further specialisation and to the formation, by 1854, of fixed departments: the Public Bill Office, the Private Bill and Committee Office, the Judicial Office, the Journal Office, and the Accountant's Office. To these departments a Record Office was added in 1946.

All assistants in the Parliament Office were appointed solely by the Clerk of the Parliaments, and a number of deeds of appointment by him survive. The House, however, in the 18th c. was frequently petitioned by junior clerks for support against the Clerk of the Parliaments, and the House came to concern itself increasingly with its own clerical staff, normally by appointing a Select Committee to inquire into some specific issue and then to report back to the House, which thereupon made an Order. From 1824 onwards, a Select Committee on the Parliament Office (usually known as the 'Offices Committee') has been appointed each Session, and this Committee exercises a general supervision over the work of the office (*see* COMMITTEE RECORDS, and below).

In 1824 the Clerk of the Parliaments Act, 5 Geo. IV, c. 82, provided that the Clerk himself should continue to be appointed by Letters Patent, but that from the next appointment he should execute the duties of the office himself, and not by deputy (as he had done for a century), whilst those of his colleagues who were in attendance at the Table of the House should be appointed by the Lord Chancellor. In practice, this has meant that the Clerk Assistant, the Reading Clerk and the Fourth Clerk at the Table have been so appointed; other clerks and officials in the Parliament office are still appointed by the Clerk of the Parliaments, with a report to the Offices Committee and the House.

The traditional system of remuneration was for the Clerk of the Parliaments to receive £40 a year under his Patent. In addition, he received fees from the public in accordance with scales approved by the House, as did also his two senior assistants, the Clerk Assistant and the Reading Clerk. Other members of the staff received salaries from the Clerk. From 1824, however, all the approved fees received by the Clerks at the Table were paid by them into a General Fee Fund. This, when necessary, was subvented by the Treasury, in order that all Parliament Office staff might then be paid fixed salaries from it. From 1869 onwards the Accountant's office has collected fees and paid them to the Treasury, which, through the Accountant, pays the salaries determined by the Offices Committee, with the aid of whatever sum may be voted to bring the total up to the necessary amount.

The present day work of the Clerk of the Parliaments and his staff is summarised as follows in Erskine May's *Parliamentary Practice*, 17th ed.

1. Minutes of proceedings of H.L. are prepared under the Clerk's direction and issued in his name.

2. In the House he is responsible for calling on each item of the business of the day as it is reached and keeping watch generally over the course of the business.

3. He gives advice to members of the House on points of order and procedure.

4. He has the custody of all records and documents of the House.

5. He endorses all Bills sent to H.C.

6. In his custody are placed Bills which have passed through both Houses and await the Royal Assent; and he is responsible for the subsequent promulgation of Acts.

7. At any ceremony of the Royal Assent to Bills by commission, he pronounces to each Act the words by which the Royal Assent is signified, and it is his duty by Statute to endorse on every Act the date on which it received the Royal Assent.

8. He is Registrar of the Court in respect of the Judicial business of the House.

9. He is also accounting officer for the Vote for the House of Lords.

Besides these there are several other functions of the Clerk of considerable importance, notably the following:

He may receive papers for presentation to the House; he makes and signs Orders under direction of the House, or in accordance with Statute or Standing Order; he is responsible for the production of Acts for transfer to the Public Record Office; and he makes certified copies of Acts, judgments, etc. for the use of officials and of members of the public.

In sum, the Clerk and his Office thus perform, in the care of Acts of Parliament, certain duties for Parliament as a whole. They also act as the secretariat of the House of Lords, working, where necessary, in conjunction with the Office of the Clerk of the House of Commons.

The records of the Parliament Office do not form part of the official archives of the House, except where they have been produced in evidence in a dispute, or laid on the Table. They were, for the most part, preserved in the various rooms of the Office, until in 1946 they were handed to H.L.R.O. and placed in the Victoria Tower repository. A further group of 17th c. Parliament records was for long in the possession of the descendants of a clerk, John Browne, but either the originals, or photographs, of all of these have now been deposited in the Office (*see* BRAYE MANUSCRIPTS). The Parliament Office Papers which have been preserved continuously in H.L. are described below. They are classified in accordance with the department of origin, but where this is in doubt arrangement is by subject. Material relating to proceedings in the House or in Committee concerning the Parliament Office may also be found in the JOURNALS, MINUTES and other records of Proceedings.

USE. In general, Parliament Office Papers less than 30 years old are restricted, but certain papers within that category, on application being made, may be released for use.

BIBLIOGRAPHY

J. C. Sainty. 'Clerks in the Parliament Office, 1600–1900', *H.L.R.O. Memorandum no. 22* (1960).

D. Dewar, 'The Financial Administration and Records of the Parliament Office, 1824 to 1868', *H.L.R.O. Memorandum no. 37* (1967).

The following articles by M. F. Bond:

'Clerks of the Parliaments, 1509–1953,' *English Historical Review*, vol. 73 (1958), pp. 78–85.

'The Formation of the Archives of Parliament, 1497–1691', *Journal of the Society of Archivists*, vol. 1 (1957), pp. 151–8.

'The Office of Clerk of the Parliaments', *Parliamentary Affairs* (1959), pp. 297–310.

For a list of CLERKS OF THE PARLIAMENTS, *see* Appendix I, below.

LISTS. Lists and card indexes of all categories of Parliament Office Papers are available in the Search Room.

Note that certain docs. listed below appear to be official papers of the House which have never been incorporated in the official files but have been preserved with working papers in the offices concerned.

Grants of Office, etc.

1621 to 1856   54 docs.

Included in this group are Letters Patent of Grant of Office to Clerk of the Parliaments, 1715, 1 doc.; Copies of Clerks' Patents, 1635, 1638, 2 docs.; Deeds of Appointment to various clerkships, 1763–1819, 15 docs.; Oath of the Clerk of the Parliaments, etc., 1610, 1621, 7 docs.; Oath for other Clerks, 1621, 1 doc.; Declaration of Clerk of the Parliaments, 1660, 1 doc.; annotated draft of Clerk of the Parliaments Act, 1824, 1 doc.

House of Lords Offices Committees (Parliament Office Papers)

1763 to 1765, 1822 to 1902   205 items

The official records relating to the Offices Committees are preserved in the main COMMITTEE RECORDS, and Reports to the House are entered in the Journals. The papers noted here are mainly subsidiary and draft documents made or used within the Parliament Office and not laid on the Table of the House.

The principal doc. is the *Register of Offices Committee Proceedings*, 1824–1902, maintained by W. H. Haines (Clerk, 1845–91) *et al*. Other items are summaries of proceedings in the House and in committee concerning the Office (1763–5); and miscellaneous draft and printed Reports of the Committee, abstracts of its proceedings, and letters concerning it (1822–1902).

Establishment Papers

1715 to 1902   60 items

The principal items in this miscellaneous series are:

Office of Clerk of the Parliaments, Memoranda (1763).

Clerk Assistant Papers, concerning Journal entries (to 1723);
    Petitions by Clerk Assistant (*c.* 1769); Appointment by Clerk of the Parliaments (n.d.); Memo. on succession to office (1855–6).

Petitions of Clerks of the House, 1715–71, concerning their appointments and duties.

Department of Black Rod, emoluments of doorkeeper, 1850 (see also pp. 195–6).

Returns of Establishment, 1850, 1902.

Civil Service Commission, Correspondence, etc., concerning Clerkships, 1862–71, 1907.

The remaining items include Letters of Application for appointment; Obituary of H. Stone Smith (1881); and a Return, n.d., of hours of attendance, endorsed as 'Library of Fiction'.

Fee and Account Records

    c. 1619 to 1928   2,438 docs.

This miscellaneous series includes the following principal items (dates given relate to the end of the year of account):

Fee Rolls, etc., c. 1619, 1726, 1829, 1855.
    The rolls contain lists of Fees payable to the House and its Officers.

Account Books
    Salary Roll of Staff of H.L., 1845–91, with appointments to 1918.
    Fee Fund Cash Book, 1835–9; Ledgers, 1892–3, 1911–17; Cash Fee Book, 1896–1908.
    Fee Books, 1883–1908 (3 vols.).
    Salary and Income Tax Book, 1868–70.
    Journal of Daily Receipts and Payments, 1879–98.

Separate Accounts
    Schedule of Fines, 1621.
    Engrossments of Parliament Rolls accounts, 1782, 1829.
    Copying accounts, 1783, 1784, 1804, 1806, 1807.
    Statements of Committee Fees, 1801, 1803, 1829.
    Enrolment of Acts accounts, 1834–44, 1854, 1855, 1857.
    Fee Fund Certificates, 1825–50 (except 1831–2), 1867, 1868, 1870.
    Fee Fund Accounts, 1828–60, 1919–31, 30 docs.
    Fee Fund Payments and Memoranda, 1830–45. There is a complete file for 1845; other files in this series are imperfect.
    Statement of Payments for the Bill concerning The Queen, 1832.
    Charges for Certificates to Ireland, 1814–31.
    Statements of sums assessed under the 1s. and 6d. Duty, 1835, 1846, 1867, 1874.
    Assessment Sheets for salaries of staff of H.L., etc., pursuant to 49 Geo. III, c. 32, s. 110, 1825–76.
    Staff Salary Lists, 1831, 1832, 1841, 1865, 1874.
    Refreshment Room Accounts, 1835–44.
    Library Accounts, 1843–5.
    Bills of Costs (Appeal Cases), 1894–1945, 1,650 docs.
(*See* also the Rose Papers in HISTORICAL COLLECTIONS, H.L.R.O.)

Letters and Memoranda Concerning Salaries and Fees, 1825–1902.

H.C. House Papers (Accounts), printed 1866–1909.
    Estimates for the Civil Services, 1866–1909, 43 vols.
    Appropriation Accounts (Civil Service and Revenue Departments), 1868–1908, 34 vols.

Income Tax Papers, 1876–1928.

Retired Officers Income Tax claim papers, 1919–23; original Commissioners assessment of duty on salaries, etc., 1876 (in duplicate); original Commissioners statement of sums assessed for House of Lords, 1876; misc. papers relating to Income Tax and Commissioners on Offices, 1892–1919; declaration of Commissioner on Offices, 1896; appointment of a Commissioner, 1870, 1874; Schedule E, Income Tax, returns, 1900–28, with charge duplicates, 1915–27; assessors' certificate of assessments, 1899–1927 with similar certificates for Pensions, 1927–8; accounts of balances and amounts of duty under Schedule E, 1899–1918.

General Parliament Office Administrative Papers

1610 to 1934   208 docs.

The series includes letters exchanged between members of the staff on office business; lists of lords who had taken or not taken the oath, 1610 (3), 1614 (1); 2 lists of creations, 1620; title deeds (12) of the house in Abingdon St., Westminster, purchased as an addition to the Parliament Office (1744–96); a narrative by Garter on the Heralds' College, 1767; a Letter Book concerning committee work, 1819–38; a group of 16 letters to or from J. Shaw-Lefevre, 1853–56; orders and memoranda concerning the destruction of petitions, 1902; and a bundle of 14 Office letters, 1927–34.

Parliament Office Book of Returns

1813 to 1849   1 vol.

'Returns respecting Appeals and Writs of Error and other matters from 1813.' The vol. includes analytical statistics and other returns for Appeals and Writs of Error, 1813–43; with returns of stages in Public Bills, 1843–4; of Railway Bills, 1836–44; of Private Bills, 1840–5; of Opposed Bills, 1844–5; of peers who have served on Opposed Committees, 1844–5; of Railway Bill Fees, 1846; of Railway Bill Capital, 1846; of Petitions, 1846; of stages in Railway Bills, etc., 1846–9; of Petitions relating to the Navigation Laws, 1849; of Appeals and Writs of Error, 1829–49; of Proxies, 1840–9, etc.

Officers' Personal Papers

1583 to 1902   95 docs.

The principal items in this series are: Deed to levy a fine, Appleford, Berks., Anthony Mason to Yate *et al.*, 1583; Will and Probate of Sir William Oldes, Black Rod, 1716; Marriage agreement for Ashley Cowper's daughter, Harriott, 1756; Jeremy Bentham's presentation copy to W. Courtenay of his Codification Proposal, 1827; Shaw-Lefevre memoranda, etc., including 62 papers relating to the Scotch Annuity Tax, 1810–49, 10 agreements for leases on Spencer Estate, 1821–37, Accounts of Tithe Collection, Wimbledon, 1838–43, with 2 of Lefevre's personal notebooks; Notes *c.* 1956 by Miss M. Edmond on biography of John Browne, with genealogical tree.

(*see* also BRAYE MANUSCRIPTS and SHAW-LEFEVRE PAPERS)

Books of Ceremonial, etc.

1950 to date

This series includes booklets, etc., relating to Visit of the President of the French Republic, 1950; Opening of the new House of Commons, 1950; Funeral of King George VI, 1952; Visit of General de Gaulle, 1960; Opening of the 7th Commonwealth Parliamentary Conference, 1961; 700th Anniversary of Simon de Montfort's Parliament, 1965.

Deposited Papers (Library)

1896 to 1909, 1937 to date   1,800 docs.

Ministers frequently make papers available in H.L. Library in order to supply peers with additional information concerning matters raised in debate or at Question time. When papers are deposited in H.C. Library for similar reasons, duplicate copies may also be placed in H.L. Library. The class opens with 89 plans (1896 to 1909) prepared by the Department of Mines, Canada, relating to the Geological Survey of Canada. It includes 340 items deposited in the Printed Paper Office, 1952–63, also for the use of peers.

USE. Access is as stated on p. 238.

LIST. MS lists are available.

House of Lords Reform Papers

1869 to 1952

The papers include Bills, memoranda, correspondence, and papers of the Bryce Conference, 1917–18; and Minutes of the Cabinet Committees on Reform, 1921–2, 1925–7.

LIST available in H.L.R.O.

USE. Papers less than 30 years old are restricted.

Journal Committee Papers

1767 to 1863   120 items

In 1767 H.L. ordered the printing of the Rolls of Parliament then extant and the Journals of H.L. The 6 volumes of Rolls were printed by 1783, the Index in 1832; the first 13 vols. of the Journals were printed by 1771, and from 1830 onwards (by which time 61 vols. had been printed) the Journals have been printed shortly after the proceedings they record. The publication of Rolls and Journals between 1767 and 1830 was supervised in some detail by committees and sub-committees of the House. The series of papers includes a file for 1767–77, 81 docs., constituting working papers relating to the initial editing and printing of Rolls and Journals; and subsequent sessional reports from the Journals Committee of intermittent dates to 1863.

Journal Office Papers

1825 to date   60 items

The principal constituents of this series are Accounts for preparation of Journals and Indexes, 1825–42, 28 docs.; Memoranda on work of Office, *c.* 1834–1862; Correspondence concerning preparation of Journals, 1835–52, 16 docs.; Register of Divisions in the House, 1850–51; Report from Select Committee on Minutes and Journals, with Evidence, 1857; Correspondence and Memoranda concerning the Roll of the Lords, Attendances, etc., 1928–58, 9 files.

Judicial Office Papers Relating to Appeals, Peerage Claims etc.

1657 to date   1,810 docs.

The principal items in this class are:

1. *Peerage Claim Papers,* 1657 to 1912, including Ratification of Constableship of Scotland, 1681; Earl Moray claim (brief), 1791; Grandison Peerage, Letters (3), 1836; Marchmont Peerage, Letters, etc. (3), 1838; Roscommon Peerage Petition, 1853; Tracy Peerage, Letters, 1853–4; Borthwick Peerage, Letters (2), 1912.

2. *Representative Peers Papers,* 1847 to 1869, including those concerning Election of Scottish Peers, 1847, 1850, 1857; Certificates of Returns of Scottish Peers, 1853, 1857; Expenses of Claims to vote by Scottish and Irish Peers, Report from Select Committee, 1856; Hawarden's Claim, Ireland, Evidence, 1857.

3. *Dignity of a Peer Papers,* 1816–19, relating to business of the Select Committee on the Dignity of a Peer, including Account of Fees for record searches, correspondence of Rt. Hon. G. Rose, and notes made from *Rolls of Parliament, Ingulph's Chronicle,* Selden's *Titles of Honour,* and other chronicles, statutes, etc.

4. *Appeal and Writ of Error Papers,* 1705–1943, including:

    General Topics: Unbound MS. vol. of Judgments, selected cases, 1689–1825; List of amended causes, 1703–1815; Precedents for arrest, 1719–1861; General precedents (36), *c.* 1750–1850; Summary of Appeal Cases, *c.* 1814–22; Return of Appeals, 1821; Writs of Error Precedents, 1842; Printed S.O.s on Writs of Error and Appeals, 1843; Minutes of Appeal Committee, 1880–93; Forms of Bills of Costs, 1962.

    Case Papers: Affidavits in cases, 1833; Questions to Judges, 1861; Original Opinions, 1796–1873; Judgments in Error, 1812–49; incidental letters and memoranda concerning cases, including 200 docs. for 1927–43.

5. *Trial of Peers Office Papers,* 1901, 1902; Letters and Marshalled Order of Peers for Trial of Earl Russell.

6. *Judicial Miscellaneous Papers,* 1819 to 1875, including letters relating to supply of printed Cases, 1819; Account of hearing of cases, 1824–43; statement of cases heard, 1844; Letters (8) concerning preparations of J. F. Macqueen's *Reports,* 1855–6; Return of appeals, 1869–74; Expenses of litigation, memorandum, n.d.; Precedents for attachment by Black Rod, n.d.; Return of Nautical Assessors, 1892–1957.

7. *Judicial Additional Papers,* 1768 to 1891, including Affidavits, 1825–91 (51); corr., 1836–85 (85); draft Judgments, 1831–49 (118); MS Opinions, 1840–52

(12); Orders of Service, 1828–47 (51); Petitions, 1828–48 (7); Tenors of Judgments, 1796–1849 (29); Wills, 1768, 1770 (2); Writs of Error, 1812–62 (17).

LIST available in H.L.R.O.

8. *Forms of Bills of Cost in H.L.*, in Appeal Cases, 1870–date, photographic copies in 2 vols.

Library Papers[1]

1834 to 1864   37 docs.

The class includes Reports from the Offices Committee on the Library, 1834 on; Memorandum concerning Books to be sent to the French Chamber of Peers, 1836; Library Accounts (6 docs.), 1846; Letters (7) concerning exchange of books with the French Senate, 1853–4, 1864; Letter and note concerning appointment of Assistant Librarian, 1845 and n.d.

Papers Relating to the Lord Great Chamberlain

1804 to date   18 docs.

The papers include a certified copy, 1804, of an Inspeximus of Grant of Office of Lord Great Chamberlain, 1 Hen. VIII.; Warrants for the preparation of Westminster Hall for the Coronation, 1821; coloured drawings of the throne, etc., 1830; Memorandum on interior arrangement of Chamber, 1844; Warrant of Lord Great Chamberlain for occupation of apartments assigned to Parliament Office, 1857; Regulations for State Opening or Proroguing, 1859, 1860; Letters concerning Secretaryship to the Lord Great Chamberlain and Use of Committee Room, 1871; Opening of Parliament, booklets of ceremonial, etc., 1966–.

See also printed vol. entitled *Extracts from the Journals and References to Entries relating to the Lord Great Chamberlain, the Gentleman Usher of the Black Rod, and to Repairs, Alterations, and Arrangements of the House, and the Maintenance of Order therein. c. 1832.* For the records of the Lord Great Chamberlain's office (1558–date), maintained in his own separate custody at the Palace of Westminster, *see* pp. 249–55 below.

PALACE OF WESTMINSTER

The mediaeval history of the structure of the Palace is summarised in R. Allen Brown, H. M. Colvin and A. J. Taylor, *The History of the King's Works*, vol. i (1963), ch. xii. The subsequent history of the Palace will be dealt with in later vols. of the *History*. A long sequence of sessional papers of the two Houses concerns the rebuilding after the fire of 1834 (*see* the annotated LIST in H.L.R.O.). *See* also the following:

A. Barry, *The Life and Works of Sir Charles Barry, R.A., F.R.S.* (1867).

---

[1] *See* C. Dobson, *The Library of the House of Lords* (1960) and also the Introduction, pp. 5–6 above, for the history of the H.L. Library. It is administered by a sub-committee of the H.L. Offices Committee.

E. W. Brayley and J. Britton, *The History of the Ancient Palace and late Houses of Parliament at Westminster* (1836).

I. M. Cooper, 'Westminster Hall' and 'The Meeting places of Parliament in the Ancient Palace of Westminster', *Journal of the British Archaeological Association* (1936 and 1938 respectively).

B. H. Fell, *The Houses of Parliament* (var. ed., 1930–date; current ed., K. R. Mackenzie).

H. T. Ryde, *Illustrations of the New Palace of Westminster* (1849).

J. T. Smith, *Antiquities of Westminster* (1807).

O. C. Williams, 'The Topography of the old House of Commons' (1953), photostat of typescript in H.L.R.O.

The contents of the Palace have been fully described by R. J. B. Walker, *Catalogue of Paintings, Drawings, Sculpture and Engravings in the Palace of Westminster*, 7 vols. (1959–67), with supplements of additions 1959–65, 1966–7, (1965, 1967) etc. [duplicated]; a set of these vols. is available in H.L.R.O.

The original papers and plans relating to the Palace are mainly preserved in the Public Record Office amongst the papers of the Office of Works. Collections of original plans and drawings are preserved amongst HISTORICAL COLLECTIONS (H. L. LIBRARY and H.L.R.O.). In addition, the following Parliament Office Papers relate to the fabric:

Palace of Westminster (Fabric Papers)

1835 to date   102 items

Reports of permanent accommodation in the New Houses of Parliament, 1835, (4); Plan of temporary building, 1835; Reports of Commissioners for Rebuilding, 1836, 1837; Ventilation, papers, 1841–2; New Houses of Parliament and Westminster Bridge, plans, 1844; Accommodation, gas lighting accounts, 1847–51; Copy of correspondence between the First Commissioner of Works and C. M. Barry, with plans, 1869; Plan of Chamber of House of Lords, 1850; Houses of Parliament Approaches, plans, 1866; Palace of Westminster, Floor Plans (4), 1881; Palace of Westminster, Plan of proposed alterations in House of Lords, 1883; Palace of Westminster, Index and Digest of Evidence taken before the Select Committee, House of Lords 1908; Houses of Parliament Thames Flood Protection Works, 3 plans, 1931; Report of Joint Select Committee on Accommodation, with Proceedings and Evidence, 1944; Reconstruction of Victoria Tower, Plans (42) 1948–61; Houses of Parliament Floor Plans (5) 1954; Memorandum on reconstructing the Victoria Tower by J. W. Worricker, architect, 1963; Plan of Palace of Westminster, showing division between the two Houses, 1965. *See* also *Extracts from the Journals . . .*, p. 189, above.

Palace of Westminster, Second World War Records (H.L.)

1939 to 1957   1,443 docs.

Four series of papers are preserved amongst the Parliament Office Papers which relate to aspects of the war-time administration of the Palace. Two complementary series are preserved in H.C. OFFICE RECORDS. The H.L. series are:

1. War-time administrative papers concerning air-raid precautions, establishment, evacuation, etc. 1939–44, 47 items.
2. Civil Defence Papers, 1940–57 including training memoranda, Treasury circulars, plans of area patrolled, 154 docs.
3. Palace of Westminster Fire-Watching Papers, 1939–46 (including establishment papers, paysheets, photographs), 1,116 docs.
4. Papers of the Air Raid Precautions Committee, Palace of Westminster, 1937–42 (including Minutes of meetings, instructions on admission to Palace, protection of Victoria Tower), 173 docs.

Palace of Westminster, War Memorial Vols. (H.L.)

1914 to 1918, 1939 to 1945   3 vols.

The vols. are of vellum leaves, engrossed and illuminated. They contain names, arms and biographical details concerning peers, lords of Parliament, officers of H.L., and their sons, killed in the first World War (2 vols.) and the second World War (1 vol.). The vols. are displayed in the Royal Gallery.

Parliament Rolls

1610, 1844, 1856   3 docs.

For the relation of the Chancery class of Parliament Rolls to the Original Acts, *see* p. 93. Robert Bowyer (Clerk, 1609–21) described the enrolment on the Parliament Rolls as being done by an under-clerk of the Petty Bag who could write the Chancery hand, 'at the request and appointment of the Clerk of the Parliament and at his charge'. The text was copied by the under-clerk from the black-letter vol. of statutes (which had itself been printed from the Original Acts); it was then checked by the Clerk of the Parliaments with the Original Acts, corrected, if necessary, subscribed by him, and transmitted to Chancery.

Draft engrossments, not transmitted to Chancery, are preserved in H.L.R.O. for 7 Ja. I, 7 & 8 Vict., and 19 & 20 Vict., respectively. That for 7 Ja. I is of the titles of Public and Private Acts only. Elsynge's draft for the Roll for 19–27 Feb. 1624 is Braye MS. 66.

H.L.R.O. also holds a set of *Rotuli Parliamentorum*; *ut et Petitiones et Placita in Parliamento*, 6 vols. and index, published in accordance with the Order of H.L., 9 March 1767.

Precedent and Procedural Papers

1620 to date   115 docs.

General office memoranda and volumes concerning procedure of the House, together with a few misc. letters relating to it. The series includes:

John Relfe's Journals. 4 vols. of categorised extracts from the Journals relating to procedure, compiled by Relfe, a clerk in the Parliament Office, 1660–1711. *See* also the Relfe Book of Orders amongst the HISTORICAL COLLECTIONS, H.L.R.O.

Precedent Book. Contains entries for 1510–1784, and was begun *c.* 1770. Much detail is included concerning, e.g. Speakers of H.L.; Breach of Privilege; Trial of Peers; Certification of Acts; refusal of Royal Assent, etc.

John Croft's Precedent Book. Croft was Clerk of the Journals, 1772–97. His book was maintained to 1847 and includes various forms of oath and certification.

Sir John Shaw-Lefevre's Notebooks. 1 vol. on the Clerk of the Parliaments Act, the Fee Fund, etc., 1825–46; 1 vol. on Joint Addresses, Lords Speaker, etc., n.d.; and 1 vol. Index of Introductions, Peerage Claims, etc., 1835–60.

Precedents concerning the Lord Speaker, 1826.

P. J. Redford's Precedent Book. Includes brief diary 1850–98, with entries to 1918.

[Augustus Pechell's] Notebooks. 2 vols., 1856 and 1857–63, relating to Bills, Proxies, Protests, Divisions, etc.

Working Papers of H. M. Burrows, Clerk in the Parliament Office, 1925–61, and Clerk Assistant, 1961–3, 15 boxes.

Clerk's MS. Manuals of Procedure, 2 vols., c. 1858–61.

Miscellaneous Papers include Precedent notes, 1621; form of oath for witnesses before a Joint Committee, c. 1644; a printed form of 'Prayers for the Parliament'; a proxy form, and other printed forms; a bundle of 18th c. precedents; an alphabetical list of precedents on procedure, c. 1810–48; precedents for the first days of Parliament; printed and typed forms of the Oath of Allegiance, 1936; forms of Prayers for Parliament, 1936–52; memo. on forms of Appellation, 1964.

Private Bill and Committee Office Papers

1767, 1819 to date   2,710 docs.

A misc. series, mainly concerning the passage of specific Estate and Railway Bills. The following docs. are included: 9 Proof Bills, 1767 (*see* p. 84 above); powers of attorney; letters concerning deposit of plans and papers; reports by Scottish and Irish Lords on Estate Bills; receipt for deposits, etc.; copies of Resolutions and Standing Orders (Railway Bills, 1837–47, Private Bills, 1859); certified copies of Parish Registers, 1847–63; regulations etc. concerning fees, 1855, 1856, 1888, 1936, 1955 and n.d.; regulations concerning deposits, 1858; letters concerning shorthand charges, 1866; correspondence with Light Railway Commissioners concerning taxation of bills of costs, 1901, 1902; notice to Parliamentary agents, 1902; register of Special Orders, 1925–36. The following precedents are also included; Private Bill procedure, c. 1842; Red precedent book on Divorce and other Private Bills, c. 1854; Divorce Bill precedents, n.d.; Taxation of Private Bills. A continuous sequence of papers, 1875–1947, includes Bills, corr. with agents, and estimates.

Public Bill Office Papers

1811 to 1921   255 docs.

A misc. series, of which 144 docs. relate principally to the Beer-house Act, 11 Geo. IV & 1 Will. IV, c. 64, including letters from magistrates and lords lieutenant from all parts of England and Wales. Other papers include 'Private and confidential remarks on the mode of preparing Bills in Parliament with a view to its alteration' (1837); texts, proofs and drafts of specific Bills; 10 original signed Memorials from Hull etc. concerning Herring measures (1849); Shaw-

Lefevre's arrangements for preparing Vellum Acts (*c.* 1850); Address to the Queen concerning Tynemouth election (1853); Petition of Guardians of the Poor for Chester (1854).

Papers Relating to Records, H.L. and the Record Office

1827 to date 136 docs.

A misc. series including the following: Statements of Payments for removing records at the time of the fire, 1834, and for storage of records in Westminster Hospital, 1838; Correspondence concerning storage of Parliamentary Papers under Bishops' room, 1837–8; Letter concerning charge for enrolment of Acts, 1859; Letter from Duffus Hardy concerning deposit of Parliament Rolls, 1868; Correspondence with the Treasury and the Historical Manuscripts Commission, and Memoranda, concerning calendaring, 1871–95; register of productions from the Victoria Tower, 1876–1948; Correspondence concerning storage of timber, etc., in Victoria Tower, 1902; Correspondence with the Royal Commission on Public Records, with memoranda and draft reports, 1912–14; Papers of H.L. Offices Sub-Committee on the care of the records, 1924; Applications to search, etc., 1928–30; Minutes, correspondence, etc. of the Clerk of the Parliaments' Committee on the care of the records, 1948–58.

Refreshment Department Papers

1905 to date 635 docs.

Corr. and accounts relating to administration of H.L. Refreshment Department including corr. relating to advertisements, 1905–53; Sample menu cards.

Stray Papers

1704 to 1934 115 docs.

These misc. papers have been preserved within the Parliament Office (*see* also the following class of Unpresented Papers). They include:

Lists of Fees taken in the Registrar's Office (Court of Chancery), and of the
  Six Clerks' Fees, *temp.* Eliz. I, 1704.
Account of pay for 4 troops of Horse Guards, *c.* 1719.
Secret Report concerning the South Sea Directors, 1720.
Probate of Will, Nicholas Sawyer, Bromyard, co. Herts., 1753.
Probate of Will, Elizabeth Wright, Mercers Court, Bower Street, London,
  1777.
Annual summary accounts of George Talbot, Treasurer of the King's House-
  hold, 1783–98, 1800, 1804.
Lease, M. Abercorn to John Cook of lands in Strabane, co. Tyrone, and
  elsewhere, 1807–26.
Grant to E. Spencer of Rugby to Hinckley Road tolls 1825.
Lease, V. Palmerston to S. Holland of premises in Festiniog, co. Merioneth,
  1826.
Papers concerning L. Holland's Ground Rents, 1826.
Rate Vouchers, Warwick Borough, 1831.
Rental of the Estates of E. Kenmare, cos. Kerry, Cork, Limerick, Kilkenny,
  Carlow and Queen's, 1831.

Lists of voters, St. Mary's, Warwick, constituency, 1 vol., *c.* 1832.

Warrants for affixing Great Seal to: Hon. W. Temple's powers as Envoy
to the two Sicilies, 1833; ratification of convention with the Netherlands,
1833; ratification and supplementary article to the Convention of 1832
with France, Russia and Bavaria, 1833; H. C. J. Hamilton's powers to
conclude a treaty with the Province of Rio de la Plata for the abolition of
Slavery, 1834.

Plans and Elevations of proposed new building at Buckingham Palace, 1847.

Letters Patent of Invention (motive power) to P. B. Kyishogloo, 1851.

Plan of Hyde Park Corner, 1882.

Plan of new public offices in Whitehall, 1882.

Drawings of chimneys, concerning boy sweepers, 10 items, n.d.

Unpresented Papers

1702 to 1703, 1791 to 1911   120 docs.

The following returns, petitions, etc. appear to have been prepared for the
use of the House, but are not noted in the Journals as having been presented.

The items dated 1702 to 1703 are 90 Lloyd's Lists of Ships' arrivals and
departures; other docs. refer to: Slave Trade (Accounts of Voyages of individual
ships) 1791, 1792; Dioceses of Killaloe and Kelfornora, 1811–22; Maintenance
of the poor in Scotland, 1824; Sufferance goods, 1825; Quebec Militia Ordinances, 1827; Co. Wexford constabulary, 1828; Roman Catholics of Pounshall,
co. Louth, *ante* 1829; Conduct of Sir Jonah Barrington *re* Case of the derelict,
Nancy (1805), 60 docs.; Moneys raised in co. Monaghan for roads, gaols etc.,
1842; Bank of England, 1844; War Office establishment, 1844; Consumption
of Spirits, 1800–45; Duty on Malt, 1847; Sittings in City of London Churches,
1849; the Roman Republic, 1849; Vivisection, 1890; Accession Oath, 1901;
Religious Statistics, 1901; the reform of the Second Chamber, 1911.

Whips

1909 to 1914, 1938 to date   6 boxes

An incomplete sequence of Whips is preserved. These include 5 sheets,
1909–14, which are copies of duplicated letters from the Leaders of the House,
drawing the attention of peers to specific pieces of business and requesting their
support. The remaining sheets are announcements of business issued by the
Chief Whips of the Parties to peers who 'receive the whip'. The earliest of these
is E. Waldegrave's four-lined whip for the 2a of the Finance Bill, 22 November
1909. Items of business may be underlined once, twice, thrice or exceptionally
four times, in order to emphasise the degree of importance to be attached to it.
Various general announcements, e.g. concerning visits or ceremonies, may also
be included in the Whip. The Whips to 1964 are mainly from the Government Party. Subsequently the other two Parties' Whips are substantially
represented.

USE. Permission is required to consult Whips less than 30 years old.

BIBLIOGRAPHY. J. C. Sainty, 'Leaders and Whips in the House of Lords, 1783–
1964', *House of Lords Record Office Memorandum no. 31* (1964).

RECORDS OF BLACK ROD'S DEPARTMENT

The office of Gentleman Usher of the Black Rod originated shortly after the foundation of the Order of the Garter. From at least 1361 ushers were appointed by Letters Patent 'to bear the rod' in processions of the Order in St. George's Chapel, Windsor Castle, and in spite of their title as ushers 'of the King's Chapel' they were officers of the Order of the Garter and not of the Chapel. In the Constitution of the Order of 1522–3 it was provided that the usher, besides 'carrying a Black Rod before the Sovereign' at Garter ceremonies, should also 'have the care and custody and pre-eminence of keeping all our secret chambers of the House where the [Garter] Chapter is held and all the doors where counsel shall be held as well in the High Court called Parliament as in any other places'. Black Rod thus became an officer of Parliament as well as of the Order.

Black Rod's Parliamentary duties were summarised in 1726 as including (i) constant attendance on the House of Lords; (ii) the carrying of the King's commands to the Commons to attend him in the House of Lords; (iii) participation in the ceremony of introducing lords into the House; (iv) employment at the order of the House concerning the commitment of delinquents. In addition, from 1700 at least Black Rod had the privilege of appointing a Yeoman Usher of the Black Rod and all doorkeepers, domestic staff and messengers of the House. Black Rod's control of domestic staff was transferred in 1876 to the Lord Great Chamberlain, leaving only the doorkeepers and messengers to Black Rod's control. In 1970, however, the control of 'the accommodation and Services' in H.L. was re-transferred to Black Rod, acting now as Agent for the Offices Committee. Whenever the House sits, Black Rod or the Yeoman Usher is present and controls the admission of strangers.

The Offices Committees (see pp. 182, 184 above) are always attended by Black Rod as well as by the Clerk of the Parliaments and the original full title of the Committee was 'on the Office of the Clerk of the Parliaments and the Office of the Gentleman Usher of the Black Rod'.

BIBLIOGRAPHY

E. Ashmole, *Institution . . . of the Most Noble Order of the Garter* (1672).

B. Horrocks, 'Gentleman Usher of the Black Rod', *The Table*, vol. xix (1951), pp. 128–31.

B. Horrocks, 'Black Rods, Maces and Serjeants at Arms', *The Table*, vol. xxiii (1954), pp. 49–54.

Report from the Select Committee, H.L., on *The Office of the Gentleman Usher of the Black Rod*. H.L. Sessional Paper, 1906 (140).

A List of Gentlemen Ushers of the Black Rod, by G. Royle, is printed in *Notes and Queries*, vol. cxciii (1948), pp. 96–7. *See* also further *fasti*, collected by J. C. Sainty for the Gentlemen Ushers and Yeomen Ushers, in H.L.R.O.

House of Lords Offices Committees (Parliament Office Papers)

See p. 184. *See* also *Extracts from the Journals* . . ., p. 189, above.

Black Rod's Appointment Book

1751 to 1824   1 vol.

The appointments noted are of Doorkeepers, Necessary women and Fire-makers.

Letter Book

1897 to 1935   1 vol.

Book for copies of letters, memoranda and other papers concerning Black Rod's Department.

See also p. 184, and other references to Black Rod in Index.

PART
TWO

RECORDS OF THE
HOUSE OF COMMONS

RECORDS OF THE HOUSE OF COMMONS

LIST OF CLASSES

	page
Records of Proceedings in the House of Commons	
Manuscript Journals, 1547–1800	207
Speaker Abbot's additions to the Journals, 1804	211
Printed Journals, 1547–date	211
General Indexes to Journals, 1547–date	212
Minutes of Proceedings	
Minute Books, 1851–date	212
The Commons Daily Issue of Papers	
Votes and Proceedings, 1680–date	213
Appendices to Votes and Proceedings, 1826–70	214
Supplement to Votes and Proceedings, 1836–date	214
Private Business, 1847–date	214
Notices of Motions, 1849–date	214
Division Lists, 1836–date	215
Public Bill Lists, 1890–date	216
Minutes of Proceedings (Standing Committees), 1883–date	216
Reports on Private Bills, 1930–date	216
Amendments to Private Bills, 1897–1931	216
Answers to Questions, 1902–15	216
Records of Debates	217
Sound Broadcasting Records, 1968	217
Records of Proceedings in Committees of the House of Commons	
Grand Committee Proceedings Books, 1621, 1625	219
Minutes of Proceedings in Committee of whole House, 1851–date	219
Select Committee Proceedings, 1689–date	219
Kitchen Committee Proceedings, 1848–date	220
Standing Committee Proceedings (Public Bills), 1883–date	220
Standing Committee Debates (Public Bills), 1919–date	220
Private Bill Committee Books, 1841–date	221
Joint Committee Proceedings Records	222
Records of the Committees on Public Petitions	
Reports of Committees on Public Petitions, 1833–date	222
Appendices to the Reports of the Committee on Public Petitions, 1834–date	222
Indexes (Public Petitions)	223

Evidence
  Secret Committee, 1835   223
  Private Bills, 1835–date   224
  Special Procedure Orders, 1948–date   224
  Courts of Referees, 1865–date   224
Committee Papers
  Select Committee on Fees Papers, 1732   225
  Select Committee Papers, 1934–date   225
Records of Bills, H.C.
  Public Bill Records
    Bill Records, 1563–1649   226
    Bound Sets of Prints of Bills, 1731–date   227
  Hybrid Bill Records, H.C.   227
  Private Bill Records, H.C.
    Original Bills, 1927–date   228
    Printed Bills   228
    Books of Reference, 1819–date   228
    Consents Lists, 1819–date   228
    Declarations, 1819–date   228
    Demolition Statements, 1874–date   229
    Departmental Reports, 1951–date   229
    Estimates of Expense, 1819–date   229
    Estimates of Time, 1819–date   229
    Examiners' Evidence, 1847–date   229
    Examiners' Reports, 1847–date   229
    Parliamentary Agent's Book of Fees, 1879–81   229
    Petitions (Private Bills), 1857–date   229
    Plans, 1819–date   229
    Registers of Bills, 1910–date   230
    Registers of Petitions on Bills, 1945–date   230
    Sections, 1819–date   230
    Subscription Contracts, 1819–58   230
    Subscription Lists, 1819–58   230
    Taxing Officer's Register, 1846–59   230
    Taxing Officer's Fee Books, 1847–1953   230
    Indexes to Committee Papers, 1835–1941   230
    Indexes to Private Bill Deposits, 1818–66   231
Sessional Papers, H.C.
  Unprinted Sessional Papers, 1850–date   232
  Cases Presented to H.C., 1712   233
  Bills and Cases in Parliament, etc. 1720–8   233
  First Series of Reports, 1715–1801   233
  Abbot Collection of Printed Papers, 1731–1800   234
  Parliamentary Collection, 1559–1740   234
  Bound Sessional Sets of Printed Papers, 1801–date   235

Department of the Speaker

Minutes of the Commissioners for regulating the Offices of the House of
    Commons, 1835–date   237

Small Classes, H.C.

Deposited Papers (Library), 1832–date   238
Election Return Books, 1835–date   238
Certificates of By Elections, 1935–59   238
Committee Records (Elections), 1826–53   239
Court Evidence (Disputed Elections), 1869–1906   239
Election Petitions Index, 1869–86   239
House Returns, 1931–date   240
Manuals of Procedure, 1857–date   240
Petitions (Preserved with Lords Papers), 1621–49   241
Public Petitions, 1951–date   241
Standing Orders, 1801–date   242
Test Rolls, 1835–date   242
Votes of Thanks, 1858–1964   242

Office Records, H.C.

Fee Records, 1812–1937   244
Precedent Books, 1544–1895   244
Journal Office Book of Statistics, 1880–1960   245
Public Bill Office Papers, 1838–1959   245
Palace of Westminster Second World War Records, 1940–61   246

Records of the Serjeant at Arms Department

Main Registers, 1788–1914   247
Account of the Office, 1803   248
Appointment and Order Book, 1804–1929   248
Letter and Memoranda Book, 1849–73   248

THE HOUSE OF COMMONS

In 1332 for the first time, so far as is known, the knights of the shire and the
representatives of cities and boroughs deliberated alone together. These two
groups, meeting together continuously, became known subsequently as 'les
communes'. The first record of a Clerk to be assigned to the Commons occurs in
1363 and the first reference to a Speaker of the House is in 1377. Membership of
the House was standardised so far as representation of the counties was concerned; each county returned two 'Knights of the Shire'. The number of towns
represented, however, varied considerably, ranging, for instance from 71 to 81 in
Henry IV's reign. Towns or cities were represented by two burgesses or citizens,
but the City of London was represented by four citizens, and each of the cinque
ports was represented by two 'Barons of the Cinque Ports'. Considerable

additions to borough representation were made in the 16th and 17th c. Some towns were added by royal charter, some by statute, while others petitioned for the revival of disused rights to elect members. Members were returned to represent Tournai in 1514, and Calais from 1536 to 1558. County representation was also extended. In 1536 the county of Monmouth gained the right to send two members, and each Welsh county the right to send one; and the counties palatine of Cheshire and Durham, in 1543 and 1673 respectively, began to return two members to each Parliament. Separate representation was granted to the Universities of Oxford and Cambridge for the first time in the Parliament of 1604. By the end of James I's reign the total membership of the Commons had reached 489.

The union of England with Scotland in 1707 added 30 members for the Scottish counties and 15 for the burghs; that with Ireland in 1800, 64 members for counties, 35 for towns, and 1 for Trinity College, Dublin. In 1801 the total membership of the Commons was 658; this figure rose to 707 in 1918, but after the loss of membership for Southern Ireland in 1920, and of separate representation for the Universities and for the City of London in 1949, it now stands at 630.

MEMBERS OF THE HOUSE OF COMMONS

(1) *Lists of Members*

A *Return of the Names of every Member returned to serve in each Parliament from the year 1696 up to the present Time...*, together with a Return *from so remote a Period as it can be obtained up to the year 1696 ...* was issued by order of H.C. It is arranged as follows (references are to H.C. Sessional Papers):

Part i, Parliaments of England, 1213–1702, H.C. 69 (1878), vol. lxii, pt. i
Part ii, Parliaments of Great Britain, 1705–96; Parliaments of the United Kingdom, 1801–74; Parliaments and Conventions of the Estates of Scotland, 1357–1707; Parliaments of Ireland, 1559–1800, H.C. 69-i (1878), vol. lxii, pt. ii
Part iii, Index, H.C. 69-ii (1878), vol. lxii, pt. iii

The following H.C. Sessional Papers list the membership for 1880–1929

Return of Names of Members returned to serve in each Parliament, 1880–85, H.C. 21 (1887, vol. lxvi)

Return ..., 1885 to ... 1900, H.C. 365 (1901, vol. lix)

Return ..., 1900 [to 1906], H.C., 334 (1908, vol. lxxxvii)

Return ..., 1906 [to 1910], H.C. 250 (1911, vol. lxii)

Return ..., 1911 [to 1918], H.C. 183 (1919, vol. xl)

Return ..., 1919 [to 1922], H.C. 97 (1923, vol. xix)

Return ..., 1922 [to 1923], H.C. 134 (1924, vol. xviii)

Return ..., 1924, H.C. 123 (1924–5, vol. xxii)

Return ..., 1924 [to 1929], H.C. 56 (1929–30, vol. xxiv)

(No similar returns have been published for later Parliaments.)

(2) *Lists of Membership (sessional, annual)*

See those vols. listed on p. 23 which deal with Members of H.C.; also, *Parliamentary Poll Book of all Elections*, ed. F. H. McCalmont, var. edd., 1879–1910 [for Members, 1832 on].

(3) *Biographies of Members*

History of Parliament, 1439–1509, 2 vols. (1936, 1938) includes biographies of Members. The post-war History of Parliament Trust has published 3 vols., *The House of Commons, 1754–1790* (1964) and 2 vols., *The House of Commons, 1715–1754* (1970), which include full biographies of Members, and the Trust plans to issue similar vols. for other periods.

Debrett's House of Commons and the Judicial Bench, annual, 1867–1931.

See also: *The Interim Report of the Committee on House of Commons Personnel and Politics, 1264–1832* (Cmd. 4130 (1932)), and the bibliography of biographies printed in *Handbook of British Chronology*, ed. F. M. Powicke and E. B. Fryde, 2nd ed. (1961), pp. xxx–xxxiii.

LISTS OF PARLIAMENTS

See pp. 23–4 above

GENERAL BIBLIOGRAPHY

The works noted here relate to the general history of the House of Commons. For similar works concerning Parliament as a whole and concerning the House of Lords see pp. 24–5.

J. G. Edwards, *The Commons in Medieval English Parliaments* (Creighton Lecture 1957) (1958).

H. L. Gray, *The Influence of the Commons on Early Legislation* (1932).

R. James, *An Introduction to the House of Commons* (1961).

K. B. McFarlane, 'Parliament and Bastard Feudalism', *Transactions of the Royal Historical Society*, 4th ser., vol. xxvi (1944).

M. McKisack, *The Parliamentary Representation of the English Boroughs during the Middle Ages* (1932).

Sir Lewis Namier and J. Brooke, *The History of Parliament: The House of Commons 1754–1790*, 3 vols. (1964).

J. E. Neale, *The Elizabethan House of Commons* (1949).

J. E. Neale, *Elizabeth I and Her Parliaments, 1559–1581* (1953).

J. E. Neale, *Elizabeth I and her Parliaments, 1584–1601* (1957).

W. Notestein, *The Winning of the Initiative by the House of Commons* (Raleigh Lecture) (1924).

D. Pasquet, *An Essay on the Origins of the House of Commons* (translated, R. G. D. Laffan, 1925).

E. and A. G. Porritt, *The Unreformed House of Commons: Parliamentary Represent- ation before 1862* (2 vols, 1903–9).

J. Roskell, *The Commons and their Speakers in English Parliaments, 1376–1523* (1965).

J. Roskell, 'Perspectives in English Parliamentary History', *Bulletin of the John Rylands Library*, vol. xlvi, pp. 448–75 (1964).

E. Taylor, *The House of Commons at Work* (6th ed., 1965).

H. R. Trevor-Roper, 'Oliver Cromwell and his Parliaments', in *Essays Pre- sented to Sir Lewis Namier*, ed. R. Pares and A. J. P. Taylor (1956).

R. G. Usher, 'The Institutional History of the House of Commons, 1547–1641', *Washington Univ. Studies*, vol. xi (1924), pp. 187–254.

RECORDS OF THE HOUSE OF COMMONS

No official records of proceedings in the Commons in the Middle Ages have survived. A few descriptions of proceedings which were compiled by private Members, however, are known. Documents such as Bills which were handled by the Commons, and therefore in some sense were records of that House, were not then preserved in the Commons own custody but passed eventually into the records of Chancery and are now preserved in the Public Record Office (*see Guide to the Contents of the Public Record Office*, vol. i). From 1497 onwards Bills engrossed in H.C. which ultimately received the Royal Assent became a con- stituent in the class of ORIGINAL ACTS preserved as records of H.L.

The earliest domestic Commons records still extant are the manuscript Journals (from 1547), the original Papers bound in the Journals (1603–10), Onslow's Journal in the Braye MSS. (1572) and the Papers and Journals mixed with the Lords records during the 17th c. and so preserved (1576–1689).[1] The bulk of the manuscript records of the House accumulating from the later 16th c. until 1834 were destroyed in the fire of 1834. The classes of records which have been preserved are listed above, pp. 199–201.

USE. The records of H.C. are in the custody of the Clerk of the House, except that the MS. Journals of the House are in the custody of Mr. Speaker, and the series of Bills, Papers, etc., ordered to be printed by the House (together with the unprinted papers) are in the care of the Librarian. With variations that are noted below all MS. records are open to inspection after thirty years, and printed records are open without restriction. All H.C. records available to the public may be consulted in H.L.R.O.

[1] To which may be added certain 17th c. office papers (*see* HISTORICAL COLLECTIONS H.C.). *See* also PETYT MSS. (BRITISH MUSEUM), p. 282

RECORDS OF PROCEEDINGS IN THE HOUSE OF COMMONS

The first surviving vol. of manuscript Journals, that for the years 1547–67, consists initially of lists 'of the Bills, when they were read in the Commons House', but subsequently it includes entries of Orders, Divisions and Licences of Departure, and, for the Parliament of 7 Ed. VI, it also comprises an account of the Opening. The second manuscript vol. (1571–81) is marked by further developments: membership of Committees is given, and in 1581 Reports and Motions are entered *in extenso*.

The Commons Journals have always been compiled by or on behalf of the Clerk of the House. The texts preserved in the official series fall into two distinct categories: (a) Journals written rapidly with many abbreviations, corrections and interlineations, presumably while business proceeded. These were known to the Clerks as 'Originals'; some are so rapidly written and so rough that they are similar to what in the Lords were described as 'Scribbled Books'; (b) neatly written Journals, compiled after the sitting. Between 1547 and 1646 there are neatly written texts for 1547–81 and for 1604, but the remaining vols. are rapidly written Journals. From 1646 onwards without exception the Journals are neatly written copies. Occasionally in the 17th c. original documents were annexed to the Journals (*see* below, p. 207).

It was customary for two, and subsequently three, Clerks to sit at the Table so that more than one 'original' or rapidly written Journal book may survive for a given period. No such originals exist for the neatly written Journals, although the Onslow Diary in the Braye MSS indicates the extensive annotation that Fulk Onslow probably made before compiling his fair copy Journal. At first during the 16th c. in H.C. as in H.L. the compilation of the Journal was left to the private initiative of the Clerk. Then, by stages, control came to be exercised by the House. From 1572 onwards the House occasionally ordered specific entries to be included, and from 1580 searches were made in the Journals for precedents. Hooker considered that the Speaker had the final responsibility to see that true records were made and kept. Then in 1607 authority was entrusted to the General Committee for Privileges, which was ordered 'to peruse and consider of such entries as are made by the Clerk in his Journal Book', and henceforth Sessional Committees were frequently appointed to inspect the Journals weekly.

Between 1547 and 1642 the production of the Journal was by either a single or a double stage process. The double stage was unvarying between 1642 and 1680. Within the following decade, however, a considerable development took place in the recording of the proceedings of the Commons. By 1690 it was normal for manuscript Minutes to be compiled during the sitting. Within a day or so a brief printed summary of *acta*, known as 'Votes and Proceedings of the House of Commons' was published. At about the same time a draft Journal was compiled, and this, after inspection, was rewritten as the definitive Journal; the double process had become quadruple.

The Clerk was ordered to keep the Journals in his personal custody but the Journals for the sessions between 1584 and 1601 were lost at some time before 1660. Much of their contents, however, had been included by Sir Simonds D'Ewes in his *Compleat Journal of the Votes, Speeches and Debates both of the House of Lords and House of Commons*, subsequently published in 1682.

The Commons Journals, unlike those of the Lords, were not regarded as a public record, and in 1666 the House ordered that only Members might consult them. In 1742 the Journals were ordered to be printed, though for the use of Members only, and from 1762 onwards the printing of the Journals continued under Sessional Orders (*see* PRINTED JOURNALS below), and in practice they then became available to the public.

Manuscript Journals continued to be kept as master-texts in spite of the publication of printed Journals, and the series was brought to an end only in 1833. The vols. for 1801–33, however, were lost in the fire of 1834, and the extant series of Manuscript Journals now finishes in 1800[1]. No printed versions have been kept under record conditions in continuation of the manuscript series, but a set of printed Commons Journals is available in H.L.R.O.

BIBLIOGRAPHY

H. Bellot, 'Parliamentary Printing, 1660–1837', *Bulletin of the Institute of Historical Research*, vol. xi (1933–4), pp. 85–98

A Bibliography of Parliamentary Debates of Great Britain. H.C. Library Document no. 2 (1956).

E. R. Foster, *Proceedings in Parliament 1610* (1966).

S. Lambert, 'Guides to Parliamentary Printing, 1696–1834', *Bulletin of the Institute of Historical Research*, vol. xxxviii (1965), pp. 111–17.

S. Lambert, *Printing for the House of Commons in the Eighteenth Century* (1968).

S. Lambert, 'The Clerks and Records of the House of Commons, 1600–1640', *Bulletin of the Institute of Historical Research*, vol. xliii (1970), pp. 215–31.

D. Menhennet, *The Journal of the British House of Commons*, H.C. Library Document no. 7 (1971).

J. E. Neale, 'The Commons' Journals of the Tudor Period', *Transactions of the Royal Historical Society*, 4th Series, vol. iii (1920), pp. 136–70.

W. Notestein, F. H. Relf, H. Simpson, *Commons Debates, 1621* (1935).

W. Notestein and F. H. Relf, *Commons Debates for 1629* (1921).

A. F. Pollard, 'The Under-Clerks and the Commons' Journals', *Bulletin of the Institute of Historical Research*, vol. xvi (1938–9), pp. 144–67; and 'Queen Elizabeth's Under-Clerks and their Commons' Journals', *ibid.*, vol. xvii (1939–40), pp. 1–12.

Report from the Select Committee, H.C. 31 May 1742, *C.J.* xxiv, pp. 263–6.

Report from the Select Committee on Votes and Proceedings, H.C. 156 (1817), vol. iii, pp. 47–68.

Report from the Select Committee on Publication of Printed Papers, H.C. 286 (1837), vol. xiii, pp. 97–201.

[1] It is likely that a duplicate set of manuscript Commons Journals was also lost in the fire of 1834. This set originated from a report of a Select Committee in 1698 which criticised the worn and ill-written character of the original Journals.

Report from the Select Committee on Publications and Debates, H.C. 321 (1914–16), vol. iv, pp. 655–779.

For works on procedure, H.C., *see* BIBLIOGRAPHY, pp. 63–4 above, and the following:

Abraham and Hawtrey's Parliamentary Dictionary, 3rd. ed., ed. S. C. Hawtrey and H. M. Barclay (1970).

C. J. Boulton, 'Recent Developments in House of Commons Procedure' [1964–70], *Parliamentary Affairs*, vol. xxiii (1969–70), pp. 61–71.

Lord Campion, *An Introduction to the Procedure of the House of Commons*, 3rd ed. (1958).

S. Lambert, *Bills and Acts: Legislative procedure in eighteenth century England* (1971).

J. Redlich, *The Procedure of the House of Commons*, trans. A. E. Steinthal, 3 vols. (1908).

P. D. G. Thomas, *The House of Commons in the Eighteenth Century* (1971).

Manuscript Journals

1547 to 1800   241 vols.

See plate 13

The vols. are in manuscript; they are bound in a uniform blue morocco binding with gold lettering which dates from 1742 onwards. The vols. to 1640 have in the main been composed of a greater number of paper volumes of slightly varying dimensions. The present numbering from 1 to 241 is of 20th c. date. Certain vols. have indexes which appear to be mainly contemporary.

List of Journals, 1547–1660, with present enumeration

Vol. 1.   8 Nov. 1547–2 Jan. 1567. Rough notes on fly leaves. Lettered as 'SEIMOUR'.

Vol. 2.   5 April 1571–17 March 1581. Two neatly written vols. bound as one. Lettered as 'ONSLOWE'.

Vol. 3.   8 March–6 July 1604. Neatly written vol., 49 original docs. bound in (List available), parallel to no. 4.

Vol. 4.   19 March 1604–7 July 1604. Composed of 7 original roughly written books, each with a title, parallel to no. 3.

Vol. 5.   5 Nov. 1605–26 May 1606. Composed of 4 original vols.

Vol. 6.   18 Nov. 1606–5 July 1607. 2 original vols., parallel to no. 7. Rough notes on fly leaves.

Vol. 7.   22 Nov. 1606–5 July 1607. 20 original docs. bound in (List available), parallel to no. 6. Additional entries relating to this Parliament at end by Charles Abbot, Speaker, 1804, comprising extracts from Robert Bowyer's diary, formerly belonging to William Williams, Speaker, 1680–1.

Vol. 8.   9 Feb. 1610–22 July 1610. Notes on fly leaves. 3 original docs. bound in.[1]

[1] Cf. the more finished Journal for 1610, Petyt MS. 537/14, in the Inner Temple Library.

Vol. 9.   5 April 1614–6 June 1614. 2 original books. Rough notes on fly leaves.

Vol. 10. 5 Feb. 1621–22 Nov. 1621 (so lettered, but includes entries for 16, 30 Jan., 3 Feb. and 23, 24 Nov. 1621). Several original vols. Defective in places, e.g. for entries of 22–24 Nov.

Vol. 11. 26 Nov. 1621–18 Dec. 1621.

Vol. 12. 12 Feb. 1624–17 March 1624, parallel to no. 13.

Vol. 13. 19 Feb. 1624–29 May 1624, parallel to nos. 12, 14. Several original vols.

Vol. 14. 21 April 1624–29 May 1624, parallel to no. 13.

Vol. 15. 21 June 1625–11 Aug. 1625.

Vol. 16. 7 Feb. 1626–23 March 1626.

Vol. 17. 7 March 1626–15 June 1626. Imperfect at beginning.

Vol. 18. 17 March 1628–26 June 1628.

Vol. 19. 20 Jan. 1629–2 March 1629.

Vol. 20. 13 April 1640–26 June 1641. Notes on fly leaf include prayer said in the House. Indexes bound at end relating to 'Orders in Generall', and 'Reports' (entries missing for 'A').

Vol. 21. 28 June 1641–30 Dec. 1641 (so lettered, in fact to 3 Jan. 1642).

Vol. 22. 4 Jan. 1642–9 April 1642, including entry concerning the attempted arrest of five Members.

Vol. 23. 11 April 1642–8 Sept. 1642.

Vol. 24. 9 Sept. 1642–14 March 1643. Indexes bound at end.

Vol. 25. 15 March 1643–28 Sept. 1643. 1 doc. bound in; analysis of sittings 20 July–14 Aug. at end struck through. Indexes.

Vol. 26. 29 Sept. 1643–21 May 1644. 1 doc. bound in. Indexes.

Vol. 27. 22 May 1644–24 Dec. 1644. Indexes.

Vol. 28. 26 Dec. 1644–15 Aug. 1645. Indexes.

Vol. 29. 27 March 1646–4 Dec. 1646. Three pp. with deleted entries for 4 Sept. 1646 at front. Indexes.

Vol. 30. 5 Dec. 1646–2 July 1647. Indexes.

Vol. 31. 3 July 1647–9 Feb. 1648. Indexes.

Vol. 32. 10 Feb. 1648–1 Sept. 1648. Indexes.

Vol. 33. 2 Sept. 1648–13 June 1649. 2 printed Ordinances bound in. Indexes. Many entries deleted, and not subsequently printed.

Vol. 34. 14 June 1649–25 June 1650. Indexes.

Vol. 35. 26 June 1650–14 Aug. 1651. Indexes.

Vol. 36. 15 Aug. 1651–26 Aug. 1652. Indexes.

Vol. 37. 27 Aug. 1652–23 Dec. 1652.

Vol. 38. 24 Dec. 1652–19 April 1653.

Vol. 39. 5 July 1653–26 Oct. 1653, but with preliminary entry for 4 July.

Vol. 40. 27 Oct. 1653–12 Dec. 1653.

Vol. 41. 3 Sept. 1654–20 Jan. 1655. Index.

Vol. 42. 17 Sept. 1656–27 Dec. 1656. Index.

Vol. 43. 30 Dec. 1656–28 April 1657.

Vol. 44. 29 April 1657–20 Jan. 1658. Index.
Vol. 45. 20 Jan. 1658–4 Feb. 1658. Index.
Vol. 46. 27 Jan. 1659–22 April 1659.
Vol. 47. 7 May 1659–18 July 1659.
Vol. 48. 19 July 1659–30 Sept. 1659.
Vol. 49. 1 Oct. 1659–18 Feb. 1660.
Vol. 50. 21 Feb. 1660–16 March 1660.

Note that the present vol. 84, lettered as 'Journal of the Assembly', for Dec. 1688, was left unnumbered when the series was rebound in 1742.

Contents

As procedure in the House and practice in preparing the Journal evolved, considerable variation in the contents of the vols. occurred. In general, however, the following principal types of entry may be found:

Preliminary matter. Entries concerning a new Parliament (or, where appropriate, a new session) may be preluded by texts of Proclamations of dissolution, of Writs of prorogation, and of appointments by the Lord Steward of deputations to administer oaths (that for 1714 is the original Commission).

Opening of Parliament. At the Opening of a new Parliament (or session) some or all of the following entries may be found, spread over several days and arranged in a varying order: delivery of Certificates of those returned as Members; subscription of oath or affirmation by Members; reading of a Bill 1a *pro forma*; message to attend the King or Lords Commissioners; report of Speech from the Throne (or by L. Chancellor, etc.), text *in extenso*; consideration of King's Speech, with Address and Answer *in extenso*; election of the Speaker and Royal approbation, with report of the Speaker's claim to privileges; motions for the issue of new writs; the making of sessional orders and the appointment of committees.

Legislative Business. The stages in the progress of every Bill are noted. When the Bill is committed the names of members of the committee are given unless the composition of the committee (e.g. of a Standing Committee) has already been recorded. Where specific amendments are under consideration (e.g. on Report, or after 1829, in C.W.H., or on Lords amendments) the texts of the amendments may be given. Until 1849–50 these texts are specified in relation to the membranes or 'presses' of the engrossed Bill; thereafter in relation to the printed House Bill.

Divisions. Divisions are recorded for both legislative and other business, the names of the Tellers as well as the number of votes cast usually being given, but without listing those voting (for which *see* DIVISIONS below, p. 215). The earliest divisions recorded are those in 1604. Divisions in C.W.H. are given from 1829 onwards.

Committees. Until 1829 the only entries relating to committees consisted of the appointment of committees, instructions given to them and the Reports from committees. The entries of Reports often contain the complete texts of the Reports, including on occasion very full accounts of amendments to Bills, speeches by Members, general arguments, or sometimes practically verbatim Evidence given in committee. In the absence of any separate class of H.C. committee records surviving for the 18th c. these full reports are of considerable value. From the 18th c. printed surviving Sessional Papers may include Minutes of Evidence given in committee (*see* also COMMITTEE RECORDS below, p. 223). From 1829 onwards, the Journals also contain minutes of proceedings in C.W.H.

Accounts and Papers. Accounts and other papers may be presented to the House as a result of its own Order, as a result of Address to the Crown, by Command of the Sovereign, or in compliance with Acts of Parliament. The delivery of these Papers is recorded in the Journal together with the names of the individuals delivering them, and the Order that they lie on the Table, be printed, be referred to a Committee, etc. (*see* SESSIONAL PAPERS). In the 17th and 18th c. some papers were entered in the Journal *in extenso* when they were laid, and the Commons Journals for this period (to a greater extent than the Lords Journals) provide important detailed information concerning national finance, the Army and Navy, treaties, foreign trade, etc. Between 1801 and 1834 the more substantial papers were printed in the Appendix to the Journal. After 1834 the practice of including full texts of papers practically ended. Since 1801 all papers ordered to be printed are available in the bound official sets of Commons *Sessional Papers.*

Motions, Orders and Resolutions. The full texts of Motions, Orders and Resolutions are given. Speeches were briefly noted between 1581 and 1628; thereafter the House rejected 'the Entry of the Clerk, of particular Mens speeches', apart from those from the Throne, etc., at the Opening. For speeches *see* PARLIA-MENTARY DEBATES, above, pp. 36-9.

Miscellaneous. From 1571 onwards Petitions to the House are entered and from 1607 some are given *in extenso*. Those of post-1660 date concerning Disputed Elections are almost invariably *in extenso* or nearly so, as are many petitions for leave to introduce canal, railway and similar Bills in the 18th and 19th c.

What are now described as 'Public Petitions' were entered either in full or in summary until 1833 but thereafter they were either briefly listed or were noted as (e.g.) 'Several Public Petitions presented and read' with a reference to the appropriate *Report of the Committee on Public Petitions* (*see* pp. 222 below).

Entries relating to Conferences with the Lords include the Order appointing Members to confer, and the Report by those Members, sometimes giving considerable detail as to proceedings. In 19th and 20th c., Private Bill entries include the registration of Certificates that Standing Orders have or have not been complied with, and Reports from the Examiners.

Omissions and Vacations. The 17th and 18th c. manuscript Journals sometimes left space for the later inclusion of complete texts (e.g. of Reports), which the clerks then failed to enter. The printed Journals indicate these omissions by asterisks. Certain entries which were subsequently ordered by the House to be erased are similarly represented by asterisks in the printed Journals but can usually be deciphered in the manuscript Journals. The entries for 6–17 March 1679 were made in 1804 by Speaker Abbot from a MS. of Speaker Williams. (*See* below; and for other MS. Journals of the Commons *see* pp. 279-80, 295 below.)

Speaker Abbot's additions to the Journals

c. 1804   1 vol.

The volume contains the texts of material Abbot found to be missing in the Manuscript Journal[1] which could be supplied from other sources: (i) the Protestation of 20 June 1604; (ii) extracts taken from Speaker Williams's copy of Bowyer's diary for 2, 19 June and 3 July 1607; (iii) Speech by E. Salisbury to both Houses, 1609; (iv) full Journal entries for 6–17 March 1679. Abbot also entered (i) and (iv) in the appropriate Manuscript Journals. The text of (iv) is largely included under the relevant dates in Anchitell Grey, *Debates of the House of Commons*, vol. vi (1769).

Printed Journals

1547 to 1761   28 vols.

The House resolved in 1742 that the Journals should be printed, and by 1762 the Journals to date had been printed in 28 vols. In that year a reprint of vols. 1–14 with Indexes was ordered. Subsequent reprints included a complete reprint of vols. 1–58 by Luke Hansard between 1803 and 1825. In 1836 the format of the vols. was changed to a smaller size, and in the same year the Journals began to be on sale to the public. Each printed vol. was provided with an index. Vol. i included the texts of the two manuscript versions for 19 March 1604 to 5 July 1607 printed *seriatim*, the second entitled 'Diarium'; the parallel text for 21 June to 8 July 1625 was published separately and is not usually found in Library sets of Journals. A more accurate text has been published in vol. xi of the *Calendar* of Lords Manuscripts.

Capital letters, punctuation and paragraphing are very largely the work of the editors. Until 1628 practically all side-headings are editorial; from then on, the side-headings may be contemporary, subsequent, or editorial. The texts follow the originals quite faithfully, although inexplicable and irrelevant entries (e.g. a list of references to earlier Journals) may be totally omitted, vital entries (e.g. for 21, 24 May 1625) may also be omitted, misplaced items are transposed without editorial comment, and duplicated matter ignored. Any entry deleted in the original is omitted, and this may be of importance as, for instance, when lists of committee members have clearly been altered from those chosen initially. From about 1642 onwards, however, the printed Journals in general follow the manuscript original accurately. *Students are recommended in cases of doubt, and particularly for the period 1547–1642, to consult the original Manuscript Journals in addition to the printed Journals.*

1762 to date   195 vols.

These volumes have generally been printed concurrently with the proceedings which they record and have been delivered during the following session or shortly after.

---

[1] As also in the printed Journals.

15—R.O.P.

General Indexes to Journals

1547 to date   16 vols.

General Indexes were first ordered by the House in 1766, and then at several subsequent dates until, from 1880 onwards, the printing and publication of indexes prepared by the Journal Office became the invariable practice. In 1852 Th. Vardon and Erskine May prepared a revised edition of the original Index, separately compiled in 3 vols. covering 1547–1714. The vols. of Indexes now generally available are as follows:

1547–1714 (Vardon & May's revision of the 3 original Indexes for 1547–1659; 1660–1697; and 1697–1714 respectively); 1714–1774 (Edward Moore's); 1774–1800 (a revision of the original separate Indexes for 1774–1790, 1790–1800); 1801–1820; 1820–1837; 1837–1852; 1852–1865; 1866–1879; 1880–1890, 1890–1900, and thereafter decennial to the latest vol., 1950–51 to 1959–60.

The Indexes give extensive cross-references and employ elaborate classifications under main headings such as 'Committees', 'Elections', 'Privileges'.

The classified lists of 'Accounts and Papers' to 1920 are of particular importance as a guide to SESSIONAL PAPERS, H.C. The Indexes in general provide the normal starting point for research relating to the Commons.

MINUTES OF PROCEEDINGS

The Journals and (from 1680) the Votes and Proceedings have been compiled from Minutes made by Clerks at the Table. Certain of these Minute Books between 1604 and 1642 have since been preserved as part of the series of Manuscript Journals (*see* pp. 207–8 above). The return made by Arthur Benson, Clerk of the Journals, to the Select Committee on Public Records in 1800 stated that he had then in his custody 'The original Books of Minutes, taken at the Table of the House, since the year 1685; and also, Books of Minutes taken before Committees of the Whole House, from the year 1688–89 to the present time.' These and later Minute Books were destroyed in the fire of 1834. Most Minute Books since that date, with the exception of those noted below, were destroyed as part of the salvage drive between 1939 and 1945.

Minute Books

1851 to 1902 (various dates), 1921, 1936 to date   97 vols.

The vols. comprise brief entries of the business of the House, or of C.W.H., either in manuscript or in pasted-in prints from order papers, etc. The vols. are of interest to the specialist in procedure but do not contain entries other than those subsequently entered in the Votes or the Journals. The vols. of House Minutes usually are endorsed with the name of the Clerk. The early vols. are as follows: 1851, Committee of the Whole House; 1861, Mr. May and Mr. Ley, 2 vols.; 1867–8, Sir Erskine May; 1868–9, Mr. Palgrave; 1895, Mr. Milman; 1898, Mr. Jenkinson; 1902, Mr. Nicholson, Mr. Webster, 2 vols.

THE COMMONS DAILY ISSUE OF PAPERS

From 1641 the private and domestic record of proceedings in the Journal was occasionally supplemented by shorter printed and published records known as 'Votes'. Such publications were only issued when some important matter was under debate which the House wished to communicate to the public. In 1680, however, a practically continuous series of published daily Votes begins. Its inception was probably due to the desire of the House to make known the action being taken concerning the Popish Plot. Although no Votes were issued for James II's Parliaments, thereafter each day's sitting has been followed almost immediately by the issue of printed 'Votes and Proceedings'. Their text has been based on the Minute Books of the Clerks at the Table, and the Votes then serve as the outline for the Journal. Although the main text of the Votes is similar to that of the Journals the Votes are of importance in several ways. From 1819 onwards additional material concerning the programme of forthcoming business is printed which is not otherwise available. The bound set of Votes in H.L.R.O. includes also, from 1680 to 1802, Parliamentary material which is not directly related to the text of the Commons Votes, described below. From 1826 onwards various ancillary classes of printed papers begin to be issued, either to deal more fully with matters previous briefly mentioned in the Votes, or to treat new topics (such as Divisions) on which daily information is needed. The entire set of daily papers which has thus evolved from the original class of Votes is sometimes known as 'The Vote'. The separate classes are numbered below, 1 to 11.

1. Votes and Proceedings

1680 to date   292 vols.

See plate 16

The unvarying contents of the Votes are the texts of Royal Speeches, of Addresses to the Sovereign and Answers, the Orders and Resolutions of the House, and brief entries of Petitions and Papers presented to it. In addition between 1742 and 1817 the full texts of Petitions may be given (usually in an appendix). The first vol. of the Votes preserved in H.L.R.O. comprises a single issue for 21–30 Oct. 1680, and separate issues for daily sittings from 1 Nov. 1680 to 28 May 1681. The vol. also includes the Speech of the King, 21 March 1681, the Debates at Oxford, 21, 28 March 1681, and the Address of the House, 21 Dec. 1680. The second vol., for 1689, comprises (a) a MS. 8 pp. index; (b) 355 pp. MS. minutes of proceedings with reports *in extenso*, etc., for 22 Jan.–20 Aug. 1689; (c) the printed votes for 18 Feb. 1689–27 Jan. 1690; (d) 4 pp. additional MS. notes for 1 Feb.–19 April 1689.

Throughout the 18th c. vols., printed Reports from committees may be bound in the official set, and from 1735 to 1802 manuscript sheets summarising day by day proceedings in H.L. are also bound in *seriatim*.

From 1819 to 1849, at the end of each issue of the Votes, there are printed Notices of forthcoming Motions and Orders of the Day for one or more subsequent sittings. Certain 18th c. vols. contain Indexes, and MS. Indexes have been preserved in the Journal Office from 1939.

From 1818 onwards each session's Votes conclude with an appendix in which appear the texts of Addresses, of certain papers laid on the Table, and of many Petitions. This appendix may be bound separately from 1826 onwards (*see* below). *See* also p. 299.

2. Appendices to Votes and Proceedings

1826 to 1870   27 vols.

These vols. contain Petitions, at first on a wide variety of matters, but after 1833 mainly relating to Disputed Elections.

3. Supplement to Votes and Proceedings

1836 to date   214 vols.

Certain supplementary material, e.g. departmental reports, had been printed in vols. of the Votes between 1800 and 1836, but from 1836 the 'supplement' forms a distinct series. Vols. may include some or all of the following matters: Lists of Applications for Private Bills, Summaries of Election Petitions, Alphabetical Lists of Members to serve on Election Committees, Panels for Election Committees, Election Petition Notices, Rules concerning the presentation of Public Petitions, Motions, Amendments and Clauses to be proposed in Committees on Public Bills, Reports from Private Bill Committees, Extracts from Minutes of Evidence taken in Private Bill Committees. The contents of the Supplement today are confined to (1) Amendments to Public Bills set down for consideration on the current day in C.W.H. or on Report; with Notices, given on the previous day, of amendments to the above stages of bills to be considered on a future day; (2) The Amendment Papers of Public Bills under consideration on the current day in a Standing Committee, with Notices as in (1), together with the Reports from Private Bill Committees, and Division Lists, as noted below.

4. Private Business

1847 to date   121 vols.

Notices relating to Private Bills are circulated with Votes and Proceedings. From 1836 to 1847 they were bound in the vols. of SUPPLEMENT TO VOTES AND PROCEEDINGS. Subsequently they have been preserved as a separate category, one vol. being bound for each session. The contents include: Notices given by Parliamentary Agents at the Private Bill Office; lists of Printed Breviates laid on the Table (to 1850); Notices of Private Business for the next day's sitting, including times and places of Committees; Appointments of Committees on Private Bills; and a periodical List of Petitions for Private Bills and Proceedings thereupon. The last named provides dates of presentation of petitions, of 1a, 2a, 3a, and of Royal Assent. For detailed work on private legislation these vols. provide information not always available in the Journals.

5. Notices of Motions

1849 to date   350 vols.

This series of printed vols. contains the daily papers circulated with Votes and Proceedings giving information to Members concerning forthcoming business (other than that on Private Bills). Over the period the main contents have varied slightly, but include: Notices of Motions and of Questions for the day of issue; Orders of the Day for that day; lists of Sessional Printed Papers delivered to the House; lists of Public Committees for the day with hour and place of meeting; lists of Notices given on that day for future days. (Weekly consolidated lists of Notices and Orders of the Day 'which now stand in the Order Book' are also issued.) The series of vols. of Notices includes materials of importance—such as Questions that subsequently were not asked, and certain Motions for which no day, or an 'early day' has been fixed—that are not recorded either in the Journal or in the *Debates*, together with other arrangements for business which subsequently for various reasons may be altered.

The information contained in the Notices (which have always been printed on blue paper) is also contained, so far as it is still correct and relevant, on each day's order paper, printed on white paper and known as the Order Book. Daily printing of the Order Book began in 1856 and weekly circulation in 1865. No bound series of these papers has been formed and they are not included in annual sets of the Vote.

6. Division Lists

1836 to date   132 vols.

The mediaeval practice of voting in the Commons seems to have been that Members shouted Aye or No and their voices were 'weighed' by the Speaker. During the 16th c. (perhaps in about 1550) the House, although continuing to vote by voice in the first instance, began also to divide when it seemed necessary, the Noes staying in St. Stephen's Hall, the Ayes going into the ante-room, and each being counted. The earliest reference to a 'division' is in 1554. The system by which both sides leave the Chamber began in 1836, and the official recording of names also began in that year. Until 1906 Members present at a sitting were compelled under penalty to take part in every Division; abstention was not allowed.

From 1604 onwards the numbers of those voting on either side may be recorded in the Journals of the House (with tellers' names being given from 1607). Although they were not officially available until 1836, the names of those participating in Divisions were often recorded unofficially and may be recovered from private diaries and correspondence, printed manifestos, etc. A number of division lists have been recently printed or listed, notably those for the period after 1688 in the *Bulletin of the Institute of Historical Research* (cf. vols. xiv, pp. 25–36; xix, pp. 1–24, 65–6; xxx, pp. 101–2; xxxiii, pp. 223–34. *See* also Special Supplement, no. 7 (1968)). Others may occasionally be recovered from the *Parliamentary History* or from *Parliamentary Debates* (though sometimes, e.g., as a 'List of the Minority').

Each vol. in the bound series of Division Lists preserved at Westminster consists of the printed sheets for each division. These record the terms of the Question *in extenso*, and the lists of Ayes and Noes, with Tellers. Certain of these lists may also be found in *Parliamentary Debates*, but complete publication of lists in the *Debates* dates only from 1909.

BIBLIOGRAPHY. J. G. Edwards, 'The Emergence of Majority Rule in the procedure of the House of Commons', *Transactions of the Royal Historical Society*, 5th series, vol. 15 (1965), pp. 165–87.

7. Public Bills Lists

1890 to date   67 vols.

Lists are circulated weekly of all Public Bills introduced since the beginning of the session. These indicate whether the Bills are Government Bills or not, the name of the Member bringing the Bill in, and its progress to date. Similar information is given concerning Provisional Order Bills, Confirmation Bills under the Private Legislation Procedure (Scotland) Acts, 1899, etc. Lists are also appended of Bills committed or referred to Standing Committees, together with a note of their progress. Sets of these Lists may be bound together with Reports from the Committee on Public Petitions and Reports from Committees on Private Bills. The same vols. also include Lists of Members entering for the Ballot for Bills and the Results of the Ballot for Bills for the session.

8. Minutes of Proceedings (Standing Committees)

1883 to date   81 vols.

By resolution of 1 Dec. 1882 two Standing Committees for the consideration respectively of Bills relating to law and courts of justice, and of Bills relating to trade, shipping and manufacture were established. In 1888 Bills relating to agriculture and fishing were ordered to be deemed Bills relating to trade. These Standing Committees continued to be appointed until the session of 1907, when amended standing orders provided for the appointment of four Standing Committees to consider such Bills as might be committed to them.

The bound vols. contain Minutes of Proceedings (with lists of those present and division lists) and prints of clauses as amended by the Standing Committees and of new clauses adopted by them.

These papers are reprinted at the conclusion of the consideration of each Bill and published as SESSIONAL PAPERS.

9. Reports on Private Bills

1930 to date   32 vols.

This series consists of a bound set of Reports from Committees on Private Bills, with relevant appendices, e.g. specifying the manner in which the clauses relating to certain regulations had been dealt with. The most recent Reports have been bound with Reports from the Committee on Public Petitions and with Public Bills Lists.

10. Amendments to Private Bills

1897 to 1931   30 vols.

These are bound sets of papers which give the texts of Amendments which have been made in the Lords to Private Bills originating in the Commons. References are to pages of the issued texts of the Private Bills.

11. Answers to Questions

1902 to 1915   26 vols.

Questions to Ministers were printed on the Order Paper from 1835, and from 1886 notice had to be given of all Questions. Both the Questions and

Answers to them might be recorded in *Parliamentary Debates*, but this was not invariable until 1909. (Thereafter Questions for Oral Answer, Answers and supplementaries appear *in extenso* in *Debates*, as do Questions for Written Answer with the Answers.)

The vols. contain the texts *in extenso* of Questions with their Answers where no Oral Answers were desired, and Questions and Answers printed and circulated with the Votes under the then S.O. no. 9.

BIBLIOGRAPHY. D. N. Chester and N. Bowring, *Questions in Parliament* (1962).

RECORDS OF DEBATES

For Records of Debates in H.C., *see* pp. 36–9 above (H.L. Section).

Sound Broadcasting Records, H.C.

H.C. conducted an experiment in sound broadcasting, 23 April–16 May 1968, during which time a complete tape was made of proceedings in the House, and varied types of edited programmes were prepared. 284 reels of tape recording of the experiment are preserved in H.L.R.O.

USE. The use of this material is restricted.

BIBLIOGRAPHY

1st Report from Sel. Com. on Broadcasting, etc. of Proceedings in the House of Commons, H.C. Sess. Paper, 1965–6 (146).

Special Report . . ., H.C. Sess. Paper, 1965–6 (111).

9th Report from the Sel. Com. on House of Commons (Services), H.C. Sess. Paper, 1967–8 (448).

RECORDS OF PROCEEDINGS IN COMMITTEES OF THE HOUSE OF COMMONS

By at least the mid-16th c. it was customary for Bills to be referred (or 'committed') to one or more members if amendments were thought necessary. Between 1558 and 1625 the number, frequency and range of subject matter of such committees greatly increased. Three principal types of committee emerged: the Select Committee (Sel. Com.), the Committee of the whole House (C.W.H.) and the Joint Committee of the two Houses (Jt. Com.). Select Committees consist of Members named in the House in order to consider specific matters; they report back to the House and after reporting are then dissolved. By the mid-18th c. there were four main classes of business likely to be sent to a Sel. Com.: the consideration of Petitions; the drawing up of heads for proposed Bills; the consideration of the text of a specific Bill (usually after 2a); and the consideration of Papers presented to the House. With the increase in the number and complexity of Private Bills after 1794, Sel. Coms. appointed to deal with the texts of Private Bills were guided by a particularly complex system of standing orders, and Private Bill Committees were in consequence treated by Erskine May (from 1844 onwards) as a distinct class of committee.

A Standing Committee is a Sel. Com. which continues throughout a session. The most important Standing Committee in the 17th and 18th c. was the Committee for Privileges and Elections. In 1883 the House began to make use of Standing Committees for the consideration of Public Bills, an individual Bill being allocated to a committee already in being instead of (as had been previously normal) to a specially chosen committee. Since 1907 all Public Bills except those dealing with finance, or confirming Provisional Orders, have been automatically referred to a Standing Committee, unless the House decides otherwise. Certain Select Committees, re-appointed every session, are today known as Sessional Committees: those active in the 20th c. have been the Public Accounts Committee (first appointed in 1861); the Committee of Selection; the Standing Orders Committee; the Estimates Committee (first appointed in 1912); the Committee of Privileges (which has taken the place of the earlier Committee for Privileges and Elections); the Public Petitions Committee; the Publications and Debates Reports Committee; the Kitchen and Refreshment Rooms Committee; the Statutory Instruments Committee; the Nationalized Industries Committee; and the House of Commons Services Committee.

The Committee of the whole House originated in 1607 and the procedure customary today was quickly established. The Speaker leaves the Chair; a Member (now usually the Chairman or Deputy Chairman of Ways and Means or one of the temporary Chairmen) takes his place; and the rule of order that Members may normally only speak once to a Question is waived (as it also is in Select Committees). C.W.H. became an important part of the working of the House after the Restoration, and an extra degree of secrecy and freedom attached to its debates in that until 1829 its proceedings were not reported in the Journals. Between 1621 and 1832 'Grand Committees' were regularly appointed, which were in fact C.W.H., in order to deal respectively with matters relating to Religion, Grievances, and Courts of Justice, but by the early 18th c. such Grand Committees had ceased to conduct any business. C.W.H. might be appointed to consider Bills at their committee stage; and also to deal with general business, especially financial, (with a special title such as Committee of Supply, or Committee of Ways and Means).

Joint Committees of the two Houses sat frequently between 1603 and 1695. They then fell into abeyance until 1864, since when they have been frequently appointed. Procedure follows that of a Lords Sel. Com. where the two Houses differ. In the 17th c. the Commons appointed double the number of representatives of the Lords, but since 1864 the numbers have been equal. Reports are made to both Houses, and Minutes of Proceedings may be ordered to be published, which then appear in bound vols. of *Sessional Papers*.

This elaborate system of Commons Committees is not today represented by extensive records for the earliest period. Books of Evidence seem to have been preserved in the Commons from 1736 onwards, but these, together with nearly all the clerks' Committee Books, were destroyed in the fire of 1834. Surviving Committee Books are listed below.

Grand Committee Proceedings Books

1621, 1625   2 vols.

These vols. are preserved amongst the Lords MSS. That for 19 Feb.–2 March 1621 has been printed *in extenso* in W. Notestein *et al.*, *Commons Debates 1621*, vol. vi (1935), pp. 249–78. That for 23 June–8 Aug. 1625 has been printed in the *Calendar*, vol. xi (Addenda), pp. 204–7.

Minutes of Proceedings in Committees of the whole House

1851, 1920 to date   50 vols.

A sample original minute book compiled by the Clerk Assistant was preserved for the period 7 Feb.–12 July 1851. Similar minute books for 1920 onwards are preserved in the care of the Clerk of the Journals. From 1829 to date minutes have been printed in the Commons Journals.

Select Committee Proceedings

For the Minutes of the Committee of Secrecy enquiring into the conduct of E. Orford, 1742, see p. 284, below.

Minutes of the Committee on the London Merchants Petition, 1689, have survived out of custody (*see* Hofmann and Freeman, *Catalogue* no. 25 (1968), item 58) and a clerk's Minute Book has also been preserved, out of custody, for the period 3 Dec. 1697–3 May 1699 (Rawlinson A.86 in the Bodleian Library, Oxford); the text has been printed *in extenso* by Dr. Orlo Williams, 'The Minute Book of James Courthorpe', *Camden Miscellany*, vol xx. It includes proceedings on some 64 Public and Private Bills. Minutes of the Committee on the State of Gaols, 1730, are preserved in the British Museum (Stowe 373).

The following MS. Committee Books of *post-*1834 date are preserved in H.L.R.O. in addition to the Private Bill Committee Books noted below, pp. 221–2.

1865 to 1878   12 vols.

This series includes Minutes of Proceedings with, in most cases, either the full Minutes of Evidence or a summary of the Evidence. The types of Committee represented are: Select Committees on Public Bills (41 committees); Hybrid Bill Committees (28); Private Bill Committees (9); Provisional Order Bill Committees (15); Committees for drawing up reasons for disagreeing to Lords Amendments (2).

LIST. A typed list is available in H.L.R.O.

PRINTED VERSIONS. Minutes of Select Committees have with increasing frequency become available in print. After 1801 it was customary for the House to order the Minutes of Proceedings in the Sel. Coms. on Elections to be printed, together with the Reports of such committees and Evidence given before them. This practice was then followed for other types of committee, e.g. for those dealing with important Public Bills. Such printed Minutes become frequent after 1860, and normal practice after 1900. Today it is customary when the work of each Sel. Com. is complete, or when an interim report is required, for the Report to be printed by order of the House together with Minutes of Proceedings, verbatim Evidence, and, where necessary, illustrative memoranda and other papers.

Kitchen Committee Proceedings

1848 to date   15 vols.

Records of the Select Committees on Kitchens have been preserved as follows: Report and Minutes of Evidence, 1848; Minutes of Proceedings, 1895 to date.

Standing Committee Proceedings (Public Bills)

1883 to date

All Standing Committees have leave to print and circulate with the Votes the Minutes of their proceedings and any amended clauses of Bills committed to them. At the conclusion of the consideration of each Bill these are reprinted and published as *Sessional Papers* (*see* SUPPLEMENT TO VOTES and SESSIONAL PAPERS).

Since 1968 the Public Bill Office has also issued lists of Amendments with decisions on each.

Standing Committee Debates (Public Bills)

1919 to date   134 vols.

No *verbatim* reports of debates in Standing Committees were made at first, although debates on Part II of the National Insurance Bill, 1911, were included in the appropriate vol. of the H.C. *Parliamentary Debates*. In 1919 a printed series of reports began, but the decision to include any particular debate within it was left to the Speaker or the Committee itself. Subsequently it became the usual practice to publish an official report of any debate on a government bill, and since 1945 debates on unofficial Members' Bills have also been printed.

The vols. are similar to the main series of *Parliamentary Debates* (see pp. 38–9) and contain *verbatim* proceedings in Committees. Each vol. is indexed for each Bill by speakers and clauses.

1926 to 1933   2 vols.

Typescript copies, bound into 2 vols., are preserved of debates in Standing Committees on the following matters:

1926–7   Diseases of Animals Bill (Lords).
           Wild Birds Protection Bill.
1927–8   Destructive Insects and Pests Bill.
           Stabilisation of Easter Bill.
           Rating (Scotland) Amendment Bill.
           Petroleum Amendment Bill
           Rubber Industry Bill.
           Administration of Justice Bill (Lords).
           Registration (Births, Deaths and Marriages) Bill.
           Public Rights of Way Bill.
           Merchant Shipping (Line-Throwing Appliance) Bill.
           Rag Flock Act (1911) Amendment Bill.
1928–9   Appellate Jurisdiction Bill
           Superannuation Diplomatic Service Bill.
           Overseas Trade Bill.
           Reconstituted Cream Bill.
           Fire Brigade Pensions Bill.
           Police Magistrates Superannuation (Amendment) Bill.
           Salmon and Freshwater Fisheries (Amendment) Bill
1929–30 Arbitration (Foreign Awards) Bill.
           Children (Employment Abroad) Bill (Lords).
1930–1   Metropolitan Police (Staff Superannuation & Police Fund) Bill.
           Colonial Naval Defence Bill (Lords).
           Ancient Monuments Bill (Lords).
           Marriage (Prohibited Degrees of Relationship) Bill.
1931–2   Universities (Scotland) Bill (Lords).
           Rights of Way Bill.
           Public Health (Cleansing of Shell Fish) Bill.
           Marriage (Naval, Military and Air Force Chapels) Bill (Lords).
           Gas Undertakings Bill (Lords).
           Rating and Valuation (No. 2) Bill (Lords)
1932–3   Visiting Forces (British Commonwealth) Bill (Lords).
           Assurance Companies (Winding Up) Bill (Lords).
           False Oaths (Scotland) Bill.
           Cotton Industry Bill.
           Protection of Birds Bill (Lords).

Private Bill Committee Books

1841 to date   176 vols.

The Minute Books of Private Bill Committees consist of the individual minute sheets for each day's sitting on a Private Bill bound, not always in the correct chronological order, to form a sessional vol. The entries vary somewhat but always include the names of Chairman and members present, a statement of business done, members of the public called in, witnesses heard, decisions on each clause, amendment, proviso, etc. Sometimes the clerk adds explanatory matter, e.g. concerning an adjournment; he may also bind up copies of papers relating to such matters as areas of land to be inclosed. The Committee Books include information sometimes lacking in the vols. of Evidence.

JOINT COMMITTEE PROCEEDINGS RECORDS

See JOURNALS, H.C. and JOINT COMMITTEE RECORDS (above, pp. 207–12; 57).

RECORDS OF THE COMMITTEES ON PUBLIC PETITIONS

The records of Public Petitions to 1833 include a few Original Petitions of the 17th c. which are preserved with H.L. Main Papers and listed in the *Calendar* (*see* p. 241 below). In addition, all Petitions are noted in the Journals, in Votes and Proceedings and in Appendices to the Votes. Since 1833 Petitions, having been presented to the House, are then usually ordered to lie on the Table and be referred to the Committee on Public Petitions. Motions have sometimes been permitted and carried for the printing of the entire text with the Votes; but normally all Petitions are referred to the Committee, under whose directions they are classified, analysed, and, when necessary, printed at length. Three series of vols. concerning Public Petitions since 1833 have been bound and placed with the bound set of Votes: (1) Reports of the Committee; (2) Appendices to the Reports; (3) Indexes.

Reports of the Committees on Public Petitions

1833 to date   202 vols.

The Reports indicate the place of origin of each Petition, the number of signatures, its general object, and the total number of Petitions and signatures referring to each subject. The name of the Member presenting the Petition is also given.

A second set of 162 vols., 1833 to 1920, formed by the Clerk of the Journals, includes certain items missing from the main set.

Appendices to the Reports of the Committees on Public Petitions

1834 to date   63 vols. (to 1896)

In the Appendices the full texts of certain Petitions are printed 'whenever the peculiar arguments and facts, or general importance, of a Petition require it', though from 1834–9 the texts printed are, in fact, summaries. From the

17th Report onwards the total numbers of signatories are given, but the names of not more than the first three signatories. Since 1934 only the names of single first signatories to individual Petitions are given. Between 1897 and 1916 Reports and Appendices were bound together in the main set. After 1916 the number of Petitions selected for printing never exceeded 10 *per annum*. From 1933 the Appendix has been printed at the end of the Report.

Indexes (Public Petitions)

Sessional Indexes are bound with the Reports to 1932. Those for 1833–52 were cumulated and issued in the main series of Parliamentary Papers: H.C. 1854–5 (531). Sessional Indexes are bound with the Appendices from 1849 to 1928. See also PUBLIC PETITIONS, with appended BIBLIOGRAPHY, below, pp. 240–1.

EVIDENCE

The Commons, since at least the 16th c., have exercised the right to summon witnesses to give evidence, either at the Bar of the House or in committees. An order was signed by the Clerk of the House for a named person to attend; when he did so questions were put to him either by the Speaker or by Members. Witnesses examined before an Election Committee were summoned, before the appointment of the committee, by a Speaker's warrant, or, after its appointment, by the Chairman's signed order. Private Bill witnesses have usually appeared by voluntary arrangement with the promoters and opposers, but if any order to attend is disobeyed the House makes an order for the witness to be sent for in the custody of the Serjeant at Arms. H.C., unlike H.L., did not possess the right to administer oaths to witnesses, and so in the 17th c. it selected Members who were justices of the peace to administer oaths; it sent witnesses to be examined by a judge; or it had witnesses sworn at the Bar of H.L. or examined in a Joint Committee. After 1757 these and other devices to enable oaths to be administered were abandoned[1] and false evidence was treated as a breach of privilege and not as perjury. The Parliamentary Witnesses Oath Act, 1871, 34 & 35 Vict., c. 83, empowered the House and its committees to administer oaths to witnesses.

It became increasingly customary during the 19th c. for the House to order some or all of the Evidence on Public Bills and other matters given before Select Committees to be printed. It usually appeared in the same vol. as the Report of the Committee and might be accompanied by Minutes of Proceedings and selected papers. *See* SESSIONAL PAPERS.

Book of Evidence (Secret Committee)

1835   1 vol.

Verbatim evidence given before the Sel. Com. on Orange Lodges, 20 and 30 July 1835, with original letters, memos., etc., bound in.

[1] Except that by Act evidence before Election Committees was taken under the sanction of an oath.

Books of Evidence (Private Bills)

1835 to 1899, 1901   3,156 vols.

Two series of vols. of Private Bill Evidence are extant; the first of these (in H.L.R.O.) ranging in date from 1835 to 1901 consists of longhand transcripts of each day's evidence on each Bill bound in sequence. The vols. are arranged alphabetically by the short titles of Bills (or sometimes by Committees dealing with Groups of Bills) session by session. Each day's transcript usually opens with the names of the Chairman, the Parliamentary Agents and the Counsel. Proceedings other than the hearing of evidence, e.g. the reading of Petitions, may be noted. It can be assumed that evidence is preserved for every Bill that was opposed in H.C. (evidence was not normally heard on unopposed Bills). Only a single vol. is preserved for 1901.

1903 to date   427 vols.

The second series of Books of Evidence (preserved in the Committee Office, H.C.) consists of similar material, but is printed, typed or duplicated, and is entitled 'Printed Evidence on Opposed Bills'. From 1941 onwards the vols. of typed evidence from which this set is prepared are preserved in H.L.R.O.

Books of Evidence (Special Procedure Orders)

1948 to date   8 vols.

Similar books of evidence are preserved for Select Committees on Special Procedure Orders (cf. the previous entry).

Books of Evidence (Courts of Referees)

1865 to date   365 vols.

Since 1854 Courts of Referees have been appointed in H.C., when necessary, to enquire into the right of petitioners to be heard before a committee or into other matters referred to them. Thus the referees might enquire into the engineering details of all works proposed to be constructed, the efficiency of such works and the sufficiency of the estimate, as also into other particulars in the case of waterworks and gas Bills. The referees have consisted of the Chairman of Ways and Means, the Deputy Chairman and other members, originally three, now at least nine, appointed by the Speaker. The procedure of the Court is similar to that of a Private Bill Committee. Reports are made to the House, and these are then referred to the Select Committee on the Bill.

The Books of Evidence are very similar to those containing Sel. Com. Evidence and contain verbatim evidence given before the Courts. They are in manuscript to 1920, and from then on, typed.

COMMITTEE PAPERS

No separate files of original Committee Papers were preserved until 1934. The post-1939 files are not as yet available to students.

Select Committee on Fees Papers

1732   1 doc.

A transcript is preserved amongst the Parliament Office Papers of the Report of the Sel. Com. on Fees and Salaries of the Servants of the House of Commons, with abstracts of the papers laid before the Com. which were presented with the Report to the House. The H.C. material is for the most part printed by Orlo Williams as app. iv. of his *Clerical Organisation of the House of Commons, 1661–1850* (1954).

Select Committee Papers

1934 to date   2,638 files

The papers include Chairman's corr., briefs and other notes; circulars; corr. with government departments, Members and the public; unprinted memoranda and evidence; draft reports; MS. minutes of evidence and of proceedings, etc.

RECORDS OF BILLS, HOUSE OF COMMONS

Procedure in both Houses on Bills has been described above, pp. 59–62. The Bill records surviving in H.C. *c.* 1733 consisted of Paper Bills from 1558; Engrossed Bills from 1621 (together with three of the reign of Elizabeth I); files of Breviates, Amendments and Provisoes; and Ordinances of the inter-regnum period. The whole of this material was destroyed in the fire of 1834 and, as a consequence, pre-1834 Commons Bill records consist merely of (a) a few early papers which had by accident been preserved among the Lords records and (b) printed versions of Bills, accounts, reports, etc., surviving either at Westminster or elsewhere, some of which have subsequently been formed into bound series. The post-1834 Bill records consist to a large extent of printed and published material.

It should be observed that as the pre-1850 engrossments of Commons Bills and the post-1850 Commons Bills have normally been sent to H.L., they will, unless subsequently returned to H.C. and retained by that House, be preserved amongst H.L. records as ORIGINAL ACTS, ENGROSSED BILLS or HOUSE BILLS.

PUBLIC BILL RECORDS, HOUSE OF COMMONS

For Records of Proceedings on Public Bills in H.C., 1547 to date, *see*:

JOURNALS OF THE HOUSE, 1547 to date, pp. 207–12 above.

MINUTE BOOKS, 1851 to date, p. 212 above.

The relevant sections of the Vote:

VOTES AND PROCEEDINGS, 1680 to date, pp. 213–14 above.

SUPPLEMENT TO THE VOTES, 1836 to date, p. 214 above.

PUBLIC BILL LISTS, 1890 to date, p. 216 above.

STANDING COMMITTEE PROCEEDINGS, 1883–1905, pp. 220–1 above.

RECORDS OF DEBATES, pp. 36–9 above.

COMMITTEE RECORDS, 1621, 1625, 1851 to date, p. 219 above.

PRINTED EVIDENCE, 1801 to date, p. 223 above.

Bill Records (Preserved with Lords Records)

1563 to 1649

A number of Paper Bills are preserved amongst the Main Papers, H.L., and calendared as 'Draft of an Act', etc. These may sometimes be identified as Commons Bills, and the *Calendar* references in these cases are to *C.J.* and not to

L.J. Lists of the Commons committees on the Bills were frequently annexed to the Paper Bills.

Bound Sets of Prints of Bills

1731 to 1800 963 items

Four sets of printed Papers, including printed Bills, were put together on the instructions of Charles Abbot, Speaker, in 1807 from the stocks then existing. The four sets differed slightly (*see* p. 234 below). That in H.C. Library includes 30 vols. of Bills, mainly post-1750. The early years are represented as follows: 1731 (1), 1739 (4), 1740 (1), 1741 (1), 1742 (5), 1743 (6). Many other separate prints for the 18th c. are available elsewhere (cf. Sheila Lambert, *List of House of Commons Sessional Papers, 1701–1750* (1968)). The British Museum holds prints for 1641 (1), 1702 (1), 1704 (2) and thereafter in gradually increasing quantities.

1801 to date

From 1801 onwards Public Bills printed by order of the House have been arranged to form one of the four groups of Sessional Papers. The prints may be of a Bill after 1a; as amended in Committee; as amended after re-commitment; as amended on Report; as amended after 3a, etc. Each text is assigned a number, an amended text having a different number from that of the first print. Clauses proposed to be added, amended clauses as accepted, Lords amendments, Lords amendments with reasons, etc., may all be ordered to be printed separately, and be assigned separate printing numbers. The names of those who prepared and brought in the Bill are given on the dorse. Until *c.* 1830 references are given in the text to folios of the 'written copy', i.e. the official Table Bill, but thereafter clauses are numbered and sub-headed; *c.* 1878 it became customary to prefix a list of contents or 'arrangement of Clauses' to the Bill. From 1882 an explanatory memorandum may be prefixed. All Public Bills have been printed since 1800, with the exception of certain Supply Bills and Mutiny Bills.

The Lords and Commons Libraries each holds a complete series of the printed and bound Commons Public Bills for 1801 to date. For indexes see the *General Index to the Bills printed by the Order of the House of Commons 1801 1852* (1853) and the entries in the Indexes of *Sessional Papers* issued subsequently (*see* p. 236). Copies of individual prints or groups of prints, as well as further sets of the bound Bills, may be consulted in the British Museum and other public libraries.

HYBRID BILL RECORDS, HOUSE OF COMMONS

See H.L. section, above, p. 69.

PRIVATE BILL RECORDS, HOUSE OF COMMONS

See the descriptions of procedure and categories of Bills, pp. 70–82 above.

For Records of Proceedings on Private Bills in H.C., 1547 to date, *see*:

JOURNALS OF THE HOUSE, 1547 to date, pp. 207–12 above.

MINUTE BOOKS, 1851 to date, p. 212 above.

The relevant sections of the Vote:

VOTES AND PROCEEDINGS, 1680 to date, pp. 213–14 above.

PRIVATE BUSINESS, 1847 to date, p. 214 above.

REPORTS ON PRIVATE BILLS, 1930 to date, p. 216 above.

AMENDMENTS TO PRIVATE BILLS, 1897 to 1931, p. 216 above.

RECORDS OF DEBATES, pp. 36–9 above.

Committee Records:

COMMITTEE BOOKS, 1865 to 1878, p. 220 above.

PRIVATE BILL COMMITTEE BOOKS, 1841 to date, pp. 221–2 above.

BOOKS OF EVIDENCE (PRIVATE BILLS), 1835 to 1899 and 1901 to date, p. 224 above.

BOOKS OF EVIDENCE (COURTS OF REFEREES), 1865 to date, p. 224 above.

For general descriptions of classes of Private Bill Records, H.C., *see* the section on PRIVATE BILL RECORDS, H.L., pp. 83–92 above, as the records of the two Houses are similar in character. For BIBLIOGRAPHY *see* pp. 72–3 above.

Bills (Original)

1927–9, 1939 to date

The original Bills preserved for 1927–9 are 'House Bills', the official interleaved copies used in H.C. The main constituents of the series for 1939 onwards are Filled Bills, i.e. prints of Bills in the form in which they are to be submitted to the committee; and Committee Bills, i.e. prints on which the amendments made in committee are written, signed by the Chairman of the Committee.

Bills (Printed)

No official set of printed Private Bills has been formed, but the sets of printed Private Bills formed by the Lords and Commons Libraries respectively may contain prints of Commons Bills. (See p. 84.)

Books of Reference

1819 to date

Consents Lists

1819 to date

Declarations

1819 to date

Demolition Statements

1874 to date

Departmental Reports

1951 to date

The Departmental Reports (from e.g. the Board of Trade, the Home Office etc.) are in typescript. They may include those made to H.L., as well as to H.C., amended in MS. where necessary in consequence of alterations made in the first House. They have been bound in vols. entitled 'Reports on Private Bills', which include (i) the printed *Reports on Private Bills* (*see* THE COMMONS DAILY ISSUE OF PAPERS), preceded by a typescript index, and (ii) printed lists of Plans, etc. deposited in respect of Private Bills, of Applications for Private Bills, and of Private Bills listed according to the House of origin.

Estimates of Expense

1819 to date

Estimates of Time

1819 to date

Examiners' Evidence

1847 to date

Examiners' Reports

1847 to date

Parliamentary Agent's Book of Fees

1879–81   1 vol.

The fee book is that of Messrs. Merrick and Co., Parliamentary Agents; it includes daily entries for agency work, with fees charged to clients. It was probably produced as an exhibit before the Taxing Officer.

Petitions (Private Bills)

1857 to date

This class consists of the originating Petitions for Private Bills, and Petitions for additional provisions, from 1857, with petitions against from 1941. The series is fragmentary to 1904, but from then on, continuous. The Petitions for are usually handwritten on parchment; those against, handwritten, typed or printed.

Plans

1819 to date

This series is complementary to the Lords Plans; many Plans identical with those in H.L. were destroyed in 1904, but deposits missing in H.L. may often be found here. It is therefore advisable to consult both series.

Registers of Bills

1910 to date   72 vols.

The vols. contain full entries of the stages in the passage of each Private Bill through H.C.

Registers of Petitions on Bills

1945 to date   18 vols.

The vols. contain lists of Bills with dates of the presentation of Petitions concerning them, and summaries of subsequent proceedings.

Sections

1819 to date

Subscription Contracts

1819 to 1858

Subscription Lists

1819 to 1858

Taxing Officer's Register

1846 to 1859   1 vol.

The Costs on Private Bills Act, 1825, 6 Geo. IV, c. 123, and subsequent Acts have regulated the taxation of costs incurred by suitors in Parliament. In each House a clerk is appointed taxing officer with power to examine parties and witnesses on oath and to call for production of books or writings. Erskine May notes that 'Any person upon whom a demand is made by a parliamentary agent or solicitor for any costs incurred in respect of any proceedings in the House, or in complying with its standing orders, may apply to the taxing officer for the taxation of such costs'. Similarly, the agents may so apply. Taxation may take place in one House for all proceedings in both Houses. The register contains details of the fees and costs paid and allowed.

Taxing Officer's Fee Books

1847 to 1953   5 vols.

The vols. contain summary entries of fees paid for taxation and of the agents paying them.

Indexes to Committee Papers (Private Bills)

1835 to 1941   9 vols.

The Indexes provide contemporary sessional guides to the papers then preserved in the Committee Office. Vol. 1, for 1835–45, is in MS. and includes lists of Petitions, Bills, etc. as deposited with clerks (who are named), with references to relevant Minute books and Evidence books. Vols. 2–9, for 1846–

1941, comprise the bound Indexes to Committee Office Papers which were also issued as part of the Vote (*see* p. 214 above). They give details of every stage in the progress of a Bill, and, to 1899, include reference to the relevant Minute books and Evidence books. The vol. for 1900–41 is entitled 'Private Bill Proceedings, H.C.' and does not list Committee papers.

Indexes to Private Bill Deposits

 1818 to 1866   3 vols.

 The vols. contain indexes of deposited plans and other papers. They indicate those papers 1818–34 which survived the fire of 1834, and those now extant.

The papers delivered to H.C. are very similar to those delivered to H.L. and they derive from similar sources (*see* SESSIONAL PAPERS, H.L. above, pp. 127–35, for a general description). The H.C. Papers may be divided into the following principal classes:

1. Returns, made in response to the desire of the House expressed in an Order, or made pursuant to an Address by the House to the Crown.
2. Command Papers, presented by command of the Sovereign.
3. Act Papers, i.e. papers required by Act of Parliament to be laid before H.C.
4. Papers presented pursuant to a Standing Order; to a Resolution of the House; to the Report of a Select Committee; or to a Church Assembly Measure.
5. Papers laid pursuant to subsidiary legislation, *see* p. 219 above.
6. Petitions, *see* pp. 240–1 below.
7. Private Bill Papers, *see* pp. 228–31 above.
8. Public Bill Papers, *see* pp. 226–7 above.

Classes 1–4 constitute the documents described below in this section; for the remaining classes 5–8 the reader is referred to the pages of this *Guide* shown in the table above.

A catalogue of Commons Papers made *c.* 1733[1] showed that at that time Bill Papers were being preserved from 1558; Petitions from 1607; and Returns from 'the usurped times' (*sc.* 1642). These series were maintained continuously until 1834 when the entire accumulation was destroyed in the fire. The present series of manuscript Sessional Papers dates only from 1850. Very many of the earlier Sessional Papers have, however, survived in printed form. From at least 1641 the Commons ordered certain papers delivered to them to be printed, and in the 18th c. the more important papers were usually printed. Luke Hansard, printer to the House, accumulated considerable stocks of these in his warehouses, and from them, on the instructions of Charles Abbot (Speaker, 1802–17), various bound sets were prepared. Four of these sets of pre-1800 papers (which are described below) survived the fire of 1834 and are available for consultation in H.L.R.O. and elsewhere.

Hansard also began in 1801 to assemble complete annual sets of printed papers as they were published, and this series, popularly known as 'Parliamentary Papers', has been continued to the present day for both Houses. A complex series of guides and indexes to the post-1800 papers is available (*see* the LISTS and INDEXES below, pp. 235–6, and the BIBLIOGRAPHY, pp. 134–5 above).

Unprinted Sessional Papers

1850 to date   42,000 docs.

These papers are normally those not considered of sufficient importance

[1] *See* p. 298 below.

to be printed, or maps, plans and similar material which would have been too costly to print. Early papers consist of such items as an Abstract of Harbour Board accounts, a Report of the Lord Chancellor on Visits to Patients by Commissioners in Lunacy, a Return of the number of Poor Rate Collectors in Ireland recently dismissed, a Return of House Duty charged in the Inns of Court and Chancery, Copies of warrants for compensation, a Return of the number of causes in the Court of Session, an Account of moneys received by the Dublin Metropolitan Police, etc. The delivery of each paper is noted in the Commons Journal. Many items in this series to date have also been delivered to H.L. and are preserved amongst the H.L. SESSIONAL PAPERS.

LISTS. MS. Lists are preserved in H.L.R.O. for each session, 1850 to date, which from 1859 to 1908 also include lists of Command Papers.

PRINTED SESSIONAL PAPERS

Many individual printed papers exist in the British Museum and other public libraries for the period from 1641 onwards. Miss S. Lambert has compiled a guide to those of 1701–50 in her *List of House of Commons Sessional Papers, 1701–1750* (List and Index Society: Special Series, vol. i, 1968). H.L. Library holds 3 papers dated 1700, 1701 and 1704 respectively. The following sets of printed papers are also preserved at Westminster:

Cases Presented to H.C.

1712   1 vol.

This vol. includes 119 printed items prepared by private individuals or corporations and relating to actual or impending legislation or to projects for such legislation. The subjects include African Trade (14 items), Duties on materials (33), Lotteries (8), Movement for measuring time (3), Prize Goods (3).

INDEX in H.L.R.O.

Bills and Cases in Parliament etc.

1720 to 1728   1 vol.

The vol. contains 105 printed papers including Private and Local Bills, mainly of 1724; Appellants' and Respondents' Cases in H.L., 1721; and a sequence of pamphlets relating to the Public Debt, the South Sea Company, the Bishop of Bangor's Sermon, the election of a Master at University College, Oxford, etc., 1720–8.

The vol. belonged to Speaker Bromley.

The First Series of Reports

1715 to 1801   16 vols.

Luke Hansard prepared this set of papers in 1803. It consists of a selection of reprinted Reports of Committees made to the House, the texts of which were originally either printed in the Journals or printed separately.

LISTS. The Index, in vol. 16, also includes a List of the Reports inserted in the
Journals which were not selected for inclusion. The *Catalogue of Parliamentary Reports* by Hansard (1834, reprinted as *Hansard's Catalogue and Breviate
of Parliamentary Papers*, ed. P. & G. Ford, 1953) is a version of vol. 16.

The Abbot Collection of Printed Papers

1731 to 1800   111 vols.

Of the original sets of Commons Papers prepared by Hansard on the
instructions of Speaker Abbot one is still in the British Museum; the fullest—
that prepared for the Speaker's Gallery—was early in the 20th c. deposited in
University College Library, University of London; a third is now in the H.C.
Library, and the fourth is lost, having possibly been burnt in the fire of 1834. A
fifth set, less extensive than the others, was perhaps assembled on the orders of
Speaker Abbot, after his creation as Lord Colchester in 1817. It is now
preserved in H.L. Library. Dr. E. L. Erickson comments on the variations
between the sets in 'The Sessional Papers: Last Phase', *College and Research
Libraries* (Sept. 1960, vol. xxi, pp. 343–58 (also reprinted)), but does not refer
to the set in H.L. Library. The papers were classified as follows: BILLS, 30
vols. (*see* above, p. 227). REPORTS FROM COMMITTEES, 28 vols. (mainly
1771–1800, the earlier are for 1744, 1748, 1755 (2), 1757, 1758, 1760, 1763).
ACCOUNTS AND PAPERS, 52 vols. (mainly 1780–1800, the earlier are of
1750 (2) and no date (3)).

LISTS. An Index vol. entitled *Catalogue of Papers printed by order of the House of
Commons from the year 1731 to 1800 in the Custody of the Clerk of the Journals*
was published in 1807 and reprinted by H.M.S.O. 1954. The General
Indexes to the Journals, 1660 to 1800, list printed papers under the heading
'Printing' (but the revised Index for 1774–1800 does not do so).

The Parliamentary Collection

1559 to 1740   1,110 items in 91 vols.

This collection of printed papers was assembled on Speaker Abbot's instructions by 1805 and then preserved in the Speaker's Gallery. It is now in the care
of H.C. Library. It is quite distinct from the Abbot Collection described above.
The collection represents what seems to have been a very much more extensive
collection of printed papers which had previously served as an 'office library' for
the Clerk of the Journals. Roughly a sixth of the papers are non-Parliamentary
in subject matter, relating e.g. to Ireland, Convocation, the City of London, etc.
The remainder are either official prints relating to the affairs of one or both of
the Houses, or private publications concerning Parliamentary proceedings. The
main categories of the Parliamentary items, with the date of the earliest papers,
are:

Royal Speeches in Parliament, 1601 (the earliest Parliamentary paper in the
collection).
Royal Messages and Answers, 1641.
Speeches of individual Peers in the Lords, 1641.
Speeches of individual Members in the Commons, 1628.

Reports, proceedings, etc., of Conferences, 1628.
Lists of Members of both Houses, 1628.
Declarations of the Commons, 1641.
Ordinances, Declarations, of Lords and Commons, 1641.
Proceedings concerning Impeachments, 1628.
Papers laid before Parliament, 1646.
Journal H.C., 21 Oct.–30 Dec. 1678.
Reports, H.L. Committees, 1704.
Reports, H.L., 1710.
Contemporary accounts of Proceedings, Debates, etc., including 1620, 1621, 1654, 1659, 1680, 1688–9, 1702–4 (Occasional Conformity).

The present Collection also includes a vol. of Votes and Proceedings, H.C., with Proceedings at Trial of William, V. Stafford, 21 Oct. 1680–25 March 1681.

LISTS. Original MS. Catalogue of 1805 and printed Chronological list of *c.* 1860.

The Bound Sessional Sets of Printed Papers

1801 to date   9,806 vols.

From 1801 the papers printed by order of the House were numbered consecutively for each session in order of printing; these numbers are also printed in the margin of the Journal entry of the order to print. From 1833 onwards Command Papers have been separately numbered in several consecutive series (*see* SESSIONAL PAPERS, H.L., p. 128).

The Sessional Papers exist as separates in many libraries. From the separates, official 'Bound Sets' have been formed, one such set being preserved in the H.C. Library and one in H.L. Library. Complete, or almost complete, sets also exist in the United Kingdom in some 11 University and other libraries (*see* W. R. Powell, *Local History from Blue Books* (1962), app. ii).

In the official Bound Sets the papers have been reclassified for each session into

1. Bills.
2. Reports from Committees and Joint Committees and Proceedings of Standing Committees.
3. Reports from Commissioners, i.e. from non-Parliamentary Committees, Commissions, etc.
4. Accounts and Papers.

Up to 1899, Command Papers were generally included in both Lords and Commons Sessional Papers, but some 35 are listed by K. A. C. Parsons in his *Checklist of the British Parliamentary Papers* (1958) as being included in the Lords papers but not in the Commons. There is a continuous MS. pagination for each vol. of the bound set and it is customary to identify a reference to a paper by the page of the vol. and not by that of the separate.

LISTS AND INDEXES

The Bound Sets have sessional indexes from 1808, and sessional lists from 1828 onwards. The principal general indexes are the following:

General Index to the Bills printed by order of the House of Commons, *1801–1852* (1853).

General Index to the Reports of Select Committees printed by order of the House of Commons, *1801–1852* (1853).

General Index to the Accounts and Papers, Reports of Commissioners, Estimates, etc. printed by order of the House of Commons or presented by Command, *1801–1852* (1853, repr. 1938).

General Alphabetical Index to the Bills, Reports, Estimates, Accounts and Papers, printed by order of the House of Commons, and to the Papers Presented by Command, *1852–1899* (1909).

General Index to the Bills, Reports and Papers printed by order of the House of Commons and to the Reports and Papers presented by Command, *1900 to 1948–49* (1960).

DEPARTMENT OF THE SPEAKER

Records relating to the appointment and work of the Speaker may be found in various H.C. classes of records already described, and notably in the Journals. With the exception given below no separate archival class has been formed by the Speakers. *See* also, however, the Onslow Precedent Books (p. 244 below), the Bromley Book of Bills and Cases (p. 233 above) and the Papers of Speaker Brand (p. 291 below).

The salaries and conditions of service of the permanent officers of H.C. and their staffs are regulated by a Commission set up under the House of Commons Offices Act, 1812, 52 Geo. III, c. 11. The members of the Commission are the Speaker, the Secretaries of State, the Chancellor of the Exchequer, the Master of the Rolls (until 1925 only), the Attorney General and the Solicitor General. The Speaker's Secretary serves as Secretary to the Commission and the records of the Commission are in the custody of the Speaker.

Minutes of the Commissioners for regulating the Offices of the House of Commons

1835 to date   5 vols.

The Minutes for the period 1812–34 were presumably destroyed in the fire of 1834. The surviving Minutes of Commissioners' Meetings record the names of those Commissioners present or consulted, and details of proceedings and decisions relating to appointments, salaries, residences, superannuations, etc. A few original letters and memoranda are inserted in the vols. Vols. 1–3 (1835–1933) are preserved in H.L.R.O. *See* also records of the Commissioners listed on p. 245 below.

USE. The permission of the Speaker is required for production of these docs. to students in each instance.

BIBLIOGRAPHY

A. I. Dasent, *The Speakers of the House of Commons from the earliest times to the present day* (1911); includes list of Speakers from 1376.

J. A. Manning, *The Lives of the Speakers of the House of Commons* (1851).

J. S. Roskell, *The Commons and their Speakers in English Parliaments 1376–1523* (1965).

P. Laundy, *The Office of Speaker* (1964).

Deposited Papers (Library)

1832, 1845, 1847, 1864 to date   4,500 files

In the course of debates, of Question time, etc., Ministers may arrange for papers to be deposited in the Library, H.C., as in the Library, H.L. (*see* p. 187). The present numbered H.C. Library series opens with three papers of pre-1864 date and is then continuous. There are 77 files for the 19th c.; the bulk of the papers are post-1920. The subject matter is varied; early files include papers relating to the trade of Central Asia, 1864; the sanitary condition of the Bombay Army, 1864; maps relating to Commons and Open Spaces, 1866, 1870, and to British Guiana, 1867; plans of the Thames Embankment, 1869; maps and sections to accompany the Report of the Royal Commission on Coal, 1871; the Procès Verbaux of the International Metric System Commission meeting at Paris, 1869–72; Reports on trade at the Treaty Ports in China for 1876; Parliamentary Franchise, 1883; Responsible Government in Natal, 1893; Grievances of Indian subjects in South Africa, 1895, etc.

USE. In general, those papers subsequently published are open without restriction; others are subject to a 30 year restriction; individual application must be made for each paper.

LIST. Chronological lists and indexes are available.

Election Return Books

1835 to date   36 vols.

The vols. contain the returns made by the Clerk of the Crown of the names of the Members elected to serve in Parliament at each election. This constitutes the 'sufficient evidence' for the return of a Member.
See also CLERK OF THE CROWN RECORDS.

Certificates of By Elections

1935 to 1945, 1959   226 docs.

The Certificates give the names of the Member and of his constituency; they are signed by the Clerk of the Crown in Chancery or his deputy.

CONTROVERTED ELECTION RECORDS

The Commons did not insist on its claim to exercise jurisdiction over controverted elections until 1604. From then disputed returns were referred to the Committee of Privileges and Elections nominated by the House, and from

1672 this was constituted as a C.W.H. After *c.* 1727 disputes were decided in the House itself until the Parliamentary Elections Act, 1770, 10 Geo. III, c. 16, transferred disputed returns to a committee principally selected from a panel chosen by lot. No appeal lay to the House. Slight variations in the mode of appointment occurred as a result of the Controverted Elections Act, 1841, 4 & 5 Vict., c. 58, and the Election Petition Act, 1848, 11 & 12 Vict., c. 98. The right to decide controverted elections was handed over to the courts of law by the Parliamentary Elections Act, 1868, 31 & 32 Vict., c. 125 and subsequent legislation. The petition against a return is presented not to the House but to the High Court of Justice; the trial is conducted by a judge from the judiciary in the appropriate part of the United Kingdom, who then sits in the county or borough concerned. At the conclusion of the trial the judge certifies his decision in writing to the Speaker, and under certain circumstances makes a report mainly relating to corrupt or illegal practices. A transcript of evidence is also supplied to the Speaker. The Certificates and Reports are entered in the Journals; Orders are made by the House to carry the judge's decision into effect; and the Minutes of Evidence with the Judgment are usually ordered to be printed by the House, thus becoming Sessional Papers and being included in the Bound Sets.

For Records of Proceedings on Controverted Elections, 1604 to date, *see*:

> JOURNALS OF THE HOUSE, 1604 to date, which include very full detail until 1868, *see* pp. 207-12 above.
>
> VOTES AND PROCEEDINGS, 1680 to date, especially Appendices and Supplements, *see* pp. 213-17 above.
>
> SESSIONAL PAPERS, 1801 to date for proceedings of Sel. Com. and Evidence, *see* pp. 235-6 above.

In addition, the following original records are preserved in H.L.R.O.:

Committee Records

1826 to 1853   5 docs.

These miscellaneous items are preserved:

Borough of Stafford Poll Books for 1826, 1830-1; Overseer's returns of voters for Christ Church parish, n.d.; Receipt for rolls registers, 1836.
County Mayo, Minutes of Proceedings and Evidence, Sel. Com. on controverted election, co. Mayo, 1853.

See also HISTORICAL COLLECTIONS, H.L.R.O. MISC.

Court Evidence

1869 to 1906   109 files

Transcripts of evidence given before the judges, from which the Sessional Papers were prepared.

Election Petitions Index

1869 to 1886   4 docs.

The Index file contains an Index of Election Petitions, 1869-78, indicating whether the petitions were printed, withdrawn, etc.; an Index of Election

Petition Trials, 1880–6, noting details concerning judges and proceedings; an Index of Evidence and Judgments, 1869–76; and a print of the Boston Election Petition Evidence, Sess. Papers H.C., 1874 (375).

House Returns

1931 to date   3 vols.

These vols., preserved in H.C. Library, comprise Returns made by Order of the House concerning the following business: Public Bills, Select Committees, Standing Committees, Sittings of the House, Closure of Debates, Addresses and Motions, Public Petitions, Private Bills and Private Business. Certain of these Returns were ordered to be printed and are also preserved with SESSIONAL PAPERS, H.C. For similar statistical material mainly for 1801 onwards, *see* the Journal Office Book of Statistics (p. 245 below).

Manuals of Procedure

1857 to date   20 vols.

In 1857 a vol. of *Rules, Orders, and Forms of Proceedings in the House of Commons* was prepared. Between then and 1896 this manual passed through 9 editions. It was succeeded in 1904 by a *Manual of Procedure*, prepared by Sir Courtenay Ilbert, Clerk of the House. This has been reissued in revised form at irregular intervals. The *Manual* gives more detail than the published S.O.s, and is in the nature of a summary of Erskine May's *Treatise*. Unlike the Collections of S.O.s the *Manual* is not a Sessional Paper.

PETITIONS

Petitions have been presented to Parliament from the earliest days, and petitioning formed the starting point for both legislative and judicial procedure (*see* PETITIONS, H.L., pp. 172–3 above). During the 16th c. an increasing number of petitions came to H.C. and by 1571 the House was receiving sufficient to warrant the formation of a committee of thirteen 'for Motions of Griefs and Petitions'. In the same year the first petition was entered in the Journal. In 1607 a C.W.H. for Grievances was formed, and it is from this year that the extensive class of original petitions still surviving in 1834 (but then destroyed in the fire) dated. In 1621 a Sel. Com. to view and consider petitions was named. This by 1626 was established as a regular Standing Committee to receive petitions concerning the delay or obstruction of justice. The Long Parliament received a flood of petitions, and committees were appointed to regulate and sort them. The Tumultuous Petitioning Act, 1661, 13 Cha. II, sess. 1, c. 5 led to a diminution in petitioning by forbidding the 'getting of Hands or other consent' from more than 20 petitioners without the consent of justices or other authorities. In 1669 H.C. resolved that it was the right of every commoner to prepare and present petitions to the House and of the House to receive and determine them. Petitions were considered by the House and only in some cases referred to a committee. An Order of 1685 that Private Bills could be brought in only after petitions had been presented established a separate class of petitions for private legislation. In 1689 the House resolved that Petitioners must sign with their own hands. In 1713 a S.O. ruled that no petition relating to grants of public money be received without the recommendation of the Crown, and from 1770 all petitions relating to elections were transferred for final decision to a special committee for that purpose. Petitioning had been adopted as 'a weapon of agitation' by Wilkes in 1769, and from 1779 on it became the primary method by which those seeking economical and Parliamentary reform sought to gain the attention of Parliament. From then until the beginning of the 20th c. 'Public Petitions', as they were called, came to the House in very great quantities, the annual numbers of petitions after 1833 varying between 10,000 and 34,000, and of those signing between ½ and 6 million. From 1833 onwards a Select Committee has been appointed to investigate the regularity of the form of the Petitions, to classify them, to summarise their arguments and to print representative texts.

From 1571 onwards the receipt of each Petition has usually been noticed in the Journal, and from 1680 onwards also in Votes and Proceedings. Between 1742 and 1833 full texts of Petitions may be given in the Votes or in their Appendix.

See also the RECORDS OF THE COMMITTEES ON PUBLIC PETITIONS, pp. 222–3, above.

BIBLIOGRAPHY

J. B. Bull, *Orders, Resolutions and Practice of the House of Commons relating to Public Petitions* (1890).
B. J. Enright, *Public Petitions in the House of Commons* (1960), typescript in H.L.R.O. Search Room.

Petitions (Preserved with Lords Papers)

1621 to 1649   100 docs.

Petitions were preserved from 1607 onwards but the entire class was destroyed in the fire of 1834 except for the small number, pre-1649 in date, which had become mixed with the Lords Papers.

These Petitions are usually on sheets of paper, are signed by petitioners and are never dated. They may, however, be endorsed with a date and with notes of action taken. Some of those of 1640 bore many signatures and dealt with general matters such as abuses in Church government, Ship Money, the Star Chamber, Monopolies, etc. They are sometimes identical with Petitions submitted to H.L.

LIST. All Commons Petitions to 1649 are listed in the *Calendar*.

Public Petitions

1951 to date   383 files

From 1834 to 1950 the originals of Public Petitions were destroyed after the committee had reported. From 1951 the complete Petitions are preserved.

USE. The Petitions are not accessible to students for 30 years from date of presentation.

Standing Orders

1801 to date   200 vols.

The House from the 17th c. has made various orders for its own guidance. Unlike H.L., H.C. did not enrol those which were intended to be continuously observed (i.e. the Standing Orders), but merely included entries of them in the Journals. Printed collections from these entries of S.O.s were made unofficially, and copies of such collections are preserved in the British Museum for 1717, 1747, 1756, 1789, etc.[1] The complexity of Private Bill procedure from 1794 onwards made the official publication of Private Bill S.O.s necessary. An edition of these appeared before 1799, and revised editions were published by L. Hansard in 1799 and 1801.

The editions of Private Bill S.O.s published by order of H.C. between 1801 and 1945 are listed by O. Williams in *Private Bill Procedure*, vol. ii (1949), pp. 3–4. The first collection of S.O.s relating to Public Business published by the House is included in the Sessional Papers for 1810 (355). S.O.s relating to Private Bill and other [*sc.* Public] Matters were included in a Sessional Paper for 1810 (350). From 1843 onwards collections of both Public Business and Private Bill S.O.s appeared annually as House Papers until 1959. From this date the two categories have again been issued separately as House Papers.

Test Rolls

1835 to date   41 docs.

The class consists of 5 rolls and 36 books. Signatures are entered of each Member taking the oath or affirming. The rolls also contain the texts of the relevant oaths and affirmations. Until Members have taken the oath or affirmed they may not sit within the Bar of the House.

Votes of Thanks

1858 to 1921, 1964   50 docs.

The Votes are printed copies of Resolutions of H.C. that the thanks of the House be given to one or more persons. The texts of the Resolutions are printed *in extenso* in the Journals. Certain of the Votes are signed by the Clerk of the House. A vol. of Thanks voted by H.L. and H.C. to the Army and Navy, 1801–59, printed by H. Hansard (1859) is also preserved, with inset memos.

[1] Certain Private Bill S.O.s were also published by J. Debrett in *Parliamentary Papers*, vol. ii (1797), pp. 577–92.

OFFICE RECORDS, HOUSE OF COMMONS

From the 14th c. an 'Under-Clerk of the Parliaments' or 'Clerk of the House of Commons' has been appointed under Letters Patent from the Sovereign to serve the Commons. The mediaeval Clerks were clerks in Chancery, but c. 1515 the Commons Office hived off from Chancery exactly as its counterpart in the Upper House had done; from then on the Clerks of the House were frequently barristers. The first appointment of a Clerk Assistant to sit with the Clerk of the House at the Table was made in 1640, and from 1801 a Second Clerk Assistant has also been appointed to sit at the Table. John Hatsell (Clerk, 1768 to 1820) summed up the traditional duties of the Clerk of the House in 1781 in the words of the Clerk's oath to 'make true entries, remembrances, and journals of the things done and passed in the House of Commons'. The Clerk also 'signs the addresses, votes of thanks, and orders of the House, endorses the bills sent or returned to the Lords, and reads whatever is required to be read in the House. He is addressed by Members, and puts such questions as are necessary, on an election of a Speaker, and for the adjournment of the House, when it is necessitated by the death or retirement of the Speaker, or by the absence of the Speaker and the Members competent to act as Deputy Speaker. The Clerk has the custody of all records or other documents, and is responsible for the conduct of the business of the House in the official departments under his control. He assists the Speaker and advises Members in regard to questions of order and the proceedings of the House. He is, also, the Accounting Officer for the House of Commons' (Erskine May, 17th ed.).

The Clerk Assistant and the Second Clerk Assistant are appointed by the Crown on the recommendation of the Speaker. They keep the minutes of proceedings, receive notices of motions, questions, and amendments, and prepare the Notice Paper and Order Book. The Clerk Assistant officiates at the Table in C.W.H. Since 1953 a Fourth Clerk at the Table has been appointed, now known as the Principal Clerk, Table Office.

In Hatsell's time there were twelve junior clerks, divided between four offices, the Committee Office, the Ingrossing Office, the Fees Office and the Journal Office, together with a Clerk of the Elections. The work of certain of these clerks increased from the 1770s onwards as they began to act as agents for external interests concerned to promote or forward the passage of Bills. With the considerable growth in Private Bill work after 1794 'outdoor' parliamentary agents took an increasing part in the promotion of Bills, and clerks were finally forbidden in 1835 to act themselves as parliamentary agents.

The original remuneration of the clerks, apart from the small salaries payable to those who were appointed by patent, came from fees payable by those promoting Bills, etc. to the clerks as officers of the House, as distinct from in their capacity as agents. The House of Commons (Offices) Act, 1812, 52 Geo. III, c. 11, provided that such fees were to be paid into a fee fund, and this was largely achieved from 1820, clerks thereafter receiving fixed salaries from the fund. Fees continued to be paid to the Committee Office until 1837, and subsequently to the Journal Office, for copies and inspections of documents.

The office responsible under the Clerk of the House for the reception of all fees was the conjoint 'Public Bills and Fees Office'. Its work had been strengthened by the appointment of an accountant in 1833. The present organisation of the Clerk of the House's department comprises seven offices, as follows: Public Bill Office, Journal Office (including the Votes and Proceedings Office), Committee Office, Private Bill Office, Table Office, Overseas Office, and Administration (Services) Office.

BIBLIOGRAPHY

J. Hatsell, *Precedents of Proceedings in the House of Commons* (1781; 4th ed., 1818).
P. Marsden, *The Officers of the Commons, 1363–1965* (1966).
O. Williams, *The Clerical Organization of the House of Commons, 1661–1850* (1954).

For a List of CLERKS OF THE HOUSE, *see* Appendix II, below.

Fee Records

1812 to 1937   31 vols.

General Account of Fees, 1834–1931, 4 vols.

Election Committee Fee Book, 1835, with inset papers relating to Elections.

Committee Clerks' Office Fee Book (Copying and Inspection), 1837, 1 vol.

Private Bill Office Fee Book (Copying and Inspection), 1837, 1 vol.

Fee Arrears Books, 1812–85, 2 vols.

Account Books:

  'Clerk of the Fees Office', 1834–70, 1 vol.

  'House of Commons Offices', 1884–1916, 1 vol.

  'Department of the Clerk of the House; Chairman of Ways and Means; Salaries; Department of Speaker; Department of Serjeant at Arms; Witnesses, etc.', 1868–1919, 1 vol.

Salary Books:

  Clerks, 1880–1937, 1 vol.

  Messengers, 1886–1937, 1 vol.

Bank Books of Commissioners of House of Commons (Bank of England), 1812–1934, 11 vols.

Fees Office Note Books, with inset correspondence, 1844–86, and *c.* 1897.

Fee Books, Journal Office, 1844–1904, 4 vols.

Precedent Books   7 vols.

1544 to 1895

Abstract of Rules and Orders of the House of Commons and Precedents of Proceedings, 1547–1820, 1 vol.

Speaker Onslow's Precedent Books, 1547–1770, 2 vols. Vol. 1 has been preserved in the Journal Office, H.C., and deals with the period 1547–1642; original docs. are bound in, and there are some annotations by Onslow. Vol. 2 is in the possession of the Earl of Onslow at Clandon Park, Surrey, but a photographic copy is preserved in H.L.R.O. It deals with the period 1660–1710, and has extensive additions by Onslow and others to *c.* 1770, with inserted prints and docs. Some of Onslow's annotations were printed by Hatsell in his *Precedents* (*see* BIBLIOGRAPHY above).

Precedents of Proceedings in the House of Commons, 1544–1881, 1 vol.

Observations Rules and Orders collected out of the Journal Books of the House of Commons, by Ambrose Kelly [mainly 16th and 17th c.], 1 vol.

Transcript of 5 printed works in 1 manuscript vol.: *Memorials . . .* by H. Scobell; *Arcana Parliamentaria* by 'R.C.'; *The Authority etc. of Parliaments* by Sir Thos. Smith; *Opinions of Antiquaries on the Antiquity of Parliaments*; *Method of Passing Bills in Parliament* by Henry Elsynge.

Forms of Entries in Votes and Proceedings of the House of Commons, *c.* 1895.

Journal Office Book of Statistics

1880 to 1960   1 vol.

The vol. was originally compiled by A. A. Taylor, 1880–1913, but has later additions to 1960; contents include statistics of: Private Bills and Public Bills from 1801–2; Closures from 1887; days occupied by Government and Private Members from 1888; Counts Out from 1880; Divisions from 1831; strangers in the Galleries from 1914; membership of the two Houses from 1295; Numbers of Motions, from 1845; dates of Parliament from 1500; numbers of Papers presented, from 1870; numbers of Public Petitions, from 1785; Questions to Ministers, from 1847; hours and periods of sittings of the House, from 1650; longest sittings; days of sitting, etc., from 1828; duration of sittings from 1831; days of Committee of Supply, etc., from 1869; Votes of Thanks. A photographic copy in 2 vols. is available to students in H.L.R.O. The original is preserved in the Journal Office, H.C.

Public Bill Office Papers

1838 to 1959   700 docs.

This series of papers was transferred to the Victoria Tower in 1970. Many of the files were damaged in the air raid of 1941 and some are imperfect. Among the papers are the following:

Public Bill Precedent Books, 1850–1936, 1900–57, 2 vols.

Indexes of names of places returning Land Tax Commissioners, 19th c., 2 vols.

Procedure in Committees on Public Bills, part of MS. treatise by John Rickman.

Appropriation Accounts (MS. and printed) for H.C. Offices, 1869–1901.

Disposal and Custody of documents, papers concerning, 1942.

Appropriation of fees collected in H.C. Offices, corr. with Treasury, etc., 1849–73.

Commissioners, H.C., minutes of meetings, 1876–1940 (see also DEPARTMENT OF THE SPEAKER).

Commissioners, H.C., corr., 1896–1935.

Fees Office rules, etc., 1866, 1889.

Parliament Act Bills files, 1925–1948.

Duties performed in the Clerk's Office, and other establishment matters, corr., memos., 1848–1932.

Public Bill Office Letter Book, 1852–64, including notes on procedure, 1888–1940.

Palace of Westminster, Second World War Records (H.C.)

1940 to 1961   1,781 docs.

The following two series are preserved amongst the Office records, H.C.:

1. Palace of Westminster Home Guard Papers, 1940–61, 925 docs. These are the records of 'C' Company, 35th London (Civil Service) Battalion, Home Guard, and include a record of service 1940–4, general corr., orders and duties, papers concerning the bombing of the Palace, photographs and plans, and (to 1961) financial papers.

2. Records of the Munitions Factory, Houses of Parliament, 1942–5, 856 docs., including minutes of meetings of the Munitions Unit, notices, progress reports, salary papers, photographs and general corr.

The Memorial vol. containing names of Members and Servants of H.C., and of sons and daughters of Members, who were killed in the second World War, is displayed in the Lower Waiting Hall, H.C.

See also SECOND WORLD WAR RECORDS, H.L., in PARLIAMENT OFFICE PAPERS.

RECORDS OF THE SERJEANT AT ARMS DEPARTMENT

The first certain evidence of a royal Serjeant at Arms assigned to the House of Commons dates from 1414. Speaker Gargrave (1559) was normally preceded by the Serjeant at Arms[1] with the Mace and in the 17th c. it became customary for the Mace, having rested on the Table when the House was in session, to be moved by the Serjeant at Arms when the Commons went into C.W.H. The Serjeant has customarily been responsible for the maintenance of order in the House. He keeps gangways clear, gives orders to doorkeepers and others in connection with divisions, serves Orders of the House on those whom they concern, regulates, under the Speaker, admission to the Press gallery and lobby, and has control of the arrangements for the admission of strangers. In addition he is the housekeeper of the Commons, and has charge of its committee rooms and other parts of the building used by the House. The Serjeant is appointed by Letters Patent 'to attend upon Her Majesty's person when there is no Parliament, and at the time of every Parliament to attend upon the Speaker of the House of Commons'.

A typescript list of Serjeants and Deputy Serjeants by J. C. Sainty may be consulted in H.L.R.O.

BIBLIOGRAPHY. P. F. Thorne, 'Maces: Their Use and Significance'. *Journal of the Parliaments of the Commonwealth*, vol. xliv (1963), pp. 25–30; and *The Mace in the House of Commons*, House of Commons Library Document, no. 3 (1957).

Main Registers (Serjeant at Arms)

1788 to 1914   24 vols.

The vols. were assembled as a series in the 20th c. Their contents are:

Vol 1. 'Officers and Usages of the House of Commons, 1805'. Notes copied 'from Mr. Colman's and Mr. Clementson's Books' relating to the Clerks at the Table, the Serjeant at Arms, the Chaplain, and the Clerk of the Crown. The vol. was probably prepared under the direction of Speaker Abbot.

Vol. 2. Accounts of the Serjeant at Arms, 1813–34 (damaged in fire).

Vol. 3. Book of Salaries and Fees, 1819–34 (damaged in fire).

Vol. 4. Register of Correspondence with Office of Works, 1828–42.

Vol. 5. Bills and Disbursements, 1834–42.

Vol. 6. Fees and Emoluments, 1834–8.

Vol. 7. Estimates and Payments, 1836–42.

Vol. 8. Estimates and Payments, 1836–49.

---

[1] In H.C. hyphens are not used in the title.

Vol. 9. Estimates and Payments, 1837–55.

Vol. 10. Estimates and Payments, 1842–9.

Vol. 11. Estimates and Payments, 1855–69.

Vols. 12–23. Printed Sessional Papers relating to H.C. and the Serjeant at Arms Department, 1788–1914.

Vol. 24. Vol. of Statistics relating to sittings of House, Bills presented, closures, counts out, divisions, etc., 19th c.

Account of the Office

1803   1 vol.

'An Account of the Office and Duty of the Serjeant at Arms attending the House of Commons', probably prepared by Edward Colman, Serjeant (1775–1805), under the direction of Speaker Abbot.

Appointment and Order Book

1804 to 1929   1 vol.

The vol. contains entries of appointments, and of orders to police, messengers, etc.

Letter and Memoranda Book

1849 to 1873   1 vol.

Memos. on duties of doorkeepers, messengers, police, etc., and on control of galleries and other parts of the building, followed by entries of outgoing letters, with some original letters annexed.

PART
THREE

RECORDS OF THE
LORD GREAT CHAMBERLAIN

RECORDS OF THE LORD GREAT CHAMBERLAIN

The office of Lord Great Chamberlain of England is one of the great offices of State. A 'Master Chamberlain' officiated as a member of the Royal Household from *temp*. William I, and in 1133 Henry I granted the office to Aubrey de Vere II, a grant which became the foundation of all subsequent claims to the office. Within a century it seems likely that the Master (or Great) Chamberlain officiated in person only at Coronations, his remaining original Household duties passing to other officers. The first trace of a Lord Great Chamberlain exercising any role within the Palace of Westminster (other than at Coronations) is in 1641 when the then holder of the office was required to see that Orders of the House were correctly exhibited. After the Restoration the Lord Great Chamberlain came to exercise general supervision over the use and preservation of the Palace, acting increasingly as an intermediary between the Sovereign and the House of Lords, and issuing warrants for building or decorating and for the occupation of accommodation within the Palace. In addition, in 1876 the House of Lords transferred to the Lord Great Chamberlain the responsibility for housekeeping within the House, previously exercised by Black Rod. In 1965, however, the Lord Great Chamberlain's custody of the Palace was vested in the two Houses acting separately, and the Lord Great Chamberlain's housekeeping functions were transferred to the Offices Committee of the House of Lords. The Lord Great Chamberlain since 1965 has continued to have custody of the Robing Room, Royal Gallery and certain other parts of the Palace[1] and he remains responsible for the ceremonial on occasions when the Sovereign is present in Parliament.

The office of Lord Great Chamberlain ceased to be held on a unitary basis on the death of the 3rd D. Ancaster in 1779. In 1781 it was decided that the office should be vested in the two sisters of the late duke and their representatives; further subdivisions occurred in 1870 and 1928. The mode of appointment since 1781 has been for the heads of the families in which the office is vested, taking into consideration existing arrangements for rotation, to execute a deed nominating a person to exercise the office. The Crown then approves the nomination, during pleasure, by Royal Warrant. The principal families at present concerned in the nomination are those of M. Cholmondeley and E. Ancaster.

LIST. A typed list of Records of the Lord Great Chamberlain is available in H.L.R.O.

USE. Application to consult specific records should be made to the Clerk of the Records.

---

[1] Control of Westminster Hall and the Crypt Chapel is vested jointly in the Lord Great Chamberlain, the Lord Chancellor and the Speaker.

BIBLIOGRAPHY

(for descent of office)
G.E.C., *The Complete Peerage*, vol. x (1945), App. F.

(for duties within Parliament)
Extracts from the Journals . . . relating to the Lord Great Chamberlain . . . (n.d.), a
print available in H.L.R.O.

Accounts with the Treasury

1830 to 1869   1 vol.

This vol. comprises accounts of the Lord Great Chamberlain relating to
payments in connection with the Opening and Prorogation of Parliament,
Coronations, etc.

Admission Registers, etc.

1880 to 1961   20 vols.

This incomplete series includes records of admissions to the Chamber, the
Opening of Parliament, the Palace of Westminster, etc., with records of
statistics, 1919–37, 1951–61.

Letters and Papers

1558 to 1937   6,500 docs.

The incoming letters and papers, together with a certain number of office
copies, have been affixed to the leaves of 26 large registers, in date order, as
follows:

> Vol. 1. 1558–1820
> Vol. 2. 1705–1823
> Vol. 3. 1830–7
> Vol. 4. 1837–51
> Vol. 5. 1849–59; with 11 docs., 1661, 1822–35
> Vol. 6. 1860–71
> Vol. 7. 1872–4

The series is maintained for subsequent years to 1937.

The main subject categories of the series are as follows:

Office of Lord Great Chamberlain (Claims, Royal Warrants, Grants, etc.)

Petitions and Claims at Coronations, 1558, 1603, 1689, 1702, 1714, etc.;
memo. by Sec. of State concerning L.G.C.'s precedence at court, 1685; memo.
on right to appoint a housekeeper, H.C., *post* 1703; memos. etc. on rights of
L.G.C., var. dates, 1715 on; Royal Warrants to L.G.C. for seats in H.L. for Dukes
of Kent, Cumberland, Sussex and Cambridge, 1799, 1801; Royal Warrants for
altered or additional accommodation in the Palace of Westminster, 1792, 1800,
1820; Royal Warrant for deputy, 1781; Royal Warrant for L.G.C., 1821;
Order in Council respecting claims of E. Marshal and L.G.C., 1821; Royal
Approval of appointment of M. Cholmondeley as L.G.C., 1830; copy of

Warrant of sanction of deputy, 1844; precedents on authority of L.G.C. (1441–1882), 1852 with earlier memos.; ditto (1843–51), 1859.

General Administrative Papers

These in part supplement the more formal Warrants of the L.G.C. series (*see* below) and relate to very similar matters, but consist chiefly of letters and memoranda. They date from 1678 and deal with misc. topics, including: E. Pembroke's trial, 1678–9; furnishing the House, 1678, 1744, etc.; altering seats, 1679; dispute with Lord Chamberlain, 1686; Painted Chamber and Lords Lobby, [1688]; Court of Wards, 1689; furniture at trials of impeached peers, 1701; claims of L.G.C. to furniture in Westminster Hall, 1748; 'Proceedings to be observed at the King's going to the House of Peers, and on the introduction of a Peer', 18th c., subsequently approved by William IV, 1830; additional buildings near H.L., 1812; claim of E. Yarmouth to carry crown before P. Wales, 1812; ceremonies and order (including search of vaults) at State Openings, Prorogations etc. for 1815 and most subsequent openings and prorogations; alterations in Old Robing Room, 1820; the new Throne, 1830; preparation of H.L. after the fire, 1834, and some corr. concerning designs for new Palace, 1835 on; letters from Barry concerning occupation and furnishing of new H.L., 1846–9; letter and memo. concerning search of vaults, 1854; sale of guide books, 1865, 1872, 1873; admission of scholars of Westminster School, 1870; services in Crypt Chapel, 1870–1; keepership of Westminster Hall, and stalls in it, 1873; letters requesting and acknowledging warrants for accommodation.

Admission to the House

Letters, etc., requesting tickets or places for various Parliamentary proceedings, 1776 on, including Warren Hastings Trial, 1788, etc., State Openings, 1795, 1802, 1817, etc., and Trial of Queen Caroline, 1820.

Coronation Papers

These Papers date from 1689 and concern the ceremonies in Westminster Hall and Westminster Abbey at Coronations. The principal subjects are the printing and distribution of tickets of admission; arrangements for the regalia and robes, for the provision of guards and for the erection of scaffolding; the delivery of the keys of Westminster Hall to the L.G.C. by the Warden of the Fleet Prison; the removal and reinstatement of the courts of justice in Westminster Hall; the Coronation banquet; the Coronation procession. *See* also p. 255.

Orders, H.L.

Original or copy Orders of the House concerning 'maintenance of order and regularity', for structural alterations, for provision of seats in Westminster Hall, etc., 1674 on.

Plans and Engravings

Plans include those relating to alterations for the old Robing Room, 1820; lines of approach to Westminster Hall, 1821; Coronation procession routes

[1821]; temporary H.L., 1834; temporary Houses of Parliament, showing exact area of fire, 1835; general plan of R. Smirke's temporary buildings, approved by Sign Manual, 1835; plans of ground floor, principal floor, chamber, etc., H.L., 1851; plan of Chamber showing accommodation on State occasions, 1851. The engravings, lithographs, etc. mainly relate to the fire of 1834.

Privy Council Papers

Certificates of L.G.C.'s being sworn Privy Councillor; copies of Orders in Council; minutes of L.G.C. taking his place as Privy Councillor; notes of fees for oath, summonses to Council, etc., 1682 on.

State Trial Papers

In addition to the papers relating to the furnishing of Westminster Hall for State Trials and admission to sittings noted elsewhere in this section, the following Trial Papers survive: memos. and papers at the trial of the Scottish peers, 1746; E. Ferrers, 1760; L. Byron, 1765; and Dss. Kingston, 1776.

Warrants of the L.G.C.

Copies of Warrants, Orders and Certificates issued by L.G.C., including Warrants for Writing Rooms in H.L., 1660; for preparation of rooms at Oxford for Parliament, 1668; for erection of a building for L.G.C. by Christopher Wren, 1672; for the erection of a scaffold at E. Pembroke's trial, 1678; to clear cellars in H.L., 1678; for the making of coffee, tea, etc. for members of H.C., etc., 1681; to prepare for installation dinner for Knights of the Bath, 1744; to refurnish H.L., 1744; for a new Throne in H.L., 1761; to require attendance of Life Guards, 1814; to refurnish H.L., 1820; form of Warrant, 1852; two original Warrants delivered up, 1857, 1859; warrants of revocation and removal, 1873 (*see* also *General Administrative Papers* above and REGISTERS OF OUTGOING WARRANTS AND LETTERS below).

LIST of this class is available in H.L.R.O.

Minute Books
1820 to 1837   7 vols.

The vols. contain detailed daily entries of business transacted by the L.G.C.'s department, entered by W. D. Fellowes, Secretary to the L.G.C. They include copies of letters and memos. dealing mainly with Coronations and with State Occasions in Parliament, but with occasional references to the business of the House.

Registers of Outgoing Warrants and Letters
1559–1929   19 vols.

Vol. 1 includes entries for the period from 1559–1874 and is selective; the other vols. cover the periods 1697–1727 and 1820–1929 in detail. 2 vols. deal with the Coronation of George IV and the Trial of Queen Caroline.

Registers (Chapel of St. Mary Undercroft)

1925 to date   3 vols.

Marriages which have taken place in this chapel (generally known as the Crypt Chapel) are recorded in the Registers of the parish of St. Margaret, Westminster, for the period subsequent to the restoration of its fabric in the mid-19th c. Baptisms from the same date to 1925 were also recorded in the parish registers, but since 1925 they have been recorded in Registers kept by the Lord Great Chamberlain.

Miscellaneous Records

1735 to date   88 vols.

The records of the L.G.C. also include the following misc. vols.: Trials of peers (E. Ferrers, 1760; L. Byron, 1765; V. Melville, 1806), 3 vols. of collected letters, memos. and prints; Standing Orders, H.L., MS. vol. 1735–42; 'Law Papers', vol. of docs. relating to cases of claim to office of L.G.C., 1780–1, 1816, with a plan of Palace of Westminster, 1834; MS. 'General account of Governor Hastings' Trial', 1788; MS. 'Succinct Notices of the High Hereditary Office of Lord Great Chamberlain in England in the Noble Families of de Vere and Bertie', c. 1781; MS. 'Discussion relating to the Office' of L.G.C. by W. D. Fellowes, 1820–1; Coronation of George IV, files of papers, tickets, prints, etc. with lists of pages and doorkeepers; Coronation of Edward VII, lists of peers and peeresses; Coronations, 1685 to date, contemporary printed works; etc.

PART
FOUR

RECORDS OF
THE CLERK OF THE CROWN

RECORDS OF THE CLERK OF THE CROWN

The Clerk of the Crown in Chancery performs two related functions; he attends continuously on the Lord Chancellor, and he serves as an officer of the two Houses of Parliament. The earliest known Clerk of the Crown in Chancery occurs in 1350; in the reign of Richard II the Clerk both wrote and read aloud certain documents in Parliament, and from the 16th c. onwards he exercised his present function at ceremonies of Royal Assent of reading aloud the titles of Bills presented for assent. The Clerk of the Crown in addition issues writs out of Chancery for elections to be held, subsequently delivering to the Clerk of the House of Commons a Return Book of the names of members elected. He issues writs under warrant from the Speaker when vacancies occur in membership of the Commons, and delivers certificates of the return to the Clerk of the House. At State Openings the Clerk of the Crown sits at the Table. For details of records made by him in his extra-Parliamentary capacity see the *Guide to the Contents of the Public Record Office*, vol. i; records of the Clerk preserved at Westminster and available for use in H.L.R.O. are noted below. A typescript list of Clerks and Deputy Clerks by J. C. Sainty is available in H.L.R.O. Search Room.

BIBLIOGRAPHY. A. F. Pollard, 'The Clerk of the Crown', *English Historical Review*, vol. lvii, pp. 312–33.

Parliamentary Election Return Books

1837 to 1929   20 vols.

The entries in these vols. include details of the Indenture of return from the constituency (to 1868), the name of the returning officer and the names of those elected to serve in the House of Commons. See also p. 238 above for similar vols.

Speaker's Warrants

1895 to 1899   1 bundle

The bundle consists of signed warrants by Mr. Speaker Gully for the making out of new writs by the Clerk of the Crown, together with a MS. index.

Note that the non-Parliamentary records of the Clerk are preserved in the Public Record Office, and that recent Parliamentary and non-Parliamentary records are in the immediate charge of the Crown Office at the House of Lords.

PART
FIVE

OTHER RECORDS OF
THE PALACE OF WESTMINSTER

OTHER RECORDS OF
THE PALACE OF WESTMINSTER

The records described above have accrued within the Upper or the Lower House of Parliament, or within the offices attached to them. The groups of records described in this section, although all preserved continuously within the Palace of Westminster, have a less direct relation with the two Houses, the final group (that relating to the office of Exchequer Chief Usher) being entirely non-Parliamentary in character.

USE. All records described in this section are available for use in H.L.R.O. subject, in the case of Statute Law Committee Papers only, to a 30 year limitation.

STATUTE LAW COMMITTEE PAPERS

The following papers were transferred to H.L.R.O. by the Statute Law Committee in 1966. This Committee, which originated in 1868, is appointed by the Lord Chancellor, and comprises members and officers of both Houses together with external members of the legal profession and others. It is responsible for making proposals for the revision of Statute Law, and for supervising the Statutory Publications Office which publishes *Statutes Revised*. It has inherited some of the functions and certain of the papers of various earlier bodies, notably of the Commissioners for digesting and consolidating the Statute Law, appointed 23 July 1833; of the Commissioners to consolidate the Statute Law, appointed 23 August 1854; and of the Commissioners to inquire into a Digest of Law, appointed 22 November 1866.

Commissioners' Papers

1835 to 1870   130 docs.

The papers include copies of relevant Sessional Papers (Returns and Reports of the Commissioners, etc.); confidential memoranda to the Lord Chancellor concerning revision; minutes of the meetings of the Law Digest Commission, 1866–70; examples of digested laws; and draft and final reports of the same Commission.

Statute Law Committee Papers

1868 to 1954   1,500 docs.

The papers include Minutes of Committee or Sub-Committee meetings, 1868–78, 1889, 1892, 1938, 1950–4; memoranda and corr., 1868–1954; establishment papers, 1923–50; papers concerning the citation of Statutes, 1930–43;

Statute Law Revision Bills, including collected series, 1861–91, 3 vols; minutes and papers concerning the State Trials Committee, 1897–9.

LIST. A summary list is available in H.L.R.O.

USE. Papers less than 30 years old are restricted.

SCOTTISH COMMISSIONS RECORDS

Scottish Commissions Records

1803 to 1856   1,700 docs.

The Scottish Highland Roads and Bridges Act, 1803, 43 Geo. III, c. 80, established a Commission (which included the Speaker of the H.C.) to supervise the expenditure of moneys on the construction of Highland roads and bridges. Their work was transferred to the local authorities by the Highland Roads and Bridges Act, 1862, 25 & 26 Vict., c. 105, and on 31 December 1862, the Commission was dissolved. The Caledonian Canal Act, 1803, 43 Geo. III, c. 102, established a similar but separate Commission to construct a canal 'from the Eastern to the Western sea', again including the Speaker of the Commons. This canal was opened in 1822. Reports from each body of Commissioners were laid before both Houses and survive in the class of SESSIONAL PAPERS from 1803 to 1852. Non-Parliamentary as well as Parliamentary manuscript sources for the work of the Commission are described and used by Dr. A. R. B. Haldane in *New Ways through the Glens* (1962). The records now in H.L.R.O. were probably preserved within the Palace of Westminster as a result of both Commissions being composed of Members of the two Houses, and their Chairman being Speaker of the Commons. The records comprise miscellaneous series of papers relating to the work of both Commissions, including original letters of Thomas Telford and others, reports, memoranda, contracts, etc. *See* also the 3 bundles of documents, 1803–25, relating to the Commission, noted in the *Guide to the Contents of the Public Record Office*, vol. ii, pp. 296, 298, 300.

THE SHAW-LEFEVRE PAPERS

The Shaw-Lefevre Papers

1575 to 1857   3,617 docs.

Sir John George Shaw-Lefevre, Clerk Assistant, 1848–55, and Clerk of the Parliaments, 1855–75, held various additional public offices, including those of Poor Law Commissioner (1834); Commissioner for South Australia (1834); assistant Secretary, Board of Trade (1841); Vice-Chancellor of London University (1842); and Civil Service Commissioner (1855). He also served as Auditor of the estates of the Earls Spencer. The series of Shaw-Lefevre Papers, which accumulated within the Palace during Shaw-Lefevre's lifetime, consist of the following main items:

Public Office (other than his Clerkship)

Board of Trade. Drafts, memos. and letters concerning: Corn Importation Act, 1842; Joint Stock Companies Act, 1844; the post of Registrar of Joint Stock companies, 1844–6; preparation of Bills, 1844, 1848; Bahamas Act, 1842; Bermuda Act, 1845; Jamaica Act, 1842; Customs duties, 1844–8; Merchant Service, 1844–8; Steam Navigation, 1848; Government School of Design, 1844–8; misc. 1843–8.

Cambridge University Election. Minutes, letters, etc., 1847.

Poor Law Commission. Letters addressed to Shaw-Lefevre as Poor Law Commissioner, 1834–41, with a copy of letter from Shaw-Lefevre to the Treasury concerning his appointment, 1835.

Royal Scottish Academy. Letters concerning a dispute with the Royal Institution, 1846, 1848.

South Australia Commission. Corr., 1835–41.

University of London. Copy of Patent of Incorporation, 1836; letters concerning appointment of Registrar, 1838; letter from Chancellor of the Exchequer to the Chancellor of the University, 1841.

Private Papers

Burley Estate, co. Hants. (bequeathed to C. Shaw-Lefevre, father of Sir John, in 1807).

Manorial documents, 1661 to 1839, including survey, 1808; descent for 1575–1823; rentals, 1661–1839.

Title deeds and miscellaneous papers, 1764–1852.

Church, erection of, papers, 1835–41.

Thomas Eyre Charities in Burley, papers, 1823–56.

Other Properties of Shaw-Lefevre. Letters and deeds concerning properties in Hyde Park Gardens, Whitehall Place, and Battersea, London; Leyton Grange, Essex; Hartley Westpall, Hants.; Sutton Place, Surrey, 1834–57.

Family Papers, tradesmen's accounts and other personal papers, 1827–56.

Estates of Earl Spencer. Grant to E. Spencer of certain tolls on Rugby to Hinckley Road, 1825.

Rentals of Wimbledon Estates, 1831; of St. James Place and the Spencer Estates in Surrey, 1826–33.

Inclosure Acts, Cases and Opinons, 1810–33.

Papers relating to sale of Wimbledon Estate, 1845.

Memoranda Books, 1826–30.

Pass Books, 1818–34.

Letter Books, 1827–35.

Correspondence with 2nd, 3rd, and 4th E. Spencer; with local agents, tenants, lawyers, etc., 1828–46.

Trusts. Miscellaneous papers concerning trusts of Rev. the Hon. Richard Carleton, 1832–56; Rev. John Field, 1854–7; Henry Kett Tompson, 1853; the Promoter Life Assurance Society, 1840, 1854.

LIST. A summary list is available in H.L.R.O.

EXCHEQUER CHIEF USHER RECORDS

An account of the Court of Exchequer and a description of those of its records there preserved are provided in the *Guide to the Contents of the Public Record Office*, vol. i. Two small series of records originally belonging to the archives of the Court of Exchequer, however, have been preserved in the House of Lords. They relate almost entirely to the work of the Chief Ushers and their deputies in the Court who, together with the Court itself, were established within the Palace of Westminster.

Chief Usher Papers

1770 to 1824   500 docs.

The first series, preserved amongst the Main Papers, H.L., principally comprises accounts and corr. concerning the payment of fees to Exchequer Officers and concerning the supply of 'necessaries' to them; it also includes several patents of appointment as Messenger.

1823 to 1841   32 docs.

A separate series of Exchequer Court records, preserved amongst the Parliament Office Papers, includes deeds of constitution of Messengers; accounts of G. H. W. Heneage, Chief Usher, 1830–7; and bill of necessaries, 1840–1.

See also HISTORICAL COLLECTIONS, p. 286, below.

The House of Lords Record Office and the Libraries of the two Houses have acquired by gift or purchase a number of manuscripts, most of which relate to the history of Parliament or to the work of members and officials of the Houses. These manuscripts are available for use by students in the Search Room of the Record Office.

HISTORICAL COLLECTIONS OF THE HOUSE
OF LORDS RECORD OFFICE

The main collections of the House of Lords Record Office are listed alphabetically; small collections or individual documents are grouped under the subheading MISCELLANEOUS.

American Papers (Russell, Edwards, etc.)

1732 to 1836   192 docs.

This collection consists of (1) two packets of papers relating to the affairs of James Russell, Ironmaster, of Nottingham, Maryland, U.S.A., including letters, lists of bonds, current accounts, certificates and valuations of confiscations, 1764–1804, 85 docs; (2) a brief for counsel appearing before the Privy Council relating to grants made by proprietors of Carolina in South Carolina in support of the confirmation of a Quit Rent Act, c. 1732; (3) deeds, letters of attorney, etc. relating to affairs and property of Thomas Pruson, Northampton, Virginia; William Walter of Williamstown, Virginia; *et al.*, 1745–78, 17 docs.; (4) the Edwards Partnership papers, including articles of co-partnership between John Edwards of Charles Town, South Carolina, and Charles Goodwin and Walter Thomas of the city of Chester, 1755, and similar articles between J.E., C.G., James Fisher and James Ballantine, all merchants of Charles Town, 1772; file of letters and accounts of the partnership; bill in equity concerning partnership in Circuit Court for South Carolina, 1755–94, 37 docs.; (5) Lee Family papers including declaration of trust as to 10,400 acres, co. Mason, Kanawha, and Fayette, States of Virginia and Kentucky, property of John Lee, LL.D., of Hartwell House, co. Bucks., 1778–1836, 52 docs.

LIST available in H.L.R.O.

The Atkin Papers

1883 to 1913   17 docs.

These papers, found amongst the Judicial records, H.L., largely concern the legal practice of J. R. Atkin, K.C., the first Lord Atkin (1867–1944), appointed a Judge in the King's Bench Division in 1913, a Lord Justice of Appeal in 1919, and, in 1928 a Lord of Appeal in Ordinary.

The items include Barristers' Fee Books and Account Books, a legal note book and an Inventory of valuation of 16 Southwell Gardens, London SW7.

The Braye Manuscripts

1572[1] to 1748   940 items

These documents were originally in the possession of John Browne, Clerk of the Parliaments, 1638–49, 1660–91, or his descendants. The greater proportion

[1] Included in this series are many later copies of pre-1572 documents.

were official records of the House of Lords, some were Parliament Office Papers, and a few personal family papers. They were discovered *ante* 1887 at Stanford Hall, Northamptonshire, in the custody of Browne's descendant, the then Lord Braye. Between 1947 and 1962 these MSS. (together with others owned by L. Braye) were sold at a sequence of auctions and private sales. The whole of the Browne papers were acquired, or the originals photo-copied, by H.L.R.O. The resulting acquisitions are kept in a numbered series as a Historical Collection named 'The Braye Manuscripts'. A considerable part of the collection had been calendared in the *10th Report* of the Historical Manuscripts Commission, app., pt. vi (1887); and further references, together with transcripts of certain important documents, are given in vol. xi of the *Calendar*.

The Braye Manuscripts are arranged in the following sequence:

Vol.
1. Letters and State Papers, 1572–1636. (Calendared in H.M.C., *10th Rept.*, *ut supra*, pp. 125–34.)
2. Letters and State Papers, 1637–41. (*Ibid.*, pp. 134–45.)
3. Letters and State Papers, 1648–1710. (*Ibid.*, pp. 167–87.)
4. Lords Journal Extracts, 1558–1604; Extracts from Bowyer's Reports, 1605, etc.
5. (a) 'Privileges of the Lords of Parliament' (MS. treatise concerning the Trial of Peers, the bringing up of writs of error, the form of swearing, etc., *temp*. Cha. I).

    (b) 'Discourse of the Privelidge and practice of the high Courte of Parleamente in Englande Collected out of the common Lawes of the lande', a version of the tract of this name by Ralph Starkey.
6. 'Treatise on Judicature in Parliament', ascribed to J. Selden, MS. copy, 17th c.
7. Declaration of both Houses, 19 May 1642.
8. Original record of the trial of Archbishop Laud, 1644 (printed *in extenso*, *Calendar*, vol. xi, pp. 364–467); with a 17th c. MS. version of the trial of E. Strafford, 1641.
9. Parliamentary Records, 1660–94 (listed in *Calendar*, vol. xi, *passim*).
10. Parliamentary Records, 1635–89 (listed in *Calendar*, vol. xi, *passim*).
11, 12. MS. Draft Journals, H.L., 1621
13–15. MS. Draft Journals, H.L., 1624–8.
16–21. MS. Draft Journals, H.L., 1640–1.
22, 23. MS. Draft Journals, H.L., Photographic copies, 1641–2.
24, 25. MS. Draft Journals, H.L., 1642.
26–44. MS. Draft Journals, H.L., 1660–90.
45–55. Files of Parliamentary and other records, 1601–1748, 345 docs. (photographic copies). They include 'Breife Collection of all generall Penall statutes now in force and in use', early 17th c.; Clerk's memoranda concerning Mompesson Impeachment, etc., 1621; vol. of speeches, etc., 1627–8; 2 Lists of Peers, 10 Cha. II; Fees payable to the Clerk by the Lords at their first coming, n.d.; Clerk's Fees, 1619; Henry Elsynge's draft chapter on 'Summons of Peers to Parliament'; original Minute

sheets, H.L., 1640, 1641, 1660–88; 7 briefs of Bills, 1670, etc.; original letters of the King of Spain etc., 1624, 1661, 1665; papers concerning conferences of the two Houses; Bowyer's note on Parliament Rolls, 1606–7; Bowyer's agreement with Owen Reynolds, deputy Clerk of the Parliaments, 1610; Minutes of proceedings, 1614; and copies of various papers as entered *in extenso* in the Journals, 1642–9.

56. Trial of E. Strafford. Photographic copy of part of vol. 8 above.

57, 58. Photostats and typescript of those Braye MSS. purchased by Sir William Teeling, M.P. in 1947, 1642 to 1647, 52 docs. For the originals *see* p. 272 below.

59, 60. Robert Bowyer's Parliamentary Diary, H.C., 1606–7 (original MS.). These 2 vols. are Books 1 and 3, respectively, of the diary printed by D. H. Willson in *Parliamentary Diary of Robert Bowyer, 1606–7* (1931).

61. Robert Bowyer's Minutes of Proceedings, H.L., 1610 (printed by E.R. Foster, *Proceedings in Parliament 1610*, vol. i (1966), pp. 177–240).

62. Committee Appointment Book, H.L., 1610.

63, 64. Books of Journal Extracts, H.L., 1621–2.

65. John Browne's Book of Procedure, H.L., *c.* 1638–42.

66. Henry Elsynge's draft of the Parliament Roll, 19–27 Feb. 1624.

67. Protestations of the Commons, 1 & 18 Ja. I.

68. Minutes of Proceedings, H.L., 5, 23 March 1623.

69. Henry Elsynge's first Draft Journal, H.L., 12 March 1621.

70. The Address to the King, and the Royal reply, H.L., 14 March 1624.

71, 72. Minutes of Proceedings (annotated and corrected), H.L., 19, 21 Feb. 1624.

73. MS. Journal H.C. (contemporary, clerk's draft), 12–25 Feb. 1624.

74. Clerk's Roll of Peers, with notes of the taking of oaths, 17 March–7 May, 1628.

75. Sir John Coke's speech at Oxford, H.L., 4 Aug. 1625.

76. Clerk's book of Notes on 'The State of the Bills', 3 & 4 Cha. I.

77. Draft Journal, H.L., 12–27 May 1679.

78. Vol. entitled 'The Habeas Corpus, 1627' concerning 'The Five Knights Case' (cf. T.B. Howell, *State Trials*, vol. iv (1816), cols. 1–59).

79. Vol. of Elizabethan transcripts, including Instructions for E. Essex and L. Howard, 1596; Epistle dedicatory to L. Howard, n.d., etc.

80. Classified Index of Private Acts, 1509–90, perhaps compiled for Sir Thomas Smith (Clerk, 1597–1609).

81. Draft message from Charles I, 2 May 1626.

82. Notes of Proceedings, H.L., concerning the case of E. Middlesex (1624) and E. Bristol (1626).

83. Draft Journal, H.L., 21 Oct.–20 Nov. 1680.

84. Petitions of Grievances, etc., H.C., 1606–10.

85. State of Public Accounts, H.L., presented 26 Oct. 1669, with copies of Roos Illegitimation Act, 18 & 19 Cha. II, no. 21; and Roos Marriage Act, 22 Cha. II, no. 14.

86. John Browne's Book of Journal Extracts, H.L., 1640, 1641, 1645–7.
87. John Browne's Book of Precedents, H.L., 1377–1629.
88. Journal Extracts, H.L., the Short Parliament, 1640.
89. Journal Book, H.C., 17 March–25 June 1628 (the text is similar to that printed in T. Fuller, *Ephemeris Parliamentaria* (1654)).
90. Draft Journal, H.L., 25 Oct. 1641–14 Jan. 1642.
91. Journals, H.C., 7 March–10 April 1593; photographic copy of MS. version of Hayward Townshend's Diary, 1601.
92. 'Some Parliament Passages', including Elsynge's *Modus tenendi Parliamentum*, and speeches in both Houses, 1621, 1625.
93. 'Fragmenta Parliamentaria', Privileges and Rights of Parliament, and Orders, in J. Browne's hand, with entries relating to 1510–1645.
94. 'Extracts, Edward I to Elizabeth', including Elizabethan MSS. on H.C. procedure, 1571–86 and *post* 1581. Photographic copies. The originals of nos. 94 and 95 are preserved amongst the Osborn MSS., Yale University.
95. 'Parliamentary 1599–1644', including Strafford trial papers, 1641, and Clerk's Diary Sheets, 1641. Photographic copies.

LISTS AND MEMORANDA available in H.L.R.O.

The Braye-Teeling Manuscripts

1642 to 1647   52 docs.

Items from the Braye collection, purchased by Sir William Teeling in 1947, and from him by H.L.R.O. in 1968. The collection is that calendared in H.M.C., *10th Rept.*, app., pt. vi, pp. 145–167, but with the omission of some items noted there. It includes a draft by John Pym, 1643; Memoranda at a Conference, 1642; copies of Examinations, 1646–7.

LIST available in H.L.R.O.

The Bromley Precedent Book

1547–1731   1 vol.

The vol. was compiled by William Bromley (M.P. 1690–1732; Speaker, 1710–13; d. 1732). It comprises his classified digest of precedents concerning H.C. procedure from the Journals, D'Ewes' *Debates*, and probably from an earlier precedent book for 1547–1640 similar to that used by Speaker Onslow (see p. 244 above). There are also copies of E. Leicester's letter to the Borough of Andover, 12 Oct. 1584, and of a writ for proroguing Parliament, 2 Jan. 1714, together with Bromley's own index. The vol. was bought by Mr. F. C. Holland, a clerk in H.C. 1888–1926, and was placed on loan in H.L.R.O. by his nephew, Mr. David Holland, the present Librarian, H.C.

The Catesby Collection

1580 to 1910   190 items

In 1965 Messrs. Catesby Ltd. deposited in H.L.R.O. a collection of prints, photographs, books, etc., relating to the Gunpowder Plot and to the conspirator, Robert Catesby (1573–1605).

The collection includes an original deed, par. Nether Heyford, co. Northants., of 1580; Plans of the Palace of Westminster, published 1804, 1807, 1825; a series of 18th–20th c. engravings, drawings and photographs concerning localities associated with the Plot, and 28 books relating to the history of the Plot.

List available in H.L.R.O.

Commonplace Note Book Collection

1668 to 1925   159 vols.

The following collection, formed in the 20th c., comprises the five series of note books, letters and papers listed below.

1. *Commonplace Books*

1740 to 1878   16 vols.

Commonplace note books of Henry Bird (1814), Georgiana Cook (1838), Gardine Isabella Edward (1856), Humphrey William Fielding (1863), Edmund Pitts Gapper (1788), E. Hayward, (*c.* 1819), Rosa Isabella Ilduton (1829), Lucinda Cowan Macy (1851), W. H. Maxwell (1820), Edward Marshall (1849), Rev. Octavius Winslow, D.D. (1878), Harriet Yonge (1860), anon., 4 vols. (1740, 1810, 1820, 1868).

2. *Personal Note Books*

1707 to 19th c.   19 vols.

This series includes a book of medical formulae (1826), legal note books, 4 vols. (1707–14), cookery recipe books (1722 of Joanna Clay, and 1867), classical note book (1756), scrap book (S.S. Bunting, 1842), philosophical note books (2 vols. Alexander Clark, 1670 and 17th c.), travel diaries, 4 vols., 19th c.

3. *Literary Manuscripts*

1800 to 1925   26 vols.

The original manuscripts in this series includes stories by Catherine Eden, 1803; verses by Annie J. Glascock, 1853, and by Adelaide Glascock, 1855; poems by Mrs. M. Robinson, *c.* 1800; poem, 'The Mysteries of Eleusis' by Alfred Addis, 1854; miscellaneous compositions by 'Edward B.P.' with diary notes, 1817–20.

4. *Clerical Notebooks*

1668 to 1755   6 vols,

The vols. comprise sermons of Rev. John Powell (1712–35); clerical notebook, including prayers, and rents for Thornhull, Gomershay, Weston and Town Tithings (1708–9); sermons preached mainly in Chichester diocese (*c.* 1707–55); sermons of Rev. James Badger, 1668 and 1676; sermons preached at Bexley and elsewhere, co. Kent (1720–31).

5. *Miscellaneous Manuscripts*

1781 to 1887   92 items

This series includes 4 vols of children's notebooks and exercise books (Charlotte and Elizabeth Caton), 1797–1808; 4 vols. private family magazines, 1880, 1887; 1 vol. copies of letter from Rev. Robert Newstead, first Wesleyan missionary to Colombo, 1816–9; 38 letters from William Wetherall of Upper Lambourne, co. Berks. and others to T. M. Robinson of Reading, principally concerning horse-racing, 1862–5.

LIST available in H.L.R.O.

'The Complete Peerage' Materials

1910 to date   332 docs. and 64 files

Between 1910 and 1959 a thoroughly revised edition of G. E. Cokayne's *The Complete Peerage of England, Scotland, Ireland, Great Britain and the United Kingdom* was published in 13 vols. under the authority of the Complete Peerage Trust. On the completion of the work the Trustees deposited materials relating to the Trust and its publications in H.L.R.O. The deposit includes the corr. and administrative papers of the Trust; an annotated set of the *Complete Peerage* vols.; a second set with press cuttings concerning peers; 3 files with a Card Index of Corrigenda for the series. Certain further corrigenda sheets are added to the files of H.L.R.O. from time to time.

USE. With the exception of the general corr., accounts, and Minutes of meetings of the Trust, this class is available for inspection.

Forest and Commons Papers

1720 to 1931   2,801 docs.

These papers were formerly in the possession of the Commons and Footpaths Preservation Society, and relate to its own work or to that of earlier or allied societies, and to law suits in which they were involved. The principal constituents are:

Epping Forest Commission Papers, 1720–1882, including Arbitration Proceedings, 1879–82. (*See* also HISTORICAL COLLECTIONS, H.C.)

Papers concerning Ken Wood and the extension of Hampstead Heath, 1871–1925.

Papers concerning Town Meadows, Fulham, 1888–90.

Epsom Common Preservation Committee Papers, 1856–99.

Bundle of papers relating to commons in Frydinghurst, Haslemere, Chiddingfold and Thursley, co. Surrey, 1781, 1884–7, with Haslemere Common Committee Papers, 1879–1906.

Papers relating to Nettlebed and District Commons (Preservation) Act, 1906.

Misc. papers relating to Vale Royal Park footpath, 1903; Northwich, co. Cheshire, 1902–3; Eastbourne, co. Sussex, 1902; Hurley, co. Berks., 1903–5, etc.

Papers relating to the Stray at Harrogate, co. Yorks. 1891–1911; Harrogate and the Forest of Knaresborough, 1770–1901; Landiway, co. Cheshire, 1902; Fakenham, co. Norfolk, 1838–71; Medmenham, co. Bucks., 1778–1898; the Commission on London Squares, 1926–31; the Foundling Hospital, London WCI, 1925–8; Malvern Hills, co. Worcs. and Heref., 1877–83; Limpsfield, co. Surrey, 1846–99.

A second deposit of papers relating to the work of the Commons and Foot-paths Preservation Society was received in 1970. It consists of 1,660 docs., dating from 1866–1908, and concerning the following places or subjects: Medmenham Ferry; Burnham Beeches, co. Bucks.; Ashdown Forest; West Wellow, co. Hants.; Anglesey; Hampstead Heath; Banstead, co. Surrey; Malvern Chase, co. Worcs.; and Thames Reservoirs.

LISTS available in H.L.R.O.

The Hardman Drawings

1835 to 1855   120 items

A file of drawings, deposited by Messrs. John Hardman Studios (Birmingham), containing working drawings prepared in their studios, relating in part to the provision of stained glass and other ornamentation for the new Houses of Parliament. The drawings are by A. W. Pugin and others; some refer to work undertaken by Hardman Studios elsewhere.

The Lee Papers

c. 1738 to 1745   9 docs.

Sir George Lee, D.C.L. (1700–58), was M.P. for Brackley, Northamptonshire from 1733 to 1742, for Devizes, 1742 to 1747, for Liskeard, 1747 to 1754, and for Launceston, 1754 to 1758. He was Dean of the Arches, 1751 to 1758. The papers include notes for a speech on Placemen in H.C., notes on proceedings on the deaths of Sovereigns, 1701 to 1727, and drafts for Bills concerning relief of prisoners, suppression of piracy, prizes, etc. The docs. are mainly holograph.

The Leveson Gower Papers

1890 to 1920   55 items

William George Gresham Leveson Gower, b. 12 March 1883, was appointed a clerk in the Parliament Office on 1 May 1908 and held this post until his death on active service, 9 Oct. 1918. He also served as a lecturer at the Working Men's College, London. The deposited papers include his diaries 1894–1918, 24 vols.: bound vols. of letters to, from, and concerning him, 1890–1907, 1918–20, 15 vols.; file of obituary notices, etc., 1918; file of 22 photographs, photograph album, etc. Deposited by Miss V. Leveson Gower. (*See* BAILEY PAPERS for a similar deposit concerning a clerk of H.C.)

The E. Manchester Papers

1606 to 1645   16 docs.

Photocopies of a group of misc. papers of 1st E. Manchester of which the

19—R.O.P.

originals are preserved in Huntingdonshire Record Office. They include the Declaration of H.C. on foreign affairs, 4 July 1621; the H.C. Diary of Sir Nathaniel Rich, 1628; the Minutes of H. C. Committee on Charges against E. Strafford, with Notes of a Conference, 1640–1; Memorandum on Parliamentary affairs of J. Williams, Bp. Lincoln, 1641; Complaint by Keeper of the Palace against J. Browne, *c.* 1642.

See also PARLIAMENTARY JOURNALS AND DIARIES, below, pp. 279–80, and WILLCOCKS PAPERS, p. 284.

Marriage Law Papers

1819 to 1836   3 vols.

The vols. were originally formed by a firm of Parliamentary Agents. They contain *c.* 450 items relating to the efforts of Unitarians and other protestant non-conformists to obtain reforms in the marriage laws. They include a copy of the rules of the Unitarian Association, 1819; corr. concerning petitions to relieve dissenters from some parts of the marriage ceremony, 1819; draft Bill, with corr. with Archbishop of Canterbury, 1822; proceedings concerning Marriage Bill, 1823; corr., etc., with Duke of Wellington, 1828; discussion with the Bishop of London, 1831; memorandum concerning parochial registers, *c.* 1831; report of sub-committee of Unitarian dissenters on Peel's Marriage Bill, 1835; papers relating to Marriage Act, 1836, 6 & 7 Will. IV, c. 85.

LIST available in H.L.R.O.

The Mattinson Letters

1884 to 1896   18 docs.

Sir Miles Mattinson, Q.C. (1854–1943), was M.P. for Walton Division of Liverpool, and Recorder of Blackburn. Letters are included from Lord Randolph Churchill (1884–5), Mr. Speaker Gully (1895–6), and others.

Miscellaneous

1300 to date   404 items

Act of Resumption. Enrolled Act of Resumption, 29 Hen. VI, as in *Rotuli Parliamentorum*, vol. v, pp. 217–20, but lacking preamble and provisoes. 1 doc.

E. Aldborough *v.* Trye *et al.* Petition of Mason Gerard, 5th E. Aldborough, [1839].

Ascot Authority Bill, Petition against (H.L.), 1913.

Autograph vol. containing 160 autograph letters, signed, engraved portraits, etc., collected by Sir Frederick Stovin, and relating to members of the Royal Family and to members of the two Houses of Parliament, etc., 1796–1856.

Autographs of peers and others, with 11 letters, in 1 vol., 1809–74, deposited by Miss F. M. Gough.

Autographs of Prime Ministers. 1 file of photographic copies of documents, containing autographs of Ministers and Prime Ministers from Cardinal Wolsey to E. Attlee. (The originals are in the collection of V. Mersey.)

Beauclerk Letters. Letters from Major A. W. Beauclerk, M.P., to George Corner, his solicitor, 1834–7, 8 docs.

Bishop of Chichester's Estate Bills, 1698, 1703. 4 docs. relating to the Bills; with photostat copies of 12 other docs. concerning them now in the custody of the City of London Guildhall Library.

A. Boyer, letter from, concerning D'Avenant's *Essays upon Peace at Home and War*, 1703, 1 doc.

British Railways (Eastern Region). Plans, Books of Reference and other Parliamentary deposits, previously in the custody of British Rail, 1847–1924, 133 docs. (duplicates of H.L. and H.C. archives).

Bromley Estate Bill. List of Committee, H.C., 26 March 1728, 1 doc.

Burke, Edmund. *A Letter from the Right Honourable Edmund Burke to a Noble Lord on the attacks made upon him and his pension in the House of Lords by the Duke of Bedford and Earl of Lauderdale Early in the present Session of Parliament.* (1796). 1 vol.

Chippenham Elections. Disputed Elections, Select Committee, H.C., Evidence (imperfect), 1802, (3 vols.), 1806 (1 vol.).

Declaration of James Stuart, the Old Pretender, from 'our Court at Plumbiers' 29 Aug. 1714. Photographic copy.

Duchy of Lancaster Deposited Plans. Plans deposited in the Duchy of Lancaster Office in connection with Private Bills relating to the Duchy (transferred from the Duchy Office to H.L.R.O.), 1863–1914, 75 docs.

Ecclesiastical Archives. Report of the Committee appointed by the Pilgrim Trustees in 1946 to carry out a survey of the Provincial, Diocesan, Archidiaconal, and Capitular Archives of the Church of England; together with the Survey, 1951, 4 vols. (typescript).

The Entwistle Statute Roll. Photographic copy of the Entwistle Roll of Statutes, 1235–97 (compiled *c.* 1300), preserved in the Lancashire Record Office, 1 vol.

Grant of Arms to City of Westminster. Letters Patent, 1601. (Photographic copy.)

'The Jurisdiction of the House of Peers'. Copy of 'imperfect' tract by L. Keeper Guilford, probably written in answer to L. Holles's 'Case Stated concerning Judicature of the House of Peers in the Point of Appeals' (1675), late 17th c.

Merchants' Petitions and affairs of the Navy, summary of proceedings in Parliament concerning, 1692, 1693, 1707, 1 doc.

Mildmay Speeches. Photographic copy of vol. of speeches of Sir Walter Mildmay M.P., and others, in H.C., 1570–93, 1 vol.

Minute Sheets, H.L. Photographic copies of Minute Sheets sent in letter form by the Clerks in the Parliament Office to D. Somerset, 1696–7, 20 docs.

Modus tenendi parliamentum. Photocopy of Harleian MS. 930, British Museum.

Newcastle Waterworks Bill, 1834. Evidence given before Sel Com., H.C., 1 vol.

Bishop Nicolson Diaries. Photocopies of diaries of William Nicolson, Bp. Carlisle (1702–18), 1701–14, 10 vols.

Orders of the House of Lords. Original printed Orders, broad-sheet, each on one leaf, 1678–80, 5 docs.

Protector Somerset, letter from, to Sir Edward North, concerning delivery of the records of Parliament, 1548. Photocopy, 1 doc.

Protest Book. 'A Collection of all the Protestations Entered in the Journals of the House of Lords', 1641–1741, recently in the possession of Lady Ramsden, 1 vol.

Protests. Clerk's Protest Sheets for Protests of E. Temple and L. Talbot, 1755, 2 docs.

Redesdale Letters. Photographic copies of correspondence of John Thomas Freeman-Mitford, 2nd L. (later E.) Redesdale, 1837–82 (originals in Gloucestershire Records Office), 114 docs.

Report of the Commissioners of Fine Arts concerning the sculpting of statues for St. Stephen's Hall, etc., sealed by Commissioners, 25 April 1845.

Ryder Notebook. Notebook of Sir Dudley Ryder (1691–1756), Lord Chief Justice, King's Bench, 1754, concerning procedure, H.L., with journal of his sitting as Speaker, H.L. etc. 1754–5. Typescript of doc. 35 (q), among records of E. of Harrowby, Sandon Hall, co. Staffs.

Speeches in H.C. Two speeches by anon. M.P., subsequently 'wrote out from Memory', delivered 25 and 26 March 1755, 2 docs.

Teller of the Exchequer, Report by Spencer Compton to the Lord Treasurer on an appointment to this post, n.d. [1711–14], 1 doc.

Tenterden Letters. Letters from John Henry Abbott, 2nd L. Tenterden to Sir Egerton Brydges, bart., L. Chandos of Sudeley, 1832–4, 3 docs.

Townshend Papers. 5 docs. from papers of M. Townshend, Raynham Hall, co. Norfolk, deposited by Dr. B. Crick, including printed Case of the British Northern Colonies, 1732; printed Representation of the Commissioners of Trade, 1735; printed Quebec Bill, 1791.

Trial of Mary Queen of Scots. Photographic copy of the record of the trial, 1586, British Museum, Cottonian MS., Caligula, C. ix, ff. 36–501, 1 vol.

Trials of Peers. Passes for trials of E. Ferrers (1760), L. Byron (1765) and Duchess of Kingston (1776), 3 docs.

Warrant under Signet to Keeper of Privy Seal to issue warrant under Privy Seal to L. Chancellor for Letters Patent creating Charles V. Whitworth, Baron Adbaston of Adbaston, 21 Nov. 1815.

Williams Deposit. Lantern slides and microfilm relating to the history of the fabric of the Palace of Westminster, 1967. Deposited by the Executors of Dr. Orlo Williams, 5 items.

The Nalson Papers

1628 to 1660   80 vols.

John Nalson, antiquary, and Canon of Ely, borrowed from John Browne, Clerk of the Parliaments, an extensive series of Parliamentary records in order to prepare an 'antidote to Rushworth'. Two volumes were published by Nalson in 1682–3, entitled *An Impartial Collection of the Great Affairs of State from the beginning of the Scotch Rebellion in the year 1639 to the Murder of King Charles I. . . .* The records were not, however, returned, and were found, *ante* 1891, in the possession of the Duke of Portland at Welbeck Abbey. They are now on deposit in the Bodleian Library, Oxford. The most important concern relations between Parliament as a sovereign body and the European powers, 1649 to 1659. The vols. in H.L.R.O. comprise photocopies made by permission of the Duke of Portland and of the Bodleian Library.

CALENDAR. The docs. are fully calendared in the H.M.C., *13th Rept.*, app., pt. i.

Parliamentary Journals and Diaries

1510 to 1750   132 vols.

The official classes of Journals are noted above under RECORDS OF PROCEEDINGS, H.L. and H.C.; the following vols. have been acquired by gift or purchase. (*See* also Journals, Minutes and Diaries listed amongst the BRAYE MSS. and the PETYT MSS.)

The Harcourt Journals, 1510–1750. Copies of the official Journals, H.L., without Presents. On fo. 1 of vol. 1 is a 'List of the severall Journals in the Parliament Office', *sc.* before they were bound in the present series. The set of vols. belonged to Edward William Harcourt of Stanton Harcourt, co. Oxon (M.P., 1878–86) and may have been written for the 1st E. Harcourt (*cr.* 1749). 124 vols.

Journal Book of the House of Peers during the Reign of Queen Mary, 1553–8. A late 17th c. MS. probably written in the Parliament Office, containing an abbreviated version of the Original Journals, with some commentary. 1 vol.

Proceedings in Parliament, 1601. A contemporary version of Hayward Townshend's Diary or Journal of H.C. for 27 Oct.–29 Dec. 1601, as printed with slight variants in his *Historical Collections*, 1680. 1 vol. Cf. J. E. Neale, 'The authorship of Townshend's Historical Collections', *English Historical Review*, vol. xxxvi (1921), pp. 96–99. Cf. also BRAYE MSS. no. 91.

Commonplace Book. This was formerly in the possession of Mr. Percy Millican; it contains proceedings from several parliaments, Ja. I and Cha. I, including notes from a Journal of H.C. 4 Ja. I, notes from Journals of H.L. and H.C. 1621 ('lent by Mr. Cotton'), notes from Journal of H.C. 3 Cha. I. There are also notes of cases in Star Chamber 1608–1640 and miscellaneous notes. This MS. is referred to in *Commons Debates 1621*, ed. W. Notestein, F. H. Relf, H. Simpson (1935), i, 14–15.

Proceedings in Parliament, 1628. A contemporary collection of some 103 speeches etc. made in H.C., 1628. 1 vol.

The Manchester Proceedings in Parliament, 1628. Photocopy of vol. in MSS. of E. Manchester (Hunts. Record Office MS. M 36/4).

The Manchester True Relation, 1629. 'A true relacion of everie daies proceedinge in Parlyament since the Session begunne the 20th of Januarie 1628'. A contemporary version, formerly amongst the MSS of E. Manchester, of a narrative of proceedings and debates, mostly in H.C., 20 January–10 March 1629 (collated by W. Notestein and F. H. Relf in their edition of the 'True Relation' in *Commons Debates for 1629* (1921) pp. 1–106).

The Grosvenor Journals, 1 vol. comprising 7 MSS. collected *c.* 1634–42, probably by Sir Richard Grosvenor, 1st bart. (1585–1645). The vol. is lettered 'Eaton MS. 24'. Its contents are:

> The order of passing of Bills in Parliament [by William Hakewill]
> 'A briefe discourse proveinge that the house of Commons hath equall power with the Peeres in point of Judicature. Written by Sir Robert Cotton to Sir Edward Mountague Anno 1621.'
> The Submission of V. St. Albans, April, 1621.

The Submission of Sir Henry Yelverton, 27 Oct. 1620.

Sir Walter Raleigh's Apology.

A letter of advice to the H.C.

Journal of H.C. 19 Feb.–9 April 1593; the version in part used by Sir Simonds D'Ewes in his *Journal of . . . the House of Lords and House of Commons* (1682) and described by him as the 'anonymous' diary.

Journal of H.L., 24 Oct. 1597–9 Feb. 1598, following the official Journal in summary form.

L. Wentworth's speech to Irish Parliament, 15 July 1634.

Proceedings on the choice of a Speaker, H.C., 1553–1734. Photocopy of Lansdowne MS. 507., British Museum.

Reports of H.C. Conferences with the Lords, 1660–1732. Photocopy of Lansdowne MSS. 550–2, British Museum.

Notes on Proceedings in the House of Lords, 1640–1. Photographic copy of Salt Library, Stafford, MS. 266, including
  (a) Standing Orders of H.L., 1624.
  (b) Notes on proceedings, in H.L., 3 Nov. 1640, 25 Jan., 24 March and 2 Aug. 1641.

The Tangye Journal, H.L., 1658–9. MS. copy of the original Journal of H.L., 20 Jan. 1658–22 April 1659 formerly in the possession of Lady Tangye, now in the London Museum, printed *in extenso* in vol. iv of the *Calendar*, pp. 503–67. 1 vol.

Leaves of Journal, H.L., 3 and 27 Henry VIII, photocopies of Harleian MS. 158, ff. 141–4, British Museum.

An Account of the Commons Journals, written *c.* 1710. It lists the individual vols. extant before the loss of the Elizabethan Journals, and before the present rebinding.

John Relfe's Book of Orders, 1710. A transcript of Standing Orders, H.L., to 1710, followed by categorised extracts from the Journals, many of which are similar to those in vol. ii of John Relfe's Journals (*see* PARLIAMENT OFFICE PAPERS). There is also additional matter, especially for *post*-1700 dates, and some variations. 1 vol.

The Petyt Manuscripts (Inner Temple)

1510 to 1704   31 vols.

William Petyt (1636–1707), Keeper of the Records at the Tower of London, bequeathed an extensive collection of manuscripts to the Inner Temple, including many relating to the affairs of Parliament in the first half of the 17th c. Certain of these were records and memoranda compiled by Robert Bowyer, Clerk of the Parliaments (1609–21), who had previously served as M.P. for Steyning (1601) and for Evesham (1605), and as Joint Keeper of the Rolls (from 1604).

Photo-copies have been made, by permission of the Benchers of the Inner Temple, and are preserved in H.L.R.O., of the principal Parliamentary docs. amongst the Petyt MSS. The vols. in the sequence 537 noted below as 'H.L.' or 'H.C. Journals' are early 17th c.; except where indicated they follow the texts of the Original Journals closely, but some matter is omitted, numbers are added for ease of reference, and some comment is interpolated. The vols. in the sequence 538 are calendared with varying degrees of detail in the H.M.C., *11th Rept.*, pt. vii, *sub*. 'MSS. of the Inner Temple'. The vols. in H.L.R.O. are as follows (in their original Inner Temple Library numeration):

537. 1. H.L. Journals, 1510–39.
537. 2. H.L. Journals, 1540–7.
537. 3. H.L. Journals, 1548–53.
537. 4. H.C. Journals, 1547–58.
537. 5. H.L. Journals, 1553–8.
537. 6. Bowyer's annotated Abridgement of H.L. Journals, 1553–1600, containing material additional to that in the Lords Journals (ed. E. Jeffries Davis, in 'An Unpublished Manuscript of the Lords' Journal for April and May 1559', *English Historical Review*, vol. xviii, pp. 531–42, and by J. C. Sainty, in *House of Lords Record Office Memorandum no. 33*).
537. 7. H.L. Journals, 1558–81.
537. 8. Bowyer's annotated Abridgement, H.L. Journals, 1603–14. (Material for 1610 is printed in E. R. Foster, *Proceedings in Parliament, 1610*, vol. i (1966), pp. 240–55.)
537. 9. H.L. and H.C. Journals, 1601.
537. 10. H.C. Diary, 1621.
537. 11. H.L. Journals, 1624.
537. 12. H.C. Journals, 1604.
537. 13. H.C. Journals, 1606–7.
537. 14. H.C. Journals, 1610, with additional material relating to Cowell's *Interpreter*, and including original entries for 9–15 Feb. and 4–6 June 1610, printed *in extenso* in E. R. Foster, *Proceedings in Parliament, 1610*, vol. ii (1966), pp. 3–9, 126–31.
537. 15. H.C. Diary, 1621.
537. 16. (a) H.L. Journal Extracts, 1621;
        (b) H.L. Standing Orders, 1–34;
        (c) H.C. Diary, 1601.
537. 17. H.C. Journal, 1624.
537. 18. H.C. Original Book of Orders, 5 Feb.–7 Dec. 1621,[1] Journal Extracts, 1610–21, and misc. papers, 1607–26.
537. 19. H.C. Journal, 1624.
537. 20. Extracts, etc., relating to proceedings in Parliament, mainly 1601–5.
538. 2. Misc. papers relating to proceedings in Parliament, 1603–16.
538. 3. Misc. papers relating to proceedings in Parliament, 1614–21.
538. 4. MS. text of ch. 5 of Book ii of Elsynge's *Manner of Holding Parliaments in England*, almost identical with the text printed by C. S. Sims, in *Expedicio Billarum Antiquitus* (1954).
538. 5. Precedents, mainly concerning taxation, *temp*. Ja. I.
538. 7. Journals, etc., H.L., 1620–8, including
        (a) Rough Minutes, 1628, printed in *Notes of Debates . . . 1621, 1625, 1628*, ed. F. H. Relf (1929).

---

[1] The Book of Orders has been printed *in extenso* in W. Notestein *et al.*, *Commons Debates 1621*. vol. vi (1935), 443–82.

(b) Rough Minutes, 1621, printed in Relf, *op. cit.*
538. 10. Bowyer's annotated Abridgement, H.L. Journals, 1604–6, and other papers (11th *Rept.*, H.M.C., pt. vii, pp. 236–7).
538. 16. Misc. notes and memoranda, 1628–81, (*ibid.*, pp. 238–44).
538. 18. Journal Extracts, H.L., 1623–28, and misc. papers (*ibid.*, pp. 244–5).
538. 19. Misc. papers, *c.* 1590–1623 (*ibid.*, pp. 245–6).
538. 20. Private Diary, H.C., 1593; 'Diurnal occurrences, or, The heads of proceedings, of both houses . . .', 1640–1; and other papers, 1620, 1628, etc. (*ibid.*, pp, 246–8).
538. 22. MS. of text of Book i of Elsynge's *Modus Tenendi Parliamentum apud Anglos,* as printed in 1660.

For other Petyt Parliamentary MSS. *see* the following entry, and also docs. amongst the collection of Lansdowne MSS., 510–21, in the British Museum.

The Petyt Manuscripts (P.R.O.)

1566 to 1614   2 vols.

Photocopies have been bound in 2 vols. of those papers of William Petyt, now preserved in the Public Record Office, which relate directly to the work of Parliament. They include:

An Anonymous Diary, H.C., 2–21 April 1571.
Robert Bowyer's Journal, H.C., 27–30 Oct. 1601.
Elsynge's Abstracts of Journals, H.L., 19 March 1604–4 July 1607.
Copy of Robert Bowyer's Notes of Bills, etc., 1606.
Proceedings in H.L., 30 March 1607.
Journal, H.L., 9 Feb.–18 June 1610, 30 June–10 July 1610.

LIST. The papers are fully listed in vol. 33 of the Lists published by the List and Index Society: *Descriptive List of State Papers Supplementary (S.P. 46), Private Papers, Series I, 1535–1705.* (1968), ff. 238, 239.

Proxy Deeds

1767 to 1816   160 docs.

A collection of signed deeds of appointment of lords as proxies, strays from the official class (*see* PROXY RECORDS), recently owned by Mr. H. S. Semple and acquired by H.L.R.O., 1968.

LIST available in H.L.R.O.

The Ratcliff Charity Trust Papers

1730 to 1954   821 docs.

The Ratcliff Educational Foundation has maintained schools in Stepney since 1862, in succession to the Ratcliff Charity School, founded 1710. The papers include apprenticeship indentures for 1730–1851; deeds of property in Stepney, accounts, corr. for 1862–1954.

LIST available in H.L.R.O.

The Rose Papers

1736 to 1817 2 vols.

The vols. contain photographic copies of the papers of George Rose, Clerk of the Parliaments (1788–1818), preserved in the British Museum as Add. MSS. 42,779, ff. 1–179. The papers are strays from the class of PARLIAMENT OFFICE PAPERS. They include docs. relating to the State of the Parliament Office, 1763; a warrant for settling the precedence of peers, 1776; a list of Peers' Pedigrees, 1767–80; account of stationery in the office, 1784–5; proceedings of Com. Priv. on Anglesey Peerage, 29–31 Jan. 1771; statements of fees and accounts, 1773–4, 1790, 1796, 1799, 1800, 1812, 1813, 1814, 1815, 1816, 1817.

LIST available in H.L.R.O.

The Samuel Papers

1883 to 1962 2,190 items

See plate 15

The papers of Herbert, 1st Viscount Samuel were deposited by his executors in 1963. They comprise the following series:

The Political Papers. (a) Papers classified in subject files, 1890–1962, 154 files; (b) General Political Papers, 1888–1962, 13 files; (c) Family Letters of political interest, 1881–1938, 1,945 items.

Personal Papers, including newspaper cuttings, other family corr., misc. corr., 1871–1962, 22 files.

Photographs and Sketches, 1870–1961; Cleveland By-Election photographs, 1909; Palestine photographs, 1920–5; and Houses of Parliament war damage photographs, 1941, 80 items.

Press Cuttings, 1888–1961, 5 boxes.

Literary, Philosophical and Scientific Papers, 1885–1962, including a MS. of L. Samuel's book, *Liberalism*, and materials relating to other publications, including *Belief and Action*, *An Unknown Land* and *Memoirs*. 84 files.

Grants of Office and Ceremonial Records, 1906–58, including Letters Patent of grants; certificates of oath taking; papers relating to funeral of Edward VII, 1910; coronation of George V, 1911; and coronation of George VI, 1937, 54 items.

LISTS

'The Political Papers of Herbert, First Viscount Samuel', ed. H. S. Cobb, *House of Lords Record Office Memorandum no. 35* (1966).
'The Personal and Literary Papers of Herbert, First Viscount Samuel', ed. H. S. Cobb, *House of Lords Record Office Memorandum no. 41* (1969).
See also the following entry.

The Samuel Papers (Israel)

1915 to 1962 20 vols.

The original papers of the 1st V. Samuel which related to Palestine and the State of Israel were deposited by his executors in the Israel State Archives. By

courtesy of the State Archivist, microfilm and full size photocopies are held in
H.L.R.O. The full size photocopies have been bound in the following sequence:

Correspondence, 1915–62, 16 vols.; *Memoranda and Minutes,* 1919–39, 1 vol.;
Israel State Archives (Official Papers preserved there) 1920–44, 1 vol.; *Press
Cuttings,* 1917–62, 2 vols.

The Tickell Papers

1709 to 1733   9 files

Thomas Tickell (1686–1740), poet, and friend of Addison, was Assistant
Secretary to the Lords Justices of England in 1714, and Secretary of the Lords
Justices of Ireland, 1715–16. His papers are now in the custody of his descendant,
Sir Eustace Tickell. The series preserved in H.L.R.O. comprises photographic
copies of the political papers only. They belong to three groups: (1) Papers
of the Lords Justices of England; minutes and correspondence, 1714. (2) Irish
Papers, 1709–33, including the correspondence of the Lords Justices of Ireland
and Lord Lieutenant of Ireland. (3) Miscellaneous official papers, 1714–20.

BIBLIOGRAPHY. R. E. Tickell, *The Tickell and Connected Families* (1948).

The Walker Papers

1643 to 1649   2 vols.

Sir Edward Walker (1612–77), Garter King of Arms, 1645–77, was in attendance as secretary on Charles I at various periods from 1642–8. The following
draft papers comprise two separate small collections, deposited in H.L. in 1922
and 1953 respectively. The vols. contain draft commissions, warrants, letters,
etc., mainly in the hand of Edward Walker, which were prepared on behalf
of Charles I.

Walpole, Sir R. (E. Orford), Committee of Secrecy Minutes

1742   1 vol.

Minutes of proceedings of the Committee of Secrecy, H.C., enquiring into
the conduct of E. Orford, 31 March–15 July 1742.

The Willcocks Papers

1528 to 1805   270 docs.

Photocopies of docs. in the possession of Mr R. M. Willocks: (1) docs. from
the archives of D. Manchester, calendared in H.M.C., 8th Rept., app., pt. ii,
pp. 55–66 (some omitted); (2) docs. from the archives of R. Cholmondeley,
including some calendared in H.M.C., 5th Rept., app. pp. 345–7, 354–5; (3)
misc. docs. including letter from Tho. Heneage to Cardinal Wolsey, 1528;
letter from E. Essex to R. Bagot, 1588; Warrant for arrest of 5 Members, 1642;
and docs. concerning the civil war, the Monmouth rebellion, the South Sea
Company, and the 1715 and 1745 rebellions, etc.

LIST available in H.L.R.O.

USE. The following collections are in the custody of the Librarian of the House of Lords to whom application by intending students should be made.

BIBLIOGRAPHY

C. Dobson, *The Library of the House of Lords* (1960).
E. Gosse, *Catalogue of the Library of the House of Lords* (1908).

Abergavenny Peerage

MS. notes in connection with the Abergavenny Peerage Claim, 1587–1604, early 17th c. Presented by V. Mersey, 1935.

Appeal Cases

1. MS. alphabetical index to printed Appeal Cases in the Library, H.L., 1702 to 1835.
2. 'A Table to the most remarkable points in the Printed Cases upon Appeals to the House of Lords from 1701 to 1728 . . .', MS., c. 1768.

Armorial

Alphabet of Arms, labelled 'Symonds's Alphabet of Arms', listing about 8,500 Coats of Arms, mid-17th c.; formerly in the possession of Richard Symonds, 1617–92, royalist and antiquary. Purchased, 1964.

Chairmanship of Committees (Memorandum)

Notes by (Sir) Edmund Gosse (Librarian, H.L., 1904–14) on the history of the Chairmanship of Committees, H.L., compiled on the appointment of E. Donoughmore as Chairman, 1911.

Debates, H.C.

Photostat copies of Notes of Proceedings in the House of Commons, Nov. 1770–May 1774, by Matthew Brickdale, M.P. for Bristol. Presented by Sir Charles Fortescue Brickdale, 1931. The original MSS. in 11 vols. are in Bristol University Library.

The Denman MS.

MS. by Ist L. Denman, 6 May 1801, consisting of a summary of Littleton's *Tenures*, together with opinions by judges in relevant cases, lettered on spine 'Readings on Littleton'.

The Drummond Collection

A collection of 150 notebooks, with additional sheets, containing extracts from printed books on the peerage, heraldry, genealogy and allied subjects, by Francis Drummond (1839–1921, Editor of *The World*, genealogist and heraldic student). The collection was placed in the Library on indefinite loan by the Athenaeum, 1957.

Ecclesiastical Law (Treatise)

A treatise in 27 chapters, relating to ecclesiastical benefices: presentations, inductions, alienations, profits, etc., 17th c., *post*-1628.

Exchequer, Offices in the Court of

1. 'A Book of all the severall offices of the Court of Exchequer, together with the names of the present officers . . . with a brief collection of the Chief Heads of what every officer usually doth . . .', compiled by Samuel Edwards, First Clerk of the Exchequer, for George Hay, V. Dupplin, M.P. (Teller of the Exchequer), *c.* 1711. The MS. was presented to the Library by J. Perceval Esq., 1932.

2. A similar MS., 18th c., previously in the Library of Thomas Wilde, 1st L. Truro, Lord Chancellor, 1850–2. Presented to H.L. Library, 1856.

Gibbs (Sir Vicary), Opinions

MS. Opinions of Sir Vicary Gibbs (1751–1820), Chief Justice of the Common Pleas, etc., 2 vols. (duplicates)

Gosse (Sir Edmund), Diary

Private diary written by Gosse, when Librarian, between 1904 and 1906, with two later entries, and a memorandum concerning his appointment in 1904. Presented by his son, Dr. Philip Gosse, in 1938.

USE. It is intended to publish the Diary in due course; in the meantime special application to consult it must be made to the Librarian, H.L.

House of Lords (Theses)

1. 'The Idea of an Aristocratic Second Chamber in a Democratic Constitution: its emergence in the major concepts of political theory from Plato to the American founders.' By A. J. Leonardy. (Submitted in partial fulfilment of the requirement for the degree of Master of Arts, University of Kansas, 1962. Typescript.) Presented by the author through the Lord President of the Council, 1962.

2. 'The present status of the House of Lords.' By Erling Jorstad (typewritten, submitted in requirement of Foreign Studies, University of Minnesota, Minneapolis, 1952). Presented by V. Furness, 1953.

3. 'The Reform of the House of Lords. Mémoire pour le Diplôme d'Etudes Supérieures d'Anglais presenté à l'Institut d'Etudes Anglaises et Américaines'. By Victor Thomas de Pange, typescript, 1949.

House of Lords War Memorial

Typescript copy of the text of the two vols. of House of Lords War Memorial Books (1914–18) which are placed in the case in the Royal Gallery (*see* p. 191). A duplicate copy is deposited in the British Museum.

Epitome of the Knighthood

MS. compilation entitled 'An Epitome of the several different military Orders of Knighthood,' prepared for a projected general History of Knighthood by 'D. W. Smith'. The vol. contains MS. notes, and mounted engravings of the insignia, etc., of Orders of Knighthood of the world, *c.* 1835.

Lloyd George (David), 1st Earl, Speech

Rough notes, pencil, for his speech on the 'Agadir' Crisis at the Mansion House on 21 July 1911, holograph, with other memoranda. Presented by 3rd V. Elibank, 1959.

The Duke of Marlborough Album

A folio album, lettered on front cover 'Illustrations and Notes relative to the Duke of Marlborough in 1711 by W. D. Fellowes', and on spine 'Historical Sketches of the Reign of Queen Anne and Louis XIV illustrated by Dorset Fellowes'. Dorset Fellowes (1769–1852), Captain, Royal Navy, was Secretary to the Lord Great Chamberlain in the reign of George IV. The contents include a contemporary copy of Marlborough's answer to accusations made against him concerning payment of an alleged bribe of £5,000, an original letter from E. Arlington, Lord Chamberlain, to E. Lindsey, Lord Great Chamberlain, arranging the trial in Westminster Hall of the 7th E. Pembroke and Montgomery for manslaughter; with two other docs., other prints, facsimiles of letters, press cuttings and extracts in Fellowes's hand from printed sources, compiled 1843–50. The album was found in 1944, in H.L., and deposited in the Library.

Book of Rates

'The Rates of Merchandize... As they are rated and agreed on by the Commons House of Parliament...', subscribed by Sir Harbottle Grimston, bart., Speaker, H.C. 1660–1. Duplicate of version preserved in H.C. (*see* p. 291).

Photographs of Members of the Two Houses

Photographs of Members of the House of Lords in 3 vols., and photographs of members of the House of Commons in 5 vols., *c.* 1865–75.

Postal Franks

Two albums, one for each House of Parliament, containing mounted 'fronts' of envelopes signed, and in most cases addressed, by Members of the Lords or Commons; almost complete collection for 1834 to 1837. The collection was made by Robert Needham Cust (1821–1909), Indian Civil Servant, barrister and author, while a boy at Eton. Cust's letter presenting the collection, and a printed copy of this letter and the Librarian's reply, are also preserved with the albums.

Protests, H.L.

Vol. of Peers' Protests, 1641–1799, copied by Parliament Office copying clerks from the Lords Journals, 18th c.

The Round Reports

Reports in four vols. by J. Horace Round (1854–1928) on Peerage Cases (vols. i–iii) and Baronetcies (vol. iv). Each vol. contains an Index.

These vols., together with six accompanying envelopes of MS. drafts and letters, were deposited under conditions in 1930 by William Page, who collected and edited Round's later work under the title *Family Origins and Other Studies* (1930).

USE. The Reports in vols. iii and iv can be inspected only with the special permission of the Librarian, H.L.

The Spencer Memorial

MS. record of the memorial bust of the 5th E. Spencer, placed in the West Front Corridor, H.L. in 1933; with list of 27 donors. Presented by the 7th E. Spencer, 1933.

The Stafford Barony Case

MS. case as to the 'Claim of Richard Stafford Cooke Esq. to the ancient Barony of Stafford . . . for Counsel's Opinion'. Purchased from the Executors of W. A. Lindsay, 1927.

Standing Orders, H.L.

'Remembrances for Order and Decency to be kept in the Upper House of Parliament', MS. Standing Orders of H.L., 12 copies, various dates, 1678–1767 (*see* pp. 177–8).

Trial by Peers (L. Morley)

Contemporary MS. describing proceedings in the trial of L. Morley in Westminster Hall, 30 April 1666. Presented by V. Clifden, 1946. (Published as an Appendix to *Trial by their Peers* by Rupert Furneaux (1959).)

The Truro Collection

The Library of Thomas Wilde, 1st L. Truro was presented to H.L. Library by his widow in 1856. L. Truro had been Serjeant at Law, 1824; King's Serjeant,

1827; Attorney General, 1841, 1846; Chief Justice of Common Pleas, 1846–50; L. Chancellor, 1850–2. He died in 1855. The collection includes:

General Legal Notebooks comprising Commonplace books, 3 vols., n.d.; Note-book of Opinions, 1825–6; Cases on Patents, 1839–41, 1 vol; Chancery Journal, 1841–50; Notebooks of 'Cases Tried', 1841–7, 2 vols.; etc. 16 vols.

The Bathurst Notebooks, a uniform series, of which vol. 1 is described as being 'from the collections of Hon. Henry Bathurst', who had been called to the Bar, 1736; and served as Solicitor General, 1746, Attorney General, 1747, Justice of the Common Pleas, 1754–70; and L. Chancellor, 1771–8. The vols. contain notes on cases in various courts, 1716–17, and 1730–74; with 3 vols. of treatises, etc. Most vols. have indexes. 25 vols.

Judge's Notebooks comprising 9 series of vols. of Sir Thomas Wilde's notes on cases heard by him as Chief Justice 1846–50, grouped as follows: Circuit (Middlesex), 10 vols.; Circuit (Nisi Prius), 10 vols.; Circuit (Crown) 9 vols.; Central Criminal Court, 1 vol.; Crown Cases Reserved, 1 vol.; Nisi Prius (London), 16 vols.; Bench Notebooks, 11 vols.; additional notebooks, 4 vols.; Judgments, 1849–50, 1 vol.

Lord Chancellor's Notebooks, 1846–50, 6 vols.

Chancery notebooks, 1850–2, 11 vols.

Miscellaneous Manuscripts

In addition, the collection contains 1 vol. legal extracts, 1817–19; 1 vol. relating to Prohibitions, etc., 17th c.; 1 vol. Reports of King's Bench, 1728–32; 2 vols. printed Appeal Cases, H.L. with MS. notes by L. Truro, 1852–3; Catalogue of L. Truro's Law Library; autograph letter to L. John Russell on L. Truro's appointment as L. Chancellor, 1850.

The Turberville Papers

In 1958 Mrs. A. S. Turberville presented to H.L. Library 43 notebooks containing Professor A. S. Turberville's notes and extracts. The collection is divided into three main categories: (a) original work unpublished, including four essays on aspects of H.L. in the 19th c., which form a nucleus for a projected but unfinished history of the House between 1837 and 1911; (b) drafts for various chapters of Turberville's published books, together with extracts from MSS. and rare books; (c) notes and extracts from other printed sources.

Westminster, Palace of

1. Copy of grant by King Charles II to Charles Whitaker of a house in the old palace of Westminster, 20 Oct. 1662. Formerly Phillipps MS. 15,788. Presented by the widow of Professor Karl Pearson, 1936.

2. The Barry-Pugin Drawings. An oblong elephant folio volume labelled 'Gothic Architecture', containing *c.* 300 drawings for the building and furnishing of the new Palace of Westminster, collected from Sir Charles Barry's drawing office. The vol. was assembled by Octavius Moulton-Barrett, (youngest brother of Elizabeth Barrett Browning), who had worked as a draughtsman for Barry.

A plan in pencil of Barry's design for the new Palace is included, which may be the earliest extant, since the Victoria Tower is marked 'King William's Tower'. Some drawings are by Augustus Welby Pugin, the majority are working drawings, many on tracing paper, by Moulton Barrett. Drawings for other buildings by Barry in the gothic style, such as Hurstpierpoint church, Sussex, are also included. Presented by Miss Elizabeth Moulton-Barrett, through her cousin, L. Mottistone, 1959.

3. Drawings for the Throne. Twenty-two highly finished original drawings (pen and ink, each 14 x 9½ inches), being Sir Charles Barry's designs for the throne in H.L., though not in Barry's hand (three of the designs differ materially from those put into effect). Bound in a red morocco album, bearing the book-plate of E. M. Barry. Presented by the family of Sir John Wolfe Barry, 1937.

4. 'The Topography of the Old House of Commons'. By Orlo Cyprian Williams, late Principal Clerk of Committees, H.C. Photostat from typescript.

HISTORICAL COLLECTIONS OF THE HOUSE
OF COMMONS LIBRARY

Unless otherwise indicated, the following collections are preserved by the House of Lords Record Office on behalf of the House of Commons Library.

USE. The collections are available to the public, without restriction, in the H.L.R.O. Search Room.

BIBLIOGRAPHY. *The Library of the House of Commons* (1970).

The Bailey Papers

Robert Neale Menteth Bailey, born 21 Aug. 1882, became a clerk in the H.C. in 1905, working in the years before 1914 in the H.C. Committee Office. In addition he taught classics at the Working Men's College, London, and lectured for the Workers' Educational Association, in company with his friend William Leveson Gower (*see* LEVESON GOWER PAPERS). Bailey served in the first World War, was wounded in Palestine and died 1 Dec. 1917. The papers consist of letters to and from his relatives and friends, with photographs, obituaries, etc., 1889–1918, 538 docs. They were presented to H.L.R.O. by Mr. James Lees-Milne.

CATALOGUE available in H.L.R.O.

Books of Rates

1. 'The Rates of Merchandize . . . As they are rated and agreed on by the Commons House of Parliament . . .' from 24 June 1660. Subscribed by Harbottle Grimston, bart., Speaker (1660–1). Originally preserved in the Speaker's Gallery, H.C. (*See* also p. 287 above.)
2. 'An Additional Book of Rates of Goods and Merchandizes . . . with Rules Orders and Regulations', n.d. Subscribed by Spencer Compton, Speaker (1715–27). Originally preserved in the Speaker's Gallery, H.C.

The Brand Papers

See plate 14

The papers are those of Henry Bouverie William Brand, 1st V. Hampden (1814–92), who was Speaker, 1872–84. They include official diaries for 1872 to 1884; and corr. 1855–92, 415 docs. (preserved in H.L.R.O. on behalf of the Journal Office, H.C.).

LIST. D. J. Johnson, *The Letters and Diaries of Speaker Brand*, House of Lords Record Office Memorandum no. 43 (1970).

The Brickdale Notebooks

Photographic copies of Notebooks of Matthew Brickdale, M.P. for Bristol, Nov. 1770–May 1774, 2 files (*see* p. 285, above).

The Bull Papers

The papers of Rt. Hon. Sir William Bull, 1st bart. (1863–1931; M.P. 1900–29).

'File A' mainly concerns House of Lords Reform, 1925–6, and includes papers of the Second Chamber Committee of the Conservative Party; papers of the Cabinet Committee on Reform (*see* p. 187 above); and papers concerning the preservation of Waterloo Bridge, 1926, *c.* 120 docs., with newspaper cuttings.

'File B' mainly concerns Proportional Representation and includes 'Minutes of the Committee appointed to organise the opposition to the Committee Stage of the Plural Voting Bill', 30 June 1913–29 April 1914; and papers concerning the opposition to the Proportional Representation Bill, 1924, 40 docs.

The Cameron Papers

Letters to Sir David Cameron, R.A., and memos., relating to the series of paintings in St. Stephen's Hall, 'The Building of Britain', 1925–7, 43 docs. Presented to the Speaker by Mr. R. C. Watt.

The Clementson Diary

Diary or Notebook of John Clementson (Deputy Serjeant at Arms, H.C., 1770–1804), 2 April 1770–11 Feb. 1802.

Cotton's 'Parliament's Antiquity'

'Parliaments Antiquity and Dignity written by Sir Robert Cotton.' 17th c. version of text as printed in *Cottoni Posthuma* (1651) and there beginning, 'That the Kings of England have been pleased, usually, to consult with their Peers in the Great Council . . .'.

Crimes Bill

The Crimes Bill, 1785. Text of bill in MS.

Debates, H.C.

Diary of Debates by Anchitell Grey for 9 Feb. 1678. Contemporary transcript; printed in *Debates of the House of Commons from the Year 1667 to the year 1694*, vol. v (1763), pp. 122–44.

Display Items

The following documents, etc., are displayed on walls of the ground floor corridors, H.C.

Sir Charles Barry's pocket Plan of the Palace of Westminster (*c.* 1840).

V. Eversley's Letters Patent of Nobility, 1857.

Matrices of 2 Great Seals, with casts, William IV, and Victoria.

10 Tally sticks, *temp.* Edward I, with 2 models (modern).

Proclamation by Queen Elizabeth I, 30 April 1573.

Speaker Lenthall's Grant of Commission to command Troops of Horse, 26 Jan. 1660.

'The Cary Scroll.' Petition of M.P.s to D. Plunket, M.P., First Commissioner of Works, drawing the attention of the First Commissioner of Works to the need for a system of telegraphic communication between House, Library and Smoking Room, signed by 400 Members, *ante*-1894. Presented by Sir Robert Cary, M.P.

Doddridge's 'Presentation'

'A true Presentation of forepast Parliaments to the view of present tymes and Posterity' by Sir John Doddridge, Justice of the King's Bench. 17th c. MS. version. (Another copy is in the British Museum, Stowe MS. 331.)

Election Papers

1. Corfe Castle: Counterparts of Returns of Burgesses for Corfe Castle, 1680, 1801, 1802, 1807, 1818, 1820, 1823, 1826, 1828, 1829, 1830, 1831, 12 docs.

2. Dundee: Election address of Winston Churchill to the Electors of Dundee, 1918. Holograph.

3. Exeter: Poll List for City of Exeter, 26–30 March 1761. *Printed*, 1 sheet, defective.

4. Lostwithiel: Letters relating to the return of Sir William Clarke, Master of the Rolls, as Member for Lostwithiel, 1754–63; from D. Newcastle (5), L. Bute (1), Charles Yorke, Attorney General (2), and copies of Clarke's letters (4).

5. Marylebone: Marylebone Election Papers, 1837, concerning disbursements by Charles John Shore, 2nd L. Teignmouth, during the election for Marylebone Borough. They comprise statements of payments for bunting and flags (12 docs.); carriage hire (25 docs.); canvassing, billposting, etc. (15 docs.); hire of club and committee rooms (25 docs.); messengers (20 docs.); printing of bill-heads, etc. (29 docs.); refreshments (7 docs.); vouchers for newspaper adverts. (71 docs.); and misc. expenses (4 docs.).

6. Wells: Letter to E. Hertford from John Horner and 99 others, dated at Wells, 14 Dec. 1620, concerning L. Beauchamp's candidature.

7. Co. York: 'Hints for the better regulating and conducting The various businesses relative to a Contested Election for the County of York', May 1784; with Appendix of papers relating to the election of H. Duncombe and W. Wilberforce, April 1784.

Election Return Register

'Returns in the Convention 16[88/9].' Copy of register of returns of elections to the Convention Parliament, 22 Jan. 1688/9 made by Paul Jodrell, Clerk of the House, 7 April 1691. Contemporary.

Elsynge Manuscripts

1. MS. text of 'Modus Tenendi Parliamentum', or The Manner of holding Parliaments in England, 17th c. by H. Elsynge.

2. MS. text of the 'Modern Form of the Parliaments of England', by H. Elsynge, dated 1658. Bought by H.C. Art Fund.

The Emmott Papers

The Papers of L. Emmott (1858–1926; Liberal M.P. for Oldham, 1899–1911, Chairman of Ways and Means, 1906–11, cr. 1st L. Emmott of Oldham, 1911) comprise 5 files:

'File A', letters and memoranda from or concerning Winston Churchill, 1900–11 (29 items); together with printed election addresses, Oldham, 1899 and 1900, photographs of Walter Runciman and Alfred Emmott, and newspaper cuttings.

'File B', 'The Votes of Alfred Emmott' marked on a series of printed records of 'the more important divisions', 1890 and 1900; newspaper cuttings of speeches by Emmott and others, 1899–1904, with text of part of speech at the Liberal League Dinner, 24 Oct. 1902, on the Irish Question.

'File C', newspaper cuttings relating to Emmott's appointment as Chairman of Ways and Means, 1906, and letters and memoranda concerning his work as Chairman, 1906–11, 55 items.

'File D', Election manifestos, photographs, press cuttings, etc., 1905–22, 15 items.

'File E', Typescripts, comprising list of additional papers of L. Emmott deposited by Mrs. Joan Simon in Nuffield College Library, 1968; typed copies of letters to Emmott, 1900–17 and of extracts from letters to Lady Emmott on his death, 1926–7, deposited in Nuffield College; correspondence with H.C. Library concerning papers 1965–8.

Epping Forest Commission Records

MS. vols. of documentary evidence presented to the Epping Forest Commissioners appointed under the Epping Forest Act, 1871, 34 & 35 Vict., c. 93. The evidence was given by (1) Lords of Manors and purchasers of inclosures, (2) the Commissioners of Sewers of the City of London and other claimants of a forestal right of Common, and (3) the Commissioner of H.M. Works. The vols. are arranged as follows. Vol. i, copies of docs. dating 1042–1629; vol. ii, 1630–98; vol. iii, 1701–1844; vol. iv, 1849–70. There are also 8 plans, and the Memorial of Owners and Occupiers within Epping Forest to the Commissioners (1 parchment roll). 1870–4, 13 items. See also pp. 274.

The Furniss Drawings

Collection of 380 original political drawings by Harry Furniss (1854–1925) for *The Graphic*, *Punch*, etc., including 36 of W. E. Gladstone; the majority c. 1887–1900.

The Gould Autobiography

Autobiography of Sir Francis Carruthers Gould (1844–1925); assistant editor, *Westminster Gazette* and political cartoonist. Holograph MSS. in two boxes with booklet of drawings of Gladstone, Rosebery, Asquith, Austen Chamberlain, Redmond and Keir Hardie.

Hardinge's 'Memorial'

MS. text of the 'Memorial concerning a King's Minority, and the Administration of Government during the King's Minority' by Nicholas Hardinge (Clerk of the House of Commons, 1731–47, and M.P. for Eye, 1748–58), with author's corrections, 1740.

The Ilbert Diaries

(a) Diaries of Sir Courtenay Ilbert (1841–1924; Clerk of H.C., 1902–21). Lett's or Stationery Office Diaries with entries of engagements, and some comment, for 1895, 1899, 1900, 1901, 1903–9, 1911–22, 23 vols.

(b) Narrative Diaries, mainly concerning business of H.C., 1896–1920, 15 vols., the first of which is brief and covers 1896–1903.

The Jennings Papers

Two notes from L. Randolph Churchill to Louis Jennings, M.P. written during proceedings on 11 March 1890, with memo. by Jennings, 1890, 3 docs. presented by L. Ritchie to the Speaker.

Journals, H.C.

1. Photographic copies of leaves of a MS. Commons Journal, 22 March and 4 April, 1604.

2. Sheets from a MS. copy of the Commons Journals with entries for 6–12 February 1641 and 18–20 March 1641, as in original Journals, *c.* 1700.

3. Extracts from the Commons Journals, 8 May 1661–20 Nov. 1685, 18th c.

4. MS. Copy of Commons Journal, 18 Feb. 1663 to 13 June 1663, with Index, *c.* 1700.

The May Notebooks

Two vols. of notebooks of Thomas Erskine May, 1st L. Farnborough (1815–86; assistant Librarian, H.C., 1831; Clerk of H.C., 1871–86; author of *Law and Practice of Parliament*, 1844, etc.).

Vol. i, 'The Manuscript Magazine', is a commonplace book for 1834–5, which also includes personal journal entries for 1 and 3 Jan. 1836.

Vol. ii is entitled 'Historical Memoranda and Extracts' and contains commonplace entries (pp. 3–45) and personal journal entries for 1857–82 (pp. 47–363).

(Typed versions of these journal entries are held in the H.C. Library and in H.L.R.O.)

Minutes, H.C.

The MS. text of 'An Exact and particular Relation, of the late Dispute, Betweene the two Houses of Parliament, In the Grand Case of Judicature, Transcribed verbatim (by way of Journal) from the Minutes of the house of Commons', 4 May–9 June, 1675; followed by the 'Votes and Resolves of the Commons', 13 Oct.–22 Nov. 1675. Contemporary.

Office Papers, H.C.

Collection of office papers including Register of amendments to draft Journals, 1678–9, etc.; Register of Divisions, 1700, 1701; notes of debates, n.d.; and observations on procedural matters for various sessions, c. 1689–90, 1695–7.

Orders, H.C.

1. The MS. text of 'A Protestation of the House of Commons . . .', 20 June 1604 (as in *C.J.*, vol. i, 243), 17th c.; followed by 'Observations, Rules and Orders collected out of divers Journals of the House of Commons . . .', 1547–1607, 17th c.

2. 'Notes of the orders, proceedings, punishments and Privileges of the lower house of Parliament', attributed to William Lambarde, 17th c. copy. Annotation of ownership by Tho. Hearne, 1731.

Parliamentary Agents

Photocopy of Rules to be observed by Parliamentary Agents, etc., as established by the Speaker, 1836.

Parliamentary Papers (Misc.)

1. Three separately paginated MSS. bound in one vol. Early 17th c.
   (a) Serjeant Glanvile's Speech on presentation as Speaker, as in *L.J.*, iv, p. 50.
   (b) Speech by Sir Harbottle Grimston, M.P. in H.C., 14 April 1640, as in *P.H.*, vol. ii, cols. 542–3.
   (c) Speech by Sir Francis Seymour, M.P. in H.C., April 1640.

2. Text of speech by Sir Benjamin Rudyerd in H.C., 7 Nov. 1640, as in *P.H.*, vol. ii, cols. 643–7. Contemporary MS. copy.

3. 'Reasons of the Prince Elector coming into England presented to both Houses of Parliament', MS. copy, early 17th c.

4. MS. statement of receipts for the payment of tax towards the maintenance of armies and navies, 5 Oct. 1653.

5. 'La Forme de La Succession de la Couronne ascordée par les Communes et par eux communiquée aux Seigneurs pour leurs consentements', with list of lords voting against the words 'abdicated and the Throne is vacant'. French. MS., late 17th c.

6. MS. text of a message of Charles II to H.C. (?1668), late 17th c.

7. MS. drafts for King's Speeches dated 10 Jan. 1716 and 20 Feb. 1717, respectively.

8. Copies of Warrants for two Messengers' Badges, Seven Boxes for the Great Seal, and for repairing and gilding the Mace belonging to H.C. Signed E. Grafton, 1734.

9. 'Lord Cromarty's Speech to the House of Lords 1745' in the course of the trial of E. Cromartie for treason, 18th c. MS. copy.

10. MS. Text of King's Speech, with covering note forwarding it on behalf of D. Newcastle, n.d.

11. Petition of the 'four Clerks without Doors attending Committees' of H.C. concerning their salary, n.d., 18th c.

Parliamentary Surveys

Copies of surveys of church lands and livings made by the Parliamentary surveyors, commissioned by virtue of ordinances of 17 Nov. 1646 and later, for the sale of Bishops' lands, 30 April 1649 and later for the sale of Dean and Chapter lands, and 8 June 1649 for the valuation of church livings. The introduction and index were prepared by Dr. A. C. Ducarel, Lambeth Palace Librarians, 1751–65. The Surveys include those of the lands of Bishops and of Deans and Chapters. The index entries refer both to the MS. Surveys preserved at Lambeth and also to these copies (which are differently paginated). The copies were probably presented to the Speaker of the Commons *c.* 1760; more recently they have been preserved in the Commons Library, 27 vols.

BIBLIOGRAPHY
S. C. Newton, *Parliamentary Surveys*, Short Guides to Records, no. 17 (1968), also printed in *History*, vol. liii (1968), pp. 51–4.

Procedural Papers, H.C.

1. 'Precedents in Parliament'. A MS. collection of precedents and memoranda of proceedings, mainly in H.C. and derived from the Journals (including Original Journals now lost, but used by D'Ewes), 2 Oct. 1566–24 Nov. 1601, the entries on pp. 1–55 by Henry Elsynge, Clerk of the Parliaments (1621–35). Phillipps MS. 11767.

2. 'Of Parliaments. A Discourse of the Priviledg and Practise of the high Courte of Parliament in England collected out of the Common Lawes of this Land.' [Ralph Starkey], early 17th c., copy of text as included in the PARLIAMENTARY COLLECTION, vol. 47 (1628). Presented by Speaker Peel, 1891.

3. 'Parliamentary Rules and Orders', a digest of extracts from the Journals under procedural headings, e.g. 'Adjourning', 'Bills', etc., *c.* 1700, with additional entries for 1707–13.

4. Three separately paginated MSS. bound in one vol.:

(a) 'Observations Rules and Orders collected out of the Journall Bookes, of the House of Commons, The Collection of Ambrose Kelly Clerk to the Committees of the House of Commons of such matters as are necessary and fitt for every member of that House touching the proceedings therein.' The extracts are arranged under procedural main headings and include some comment by the writer. The latest entry is for 1679. A text of the Commons Protestation of 1604 is included. Late 17th c. For another copy see p. 245 above.

(b) 'The Discourse of John Selden Esq.', a version of Selden's *Table Talk*, late 17th c.

(c) 'A breife Declaracion how the Kings of England have from tyme Supported and repaired their Estates and Annual Revenues being collected out of the Records of the Tower Parliament Rolls and Close Peticions, etc.' Anon., late 17th c.

Records of H.C. (Catalogue)

Catalogue of the Records of H.C. including Journals, Petitions, Paper Bills, Engrossed Bills, Ordinances, etc., 1547–1733, *c.* 1733. Photocopy of Lansdowne MS. 533, British Museum.

Selden's 'Baronage'

'Priviledges of the Baronage of England when they sitt in Parliament by Mr. Selden', contemporary transcript, perhaps made in the Parliament Office, of the report presented by Selden to H.L. in 1621 (*see Calendar* for 15 Dec. 1621) and subsequently printed (cf. *Opera omnia*, ed. D. Wilkins, 1726).

Speakers, H.C. (List)

'Speakers of the Parliament.' A List from 1260 (Peter de Montfort) to 1804, continued to 1817 and, in pencil, to 1841; annotated, with coats of arms. 1804. Compiled by G. Beltz for Speaker Abbot.

Standing Orders, H.L.

1. MS. copy of Standing Orders, H.L., 1735.
2. MS. copy of Standing Orders, H.L., 1763.

Statutes (Index)

'Repertorium sive Elenchus Parliamentorum'. MS. index to statutes, etc., Edward III–Edward IV, dealing with public matters, probably holograph, by Walter Yonge, M.P. 1644 (cf. W. Yonge's 'Parliamentary Diary', British Museum, Add. MSS. 1877–81).

Strangers' Book

Strangers' Book, 14 Feb.–3 July 1837, listing Strangers admitted to H.C. Chamber, with signature of Member sponsoring.

The Vargas Papers

The papers of Peter Vargas (d. 1879; private secretary to the Government Whips from *c.* 1820), comprising:

(a) Parliamentary Letter Books, containing copies of letters concerning forthcoming sessions which were sent from Downing Street to Members of H.C., 1783–1878, 2 vols.

(b) Peers Letter Book, containing copies of similar letters sent to members of H.L., 1837–78, 1 vol.

(c) Letter Book, containing precedent letters to urge attendance or to enquire into reasons for absence, 1839–74, 1 vol.

(d) Divisions in H.C., a Register of those voting in named divisions, 22 April 1818–19 July 1822, 1 vol.

(e) Misc. papers, including 'Times of Proceedings of Liberal Registration Association,' July 1865; Whip letter from L. Derby, 27 Feb. 1858; summary of elections of Speakers, 1817–59; invitation to a Fish Dinner at the Trafalgar, Greenwich, n.d.; and four press cuttings of obituaries of Vargas, 21 docs.

Votes and Proceedings, H.C.

1. (a) MS. text of the Votes of the House of Commons, 22 May–20 Nov. 1685, with note of dissolution on 2 July 1687, and contemporary printed list of Members, etc., pasted in. Formerly in the possession of Speaker Bromley, who represented Warwickshire from 1690, and Oxford University from 1700–32. Late 17th c.

(b) MS. text of 'The Debate at large Betweene the house of Lords and the house of Commons at the free Conference held in the Painted Chamber in the session of the Convention, anno 1688 Relating to the word "abdicated" And the Vacancy of the throwne in the Commons Vote . . .' (pp. 1–2 missing). Cf. *P.H.* vol. v, cols, 63–108. Contemporary.

2. Votes and Proceedings, H.C. MS. version of Votes for 22 Jan.–21 Oct. 1689, containing more than the official copy for this period (*see* VOTES AND PROCEEDINGS, H.C.). Contemporary index. Late 17th c.

The Weston Estate Papers

Deeds and other docs. relating to estates of the Rev. Samuel Ryder Weston, D.D., in Tetsworth, Rofford, Chinnor, Henton, and Little Milton, co. Oxon., 1710–1816, 65 docs. (preserved in H.L.R.O. on behalf of the Journal Office H.C.).

Westminster Palace

'Westminster Palace, St. Stephen's Chapel and the House of Commons', a description of buildings and decoration, with drawings in wash and water colour, *c.* 1807, [by J. T. Smith, author of *Antiquities of Westminster* (1807)].

The Wren Pedigree

Pedigree of Sir Christopher Wren, covering 16th–19th c., n.d.

APPENDICES

APPENDIX I

LIST OF CLERKS OF THE PARLIAMENTS

John Kirkby, Keeper of the Rolls of Chancery[1]	? 1280–90
Gilbert of Rothbury, Clerk of the Council	1290–1314
Robert of Ashby, senior clerk in Chancery	1315
William Airmyn	1316–
Henry of Edenstowe	*c.* 1327–*post* 1334
Thomas of Brayton	*c.* 1340–6
John of Coddington	occ. 1351, 1352
Geoffrey Martin, Clerk of the Crown	occ. 1377
Edmund Brudenell, Clerk of the Crown	occ. 1377
Richard de Ravenser	? 1372–86
John de Waltham	? *c.* 1381
John de Scarle	*ante* 1384–94
John Rome	1394–1414
John Frank	1414–23
William Prestwyke	1424–36
John Bate	1437–8
Thomas Kirkby	1438–47
John Fawkes	1447–70
Baldwin Hyde	1470–1
John Gunthorpe	1471–83
Thomas Hutton	1483–5
John Morgan	1485–96
Richard Hatton	1496–1509
John Taylor	1509–23
Brian Tuke, kt.[2]	1523–39
Edward North, kt. (1st L. North)	1531–9
Thomas Soulement	1540–1
William Paget, kt. (1st L. Paget)	1541–9
Thomas Knight	1543–50
John Mason, kt.	1550–66
Francis Spilman	1551–75
Anthony Mason (*al.* Wyckes)	1574–97
Thomas Smith, kt.	1597–1609
Robert Bowyer	1609–21
Henry Elsynge (the elder)	1621–35
Thomas Knyvett	1635–7
Daniel Bedingfield	1637

[1] The first three names in this list are of ministers or clerks who had responsibility for the business and rolls of Parliament but for whose appointment as specific *clericus parliamenti* no evidence survives.

[2] Between 1531 and 1574 several grants in survivorship of the office were made to two clerks at a time.

John Browne	1638–49;
	1660–91
Edward Norgate, clerk of the Upper House at the Oxford Parliament	1644
Henry Scobell	1649–60
Matthew Johnson	1691–1716
William Cowper	1716–40
Ashley Cowper	1740–88
George Rose	1788–1818
George Henry Rose, kt.	1818–55
John George Shaw-Lefevre, kt.	1855–75
William Rose, kt.	1875–85
Henry John Lowndes Graham, kt.	1885–1917
Arthur Theodore Thring, kt.	1917–30
Edward Hall Alderson, kt.	1930–4
Henry John Fanshawe Badeley, kt. (1st L. Badeley)	1934–49
Robert Leslie Overbury, kt.	1949–53
Francis William Lascelles, kt.	1953–8
Victor Martin Reeves Goodman, kt.	1959–63
David Stephens, kt.	1963–

BIBLIOGRAPHY

Calendars of Patent Rolls; *Lords Journals*; H. G. Richardson and George Sayles, 'The King's Ministers in Parliament, 1271–1377', *English Historical Review*, vols. xlvi, pp. 529–50, and xlvii, pp. 194–203, 377–97; A. F. Pollard, 'Fifteenth Century Clerks of Parliament', *Bulletin of the Institute of Historical Research*, vol. xv, pp. 137–61; M. F. Bond, 'Clerks of the Parliaments, 1509–1953', *English Historical Review*, vol. lxxiii, pp. 78–85.

APPENDIX II

LIST OF CLERKS OF THE HOUSE OF COMMONS

Robert de Melton	1363–?84
John de Scardeburgh	1384–1414
Thomas Haseley, kt.	1414–[40]
John Dale	1440–
Thomas Bayen	1461–1503
Thomas Hylton	1504–
William Underhill	1510–c.14
Robert Ormeston	1516–?47
John Seymour	1548–67
Fulk Onslow	1567–1602
Ralph Ewens	1603–11
William Pynches	1611–12
John Wright	1612–33
Henry Elsynge (the younger)	1639–48
Henry Scobell	1649–58
John Smythe	1658–9
John Phelpes	1659
Thomas St. Nicholas	1659–60
William Jessop	1660
William Goldsborough (the elder)	1661–78
William Goldsborough (the younger)	1678–83
Paul Jodrell	1683–1727
Edward Stables	1727–31
Nicholas Hardinge	1731–47
Jeremiah Dyson	1747–62
Thomas Tyrwhitt	1762–8
John Hatsell	1768–1820
John Henry Ley	1820–50
Denis Le Marchant, kt.	1850–71
Thomas Erskine May, kt. (1st L. Farnborough)	1871–86
Reginald Francis Douce Palgrave, kt.	1886–1900
Archibald John Scott-Milman	1900–2
Courtenay Peregrine Ilbert, kt.	1902–21
Thomas Lonsdale Webster, kt.	1921–30
Horace Christian Dawkins, kt.	1930–7
Gilbert Francis Montriou Campion, kt. (1st L. Campion)	1937–48
Frederic William Metcalf, kt.	1948–54
Edward Abdy Fellowes, kt.	1954–61
Thomas George Barnett Cocks, kt.	1962–

BIBLIOGRAPHY

Calendars of Patent Rolls; *Commons Journals*; A. F. Pollard, 'The Mediaeval Under-Clerks of Parliament', *Bulletin of the Institute of Historical Research*, vol. xvi, pp. 65–87, 'The Under-Clerks and The Commons' Journals', *op. cit.*, pp. 144–67, 'Queen Elizabeth's Under-Clerks and their Commons' Journals', *op. cit.*, vol. xvii, pp. 1–12, and 'A Protean Clerk of the Commons', *op. cit.*, vol. xviii, pp. 49–51; J. E. Neale, 'The Commons' Journals of the Tudor Period', *Transactions of the Royal Historical Society*, 4th series, vol. iii (1920), pp. 136–70; O. C. Williams, *The Clerical Organisation of the House of Commons* (1954).

TABLE OF
ACTS OF PARLIAMENT
CITED IN THE TEXT

Table of Acts of Parliament
cited in the text

1442 20 Hen. VI, c. 9. Peeresses, *page* 111
1503 19 Hen. VII, c. 7. Ordinances of Corporations, 152
1541 33 Hen. VIII, c. 21. Commission, 176
1558 1 Eliz. I, c. 1. Supremacy, 95
1585 27 Eliz. I, c. 8. Court of Exchequer Chamber, 106
1588 31 Eliz. I, c. 1. Error, 106
1609 7 Ja. I, c. 2. Naturalisation and Restoration of Blood, 79, 81
1609 7 Ja. I, c. 6. Oath of Allegiance, 179
1627 3 Cha. I, c. 1. Petition of Right, 95
1661 13 Cha. II, sess. 1, c. 1. Sedition, 111
1661 13 Cha. II, sess. 1, c. 2. Clergy, 21
1661 13 Cha. II, sess. 1, c. 5. Tumultuous Petitioning, 172, 240
1662 14 Cha. II, c. 4. Uniformity, 95
1663 15 Cha. II, c. 1. London and York Road, 77.
1666 18 & 19 Cha. II, c. 8 (private). Roos Illegitimation, 271
1667 19 & 20 Cha. II, c. 1. Public Accounts, 136
1670 22 Cha. II, c. 1 (private). Roos Marriage, 271
1672 25 Cha. II, c. 2. Popish Recusants, 179
1678 30 Cha. II, sess. 2, c. 1. Parliament, 179
1679 31 Cha. II, c. 2. Habeas Corpus, 96
1688 1 Will. & Mary, sess. 1, c. 1. Parliament, 179
1688 1 Will. & Mary, sess. 2, c. 2. Bill of Rights, 96, 170
1688 1 Will. & Mary, c. 6. Coronation Oath, 170
1694 5 & 6 Will. & Mary, c. 10. Orphans, London, 140
1695 7 & 8 Will. III, c. 3. Treason, 111
1697 9 Will. III, c. 44. East India Company, 148
1698 10 Will. III, c. 3. Exportation, 144
1698 10 Will. III, c. 6. Russian Company (Membership), 148
1698 10 Will. III, c. 9. Grant of a Sum to disband the Army, 150
1698 11 Will. III, c. 8. Debts due to the Army, 137
1698 11 Will. III, c. 2. Sale of Forfeited Estates in Ireland, 150
1700 12 & 13 Will. III, c. 2. Settlement, 170
1700 12 & 13 Will. III, c. 3. Privilege of Parliament, 124
1701 13 & 14 Will. III, c. 6. Succession, 179
1703 2 & 3 Anne, c. 12. Privilege of Parliament, 124
1706 6 Anne, c. 11. Union with Scotland, 76, 96, 114n, 137, 165
1707 6 Anne, c. 37. Duties on East India Goods, 148–9
1707 6 Anne, c. 53. Exchequer Court, 120
1707 6 Anne, c. 78. Scottish Representative Peers, 165
1708 7 Anne, c. 5. Foreign Protestants Naturalisation, 79
1710 9 Anne, c. 17. New Churches in London and Westminster, 149
1711 10 Anne, c. 20. Churches in London and Westminster, 149

1711   10 Anne, c. 35. East India Company, 149
1713   13 Anne, c. 20. Dagenham Breach, 149
1715   1 Geo. I, sess. 2, c. 50. Forfeited Estates, 150
1725   12 Geo. I, c. 37. Kensington, Chelsea and Fulham Roads (Tolls), 151
1730   4 Geo. II, c. 26. Proceedings in Courts of Justice, 95
1735   9 Geo. II, c. 29. Westminster Bridge, 158
1747   21 Geo. II, c. 29. Orphans, London, 140
1748   21 Geo. II, c. 32. Mercers, London, 151
1750   24 Geo. II, c. 14. London and Mercers Company, 151
1750   24 Geo. II, c. 25. Carlisle and Newcastle Road, 139
1750   24 Geo. II, c. 31. Linen and Hemp Manufactures, Pl. 7
1751   25 Geo. II, c. 7. Mercers Company, London, 151
1751   25 Geo. II, c. 41. Forfeited Estates in Scotland, 150
1755   28 Geo. II, c. 20. Whale Fishery, 157
1756   29 Geo. II, c. 40. London Bridge, 139
1756   29 Geo. II, c. 86. Blackfriars Bridge, 139
1757   31 Geo. II, c. 30. Militia Pay, 138
1759   33 Geo. II, c. 2 (private). Duke of Bridgewater's Canal, 73
1762   2 Geo. III, c. 21. London Streets, 158
1766   6 Geo. III, c. 26. London Paving and Lighting, 140
1766   7 Geo. III, c. 37. Thames Embankment, 139, 140.
1770   10 Geo. III, c. 16. Parliamentary Elections, 239
1770   10 Geo. III, c. 50. Parliamentary Privilege, 124
1771   11 Geo. III, c. 29. City of London Sewerage, 140
1773   13 Geo. III, c. 83. Richmond Bridge, 155
1776   16 Geo. III, c. 40. Poor, 153
1776   17 Geo. III, c. 18. Thames Navigation, 140
1778   18 Geo. III, c. 53. Recruiting, 153
1778   18 Geo. III, c. 71. London Streets, 139, 140
1781   21 Geo. III, c. 58. Growth of Hemp and Flax, 144
1782   22 Geo. III, c. 53. Repeal of Act for Securing Dependency of Ireland 114n.
1782   22 Geo. III, c. 82. Civil List and Secret Service Money, 137
1783   23 Geo. III, c. 28. Irish Appeals, 114n
1786   26 Geo. III, c. 31. National Debt Reduction, 137
1786   26 Geo. III, c. 37. Blackfriars Bridge (Sunday Tolls), 139
1786   26 Geo. III, c. 43. Hemp and Flax, 144
1786   26 Geo. III, c. 87. Crown Land Revenues, 137
1786   26 Geo. III, c. 101. Erection of Lighthouses, 156
1787   27 Geo. III, c. 13. Customs and Excise, 137
1789   29 Geo. III, c. 37. National Debt. 136
1793   33 Geo. III, c. 13. Acts of Parliament (Commencement), 94
1795   35 Geo. III, c. 126. Temple Bar, etc., 140
1795   35 Geo. III, c. 131. Blackfriars Sewer, 140
1800   39 & 40 Geo. III, c. 67. Union with Ireland, 76, 114n, 120, 167
1801   41 Geo. III, c. 33 (local and personal). Croydon and Wandsworth Railway, 79
1803   43 Geo. III, c. 80. Scottish Highland Roads and Bridges, 264
1803   43 Geo. III, c. 102. Caledonian Canal, 264
1808   48 Geo. III, c. 151. Court of Session, 114

1809   49 Geo. III, c. 32. Pension Duties, 185
1812   52 Geo. III, c. 11. House of Commons (Offices), 237, 243
1822   3 Geo. IV, c. 126. Turnpike Trusts, 77
1824   5 Geo. IV, c. 82. Clerk of the Parliaments, 182, 184
1825   6 Geo. IV, c. 67. Naturalisation and Restoration of Blood, 79
1825   6 Geo. IV, c. 123. Costs on Private Bills, 230
1829   10 Geo. IV, c. 7. Roman Catholic Relief, 79, 179
1830   11 Geo. IV & 1 Will. IV, c. 64. Beer-houses, 192
1832   2 & 3 Will. IV, c. 65. Representation of the People, 96
1832   2 & 3 Will. IV, c. 69 (local and personal). Manchester, Bolton and Bury Canal Co., 74
1835   5 & 6 Will. IV, c. 50. Highway, 76
1836   6 & 7 Will. IV, c. 85. Marriage, 276
1836   6 & 7 Will. IV, c. 115. Inclosure, 77
1840   3 & 4 Vict., c. 97. Railway Regulation, 80
1841   4 & 5 Vict., c. 58. Controverted Elections, 239
1845   8 & 9 Vict., c. 113. Evidence, 27
1845   8 & 9 Vict., c. 118. Inclosure, 77
1845   9 & 10 Vict., c. 18. Land Clauses Consolidation, 80
1847   10 & 11 Vict., c. 52. Representative Peers (Scotland), 165
1847   10 & 11 Vict., c. 108. Bishopric of Manchester, 21
1848   11 & 12 Vict., c. 98. Election Petition, 239
1850   13 & 14 Vict., c. 21. Interpretation of Acts, 98
1850   13 & 14 Vict., c. 83. Railway Abandonment, 80
1851   14 & 15 Vict., c. 87. Representative Peers (Scotland), 165, 166
1852   15 & 16 Vict., c. 76. Common Law Procedure, 120
1852   15 & 16 Vict., c. 79. Inclosure, 78
1852   15 & 16 Vict., c. 80. Court of Chancery, 22
1857   20 & 21 Vict., c. 85. Matrimonial Causes, 75
1858   21 & 22 Vict., c. 48. Oaths of Allegiance, 179
1858   21 & 22 Vict., c. 78. Parliamentary Witnesses, 46
1862   25 & 26 Vict., c. 105. Highland Roads and Bridges, 264
1866   29 & 30 Vict., c. 19. Parliamentary Oaths, 179
1868   31 & 32 Vict., c. 72. Promissory Oaths, 179
1868   31 & 32 Vict., c. 125. Parliamentary Elections, 239
1869   32 & 33 Vict., c. 42. Irish Church, 167
1871   34 & 35 Vict., c. 83. Parliamentary Witnesses Oath, 223
1871   34 & 35 Vict., c. 93. Epping Forest, 294
1871   34 & 35 Vict., c. 115. Annual Turnpike Acts Continuation, 77
1873   36 & 37 Vict., c. 48. Regulation of Railways, 74
1873   36 & 37 Vict., c. 66. Supreme Court of Judicature, 114
1876   39 & 40 Vict., c. 59. Appellate Jurisdiction, 22, 114, 115
1877   40 & 41 Vict., c. 57. Supreme Court of Judicature (Ireland), 120
1888   51 & 52 Vict., c. 25. Railway and Canal Traffic Act, 74
1888   51 & 52 Vict., c. 46. Oaths, 179
1889   52 & 53 Vict., c. 30. Board of Agriculture, 78
1889   52 & 53 Vict., c. 63. Interpretation, 98
1896   59 & 60 Vict., c. 14. Short Titles, 98n.
1896   59 & 60 Vict., c. 48. Light Railways, 80
1899   62 & 63 Vict., c. 47. Private Legislation Procedure (Scotland), 72, 216

1907 7 Edw. VII, c. 23. Criminal Appeal, 114, 120
1910 10 Edw. VII & 1 Geo. V, c. 29. Accession Declaration, 170
1911 1 & 2 Geo. V, c. 13. Parliament, 62
1914 4 & 5 Geo. V, c. 91. Welsh Church, 21
1919 9 & 10 Geo. V, c. 50. Ministry of Transport, 74, 80
1919 9 & 10 Geo. V, c. 76. Church of England Assembly (Powers), 62, 104
1919 9 & 10 Geo. V., c. 100. Electricity (Supply), 45
1920 10 & 11 Geo. V, c. 28. Gas Regulation, 45
1922 12 & 13 Geo. V, c. 4. Irish Free State (Agreement), 167
1930 20 & 21 Geo. V, c. 45. Criminal Appeal (Northern Ireland), 115
1934 24 & 25 Geo. V, c. 40. Administration of Justice (Appeals), 114
1935 26 Geo. V & 1 Edw. VIII, c. 1. Government of India, 45
1935 26 Geo. V & 1 Edw. VIII, c. 2. Government of Burma, 45
1945 9 & 10 Geo. VI, c. 18. Statutory Orders (Special Procedure), 72
1946 9 & 10 Geo. VI, c. 36. Statutory Instruments, 129
1947 10 & 11 Geo. VI, c. 49. Transport, 74, 80
1948 11 & 12 Geo. VI, c. 58. Criminal Justice, 111
1949 12 & 13 Geo. VI, c. 33. Consolidation of Enactments (Procedure), 130
1949 12, 13 & 14 Geo. VI, c. 103. Parliament, 62
1951 14 & 15 Geo. VI, c. 46. Courts Martial (Appeals), 115
1958 6 & 7 Eliz. II, c. 21. Life Peerage, 22
1960 8 & 9 Eliz. II, c. 65. Administration of Justice, 115
1962 10 & 11 Eliz. II, c. 34. Acts of Parliament Numbering and Citation, 98
1962 10 & 11 Eliz. II, c. 46. Transport, 74, 80
1963 c. 48. Peerage, 22, 165
1965 c. 43. Statutory Orders (Special Procedure), 72
1967 c. 23. Royal Assent, 94, 176
1968 c. 73, Transport, 74, 80
1969 c. 58. Administration of Justice, 114

INDEX

NOTE. Entries for the main descriptions of classes of records are given in bold figures. H.C. (House of Commons) or H.L. (House of Lords) are used for entries referring exclusively to one House. Incidental references to recurring subjects (e.g. Journals, Bills), titles of works listed in the Bibliographies, and the names listed in the Appendices have not been indexed.

Abbot, Charles, Speaker, H.C. [1st L. Colchester], 207, 211, 234, 247, 248, 298
collection of printed papers, 66, 227, **234**
Abbot, George, Archbishop of Canterbury, 150
Abercorn, John James (Hamilton), 1st M. of, 193
Aberdeen Streets Bill (1800), 48
Aberfan Disaster, report of tribunal on, 130
Abergavenny peerage claim, **285**
Acceleration, Writs in, 21
Accession Declarations, 29, **170**
Accession Oath, 194
Account of the Office [Serjeant at Arms], H.C., **248**
Account Records
H.C., **244**
H.L., **185–6**
Accountant, the, H.C., 244
Accountant's Office, H.L., 182
Accounts and Papers, 129–30; H.C., 210, 212, 234, 235; H.L., 30, 131
Accounts, Commissioners of, 136
Accounts due to the Army, Commissioners of, 137
Accounts, Public, 136–7, 271
Accounts with the Treasury, L. Great Chamberlain, **252**
Act Papers, 33, 127, **128–30**, 132, 136, 232
Acts of Parliament. *See also* Ordinances, Private Acts, Public Acts, Royal Assent
calendars of, **96–7;** the long, 96–7; the short, 96–7
certification of, 191
classification of, 98–101

Acts of Parliament *cont.*
enrolment of, 93, 94, 185, 193
history and procedure, 93–5
lists and indexes of, 30, 94, **96–7,** 98, 102–3, 133
long titles of, 97
numbering of, 97–8
Original, 3, 11, 59, 61, 66, 67, 94, **95–6,** 101, 102, 181, 191; printed (vellums), 94, **96,** 193
printed, 96, 99–102
printing of, 98–103
sent to Public Record Office, 183
short titles of, 97, 98n
Addis, Alfred, 273
Addison, Joseph, 284
Addresses to Crown, 29, 131, 209, 213, 240, 243, 271
for papers, 127, 128, 210, 232
Motions for, in H.C., 45
on Special Procedure Orders, 72
Addresses, Joint, 192
Administration of Justice Bill (1927–8), 221
Administration (Services) Office, H.C., 244
Admirals of the Fleet, 152
Admiralty, Harbour Department of the, 80
officers of the, 80
Secretary to the, 155
Admission to H.L. [L. Great Chamberlain's records], 253
Admission Registers (Opening of Parliament) [L. Great Chamberlain], **252**
Affidavits, H.L., on Private Bills, **83**
on peerage claims, 164
Affidavits of Service of Notice [Appeal Cases, H.L.], **118**
Affirmations, 29, 179, 242. *See also* Oaths

Africa
  Cape Coast, 146
  Company of Merchants trading to, 142
  Natal, Responsible Government in, 238
  Royal African Company, 142
  Scotland, Africa Company of, 142
  Sierra Leone Company, 143
  slave trade, slavery, 52, 145, 194
  Slave Trade Bills (1788–99), 47
  South Africa, Indians in, 238
'Agadir' crisis (1911), 287
Agents. *See* Parliamentary Agents
Agriculture, Bills concerning, H.C., 216
Agriculture, Board of. *See* Board of
  Agriculture
Aire and Calder Navigation Bill (1828), 50
Aldborough, Mason Gerard (Stratford),
  5th E. of, 276
Allegiance, Oath of, 179, 192
Almanza, battle of (1707), 10
Almon, John, *Debates and Proceedings of the*
  British House of Commons, 37
Amendments. *See* Bills, Private Bills,
  Public Bills.
America, North, American Colonies,
  [United States of America], 140–1,
  152, 153
  American Papers (Russell, Edwards,
  etc.), **269**
  Annapolis, Maryland, 141
  Boston, Massachusetts, 141
  British Northern Colonies, Case of, 278
  Canada, geological survey, 187
  Charles Town, S. Carolina, 269
  courts martial in, 138
  French fleets in N. America, 141
  Georgia, 141
  guides to manuscripts relating to, 135,
  140
  Kentucky, 269
  Massachusetts, House of Representatives
  of, 147
  Massachusetts Bay, 141, disturbances
  (1774), 55
  New Jersey, 141
  New York, 141, 147
  Newfoundland Expedition (1699), 55
  Northampton, Virginia, 269
  Nottingham, Maryland, 269
  Nova Scotia, 141

America *cont.*
  prizes taken, 139
  Quebec, 141; militia ordinances, 194
  Quebec Bill (1791), 278
  Saratoga campaign, 138
  South Carolina, 141, 147, 269
  Spanish coins in Georgia, 141
  trade with, 143, 144, 145, 146, 147, 148
  Virginia, 147, 269
  War of Independence, 138, 142; Ameri-
  can prisoners, 52
  Williamstown, Virginia, 269
  Yale University, 272
America, West Indies, etc.
  Bahamas Act (1842), 265
  Barbadoes, 148; General Assembly, 145
  Bermuda Act (1845), 265
  British Guiana, 238
  Dominica, 139
  Jamaica, 141, 142, 148, 153
  Jamaica Act (1842), 265
  West Indies, 145, 152, 153; bullion
  from, 143; condition of (1832), 52;
  courts martial in, 138; duties, 141;
  guide to records relating to, 135;
  privateers in, 9, 55; trade with, 147,
  148
American Papers (Russell, Edwards, etc.),
  269
Analytical Table of Private Statutes, 103
Ancaster, Peregrine (Bertie), 3rd D. of, 251
  Gilbert Henry (Heathcote-Drummond-
  Willoughby), 1st E. of, 251
Ancient Monuments Bill (1930–1), 221
Ancient Petitions [P.R.O.], 3*n*, 93
Ancillary Papers [Judicial], H.L., **109**
Andover Borough, co. Hants, 272
Anglesey, 275
Anglesey peerage, 283
Annapolis, Maryland, 141
Annual Volumes of Statutory Rules and
  Orders, 132
Annuities, 136
Answers [Appeals], H.L., 115, **117**, 118,
  119, Pl. 8
Answers of the Accused [Impeachments],
  H.L., 109, **110**
Answers to Petitions [Judicial], H.L., **108**
Answers to Questions to Ministers, 38,
  216–17. *See also* Questions to Ministers

Answers of Sovereign, 213

Antingham Inclosure Bill (1809), 48

'appeal' or private accusation, 106

Appeal, Court of, 114
Lords of, 114

Appeal Cases, H.L. (*See also* Committees, H.L.), 33, 186
bills of costs, 185, 188
history and procedure, 107, 114-15, 178, 277
judgments in, **118**, **119**, 171, 174, 188
printed, **117**, 120, 123, 233, 289
records of, 116-20, 188, Pl. 8
tables of, 32, 285

Appellate Jurisdiction Bill (1928-9), 221

Appendices to Votes and Proceedings, 213, **214**, 222

Appleford, co. Berks., 186

Appointment and Order Book [Serjeant at Arms], H.C., **248**

Appointment Book [Black Rod], 196

Appropriation accounts, H.C., 245

Arbitration (Foreign Awards) Bill (1929-30), 221

Arbuthnott, John (Arbuthnott), 8th V., 113

Arcana Parliamentaria, 245

Arches, Dean of the, 275

Arlington, Henry (Bennet), 1st E. of, 287

Armed Forces pensions, 130

armorial, **285**

Army, papers relating to, 138-9, 150, 153, 210, 242

arrest, peer's freedom from, 124

Articles of Impeachment, 109, **110**

Artillery, Royal, 138

Ascot Authority Bill (1913), 276

Ashdown Forest, 275

Asia
Bengal, Governor of, 110
Bombay Army, 238
Burma. *See* India and Burma Orders Committees
Carnatic, the, 149
Central Asia, trade of, 238
China, Treaty Ports in, 238
Colombo, 274
Committees, India and Burma Orders, minutes, **45-6**
East India, 149
East India Company, 29, 55, 57, 142,

Asia *cont.*
East India Company *cont.*
148, 149; accounts, 110; treaty, 157. *See also under* Scotland
East India Company Bill (1830), 48
East India Company, Skinner *v.*, 8, 107
Fort William, 142
Hastings, Warren, 110, 142, 253, 255
India, Committee papers on (1933-4), 55; marriages in, 75; pensions relating to (1800), 55; *see also* E. India, Indian princes *and* Indians
India and Burma Orders Committees, H.L., **45-6**
India Office, 46
Indian Princes, 110, treaties with, 157
Indians in S. Africa, 238
Madras, 149; Governor of, 110
Scotland, East India Company of, 9, 142
Skinner *v.* E. India Company (1666), 8, 107
South and South East Asia, guide to manuscripts relating to, 135
Tanjore, 149
Tippo Sahib, 149

Asquith, Herbert Henry, 1st E. of Asquith and Oxford, 295

Assent. *See* Royal Assent

assents, dissents and neuters, 77. *See also* Consents Lists

Assiento, the, 143, 148

Assignments of Errors, 121, **122**, 123

Assistance, Writs of, 22, 179-80, 181

assistants of H.L., 22, 42

Assurance Companies (Winding Up) Bill (1932-3), 221

Athenaeum Club, The, London, 286

Athlone peerage claim, 169

Atkin, James Richard (Atkin), 1st. L., papers of, **269**

Attainder, Acts of, 106
Bills of, 46
reversal of, 81
of Thomas Seymour, Pl. 1

Attlee, Clement (Attlee), 1st E., 276

attorney, powers of, 192

Attorney General, 22, 80, 114, 121, 160, 237, 289, 293
Reports of, peerage claims, **163**

Australia, South Australia Commission, 264, 265
Authority of Parliaments, by Sir Thomas Smith, 245
Avon, Kennet and, Canal Bill (1809), 49
Aylesbury Election Bill (1804), 47

Bacon, Francis, 1st V. St. Albans, Lord Chancellor, 109, 279
Badeley, Sir Henry [1st L. Badeley], Clerk of the Parliaments, 5
Baden, 157
Badger, Rev. James, 273
Bagot, R., 284
Bahamas Act (1842), 265
Bailey, Robert Neale Menteth, papers of, **291**
Baillie, Capt., 151
Baking Trade, Ireland, Bill (1831), 48
Ballantine, James, 269
ballot for Bills, H.C., 216
Balmerino [Balmerinoch], Arthur (Elphinstone), 6th L., 113
Banbury, William (Knollys), 1st E. of, patent of, 11, 164
Bangor, Bishop of, sermon, 233
Bank Cash Payments (1819), 52
Bank of England, 42, 137, 143, 194
Banstead, co. Surrey, 275
Barbadoes, 148; General Assembly, 145
Barnet Market Bill (1592), Pl. 6
Barnewell Peerage (1812), 52
baronetcies, report on, 288
baronies by writ, proceedings on claims to, H.L., **162**
barracks, 138
Barrington, Sir Jonah, Judge of the Court of Admiralty in Ireland, 52, 194
Barrow, John Henry, *The Mirror of Parliament*, 38–9
Barry, Sir Charles, 4, 293
  drawings of, 289–90
  letters of, 253
Barry, Edward Middleton, 290
Barry, Sir John Wolfe, 290
Bath, Knights of the, 254
Bath Common Leases Bill (1806), 48
Bath Road Bill (1829), 50
Bathurst, Henry [2nd E. Bathurst], L. Chancellor, notebooks of, 289

Battersea, London, 265
Bavaria, 157, 194
Beauchamp, William (Seymour), L. [1st M. of Hertford], 293
Beauclerk, Major A. W., 276
Bedford, Farringdon and, Road Bill (1833), 51
beef, 147, 148, 153
Belfast Harbour Bill (1831), 51
Bell, John, doorkeeper, 52
Beltz, George Frederick, 298
Bengal, governor of, 110
Benson, Arthur, Clerk of the Journals, H.C., 212
Bentham, Jeremy, 186
Bere Forest Bill (1810), 49
Berkeley, George (Berkeley), 1st E. of, patent of, 164
Berkeley, John *v.* Cope, Pl. 8
Berkshire Protestation Returns, 154
Bermondsey Poor Bill (1809), 49
Bermuda Act (1845), 265
Bertie, family of, 255
Bexley, co. Kent, 273
Bill Books [Private Bills], H.L., **83**
Bill Papers (Miscellaneous) [Private Bills], H.L., **84**
Bills, 3, 30, 182, 259, 271. *See also* Acts of Parliament, Hybrid Bills, Local and Personal Bills, Personal Bills, Private Bills (incl. categories, e.g. Railway Bills), Public Bills, H.C., H.L.
  amendments to, 58, 60, 61, 65, 66–7; H.C., 209, 218, 220, 226, 243; H.L., 42, 43; marshalled lists of, 33. *See also* riders.
  analyses, 61
  breviates (briefs). *See separate entry.*
  draft, 265, 275, 276
  engrossed, 59*n*, 60, 61, 94–5; H.C., 209, 226, 298
  explanatory memoranda, 227
  H.C., 28, 204, 205, 218, 219, 226, 243, 247
  H.L., 26, 28, 43
  House, 61, 66–7, 84, 94, 95; H.C., 209, 228
  message and assent formulae, 62. *See also* Royal Assent
  Original, H.C., **228**

Bills *cont.*
  Paper, 60, 61; H.C., 298, Pl. 6
  petitions for, 172
  printed, 3, 61–2; lists of, 134; sessional
    lists of, 33; H.C., 235; H.L., 131.
  procedure on, 59–62, 279
  progress of, H.C. 209; H.L., 29, 33, 34
  Table, 66, 84, 227
Bills and Cases in Parliament, etc., H.C.,
  233
Bird, Henry, 273
Birmingham Canal Bill (1791), 48; (1826),
  50
Birmingham Grammar School Bill (1830),
  51
Birmingham, London and, Railway Bill
  (1832), 51
bishops' lands, 297
Bishopstone Inclosure Bill (1809), 49
Black Rod, Gentleman Usher of the,
  186, 188, 189, 251
  appointment book, **196**
  department of, 184
  history of office, 195
  Letter Book, **196**
  Yeoman Usher of the, 195
Blackburn, Lancs., 276
Bletchingley Inclosure Bill (1810), 49
Blomfield, Charles James, Bishop of
  London, 276
Blind, School for Indigent, Bill (1829),
  48
Board of Agriculture, 78
Board of Trade, 80, 264, 265
  Librarian of, 131
Bohemia, 157
  Elizabeth, Queen of, 8
Bombay Army, 238
Book of Receipts of Rolls, H.L., **123**
Books of Ceremonial, etc., **187**
Books of Evidence. *See* Evidence
Books of Orders and Judgments [Appeals]
  H.L., **118**
Books of Orders and Ordinances. *See*
  Orders and Ordinances.
Books of Receipts [Private Bills], H.L.,
  85
Books of Reference, 71, 74, 80, 83
  H.C., **228**
  H.L., **85**

Borthwick peerage claim, 188
Boston, Massachusetts, 141
Boston, co. Lincs., election evidence, 240
Bound Sessional Sets of Printed Papers,
  H.C., **235**
Bourchier's case (1621), 107
Bowyer, Robert, Clerk of the Parliaments,
  3, 4, 31, 35, 181, 191, 270, 271, 280,
  281, 282
  diary of, 207, 211, 271
Boyer, Abel, 277
B.P., Edward, 273
Brackley, co. Northants., 275
Brand, Henry Bouverie William, Speaker,
  H.C. [1st V. Hampden], papers of,
  237, **291**, Pl. 14
Brandenburg-Anspach, 157
brandy, 143
brass, 143
Braunston, Warwick and, Canal Bill
  (1794), 48
Braye, Alfred Thomas Townshend
  (Wyatt-Edgell, afterwards Verney-
  Cave), 5th L., 270
  manuscripts of, 32, 34, 35–6, **269–72**
Braye-Teeling Manuscripts, **272**
bread, sale of (1836), evidence concerning,
  53
Brecon, Court of Chancery of, 114
Breda, Declaration of (1660), 4
Breviates (or Briefs), 60, 61, 71, 271;
  H.C., 214, 226
  H.L., **67, 85**
Brickdale, Sir Charles Fortescue, 285
Brickdale, Matthew, notebooks of, **285,**
  292
bridges, 82, 89, 129
Briefs. *See* Breviates
Bristol, co. Somerset, 292
  Cathedral, 150
  University Library, 285
Bristol Dues Bill (1825), 50
Bristol, John (Digby), 1st E. of, 271
British and Foreign Life Assurance Bill
  (1824), 47
British Gas Light Bill (1829), 48
British Guiana, 238
British Museum, London. *See* London.
British Northern Colonies, Case of, 278
British Railways Board, 80

British Railways (Eastern Region), parliamentary deposits, 277
British Transport Commission, 74, 80
British Waterways Board, 74
broadcasting, sound, records of, H.L., **39**; H.C., **217**
Bromley [William] Estate Bill (1728), 277
Bromley, William, Speaker, H.C., 299
  Book of Bills and Cases of, **233**, 237
  Precedent Book of, **272**
Bromyard, co. Herts., 193
Browne, John, Clerk of the Parliaments, 30, 181, 183, 186, 269–70, 271, 272, 276, 278
Browning, Elizabeth Barrett, 289
Brunswick, 157
Brunswick-Luneburg-Wolfenbuttel, 157
Bryce Conference (1917–18), 187
Brydges, Sir Egerton, 278
Buckingham Palace, conference at, Pl. 15
  plans of, 194
Buckinghamshire Protestation Returns, 154
Bull, Sir William, papers of, **292**
bullion, 143
Bunting, S.S., 273
burgesses or citizens [Members, H.C.], 201
Burgoyne, Sir John, General, 141
Burke, Edmund, 141, 277
Burley estate, co. Hants., 265
Burma. *See* India and Burma Orders Committees.
Burnham Beeches, co. Bucks., 275
Burrows, Henry Montagu, Clerk Assistant, H.L., papers, 192
Bute, John (Stuart), 3rd E. of, 293
Bute Ship Canal, 1830, 51
By Elections, Certificates of, **238**
Byng, John, Admiral, court martial of, 153
Byron, John, Rear-Admiral, 153
Byron of Rochdale, William (Byron), 5th L., 113, 254, 255, 278

Cabinet Committee on Reform of H.L., 187, 292
Cadiz, 153
Calais, 202
Calder, Aire and, Navigation Bill (1828), 50

Calder and Hebble Navigation Bill (1834),
Caldon, co. Staffs., 79   [52
calicoes, 149
Callan Common Bill (1829), 51
Camberwell Poor Bill (1833), 51
Cambridge Canal Bill (1812), 49
Cambridge Road Bill (1823), 49
Cambridge University, 202
  election, 1847, 265
  Protestation Returns, 154
  Trinity College, manuscript of, 170*n*
Cambridge, D. of, Prince Adolphus Frederick, 252
Cambridge, James, E. *See* Hamilton, 1st. D. of
Cameron, Sir David, papers of, **292**
Canada, geological survey, 187
canal Bills, 71, 73–4, 85, 89, 90, 210
  evidence on, 53
canal companies, 79
candles, 146
Canterbury, Archbishop of. *See* Abbot, G.; Laud, W.; Manners Sutton, C.; Secker, T.; Sheldon, G.
  Cathedral, 150
  Convocation of, 178
Cape Coast, Africa, 146
Capell, Arthur (Capell), 1st L. Capell of Hadham, 151
Cardigan, James Thomas (Brudenell), 7th E. of, 113
Carew Manuscripts, 35
Carleton, Hon. Richard, 265
Carlisle, William Nicolson, Bishop of, 277
Carlisle to Newcastle Military Road, 139
Carlow co., 193
Carnatic, the, India, 149
Caroline, Queen, 42, 47, 253, 254
Cartwright's Patent Bill (1801), 48
Cary, Sir Robert, scroll of, 293
Cases, Appeal, printed, 117
  [Irish Peerages], **168**
  [peerage claims], 162, **163**, 167
  presented to H.C., **233**
  [Public Bills], H.L., **67**
Catesby Collection, **272–3**
Catesby, Robert, 272
Caton, Charlotte, 274
Caton, Elizabeth, 274
Cause Sheets, 34

Causes, index of, 32

Census Reports, 130

Central Asia, trade of, 238

Ceremonial, Books of, H.L., **187**

Certificates of Election [Scottish Representative Peers], H.L., **166**

Certificates of receiving Holy Communion (Sacramental certificates), 79, **85**

Certificates of Secretary of State, 79, **85**

certiorari, Writs of, 111; in trials of peers, **113**

Chairmanship of Committees (Memorandum), H.L., **285**

Chalmorton Inclosure Bill (1805), 48

Chamberlain, Sir Joseph Austen, drawings of, 295

Chancellor of the Exchequer, 237, 265

Chancery, 3, 20, 30, 93-4, 96, 102, 191, 204, 259

  clerks of, 3, 181, 243

  Courts of, 48, 55, 106, 107, 114, 120

  Masters in, 22, 181

  Registrar's office, 193

Chancery, Court of, Regulation Bill (1833), 48

Chandler, Richard, *History and Proceedings of the House of Commons*, 37

Chandos peerage claim, 52

Chandos of Sudeley, L. *See* Brydges, Sir Egerton

Change of Name Bills, 70, 78

Chantries Bill (1547), 66

Charing Cross Bill (1826), 50

Charles I, King, 4, 156, 271

  death warrant of, 6, 11, 151-2

  goods of, 8, 152

  portrait of, 11

  secretary to, 284

  trial of, 10

Charles II, King, 296

Charles, the 'Young Pretender', 158

Charles Town, South Carolina, 269

Charlwood Inclosure Bill (1828), 50

charters of liberties, 102

Chelsea roads, London, 151

Chelworth Inclosure Bill (1789), 48

Cheshire, county palatine of, 202; Protestation Returns of, 154*n*

Chester, co. Cheshire, 269

  Court of Vice-Chancellor of, 114

  poor of, 193

Chester *cont.*

  Protestation Returns, 154

Chichester, Bishop of, Estate Bills, 277

  Cathedral, 150

  diocese, 273

Chiddingfold Common, co. Surrey, 274

Chief Clerk, H.L., 181

Chief Usher Papers [Exchequer], 266

Children (Employment Abroad) Bill, (1929-30), 221

children's notebooks, 274

chimneys, boy sweepers of, 194

Chimney Sweepers Bill (1834), 48

China, Treaty Ports in, 238

Chinnor, co. Oxon., 299

Chippenham, disputed elections evidence, 277

Cholmondeley, M. of, family of, 251

Cholmondeley, George Horatio (Cholmondeley), 2nd M. of, 252

Cholmondeley, R., 284

Chronicle of the Kings of England, 30

Chronological Table of the Statutes, 98, 99, 101, 102

Church Assembly [General Synod], 104

  Measures, 103, 130; lists of, 134; papers pursuant to, 232; printed, **104**; records of, **104**

church, government (abuses in), 241

  lands and livings, 297

Churches, Commissioners for building, 149

  new, 76

Churchill, L. Randolph, 276, 295

Churchill, Sir Winston Spencer, 293, 294

Cinque Ports, co. Kent and Sussex, barons of, 201

Civil Defence papers, H.L., 191

Civil Lists, 136

Civil Service Commission, 185. *See also* Shaw-Lefevre, Sir John George, Civil Service Commissioner.

Civil War (1642-9), the, 284

  death warrants, 151-2

Clackmannan and Kinross Parishes Bill (1833), 51

Claims, Register of [Irish peers], H.L., **168**

Clandon Park, co. Surrey, 244

Clarence and Avondale, D. of, Prince Albert Victor Christian Edward, 43

Clarence Railway Bill (1829), 51
Clarence, Tees and, Railway Bill (1828), 50
Clarendon, Edward (Hyde), 1st E. of, 8, 178
Clark, Alexander, 273
Clarke, Sir William, 293
classical note book, 273
Clay, Joanna, 273
Clementson, John, notebook, of, 247, **292**
clerical notebooks, 273
Clerk Assistant, H.C., 219, 243
Clerk Assistant, H.L., 26, 33, 181, 182, 192, 264
  Minutes or Sheets, **33**
  papers, 184
Clerk of Committees, H.C., 290, 297
Clerk of the Crown, 94, 166, 179, 238, 247
  history and duties of, 259
  records of, 6, 259
  See also under Ireland
Clerk of the Elections, H.C., 243
Clerk of the House of Commons, 5, 20, 94, 201, 204, 205, 206, 223, 240, 242, 259, 293, 295, app. II
  history and duties of, 181, 243–4
  office of, 183
  See also Hardinge, N.; Hatsell, J.; Ilbert, C.; Jodrell, P.; Ley, J.H.; May, T. E.; Onslow, F.; Palgrave, R. F. D.; Webster, T. L.
Clerk of Ingrossments, H.L., 181
Clerk of Inrollments, H.L., 94*n*
Clerk of the Journals, H.C., 212, 219, 222, 234
Clerk of the Journals, H.L., 26, 181, 192
Clerk of the Parliaments, 5, 7, 26, 46, 61, 80, 86, 88, 91, 94, 95, 108, 121, 123, 125, 132, 168, 171, 175, 179, 191, 193, 264, 269, 278, 280, 283, 297, app. I
  fees of, 270
  history of, 3, 181–3
  letters patent of, 184
  office of 52, 195,
  See also Badeley, H.; Bowyer, R.; Browne, J.; Cowper, A.; Cowper, W.; Elsynge, H.; Goodman, V. M. R.; Hatton, R.; Mason, A.; North, E.; Rose, G.; Scobell, H.; Smith, T.; Taylor, J.; *and* Deputy Clerk of the Parliaments

Clerk of the Parliaments Act (1824), 192
Clerk of the Parliaments Rolls, 23, 29, **170**, 188, 271
Clerk of the Records, 5, 6
Clerk, Reading. *See* Reading Clerk
Clerks of the Peace, 80
Clerks of Session [Scotland], 165
Clerkenwell Improvement Bill (1829), 50
Cleveland, co. Yorks., 283
Clifden, Victor (Agar-Robartes), 8th V., 288
Clifford, de, Edward Southwell (Russell), 26th L., 111, 113
Close Rolls [P.R.O.], 180
closures, H.C., 240, 245
coach duty, 149
coal, 143
  Royal Commission Report on, 238
  trade, 29, 52, 55
Coal Trade Bill (1829), 48
coats of arms, 162, 164
Cobbett, William, *Parliamentary History of England*, 30, **37**
Coercion Bill (1881), Pl. 14
coffee, 146
Coke, Sir John, 271
Colchester, Charles (Abbot), 1st. L. *See* Abbot, Charles
Colman, Edward, 247
Colombo, 274
Colonial Naval Defence Bill (1930–1), 221
Colonies, H.L. Sessional papers concerning, 136, 140–1
Command Papers, 29, 33, 127, **128**, 131, 132, 133, 232, 233, 235
  lists of, 134
commercial distress (1847–8), 42
Commercial Docks Bill (1810), 49
Commercial Road Bill (1824), 49; (1828), 50
Commissions, Commissioners, accounts or reports of, 129, 131, 132, 235. *See also under* particular names *and* Royal Commissions
Commissioners' Papers [Statute Law], **263**
Committee Bills, H.C., 228
Committee Clerks, H.C., 297; H.L., 181
Committee Office, H.C., 224, 230–1, 243, 244, 291
Committee Office, Private Bill and, H.L., 182

Committee Office, Private Bill and, H.L.
  Amendment Book of, **85**   [*cont.*
  Notice Books of, **86**
  Petition Books of, **86**
Committees, H.C., 41, 60, 61, 62, 109, 205,
    209, 210, 212, 218–20, 223, 227, 239,
    276, 277
  Debates, 38
  Election, 214, 218, 220, 223, 238;
    evidence, 277; records, **239**, 244
  Estimates, 218
  evidence in, 210, 219, 220
  Fees and Salaries, **225**
  grand, 218–19; proceedings, **219**
  Hybrid Bill, 220
  Journal, 205, 206*n*
  Kitchen and Refreshment Rooms, 218
  lists of, 68
  Local Legislation, 82
  minutes, 4, 219–22
  Nationalised Industries, 218
  'out of the House', 'outdoor', 60
  papers, **224–5**
  for petitions, 173, 240–1. *See also* Public
    Petitions *infra*
  Police and Sanitary, 81
  printed reports, 213, 220, 234, 235
  Private Bill, 214, 216, 218, 219, 224,
    228; deposits, Indexes, **231**; evidence,
    214, 224; minutes, 220, **221–2**; papers,
    Indexes, **230**; reports, 214, **216**
  of Privileges (and Elections), 205, 218,
    238
  Provisional Order Bill, minutes, 220
  Public Accounts, 218
  Public Bill, 214, 215, 218; minutes, 220,
    245
  Public Petitions, 173, 218, 240–1;
    reports, 216, **222–3**
  Publications and Debates Reports, 218
  Second Reading, 62
  Secret, 223–4; minutes, 284
  Select, 38, 46, 206*n*, 212, 218, 224, 240,
    241; evidence, 225, 277; minutes,
    219–20; papers, 225, 232; proceedings,
    219–20
  of Selection, 218
  Services, 218
  Sessional, 205, 218
  Special Procedure Orders, evidence, 224

Committees, H.C. *cont.*
  Standing, 209, 214, 216, 218, 240; de-
    bates, **220–1**
  Standing Orders, 71, 88, 218
  Statutory Instruments, 218
  of Supply, 219, 245
  of Ways and Means, 219
  of the whole House, 60, 109, 209, 210,
    212, 214, 218, 219, 239, 243, 247;
    minutes, 213, **219**
Committees, H.L., 3, 29, 34, 41–56, 86,
    173, 186
  Appeal, 41, 115; evidence, 116; minutes,
    44–5; proceedings, **116**; reports, 116
  Appellate, 41, 115; proceedings, **116**;
    reports, 116
  Appointment Books, **42**, 177*n*, 271
  Dignity of a Peer, 160, 188
  Estate Bill, 47, 85; minutes, **44**
  fees of, 185
  indexes of, 46
  India and Burma Orders, minutes, **45–6**
  for the Journals, 26, 28*n*, 41, 53, **187**, 188
  'judicial', 107; order books, **108**
  Leave of Absence, 41
  lists of, 34, 68
  L. Chairman of, 44, 72, 84, **285**
  minutes, **42–6**
  Offices, 41, 44, 55, 182, 189, 193, 195,
    196, 251; papers, 184
  'out of the House', 'outdoor', 41, 60
  papers of, **54–6**
  Personal Bills, 41, 76
  for Petitions, 41, 106, 107, 108, 118, 172,
    173; minutes, **43**
  printed reports of, 42, 131, 132, 235
  Private Bill, 47, 83, Pl. 3; Opposed, 186,
    minutes, **44, 45**; Unopposed, 69,
    minutes, **44**, 83, **92**
  for Privileges, 26, 41, 52, 55, 108, 112, 115,
    160, 161–2, 164, 165, 166, 167, 283;
    minutes, **43, 125, 161**; reports, **164**, 167
  Procedure, 41
  Secret, 42, 52, 55
  Select, 29, 41–2, 46, 54, 55, 69, 70, 76,
    112, 116, 130, 182, 188, 190, 219;
    evidence, **47–53**; minutes, **43–6**, 83;
    on Public Bills, 34
  of Selection, 41; minutes, **44**
  Sessional, 41–2, 44, 116

Committees, H.L. *cont.*
  Special Orders, 41, 56; minutes, **45**
  Standing, 41–2, 70; minutes, 43–6
  Standing Orders, 41, 71, 74, 75, 79, 80, 88; minutes **44, 45**
  S.O.s concerning, 41, 54
  on State of the Nation, 9
  of Whole House, 29, 33, 41–2, 60, 69, 70, 75, 174; evidence, 46–8, 52–3; minutes, **42**
Committees, Joint, 28, 29, 41, 55, 57, 132, 173, 190, 192, 218, 219, 222, 223, 235
  minutes and other records of, **57**
Common Pleas, court of, 22
  Chief Justice of, 286
Common Prayer, Book of (1662), 4, 95, (1927), 104
Commonplace Book, parliamentary, 279
Commonplace Note Book Collection, **273–4**
Commons, House of. *See* House of Commons
Commons and Footpaths Preservation Society, 274, 275
Commons and Open Spaces, 238, **274–5**
Commonwealth Parliamentary Conference (1961), 187
companies, trading, 142
compensation, warrants for, 233
Complete Peerage Trust, materials, **274**
Compton, Spencer, [1st E. Wilmington], Speaker, H.C., 278, 291
Conferences between Houses, 41, 58, 61, 210, 235, 271, 272, 276, 280, 299, Pl. 13
  ancillary papers, **58**
  reports, **58**
Conformity, occasional, debates concerning, 235
Consents Lists, 74, 80, 83, **86, 228**
Conservative Party, Second Chamber Commission of, 292
Consolidated Fund, 137
Consolidation Bills, 57
conspiracy, in favour of the Pretender (1723), 55
Continental Gas Bill (1833), 51
Controller and Auditor General, 130
Controverted Elections, 210, 214, 277. *See also* elections, H.C.
  records, H.C., 238–40

Convention Parliament (1660), 21, 37; (1689) 293, 299
Conventions, texts of, 157–8
Convocations of the Church of England, 178, 234
convoys, 9
Cook, Georgiana, 273
Cook, John, 193
Cooke, Richard Stafford, 288
Cooke, Sir Thomas, 57
cookery recipe books, 273
Cope, Jonathan, *v.* Berkeley, Pl. 8
Corfe Castle, co. Dorset, election returns, 293
Cork, estates in co., 193
Corn Importation Act (1842), 265
Corn Laws, 144
corn trade, 52, 144, 148
Corner, George, 276
Cornwall Protestation Returns, 154
Cornwallis, Charles (Cornwallis), 3rd L., 111
Cornwallis, Charles (Cornwallis), 2nd E., 138, 153
coronations, 6, 29, 151, 170, 189, 251, 252, 254, 255, 283
  L. Great Chamberlain's papers concerning, 253
Corporation Act (1828), 172
Cotton Factories Bill (1819), 47
Cotton Factory Bill (1825), 47
Cotton Industry Bill (1932–3), 221
Cotton, Sir Robert, 279
  'Parliament's Antiquity', **292**
cotton wool, 144, 147
Counsel, King's or Queen's, 44, 45, 46, 53, 60, 67, 86, 109, 113, 115, 116, 121, 122, 123, 161, 224
  names of, 33
  speeches of, 43
counts out, H.C., 245, 248
County Rates Bill (1834), 48
County Record Offices, 78
Court Evidence [Controverted Elections], H.C., **239**
Court Proceedings (Divorce), **86**
Court of Wards, 253
Courtenay, William, Deputy Clerk of the Parliaments, 186
Courthorpe, James, minute book of, 219

courts of equity, 54, 106
courts of justice, 54, 216, 219
Courts Martial, 138
Courts Martial Court, 115
covenant lists, 151
Covenham St. Bartholomew, co. Lincs., Pl. 10
Covent Garden Vestry Bill (1829), 50
Coventry, co. Warwick, Protestation Returns, 155
Cowell, John, *The Interpreter*, 281
Cowper, Ashley, Clerk of the Parliaments, 186
Cowper, Harriott, 186
Cowper, William, Clerk of the Parliaments, 97
Crediton, Exeter and, Railway Bill (1832), 51
Crick, Dr. Bernard, 278
Cricklade Election Bill (1782), 47
Crimes Bill (1785), **292**
Criminal Appeal, Court of, 114, 115
Croft, John, Clerk of the Journals, precedent book, 192
Cromartie, Cromarty, George (Mackenzie), 3rd E. of, 113, 297
Cromford Canal Bill (1789), 48
Crown estates, 141
Crown Office, 180, 259. *See also* Clerk of the Crown
Cumberland Protestation Returns, 154
Cumberland, D. of, Prince Ernest Augustus, 252
Cupar Gaol Bill (1812), 49
Curtis, Sir Roger, Admiral, 153
Curwen's Exchange of Living Bill (1797), 48
Curzon of Penn, Assheton (Curzon), 1st L., pedigree of, Pl. 12
Cust, Robert Needham, 288
customs and excise, produce of, 137
customs and trade, H.L. sessional papers concerning, 136, 142–9
general accounts, 148–9
customs duties (1844–8), 265

Dagenham Breach, co. Essex, 149
Act (1717), 129
D'Avenant, Charles, *Essays upon Peace at Home and War*, 277
Darlington, Stockton and, Railway Bill (1828), 50

Dartmouth, William (Legge), 3rd L., 131
Dean and Chapter lands, 297
death warrants (Civil War), 151–2
debates, records of, H.C. and H.L., **36–40**
H.C., 217, 220, 240, 285, **292,** 296
H.L., 160
Debrett, John, *History, Debates and Proceedings of both Houses of Parliament*, 37
Debtors, Insolvent, Bill (1820), 47
declaration against transubstantiation, 29, 179
Declaration of James, Prince of Wales, the 'Old Pretender', 277
Declaration of Rights (1689), 152, Pl. 11
Declarations, Accession, 29, **170**
'of Grievances', 110
of H.C., **228,** 235, 276
Declarations (Private Bill), H.L., **86**
Delamer, Henry (Booth), 2nd L., 111
De La Warr peerage claim (1597), 160, 163
Delegated Legislation, **129,** 130
printing of, 132
Demolition statements, 71, 80, **86, 229**
Denbighshire Protestation Returns, 154
Denman, Thomas (Denman), 1st L., manuscripts of, **285**
Denmark, 157
Departmental Reports. *See* Reports, Departmental
Deposited Papers (Library), H.C., **238**
H.L., **187**
Deptford Road Bill (1812), 49
Deputy Clerk of the Parliaments, 271. *See also* Courtenay, William
Deputy Lieutenants, papist, 150
Derby, Edward Geoffrey (Smith-Stanley), 14th E. of, 299
Derwentwater Estate, co. Derby, 151
Design, Government School of, 265
Destructive Insects and Pests Bill (1927–8), 221
Devizes, co. Wilts., 275
Devon Protestation Returns, 154
D'Ewes, Sir Simonds, 37, 206, 280, 297
Diaries and Journals (unofficial), Parliamentary, 10, 270–2, 276, **279–80,** 281–2
Dignity of a Peer, papers concerning the, 188

Directory for Public Worship (1645), 150
Diseases of Animals Bill (1926–7), 221
Display items, H.C., **292–3**
disputed elections. *See* Controverted Elections
Distillers' Company, ordinances of, 152
divisions, 37, 38, 39
  H.C., 205, 209, 213, 214, 215, 245, 247, 299; lists, **215**; register of, 296; H.L., 29, 33, 43, 192, Pl. 2; lists, 34, 174; register of, 188
divorce, Court proceedings, records of, **86**
Divorce Acts, 102
Divorce Bills, 30, 44, 46, 60, 75, 88, 192
  evidence on, 53
Dobson, Hart and, trial (1805), 52
Dock Bills, 71, 82
Dock Boards, 130
docks, 89
Doddridge, Sir John, Justice of the King's Bench, *A True Presentation of forepast Parliaments*, **293**
Dominica, 139
Don Bridge Bill (1825), 50
Doncaster and Thorne Road Bill (1825), 50
Donoughmore, Richard Walter John (Hely-Hutchinson), 6th E. of, 285
doorkeepers, H.C., 247, 248; H.L., 184, 195, 196
Dorset Protestation Returns, 154
Draft Journals, H.L. *See* Journals, Draft
Drummond, Francis, collection of, **286**
Dublin, Metropolitan Police in, 233
  Trinity College, 202
Dublin Equitable Loan Bill (1824), 47
Dublin Railroad Bill (1831), 51
Dublin Steam Packet Company Bill (1833), 51
Ducarel, Andrew Coltee, Keeper of Lambeth Palace Library, 297
Dugdale, Sir William, 171
Dunbar Harbour Bill (1827), 50
Duncombe, Henry, 293
Dundee, 293
Dundee Harbour Improvement Bill (1814), deposits, Pl. 4, 5
Dunkirk, 10, 143, 149, 158
Dupplin, George (Hay), 1st V., 286
Durham, county palatine of, 202
  Court of Chancery of, 114

Durham *cont.*
  Protestation Returns, 154
Durham Railway Bill (1834), 52
Durham Yard Embanking Bill (1771), 48
Durye, John, mission papers, 8, 150

Earl Marshal, 160, 170, 252
'Early Day' motions, H.C., 34
East India, 149
East India Company, 29, 55, 57, 142, 148, 149
  accounts, 110
  treaty, 157
  See also under Scotland
East India Company Bill (1830), 48
East India Company, Skinner *v.*, 8, 107
East Retford Election Bill (1830), 48
Eastbourne, co. Sussex, 274
Eau Bank Drainage Bill (1831), 51
ecclesiastical archives, Pilgrim Trust survey of, 277
Ecclesiastical Bills, 82
Ecclesiastical Committee (Joint), 55, 104
  Reports and Proceedings, **104**
ecclesiastical law, treatise concerning, **286**
Eckington Inclosure Bill (1810), 49
Eden, Catherine, 273
Edinburgh, 155, 156
Edinburgh Roads Bill (1803), 48
Edmond, Mary, 186
education, 172
Edward VII, King, coronation of, 255
  funeral of, 283
Edward VIII, King, 170
Edward, Gardine Isabella, 273
Edwards, John, 269
Edwards, Samuel, 286
Election Papers, H.C., **293**
Election Returns, Irish Representative Peers, H.L., **168**
elections, H.C., 238–40, 241, 259, **293**
  Bills concerning: Aylesbury Election Bill (1804), 47; Cricklade Election Bill (1782), 47; East Retford Election Bill (1830), 48; Helleston Election Bill (1814, 1815), 47; Nottingham Election Bill (1803), 47; Shaftesbury Election Bill (1775), 47
  By Elections, Certificates of, **238**
  Clerk of the Elections, H.C., 243

elections, H.C. *cont.*
  Committees, Election, H.C., 214, 218, 220, 223, 238; evidence, 277; records, **239**, 244
  disputed elections. *See* elections, controverted, *infra*
  elections: Cambridge University, 265; Corfe Castle, 293; Dundee, 293; Exeter, 293; Lostwithiel, 293; Marylebone Borough, 293; Mayo County, 239; Tynemouth, 193; Wells, 293; Yorkshire, 293
  elections, controverted, 210, 214, 277; records, H.C., 238–40; Court Evidence, H.C., **239**; Boston, Lincs., evidence, 240; Chippenham, evidence, 277
  petitions, 214, index, 239
  Return Books, 4, 238, **259**
  Return Register, **293**
Electricity Commissioners, 45
Elibank, Patrick (Murray), 3rd L., 287
Elizabeth I, Queen, 293
Elizabeth II, Queen, 170
Elsynge, Henry, sen., Clerk of the Parliaments, 3, 4, 35, 181, 191, 270, 271, 297
  author of *Manner of Holding Parliaments*, 281; *Method of Passing Bills in Parliament*, 245; *Modern Form of the Parliaments of England*, 294; *Modus Tenendi Parliamentum apud Anglos*, 272, 282, 294
Ely, canon of. *See* Nalson, John
Ely Drainage Bill (1823), 49
Ely peerage claim, 169
Emmott, Alfred (Emmott), 1st L., **294**
Empire, Holy Roman, 157
Ensham Inclosure Bill (1800), 48
Entwistle Statute Roll, 277
Epping Forest Commission Papers, 274, records, **294**
Epsom Common Preservation Committee Papers, 274
Equitable Loan Bills (1824, 1825), 47
Equivalent, Commissioners of the, **137**
Erickson, Dr. E. L., 234
Error, Cases in, judgments, 171; jurisdiction of H.L., 106; printed, 117, 121, **123**; procedure in, 120–1; records of, 119, **121–3**; S.O.s concerning, 174. *See also* Standing Orders

Error, Cases in *cont.*
  Commissioners of, 120
  Writs of, 55, 106, 114, 115, 120, **121**, 122, 123, 186, 270, Pl. 9; papers concerning, 188; tables of, 32
Essex, Robert (Devereux), 2nd E. of, 271, 284
Essex, Robert (Devereux), 3rd E. of, letters of, 8
Essex Protestation Returns, 154
  county rates, western division, 52
Establishment Papers [Parliament Office], H.L., **184–5**
Estate Acts, 102
Estate Bills, 46, 59, 70, 75–6, 83, 88, 92, 192. *See also* Committees, H.L.
Estimates of Expense [Private Bills], 74, **87**, **229**, Pl. 5
Estimates of Time [Private Bills], **87**, **229**, Pl. 5
Eton College, co. Bucks., 150
Evesham, co. Worcs., 280
Eversley, Charles (Shaw-Lefevre), 1st V., [Speaker, H.C.], 293
Evidence, H.C., 223–4; H.L., 41, 42, 43, 44, 45, 46–54
  Book of (Secret Committee), H.C., **223**
  Books of, H.L., 47, **53**
  Books of (Courts of Referees), H.C., **224**
  Books of (Private Bills), H.C., **224**
  Books of (Special Procedure Orders), H.C., **224**
  Examiners', H.C., **229**; H.L., **87–8**
  (Main Papers), H.L., **53**
  manuscript, H.L., **47–54**, H.C., 223
  on peerage claims, **161–2**, 164, Scottish, **166**, Irish, **168**
  printed, H.C., 223; H.L., 46
Evidential Documents [Impeachments], **110**
Evidential Papers [Peerage Claims], H.L., **164**, 167
Examinations, copies of (1646–7), 272
Examiners of Private Bills, 44, 45, 69, 71, 74, 75, 79, 83, 88
  affidavits of, 83
  certificates of, 83, **87**
  evidence of, **87–8**, **229**
  reports, of, 88, **229**
Exchequer, 4, 22, 93, 136

Exchequer *cont.*
  bills, 54
  Book of the, 99
  Court of, 114, 266; Chief Usher of,
    records, 6, 263, **266**; offices in, **286**
  Teller of, 278
Exchequer Chamber, Court of, 106, 114,
    120, 122
Exclusion Bill (1680), 9
Exeter, Cathedral, 150
  city, poll list, 293
Exeter and Crediton Railway Bill (1832),
    51
Expedicio Billarum Antiquitus, by H.
    Elsynge, 281
Expenses. *See* Estimates of Expense
Eye, co. Suffolk, 295
Eyre, Thomas, 265

Fagg, Shirley *v.* (1675), 107
Fakenham, co. Norfolk, 275
Falkland Island, 141
False Oaths (Scotland) Bill (1932–3), 221
'Fane Fragment', 26
Farnborough, 1st. L. *See* May, Thomas
    Erskine
Farrer's Estate Bill (1809), 49
Farringdon and Bedford Road Bill (1833),
    51
fee fund, H.C., 243–4
  H.L., 182, 192
Fee Receipt Books (Light Railway Com-
    mission), 92
fees and accounts, H.C., 225, **244**
  H.L., 52, 185–6, 283
Fees Office, H.C., 243, 245
Fellowes, W. Dorset, Secretary to the
    Lord Great Chamberlain, 254, 255,
    287
felony, 111, 124
Fergusson of Kilkerran, Sir James, *The
    Sixteen Peers of Scotland*, 166
Ferrers, Laurence (Shirley), 4th E., 112,
    113, 254, 255, 278
ferries, 82, 89
Festiniog, co. Merioneth, 193
Field, Rev. John, 265
Fielding, Humphrey William, 273
Filled Bills, H.C., 228
  H.L., 84

Fine Arts, Commissioners of, 278
Fire Brigade Pensions Bill (1928–9), 221
First Fruits Office, accounts of, 137
First Series of Reports [Sessional Papers],
    H.C., **233–4**
fish, 144, 148
Fisher, James, 269
Fishery, Fishing Bills, 82, 216
Fitton *et al., v.* L. Gerard of Brandon
    (1663), 108
Five Knights Case (1627), the, 271
five Members (1642), warrant for the
    arrest of the, 284
Five Oaks Road Bill (1832), 51
Flanders, trade with, 147
flax, 144
Fleet and Fortifications (1699), papers
    concerning, 55
Fleet Market Bill (1824), 50
Fleet Prison, 152
  warden of, 253
Flour Company Bill (1800), 47
flour imports, 144
Flourdew's case (1 Hen. VII), 106
Floyd's case (1621), 106
Forest and Commons Papers, **274–5**
Forfeited Estates, 150
  in Scotland, 156
Forms of Appeal, 178
*Forms of Entries in Votes and Proceedings of
    the House of Commons*, 245
Fort William, Calcutta, 142
Fort William, co. Inverness, 155
Fortifications, Fleet and, (1699), papers
    concerning, 55
Fox, Mr. Justice, 52
France, President of, 187
  Senate and Chamber of Peers of, 189
  trade with, 143, 147
  treaties, etc., with, 10, 58, 157, 194
  war with (1798), 79
  See also French
franchise, parliamentary, 238
Frauds, Statute of, (1677), 9
French fleets, shipping, etc., 153, 158
  in N. America, 141
  invasion of Scotland, 9, 156
  prisoners of war, 158
French Trade Bill (1690), 9
Frodingham Inclosure Bill (1831), 51

Froghall, co. Staffs., 79

Frydinghurst Common, co. Surrey, 274

Fulham roads, London, 151
  Town Meadows, 274

Fuller, Thomas, *Ephemeris Parliamentaria*, 272

Furness, William Anthony (Furness), 2nd V., 286

Furness, Harry, drawings by, **294**

Game Laws Bill (1828), 48

Gaol Fees Abolition Bill (1815), 47

gaols, state of, 219

Gapper, Edmund Pitts, 273

Gargrave, Sir Thomas, Speaker, H.C., 247

Garter, Order of the, 195

Garter King of Arms, 26, 160, 170, 186, 284

Garter's Rolls, 23, 29, **170**

Gas Bills, 224

Gas Light and Coke Company Bill (1810), 49

Gas Light, British, Bill (1829), 48

Gas Light Company Bill (1816), 47

Gas Undertakings Bill (1931–2), 221

Gaulle, de, Charles, General, 187

Gayton Inclosure Bill (1810), 49

Geldart, Thornton and, Land Exchange Bill (1798), 48

general fee fund, H.L. *See* fee fund

General Synod of the Church of England, 104
  Measures of, **104**
  See also Church Assembly

Genoa, 157

George IV, King, coronation of, 254, 255

George V, King, 43; coronation of, 283

George VI, King, coronation of, 283
  funeral of, 187

Georgia, North America, 141

Gepp, Mr., 52

Gerard, L., of Brandon, *v.* Fitton *et al.* (1663), 108

Germany, trade with, 143, 147

Gertruydenberg Conference (1710), 10

Gibbs, Sir Vicary, Chief Justice, Common Pleas, Opinions, **286**

Gibraltar, Courts Martial, 138

Gladstone, William Ewart, drawings of, 294, 295

Glanville, Sir John, Speaker, H.C., 296

Glascock, Adelaide, 273

Glascock, Annie, J., 273

Glasgow and Portpatrick Roads Bill (1824), 49

Glasgow Harbour Bill (1830), 51

Glasgow Road Bill (1830), 51

Gloucester Cathedral, 150

Gloucestershire Records Office, 278

gold and silver thread, 110

Goodman, Sir Victor Martin Reeves, Clerk of the Parliaments, 5

Goodwin, Charles, 269

Gosse, Sir Edmund, Librarian of the House of Lords, 285
  diary, **286**

Gosse, Dr. Philip, 286

Gough, Miss F. M., 276

Gould, Sir Francis Carruthers, autobiography of, **295**

Government Orders, indexes, 133

Government Publications, Catalogue of, 133

Government Reports and Accounts, **129–30**

Grafton, E., 297

Grampound Disfranchisement Bill (1821), 47

Grand Junction Canal (Waterworks) Bill (1819), 49

Grand Surrey Canal Bill (1811), 49

Grandison peerage claim, 188

Grants of Office [Parliament Office], **184**

Gravesend Pier Bills (1832, 1833), 51

Greenwich, co. Kent, The Trafalgar, 299

Greenwich Ferry Bill (1812), 49

Greenwich Hospital, co. Kent, 52, 150–1

Grey, Anchitell, *Debates of the House of Commons*, 37, 292

grievances in Grand Committees, H.C., 219

Grimston, Sir Harbottle, Speaker, H.C., 287, 291, 296

Grosvenor, Sir Richard, journals of, 279

Guilford, Francis (North), 1st L., L. Keeper, 277

Gully, William Court, [1st V. Selby], Speaker, H.C., 259, 276

Gunpowder Plot, 272–3, 284

Habeas Corpus Act (1679), 9

habeas corpus, Writs of, 125

Hackney Coach Office, accounts of, 137

Haddock, Nicholas, Admiral, 152, 153

Hailsham, Quintin (Hogg), 2nd V., [L. Hailsham of St. Marylebone], 5

Haines, William Henry, Clerk in the House of Lords, 184

Hakewill, William, 'The Order of passing of Bills in Parliament', 279

Hamilton, James (Hamilton), 1st D. of, and 1st E. of Arran and Cambridge, 151

Hamilton, H. C. J., 194

Hammersmith Bridge Bill (1824), 50

Hampden, 1st V. *See* Brand, H. B. W.

Hampshire Protestation Returns, 154

Hampstead Heath, London, 275
  extension, 274

Hanover, 138, 157

Hansard, Henry, 242

Hansard, Luke, 211, 232, 234, 242

Hansard, Thomas Curson, etc., *Parliamentary Debates*, 27, 30, **38–9**, 42

Harbour Bills, 71, 73, 82, 89

Harbour Board Accounts, 233

Harbour Boards, 130

Harbour Department of Admiralty, 80

Harcourt, Simon (Harcourt), 1st E., 279

Harcourt, Edward William, 279

Harcourt Journals, H.L., 279

Hardie, Keir, 295

Hardinge, Nicholas, Clerk of the House of Commons, 'Memorial concerning a King's Minority', **295**

Hardman, John, Studio drawings, **275**

Hardy, Sir Thomas Duffus, 4, 193

Harefield Inclosure Bill (1811), 49

Harrogate, co. Yorks., The Stray, 275

Harrowby, Dudley (Ryder), 6th E. of, 278

Harston Inclosure Bill (1798), 48

Hart and Dobson trial (1805), 52

Hartlepool Dock Bill (1832), 51

Hartley Westpall, co. Hants., 265

Hartwell House, co. Bucks., 269

Haslemere Common, co. Surrey, Committee Papers, 274

Hastings, Warren, 110, 142, 253, 255

Hatsell, John, Clerk of the House of Commons, 243

Hatton, Richard, Clerk of the Parliaments, 3

Hawarden, Cornwallis (Maude), 3rd V., 52

Hawarden peerage, claim to vote, 188

Hayward, E., 273

Hearne, Thomas, 296

Hebble, Calder and, Navigation Bill (1834), 52

Helleston [Helston] Election Bill (1814, 1815), 47

hemp, 144, 147

Heneage, G. H. W., Chief Usher, Court of Exchequer, 266

Heneage, Thomas, 284

Henton, co. Oxon., 299

heraldry. *See* armorial, coats of arms

Heralds, College of, London, narrative of, 186

herring, measures concerning, 192

Hertford, Edward (Seymour), 1st E. of, 293

Hertfordshire Protestation Returns, 154

Hesse-Cassel, 157

Hesse-Darmstadt, 157

Highland clans, 155

Highway Bills, 76–7. *See also* turnpike roads

Hinckley Road, Rugby to, 193, 265

Historical Manuscripts, Royal Commission on, 193
  Reports, 4, 8–9

Holland, relations with, 158
  trade with, 143, 147
  See also Netherlands, *and* States General

Holland, Henry (Rich) 1st E., 151

Holland, Edward (Rich), 3rd E., 113

Holland, Henry Richard (Fox), 3rd L., 193

Holland, D. C. L., Librarian of the House of Commons, 272

Holland, F. C., Clerk in the House of Commons, 272

Holland, S., 193

Holles, Denzell (Holles), 1st L. Holles of Ifield, 152, 277

Hollingrake's Patent Bill (1830), 51

Hollyn Inclosure Bill (1793), 48

Holstein, 157

Holstein-Gottorp, 157

Holyhead, London to, Road, 77n, 130

Holyhead Road Bill (1830), 51

Holy Roman Empire. *See* Empire, Holy Roman

Home Guard Papers, 246
Home Office, Library, 131
Home Department, Secretary of State for the, 85
Hooker, John, 205
Horner, John, 293
horse guards, pay of (1719), 193
horse racing, 274
Hosier, Vice Admiral, Sir Francis, 152
House Bills, H.C., 209, 228
H.L., 61, 66–7, 84, 94, 95
House of Commons. *See also* Palace of Westminster, *and* Parliament
clerks of, 205, 237, 243, 244, 247, 272, 291. *See also* Clerk of the House of Commons
Commissioners of, 244, 245; Bank Books of, 244
fire at (1834), 4, 204, 206, 212, 226, 232, 237, 240, 241
history of, 20
Members of, 201–2, 245; autographs of, 276; lists, 37, 202–3, 209, 235; photographs (1865–75), 287; Placemen among, 275; statistics of, 23
Office, 243–4, 245. *See also* clerks *above*
records of, history of, 3–6 *passim*, 204
sittings of, returns of, 240
statistics of business etc., 24, 245, 247
Strangers' Book, 298
telegraphic communications in, 293
House of Lords (*See also* Palace of Westminster, Parliament, *and* Parliament Office)
contempt of, 124
history of, 20–2, 289
jurisdiction of, 114–15, 120
Leaders of, 194
members of, 20–3, 235, 245; Irish 167; Scottish, 165; autographs of, 276; photographs of (1865–75), 287. *See also* peers
records of, history of, 3–11, *passim*
reform of, 55, 187, 194, 286, 292
theses concerning, 286
House Returns, H.C., 240
Houses of Parliament. *See* Parliament, House of Commons, House of Lords
Howard, Charles (Howard), 2nd L. Howard of Effingham, 271

Howe, William, [5th V. Howe], General, 138
Hull, co. Yorks., 149, 192
Hungary, 157
Huntingdonshire Protestation Returns, 154
Record Office, 276, 279
Hurley, co. Berks., 274
Hurstpierpoint church, co. Sussex, 290
Hutchinson, Col. John, letters, 8
Hybrid Acts, 99
Hybrid Bills, 220
procedure and records, 69, 227
Hyde Park Corner, London, plan, 194

Ilbert, Sir Courtenay, Clerk of the House of Commons, 240
diaries of, 295
Ilduton, Rosa Isabella, 273
Impeachments, 54, 58, 106, 131, 235
procedure, 109
records of, 109–11
Imperial Loan (1797), 158
'Incident', the (1641), 8, 156
Incidental Petitions [Appeal Cases], H.L., 119
[Cases in Error], H.L., 123
Inclosure Acts, 102
Awards, 78
Bills, 77–8, Pl. 3; Cases and Opinions on (1810–33), 265
Inclosure Commissioners, 77–8
Indemnity, Act of (1660), 8
Index to Local and Personal Acts, 103
Index to the Statutes in Force, 102
Indexes to Committee Papers (Private Bills), H.C., 230
Indexes to Private Bill Deposits, H.C., 231
India, committee papers on (1933–4), 55
marriages in, 75
pensions relating to (1800), 55
See also East India, Indian princes *and* Indians
India and Burma Orders Committee, H.L., records of 45–6
India Office, 46
Indian princes, 110
treaties with, 157
Indians in South Africa, 238
Indictments and Inquisitions, trials of peers, H.L., 112, 113

Ingrossing Office, H.C., 243

Inner Temple Library, London, 281
  Petyt manuscripts in, 280–1

innkeepers, 110

Inns of Court and Chancery, 181, 233

Inquisitions, Indictments and, trials of
  peers, H.L., **113**

Inspections, Sel. Committee on, H.L.,
  1689, 54

International Metric System Commission,
  238

Invention, Letters Patent of, 194

Ireland, 151, 152, 158, 185, 234
  appeals from, 9, 54, 114–15
  army service in, 139
  Church disestablishment, 21
  circulation of papers in (1804), 52
  Clerk of the Crown, 167, 168
  Court of Admiralty, 52
  Court of Appeal, 115, 120
  Court of Chancery, 54, 114
  Court of Exchequer, 114
  Courts Martial in, 138
  education in (1837), 53
  forfeited estates in, 150
  guide to manuscripts relating to, 135
  House of Lords in, 114, 120
  judges in, 76
  King's Bench in, 120
  Lord Lieutenant of, 284
  Lords Justices, secretary to, 284
  marriages in, 75
  Orange Lodges, 223
  Parliament of, 280
  peerages, 55, 167, 170. *See also* Repre-
    sentative Peers
  plans (Private Bill) concerning, 73
  poor rate collectors, 233
  promissory notes in (1826), 52
  state of (1824, 1825), 29, 52
  tithes in (1832), 52
  trade, 48, 52, 147
  union with, 52, 202
  writs of error from, 120

Irish Commercial Propositions (1785), 52

Irish Question, 294

iron, 144

Isle of Man Bill (1781), 48

Israel, State of, 283
  archives of, 283–4

Israel, State of *cont.*
  See also Palestine

Itchen Bridge Bill (1834), 52

Jacobites, 9, 10
  rebellions of, 284

Jamaica, 141, 142, 148, 153

Jamaica Act (1842), 265

Jenkinson, Mr., 212

Jennings, Louis, papers, **295**

Jodrell, Paul, Clerk of the House of
  Commons, 293

Joinders in Error, 121, **122**

Joint Committees. *See* Committees, Joint

Joint Stock Companies Act (1844), 265

Joint Stock Companies, Registrar of, 265

Jorstad, Erling, 286

Journal Committee Papers, H.L., **187**

Journal Office, H.C., 212, 213, 243, 244,
  245, 291, 299
  Book of Statistics, 240, **245**

Journal Office, H.L., 182
  papers, **188**

Journals, H.C., 4, 10, 213
  catalogue of, 298
  draft, 205
  'Journal of the Assembly' (1688), 209
  Manuscript, 5, 204, 205–6, **207–10**, 211,
    212, 271, 272, Pl. 13; copies of,
    279–82, 295, 296, 297; vacations in,
    210, 211; Abbot additions to, **211**
  Printed, 206, 210, **211**, 235, indexes,
    212
  See also Parliamentary Diaries and
    Journals

Journals, H.L., 3, 8, 9, 26–7, 41, 42, 43, 46,
  97, 281
  calendars, **32**
  draft, 26, **34–6**, 270, 271, 272
  indexes, **32**, 33
  Manuscript, Original, **28–31**, Pl. 1;
    copies of, 279–82; vacations in, 30, 31
  Printed, 28, **31**; record copy of, 28
  printing of, 53, 55, 187, 188
  See also Parliamentary Diaries and
    Journals

Judges, as members of H.L., 22, 179–80
  as assistants to H.L., 33, 42; on Appeal
    Cases, 33, 119; on Private Bills, 42,
    46, 70, 76, reports, **88**; on peerage

Judges *cont.*
  as assistants to H.L. *cont.*
    claims, opinions of, 160, 164; on privilege, opinions of, 43
  examining witnesses, H.C., 223
Judgments, Appeals, 118, **119–20**
Judgments, Impeachments, **111**
Judicature, dispute between H.L. and H.C. (1675), 296
udicial business, H.L., 27, 29, 33, 34, 106–26, *passim*
Judicial Office, H.L., 116, 178, 182; papers, **188–9**
judicial records, 108–26
jurisdiction of H.L., 106–7, 111, 277
Justices of the Peace, 153, 172, 192, 240
  Members of Parliament as, 223
  papist, 150
  See also Peace, Commissions of the

Kelfornora, diocese of, 194
Kelly, Ambrose, collection of, 297
  precedent book of, 245
Ken Wood, Hampstead, London, 274
Kenmare, Valentine (Browne), 2nd E. of, 193
Kennet and Avon Canal Bill (1809), 49
Kensington roads, London, 151
Kensington Roads Bill (1824), 49
Kent, Edward, D. of, 252
Kent, parish registers of, 150
  Protestation Returns, 154
Kent Street, Southwark, Lighting Bill (1812), 49
Kentucky, North America, 269
Keppel, Augustus, [1st V. Keppel], Admiral, court martial of, 153
Kerry co., estates in, 193
Kidwelly [co. Carmarthen] Road Bill (1831), 51
Kilkenny co., estates in, 193
Killaloe, diocese of, 194
Kilmarnock, William (Boyd), 4th E. of, 113
Kilmore Peerage (1812), 52
Kiltarton of Gort, John (Prendergast-Smyth), 1st L., patent of, 164
King's (Queen's) Bench, 22, 106, 115, 120, 122
  Chief Justice of, 106, Pl. 9
  Justice of, 293

King's (Queen's) Bench *cont.*
  Plea Rolls of, Pl. 9
  reports of, 289
King's Household, Treasurer of, 193. *See also* Royal Household
King's Lynn Paving Bill (1806), 48
Kingston, Elizabeth (Chudleigh), Dss. of, 113, 278
Kingston, Cambridge, Inclosure Bill (1810), 49
Kinross, Clackmannan and, Parishes Bill (1833), 51
Kitchen Committee Proceedings, H.C., **220**
Knaresborough, Forest of, 275
Knighthood, 'Epitome' concerning, **287**
knights of the shire, 201
Koop's Patent Bill (1801), 48
Kyishogloo, P. B., 194

Lambarde, William, 59, 296
Lambeth Palace, London, Librarian of, 297
Lancashire Protestation Returns, 154
  County Record Office, 277
Lancaster, Duchy of, deposited plans, 277
  Court of, 114
Lancaster Justices Bill (1805), 47
Land Commissioners, 78
Land Revenue, Commissioners of, 137
  surveyor of the, 137
Land Tax Acts, 102
Land Tax Commissioners, 245
Landiway, co. Cheshire, 275
Langton's Discovery Bill (1829), 50
Laud, William, Archbishop of Canterbury, trial of, 10, 270
  visitations of, 8, 150
Launceston, co. Cornwall, 275
Law Digest Commission, 263
Law Officers, 179–80
Law Reports, 116, 117, 162
Leaders of the House, H.L., 194
leather, 149
Leave of Absence, H.L., 34, 41, 55
Lee, Sir George, papers, **275**
Lee, John, 269
Leeds and Liverpool Canal Bill (1809), 49
Leeds and Selby Railway Bill (1803), 51
Lees-Milne, James, 291
legal note books, 273

Leicester, Robert (Dudley), 1st E. of, 272
Leicester and Swannington Railway Bill (1833), 51
Leiston Inclosure Bill (1810), 49
Leith Police Bill (1827), 48
Leith Reservoir Bill (1825), 50
Lenthall, William, Speaker, H.C., 293
Leonardy, A. J., 286
Letter Book [Black Rod], **196**
Letter and Memoranda Book [Serjeant at Arms] H.C., **248**
Letters and Papers [L. Great Chamberlain], **252–4**
Letters Patent, 29, 175
    of grants of office, 181, 182, 243, 283
    of nobility, 29, 164, 180, 293
    Royal Commissions, 29, **175**
Leveson Gower, William George Gresham, Clerk in the House of Lords, papers of, **275,** 291
Leveson Gower, Victoria, 275
Ley, John Henry, Clerk of the House of Commons, 212
Leyton Grange, co. Essex, 265
Libels [H.L. Privilege], 126
    printers of (1675–7), 54
Liberal League, 294
Liberal Registration Association, 299
Library, H.C., 5, 11, 101, 222, 227, 228, 234, 235, 238, 267, 291–9 *passim*
    Deposited Papers, 187, **238**
    Librarian, 204, 272
Library, H.L., 5, 11, 97, 101, 131, 133, 163, 166, 168, 227, 228, 233, 234, 235, 238, 267, 285–90 *passim*
    accounts, 185
    Deposited Papers, **187**
    Librarian, 285, 286, 288
    papers, **189**
licences of departure, H.C., 205
Lichfield Cathedral., co. Stafford, 150
Lieutenancy, commissions of (1642), 151
Life Guards, 254
Light Railway Bills, 92
Light Railway Commission, 80, 192
Lighthouses, Northern, 156
Lighting Bills, 82
Limerick co., estates in, 193
Limerick Regulation Bill (1823), 49
Limerick Road Bill, (1830), 51

Limpsfield, co. Surrey, 275
Lincoln, Bishop of, [John Williams], 276
Lincolnshire Protestation Returns, 154
Lindsay, W. A., 288
Lindsey, Robert (Bertie), 4th E. of, 287
Linen and Hemp, Ireland, Bill (1828), 48
Linen and Hemp Manufactures Act (1750), Pl. 7
linen cloth, 147
Liskeard, co. Cornwall, 275
Listowel peerage claim, 169
literary manuscripts [Commonplace Note Book Collection], 273
Little Milton, co. Oxon., 299
Littleton, Sir Thomas, *Tenures*, 285
Liverpool, Leeds and, Canal Bill (1809), 49
Liverpool and Manchester Road Bill (1826), 50
Liverpool Buildings Bill (1825), 50
Liverpool Court of Passage Bill (1834), 52
Liverpool Tractate, The, 70
Llanelly Roads Bill (1828), 50
Llanelly Tithes Bill (1831), 51
Lloyd George, David, 1st E. Lloyd George of Dwyfor, speech (1911), **287**
Lloyd's *Lists of Ships*, 194
Local Acts, lists of printed, 134
    sessional vols. of, collected, **101**
    See also Local and Personal Acts
Local and Personal Acts, 100–1, 102
    definition of, 100–1
    sessional vols. of collected, **101**
    Index to, 103
Local Bills, printed, 233
Local Government Bills, 81
London, Bishop of [Charles James Blomfield], 276
London. *See also* Metropolis
    The Athenaeum Club, 286
    Battersea, 265
    Bower Street, 193
    British Museum, documents in, 35, 131, 227, 233, 234, 242, 277, 278, 280, 282, 283, 287, 293, 298
    Buckingham Palace, conference at, Pl. 15; plans of, 194
    Chelsea roads, 151
    City of, 201, 202, 234; Chamberlain of, 139, 140; Churches in, 194; Commissioners of Sewers of, 294; lieuten-

London *cont.*
  City of *cont.*
    ancy of, 9; Lord Mayor's Court, 114;
      Orphans' Fund, 129; Recorder of, 31
    Clerkenwell Improvement Bill (1829),
      50
    Commercial Docks Bill (1810), 49
    Commercial Road Bill (1824), 49,
      (1828), 50
    Covent Garden Vestry Bill (1829), 50
    Durham Yard Embanking Bill (1771), 48
    Foundling Hospital, 275
    Fulham Roads, 151; Town Meadows,
      274
    Guildhall Library, 277
    Hampstead Heath, 275; extension, 274
    Hyde Park Corner, plan, 194
    Hyde Park Gardens, 265
    Inner Temple Library, 281; Petyt
      manuscripts in, 280–1
    Ken Wood, Hampstead, 274
    Kensington Roads, 151
    Kensington Roads Bill (1824), 49
    Kent Street, Southwark, Lighting Bill
      (1812), 49
    Lambeth Palace, Librarian of, 297
    London Bridge Bill (1823), 49, (1831), 51
    London Bridge Approaches Bill (1829),
      50, (1834), 52
    London Docks Bill (1800), 48, (1810), 49
    London Museum, 9, 280
    merchants, petition of, 219
    Middle Temple, Library of, 162
    municipal jurisdiction of, 120
    Paddington (Regent's) Canal Bill (1812),
      49
    Public Record Office. *See* separate entry
    Regent Street, 77*n*
    road from, to Holyhead, 77*n*, 130; road
      from, to York, 77
    St. James's Place, 265
    St. Katherine's Docks Bill (1825), 50
    St. Pancras Vestry Bill (1819), 49
    St. Paul's Cathedral, 150
    Shadwell Church Bill (1823), 49
    Southwark Bridge Bill (1811), 49
    Southwark, Kent Street, Lighting Bill
      (1812), 49
    Southwell Gardens, S.W., 269
    Squares, Commission on, 275

London *cont.*
  Stepney, 282
  Thames, river, 142; embankment, 238;
    reservoirs, 275
  University, of, 234, 264, 265
  University College, 234
  Wandsworth, Croydon (Surrey) and,
    Railway, 79
  Waterloo Bridge, 292
  Westminster. *See* separate entry
  Whitehall, 77*n*, 194
  Whitehall Place, 265
London and Birmingham Railway Bill
  (1832–3), 51
London and Southampton Railway Bill
  (1834), 52
London Bridge Bill (1823), 49, (1831), 51
London Bridge Approaches Bill (1829), 50,
  (1834), 52
London Docks Bill (1800), 48, (1810), 49
London Gazette, The, notices in, 80, 90
Long Roll, The, (of Scottish peers). *See*
  Union Roll
Lord Advocate, Reports by, 160
Lord Chancellor, 3, 29, 106, 107, 109, 112,
  114, 160, 169, 179, 182, 209, 251*n*,
  259, 263, 278
  memoranda of, 130; report of, 233
  notebooks of (L. Truro), 289
Lord Clerk Register [Scotland], 165
Lord Great Chamberlain, history and
  duties of, 195, 251–2
  records of or concerning, 6, **189, 252–5**
  secretary to, 287
Lord High Steward, 109, 111, 112
  Court of, 111
  commissions appointing, **112**, 176
Lord Keeper, 109
Lord Steward, 209
Lord Treasurer, 29, 278
Lords, House of. *See* House of Lords
Lords Appellant, 106
Lords Justices of England, secretary to, 284
Lords Lieutenant, 192
Lords of Appeal in Ordinary, 22
Lostwithiel, co. Cornwall, election, 293
lotteries (1712), 233
Loudoun peerage claim, 167
Lovelace, Richard, petition, 1642, 11
Lower Barrier Bank Bill (1810), 49

Lunacy, Commissioners in, 233
Luneburg, Hanover, 157
Lyons, Richard, 109

Macclesfield Gas Bill (1826), 50
MacDonnogh *v.* Stafford [in error], Pl. 9
mace, H.C., repair of, 297
Macqueen, John Fraser, *Reports*, 188
Macy, Lucinda Cowan, 273
Madras, India, 149; Governor of, 110
Magna Carta, 106, 111
Main Papers, H.L., categories of, 127
  lists, 132–3
Main Registers (Serjeant at Arms), H.C.,
  247
Mainz, archbishopric of, 157
malt, duty on, 194
Malvern Hills, co. Worcs. and Hereford, 275
  Chase, co. Worcs., 275
managers, for Conferences, 58
  H.C., for impeachments, 109
Manchester, Henry (Montagu), 1st E. of,
  papers of, **275–6**, 279
Manchester, William Angus Drogo
  (Montagu), 9th D. of, manuscripts of,
  284
Manchester and Salford Improvement Bill
  (1828), 50
Manchester and Sheffield Railway Bill
  (1831), 51
Manchester, Bolton and Bury Canal Co., 74
Manchester Equitable Loan Bill (1824), 47
Manchester Improvement Bill (1830), 51
Manchester, Liverpool and, Road Bill
  (1826), 50
Manchester Waterworks Bill (1809), 49
Manners Sutton, Charles, Archbishop of
  Canterbury, 276
Manuals of Procedure, H.C., **240**
manufacture, Bills concerning, H.C., 216
Manuscript Evidence, H.C., **224**, H.L.,
  47–54
Manuscript Evidence Volumes [peerage
  claims], H.L., **161–2**
Manuscript Journals, H.C., **207–10**
'Manuscript Minutes'. *See* Minutes of
  Proceedings in H.L.
Manuscript Speeches [peerage claims],
  H.L., **162**
Manwaring, Roger, Declaration against, 96

Marchmont peerage claim, 188
Margate Pier Bill (1812), 49
Marlborough, John (Churchill), 1st D. of,
  album relating to, **287**
Marmion peerage claim (1815), 160
Marriage Law Papers, **276**
Marriage (Naval, Military and Air Force
  Chapels) Bill (1931–2), 221
Marriage (Prohibited Degrees of Relation-
  ship) Bill (1930–1), 221
Marshall, Edward, 273
Mart, Letters of, 152
Mary, Queen of Scots, trial of, 10, 127, 278
Marylebone Borough election papers
  (1837), 293
Mason, Anthony, Clerk of the Parliaments,
  186
Massachusetts, North America, House of
  Representatives of, 147
Massachusetts Bay, 141
  disturbances (1774), 55
Master of the Rolls, 22, 30, 237, 293
Mattinson, Sir Miles, letters of, **276**
Maxwell, W. H., 273
May, Thomas Erskine, Clerk of the House
  of Commons [1st L. Farnborough],
  59, 70, 212
  notebooks of, **295**
Mayo, co., election, 239
medical formulae, 273
Mediterranean sea, 153
Medmenham, co. Bucks., 275
Meltham Inclosure Bill (1830), 51
Melville, Henry (Dundas), 1st V., 255
Members of Parliament. *See* House of
  Commons, members of, knights of the
  shire *and* burgesses or citizens
Memorial Books. *See* War Memorial
  Books
Memorials [Private Bills], H.L., **88**, 91
Mercers' Company, annual accounts, 151
Merchant Service (1844–8), 265
Merchant Shipping (Line-Throwing
  Appliance) Bill (1927–8), 221
merchants, losses of, 152
  petitions of, 219, 277
Merrick & Co., Messrs., Parliamentary
  Agents, 229
Mersey, Charles Clive (Bigham), 2nd V.,
  285

Mersey, Edward Clive (Bigham), 3rd V., 276

Message and Assent formulae, 62. *See also* Royal Assent

Messages from H.C., 28, 33, 58

Messengers' badges, 297

Method of Passing Bills in Parliament, by Henry Elsynge, 245

Metropolis, water supply to (1840), 53

Metropolis Cemetery Bill (1832), 51

Metropolis Roads Bill (1829), 51

Metropolis Turnpike Road Bill (1826), 50

Metropolitan Police (Staff Superannuation and Police Fund) Bill (1930–1), 221

Middle Temple, Library of, 162

Middlesex, Lionel (Cranfield), 1st E. of, 271

Middlesex Protestation Returns, 154–5

Mildmay, Sir Walter, speeches, 277

militia, 138

Millican, Percy, 279

Ministers, Questions to. *See* Questions to Ministers

Ministry of Transport, 74, 80

minority of king, 295

Minsmere Level Drainage Bill (1810), 49

Minute Books [L. Great Chamberlain], **254**

Minute Entry Registers (Judicial Office), H.L., **161**

Minute Sheets (1696–7), H.L., 277

Minutes of Proceedings at Elections [Scottish Representative Peers], H.L., **166**

Minutes of Proceedings in H.C., 205, 213, 243

  Minute Books, **212**

Minutes of Proceedings in H.L. (Manuscript Minutes), 3, 26–7, 30, 33, 34, **35–6**, 42, 46, 270–1, Pl. 2

  summaries of, 213

Minutes of Proceedings in H.L. (Printed), **33–4**, 182

Minutes of Proceedings (MS. Papers), H.L., **34**

Minutes of Proceedings (Standing Committees), H.C., **216**

Miscellaneous Petitions and Orders, H.L. [trials of peers], 113

Modena, 157

'Modus tenendi Parliamenta' (Irish), 9

'Modus Tenendi Parliamentum', 30, 277

Mohun, Charles (Mohun), 4th L. Mohun of Okehampton, 113

Mompesson, Sir Giles, impeachment of (1621), 8, 106, 109, 110, 111, 270

Monaghan, co., 194

Money Bills, 62, 93

Monks Risborough Inclosure Bill (1830), 51

Monmouth, co., 202

Monmouth Rebellion (1685), 284

monopolies, 241, Pl. 13

Montery, Capt., 153

Montfort, Simon de, 11, 187

Moray peerage claim, 188

Morgan's Estate Bill (1825), 50

Morley, Henry (Parker), 14th L., 113

Morley, Thomas (Parker), 15th L., description of trial of, **288**

Morning Post, complaint against (1834), 53

Moses Gate Road Bill (1833), 51

Motions, H.C. *See* Notices of Motions

Motions for Addresses, H.C., 45

Motions, H.L., 30

  'No Day Named', 34

  for Papers, 128

Mottistone, John Alexander (Seely), 2nd L., 290

Moulton-Barrett, Elizabeth, 290

Moulton-Barrett, Octavius, 289–90

Mountague, Sir Edward, 279

Municipal Corporations Bill (1835), 46, 58

munitions factory, Houses of Parliament, 246

Munster, Westphalia, 157

Mutiny Bills, 227

Nalson, John, Canon of Ely, *Impartial Collection of the Great Affairs of State*, 110

  papers of, **278**

Name Acts, 102

Name Bills, 70, 78

Nancy, derelict, 194

Naples, 158

Naseby, battle of, papers, 4, 8, 152

Natal, South Africa, Responsible Government in, papers concerning, 238

Nation, State of the, Committee on, H.L., 9

National Debt, 137

national finance, papers concerning, 210
National Government (1931), Pl. 15
National Insurance Bill (1911), 220
nationalised corporations, 130
Naturalisation Acts, 102
Naturalisation Bills, 70, 79, 85
naval stores, 147, 148, 149, 153
Navigation Acts, 53, 186
Navigation Bills, 73–4
Navy, papers relating to, 9, 55, 137, 150, 152–3, 155, 210, 242, 277
Navy Dock Yards, Commissioners of, 155
Nene Outfall (Improvement) Bills (1827, 1829), 50
Nether Heyford, co. Northants., 273
Netherlands, 194. *See also* Holland *and* States General.
Nettlebed and District Commons (Preservation) Act (1906), 274
Nevin Inclosure Bill (1812), 49
New Jersey, 141
New York, 141, 147
Newbury Improvement Bill (1825), 50
Newcastle, Thomas (Pelham-Holles), 1st D. of, 293
Newcastle, Carlisle to, Military Road, 139
Newcastle Waterworks Bill (1834), H.C. evidence, 277
Newfoundland Expedition (1699), 55
Newport, co. Monmouth, Improvement Bill (1826), 50
Newstead, Rev. Robert, 274
Newton, Warrington and, Railway Bill (1831), 51
Nicholson, Arthur William, Clerk, H.C., 212
Nicolson, William, Bishop of Carlisle, diaries, 277
'No Day Named' Motions, 34
Norfolk, co., covenant lists, 151
Norris, Sir John, Admiral of the Fleet, 152
North America. *See* America
North Shields Road Bill (1831), 51
North, Sir Edward, Clerk of the Parliaments [1st L. North], 277
North Union Railway Bill (1834), 52
Northampton, Charles (Compton), 1st M. of, 75
Northampton, Virginia, 269

Northumberland Protestation Returns, 155
Northwich, co. Cheshire, 274
Norwich, Bishop of, proxy, 30–1, 175
Norwich Cathedral, co. Norfolk, 150
Norwich Navigation Bill (1827), 50
note books, classical, **273**
   clerical, **273**
   commonplace, **273–4**
   legal, 273
   philosophical, 273
Notice Paper, H.C., 243
'Notices and Orders of the Day', H.L., 34
Notices of Motions [H.C. Vote], 213, **214**
Nottingham Election Bill (1803), 47
Nottingham, Maryland, 269
Nottinghamshire Protestation Returns, 155
Nova Scotia, 141
Nuffield College, Oxford, Library of, 294

oaths, 29, 209, 223, 242
   Accession Oath, 194
   commissioners of, 118
   Oath of Allegiance, 79, 81, 179
   Oath of Supremacy, 79, 81, 179
   See also affirmations
Oaths, Abolition of, Bill (1834), 48
O'Brien of Kilfenora, Peter (O'Brien), 1st L., patent, 164
Oddie Estate Bill (1825), 50
Office Papers, H.C., 296
'Officers and Usages of the House of Commons' (1805), 247
Officers' Personal Papers, H.L., **186**
Offices Committees (Parliament Office Papers), H.L., **184**, 196
Offices of H.C., Commissioners for Regulating, minutes of, **237**
Official Report of debates, 38. *See also* Hansard
Ogle, Sir Chaloner, Admiral of the Fleet, 153
'Old Parliamentary History', 37
Oldes, Sir William, 186
Oldham, co. Lancs., 294
Onslow, Arthur, Speaker, H.C., 272
   precedent books of, 237, 244–5
Onslow, Fulk, Clerk of the House of Commons, H.C., Journal of, 204, 205

Onslow, William Arthur Bampfylde (Onslow), 6th E. of, 244
Opinions of Antiquaries on the Antiquity of Parliaments, 245
Opinions [Appeal Cases, H.L.], 118, **119–20**
Opposed Bills, H.L. (1844–5), 186
Orange Lodges, 223
Order Book (Order Paper), H.C., 215, 216, 243
Orders, H.L., printed, 277
Orders, Book of (1621), H.C., 281
Orders in Council, 55, 129
Orders of the Day, H.C., 213, 215
Orders of H.L. [Private Bills], **88**
Orders of H.L. [trials of peers], **112 ,113**
Orders, ministerial, 129
Orders and Ordinances, H.L., 30
  Books of, **171**
Orders to print, H.L., 131
Orders and Resolutions [peerage claims], H.L., **164, 167, 169**
Orders of Service [Divorce Bills], H.L., **88**
Ordinances (1641–60), 96, 102, 208, 226, 235
  Books of Orders and, **171**
  catalogue of, 298
ordnance, 139
Ordnance Survey maps, 89
Orford, Robert (Walpole), 2nd E. of, 219, 284
Original Acts. *See under* Acts of Parliament
Original Journals, H.L. *See under* Journals, H.L.
Original Orders of H.L. [Appeal Cases], 118
Original Orders of H.L. [Cases in Error], **123**
Original Petitions, Reports and Orders [peerage claims], H.L., **164**
Original Protest Books, H.L., **174**
Original Recognisances [Appeal Cases], H.L., **118**
Originating Petitions [Cases in Error], H.L., **121**
Originating Petitions [H.L. judicial], **108**
Ormonde, James (Butler), 1st D. of, 54
Osborn manuscripts, 272
Ostend, 149
'Other House', the, 21

Ottoman Porte, the, 158
Oundle Improvement Bill (1825), 50
Overseas Office, H.C., 244
Overseas Trade Bill (1928–9), 221
Overseers' Returns, 239
Owners, Occupiers and Lessees. *See* Books of Reference *and* Consents Lists
Oxford, 152, 213
  Bodleian Library, manuscripts in, 36, 219, 278
  Parliament at (1668), 254
  Protestation Returns, 155
  University, Constituency, 202, 299; University College, Master of, 233
Oxfordshire Protestation Returns, 155

Paddington [Regent's] Canal Bill (1812), 49
Page, William, 288
Palace of Westminster (*see also* House of Commons, House of Lords, Parliament), 3, 4, 5, 6, 44, 57, 252
  Chancellor's Gate, 6
  Court of Exchequer in, 266
  Crypt Chapel (Chapel of St. Mary Undercroft), 251n, 253; Registers of, 255
  drawings of, 289
  descriptions of, 299
  fabric papers, **190**
  history of building, 189–90
  house in, 289
  House of Commons Chamber, 215; admissions to, 298; new, opening of (1950), 187; furnishing of, 253; Gallery, 36; Press Gallery, 247
  House of Commons, Speaker's Gallery, 234, 291
  House of Lords Chamber, 189, 190, 252; windows of, 55; Gallery, 36
  House of Lords, warming and ventilation of (1794), 55; Lobby, 253
  illustrations of, 253, 278
  Jewel Tower, 3, 4, 61, 97
  Keeper of, 276
  King William's Tower (Victoria Tower) 290
  Old Palace Yard, 4
  Painted Chamber, 58, 253, 299

Palace of Westminster *cont.*
plans of, 253, 255, 272, 293
Prince's Chamber, 180
Robing Room, 251, 253
Royal Gallery, 191, 251, 252, 287
St. Stephen's Hall, 215, 278; paintings in, 292
stained glass in, 275
'tally-stick fire' (1834), 4
temporary Houses of Parliament (1834), 254
Throne, the, 253, 254, 290; drawings of, 189
Victoria Tower, 4, 5, 6, 61, 97, 183, 193, 245, 290, frontispiece; reconstruction of (1948–61), 190
war damage to, 283
War, Second World, records concerning, H.C., **246**, H.L., **190–1**
Westminster Hall, 189, 251*n*, 253, 254, 287, 288; courts of justice in, 253
Palatinate, the, 158
Palestine, 283, 291. *See also* Israel, State of
Palgrave, Sir Reginald Francis Douce, Clerk of the House of Commons, 212
Palmerston, Henry John (Temple), 3rd V., 193
pamphlets, political, 37
Pange, Victor Thomas de, 286
Papers presented, H.C., statistics of, 245
Papers, H.C., Daily issue of, 213
papers laid on the Table, 37, 38, 235
in H.L., 27, 33
procedure, 130–1
Papists Lists, 150. *See also* Roman Catholics
Parchment Collection, description of, 127
lists, 132–3
Pardon, Bills for, 60. *See also* Restitution of honours
Paris, 238
parish boundaries, 76
parish registers, 164, 255, 276
copies, 192
of Kent, 150
Parke, Sir James, 21
Parliament (*see also* House of Commons, House of Lords, Westminster, Palace of)
disability to sit in, 79

Parliament *cont.*
dissolution, 28, 176, 209
history of, 20–2, 160, 201–2, 267
Houses of, destruction of old, 53; New, 53
lists of, 23–4, 203
Members of. *See* House of Commons
munitions factory, 246
opening of, 29, 34, 176, 180, 189, 205, 209, 252, 253, 254, 259
prayers for, 192
prorogation of, 28, 30, 34, 176, 189, 209, 252, 272; writs of, 209
records of, history of, 3–6, 277
Rolls of, 3, 26, 31, 37, 61, 93, 99, 102, 179, 181, 185, 193, 271; draft, **191**; printing of, 55, 187
Royal Commissions concerning, 176. *See also* Royal Assent.
sessions, dating of, 97–8
the Short (1640), 272
Parliament Act Bill files (1925–48), 245
Parliament Office, 3, 4, 34, 53, 95, 96, 97, 101, 102, 123 ,163, 172, 173, 174, 181–4, 189, 190, 279, 283, 298
Book of Returns, **186**
clerks in, 33, 36, 67, 163, 181–5 *passim*, 275, 277, 288. *See also* Clerks of the Parliaments
grants of office, **184**
history of, 181–3
Papers, 54, 175*n*, 183, **184–94**, 224, 270
Parliament Pawns (Petty Bag Office) [P.R.O.], 180
Parliamentary Agents, 71, 84, 86, 89, 90, 92, 192, 214, 224, 230, 243, 276
Appearance Registers, H.L., **89**
Books of Fees, **229**
Rules of, 296
Parliamentary Collection, The, H.C., **234**
Parliamentary and Council Proceedings, [P.R.O.], 3*n*, 93
Parliamentary or Constitutional History of England, **37**
Parliamentary Debates, **38–9**, 220, 221
lists, 134
See also Hansard
Parliamentary Diaries and Journals (unofficial), 10, 270–2, 276, **279–80**, 281–2. *See also* Journals, H.C. and H.L.

Parliamentary Election Return Books, **259**

'Parliamentary hand', 95

Parliamentary Letter Books, Vargas Papers, 299

'Parliamentary Papers', 6, 232. *See also* Sessional Papers

Parliamentary Papers (Misc.), **296**

Parliamentary Proxies [P.R.O.], 175

Parliamentary Record. See Ross's *Parliamentary Record*

Parliamentary Register, The, 37

'Parliamentary Rules and Orders', 297

Parliamentary Surveys, **297**

'Parliament's Antiquity', 292

Parliaments, Clerk of. *See* Clerk of the Parliaments

passengers, censuses of, 47

patent, letters, of nobility, 29, 164, 180, 293

Peace, Commissions of the (1680), 54

Pearson, Professor Karl, 289

Pechell, Augustus, notebooks of, 192

pedigrees of peers. *See* peers, pedigrees of

Peel, Arthur Wellesley [1st V. Peel], Speaker, H.C., 297

Peer, the Dignity of a, Select Committee concerning, H.L., 160, 188

peerage (*see also* peers *and Complete Peerage* Trust), notes on, 286
  claims, individual: Abergavenny, **285**; Anglesey, 283; Athlone, 169; Barnewell, 52; Borthwick, 188; Chandos, 52; De La Warr, 160, 163; Ely, 169; Grandison, 188; Hawarden, 188; Kilmore, 52; Listowel, 169; Loudoun, 167; Marchmont, 188; Marmion, 160; Moray, 188; Queensbury, 52; Roscommon, 188; Roxburghe, 52; Stafford, 52; Tracey, 164, 188; Willoughby of Parham, 160
  claims, records of, 43, 125, **160–4**, 165, 288, indexes of, 163, 192, papers, 188; Attorney General, Reports on, 163; Cases, Irish Peerages, 168; Scottish, 167; evidence, **162**, 164, Scottish, **166**, Irish, 168; Evidential Papers, **164**, 167; Lord Advocate and peerage claims, 160; Manuscript Speeches, H.L., 162; Orders and Resolutions, H.L., **164**, **167**, **169**; Original Petitions, Reports

peerage *cont.*
  claims, records of *cont.*
    and Orders, H.L., **164**, Petitions, **162–3**, **164**; Printed evidence, H.L., **162**; *Proceedings and Minutes of Evidence* [on peerage claims], 161; Register of Claims, Irish Peers, **168**; Representative Peers for Ireland, records of claims and elections, 167–9; Representative Peers for Scotland, records of claims and elections, 165–7; Standing Orders on peerage claims, H.L., 160, 164, Irish, 167, Scottish, 165; Statements of Proof, Irish peerage claims, **168**
  creations, 22–3, 160; lists of, 22, 186
  degrees of, 21
  Papers, H.L., 162, **164**

peerages in abeyance, Sel. Com., H.L., on 55

peeresses, 111

peers (*see also* House of Lords *and* peerage)
  attendance of, 55
  autographs of, 276
  introduction of, into H.L., 195; index of, 192; procedure on, 253; tables of, 32; first sitting, record of, 33
  letters to, 299
  lists of, 170–1, 186, 270; register of, 171
  patents of. *See* patent, letters, of nobility
  pedigrees of, 160, 162, **163–4**; lists of, 283; pedigree proofs, **164**
  precedence of, 283
  proxies of, 174–5
  servants of, 124
  trials of, 106, **188**, 191, 253, 255, 270, 278, 288; printed, 114, 131; records of, 111–14, list of, 113
  War Memorial of, Sel. Com., H.L. concerning (1919–32, 1948–56), 55. *See also* War Memorial, *below*
  Writs of Summons to. *See separate entry*

Pembroke, Philip (Herbert), 7th E. of, 111, 113, 253, 254, 287

Penmorfa Inclosure Bill (1812), 49

Pennsylvania, 147

Penryn Disfranchisement Bill (1828), 48

pensions, relating to India, 55; Treasury, 137

pepper, 144

Perceval, J., 286
Personal Acts, index to, 103
Personal Bills, 44, 70, 75, 78, 79, 86, 88, 98
 indexes to, 33
 printed, **89**
 See also Committees, H.L.
Peterborough Cathedral, 150
Petitions, H.C. (*see also under* Committees,
 H.C. *and* Bills, Public Bills, *and*
 Private Bills) 4, 172–3, 210, 213, 214,
 218, 232, 239, 240–1, **241**, 271
 catalogue of, 298
 public, **241**; reports on, **222–3**
 statistics of, 245
Petitions, H.L. (*see also under* Committees,
 H.L., *and* Bills, Public Bills *and*
 Private Bills) 3, 26, 30, 45, 106, 127,
 172–3
 Answers to judicial, **108**
 in appeal cases, 115, 116, **117**, 118, 119,
 Pl. 8
 destruction of, 186
 divorce, 75
 in cases in error, 121, 123
 in impeachments, 110
 judicial, 29, 106, 107, **108**, 172, 173
 in peerage claims, **162–3**, **164**
 printed, 132
 in privilege cases, **125**, 126
 Receivers and Triers of, 26, 28, 29, 172
 concerning Representative Peers for
 Ireland, 167, **168**; for Scotland, 165,
 166–7
 in trials of peers, **112**, **113**
Petroleum Amendment Bill (1927–8), 221
Petyt, William, manuscripts of, 35, **280–2**
Phillips' Powder Bill (1781), 48
philosophical note books, 273
photographs of members, H.C., H.L., **287**
photographs of proceedings, H.L., **39**
piers, 82
Pilgrim Trust survey of ecclesiastical
 archives, 277
Plans, H.L., 44, 71, 74, 77, 80, 83, 85, 86,
 88, **89–90**, 229, Pl. 4; signed, 90
 H.C., **229**
 other copies, 277
plate in Scotland, 156
Plunket, David, 293
Plural Voting Bill (1913–14), 292

Plymouth, co. Devon, Mill Prison (1781),
 52
Plymouth Improvement Bill (1824), 50
Poland, 158
police, 248
Police Magistrates Superannuation
 (Amendment) Bill (1928–9), 221
Poor Law Amendment Act (1837–8),
 operation of, evidence concerning, 53
Poor Law Bill (1831), 48
Poor Law Commission (1834–41), 264, 265
poor, state of the, 153
Popish Plot (1678), 9, 57, 213
pork, 147, 148
Porteous riots, Edinburgh, 156
Portland, William John Arthur Charles
 James (Cavendish-Bentinck), 6th D.
 of, 278
Portpatrick, Glasgow and, Roads Bill
 (1824), 49
ports, 82, 89
Portsmouth Docks, co. Hants., com-
 missioners for, 153
Portsmouth Water Bill (1809), 49
Portugal, 158
 trade with, 148
Portuguese coins, 141
Post Office, accounts, 137, 153
 Commissioners of, 155
postal franks, **287**
potatoes and salted provisions, 144
Pounshall, co. Louth, 194
Powell, Rev. John, 273
Poyntz *et ux.* Estate Bill (1799), 48
Prayer Book. *See* Common Prayer
Precedent and Procedural Papers, H.L., **191**
Precedent Books, H.C., **244–5**
Precedent Bills, H.L., 84
precedents, H.C., 296
 H.L., 272
'Precedents in Parliament', 297
presentation of papers, H.L., 128
Presents, H.L., 28, 33
Press Gallery, H.C., 247
Preston and Wigan Railway Bill (1831), 51
Pretender, the Old, *see* James, Prince of
 Wales
Pretender, the Young, *see* Charles, the
 'Young Pretender'
Prime Ministers, autographs of, 276

Prince Elector, reasons for coming into England, 296
Printed Cases [Appeals], H.L., **117**
Printed Cases [in Error], H.L., 121, 122, **123**
Printed Cases (Bound) [peerage claims], H.L., **163**
Printed Cases (Separate Prints) [peerage claims], H.L., **163**
Printed Evidence on Opposed Bills, H.C., **224**
Printed Evidence [peerage claims], H.L., **162**
Printed Original Acts (Vellums), **96**. *See also* Acts of Parliament
Printed Paper Office, H.L., 187
indexes of, 133
Prints of (Public) Bills, Bound Sets, H.C., 227
Private Acts, 96, 98, 99–101, 102, 106. *See also* Acts of Parliament
engrossed, 84
index of, 271
mediaeval, 93
printed, 84, **101-2**
writs for certifying, 30
Private Bill Amendment Book, H.L., **90**
Private Bill Books, H.L., **83, 85**
Private Bill and Committee Office Papers, H.L., **192**
Private Bill business, H.L., 27
Private Bill Committee Books, H.C., **221**
Private Bill Office, H.C., 71, 88, 214, 244
Private Bill Office, H.L., 71, 85, 88, 182
Private Bill Papers, H.L., **84**
'Private Bill Proceedings, H.C.', 231
Private Bills (*see also* Bills, Hybrid Bills, Local and Personal Bills, Personal Bills, Committees, Standing Orders *and* under individual classes of Private Bill records), 42, 57, 70–92 *passim*, 99; H.C., 214, 216, 218, 219, 221, 222, 228–31 *passim*, 243, 245
amendments to, 44, 45; H.C., 216; H.L., **83**, 84, 85, 90, **216**
categories of, 73–82
certificates of compliance with S.O.s, 210
Committee Bills, H.C., 228
compared with Public Bills, 70
deposits, 71, 73–91 *passim*, 192, 228–31 *passim*

Private Bills *cont.*
Engrossed, 71, **84**
evidence on, H.C., **224**, 230; H.L., **48–52, 53**
Examiners of petitions. *See separate entry*
fees on, 70; H.L., 52, 192
Filled, H.C., 228; H.L., 84
House, H.C., 228; H.L., 84
opposed, H.L., 44, 45. *See also* Evidence *above*
Paper Bills, 83, **84**
petitions for and against, 59, 69, 70, 71, 72, 76, 78, 79, 81, 276; H.C., 74, 214, 224, **229**, 230, 240; Registers of, **230**; H.L., 86, 87, 88, **89**, 93–4; Registers of, H.L., **90**; sessional lists of, H.L., 33. *See also* Examiners of petitions, Memorials.
Precedent, 84
Printed, H.C., **228, 233**; H.L., 70, 71, **84**; sessional lists of, H.L., 33
procedure on, 59–62, 69, 70–2, 74–82 *passim*, 242; H.L. committee papers on, 55
proof, 84, 192
records, H.C., 5, 228–31, 232; H.L., 82–92, 127
Registers, H.C., **230**
reports on, **216**
returns of, 186, 240
taxation of costs, 192, 230
unopposed, H.L., 44, 92
Private Business, H.C., returns of, 240
Private Business [H.C. Vote], **214**
Private Business, H.L., petitions concerning, 173
S.O.s concerning, 177
privateers, 9
Privilege, cases of, H.L., 124
ancillary papers, **125**
breaches of, 36, 191
procedure in, 124
records of, **125-6**
See also Committees, H.C., H.L.
'Privileges of the Lords of Parliament', 270
Privy Council, 106, 160, 269
papers [L. Great Chamberlain], 254
prize goods, 233
prize money, 151

procedure, H.C., 272, 296
  Manuals of, **240**
  Procedural Papers, **297**
procedure, H.L., 55, **173**, 278
  J. Browne's Book of, 271
proceedings, H.L., printing of, 124
Proceedings and Minutes of Evidence [on peerage claims], 161
proceedings in H.C. (1770–4), 285
Proclamation, (1573), 293
  Writs of, 93
prohibited goods, 148
prohibitions, 289
Promoter Life Assurance Society, 265
Proof Bills, H.L., 84, 192
Proportional Representation Bill (1924), 292
Prorogation Writs, 176. *For prorogation see under* Parliament
Protection of Birds Bill (1932–3), 221
Protections, H.L., 124, 126; Registers, of, **125**
Protest Books, H.L., 30, **174**, 277
  Register, **174**
  Sheets, 278
Protestation Returns, 8, 154–5, Pl. 10
Protestations, H.C., 131, 211, 271, 296, 298; H.L., 96, 155
Protests, H.L., 30, 173–4, 177*n*, 192, **288**
  printed, 174
Provisional Order Bills, H.C., 216, 218, 220
Provisional Order Confirmation Bills, 72 H.C., 216
Provisional Orders, 71–2
provisions, dearness, dearth, of (1765), 55, (1800), 52, 55
Proxies, H.L., 29, 186, 192, Pl. 2
Proxy Books, **175**
  Deeds, **175, 282**
  form, 192
  lists, 30
  records, 174–5
Pruson, Thomas, 269
Prussia, 158
Public Accounts. *See* Accounts, Public
Public Acts, 62, 93, 96, 98, 99–101. *See also* Acts of Parliament
  black letter vols., 101
  sessional vols., 99, **101**

Public Bill Files, H.L., 67
Public Bill Lists [H.C. Vote], **216**
Public Bill Office, H.C., 220, 244; papers **245–6**
Public Bill Office, H.L., 67, 182; papers, **192–3**
Public Bill Papers, H.C., 232, H.L., 127
Public Bills (*see also* Bills, Hybrid Bills, Committees, Standing Orders and under individual classes of Public Bill records), 99; H.C., 216, 218, 219, 220, 223, 240, 245; H.L., 41, 42
  amendments to, H.C., 214, 220; H.L., **67**, Pl. 11. *See also* riders
  'cases', **67**
  compared with Private Bills, 70
  Engrossed, **65–6**
  evidence on, H.L., 47–8, 52, 53
  Files, H.L., 67
  House, 66–7
  indexes to, H.L., 32
  Paper Bills, **65**, 226, 227
  petitions concerning, 93–4; H.L., **67**, 69
  Printed, **66–7**, 131; H.C., **227**, 234; lists of, 134
  procedure on, 59
  records of, H.C., 226–7, 232; H.L., 65–8, 127
  returns of, 186
  Table, 66
Public Building and Works, Ministry of, 5. *See also* Works, Commissioners of
Public Business, S.O.s concerning, H.C., 241, H.L., 177. *See also* Standing Orders, H.C., H.L.
Public Debt, 137, 233. *See also* National Debt
Public General Acts, lists of, printed, 134
Public Health (Cleansing of Shell Fish) Bill (1931–2), 221
public income and expenditure, 137
Public Notices, H.L., **90**
public offices, reports on, 155
Public Record Office, manuscripts in, 3, 5, 78, 93, 94, 96, 102, 104, 180, 183, 204, 259, 282
Public Records
  Royal Commission on, 193
  H.C. Sel. Committee on (1800), 212
  H.L. Sel. Committee on (1719), 55

Public Records *cont.*
See also Public Record Office *and* Record Commission
public revenue, 137
Public Rights of Way Bill (1927–8), 221
public utilities (1912–43), 55
public works, 54
Pugin, Augustus Welby, drawings by, 275, 289–90
Pym, John, 272

Quakers, 179
quays, 82
Quebec, 141
militia ordinances, 194
Quebec Bill (1791), 278
Queen's Bench. *See* King's Bench
Queen's county, Ireland, 193
Queensbury Peerage, 1812, 52
Queensferry Passage Improvement Bill (1809), 48
Questions to Ministers, 30, 38
H.C., 215, 216–17, 238, 243
H.L., 27, 34
See also Answers to Questions to Ministers

Rag Flock Act (1911) Amendment Bill (1927–8), 221
Railway Bills, 44, 74, 79–80, 85, 89, 91, 186, 192, 210
evidence on, 53
Railway Commissioners, 74
Railway Department of Committee for Trade, 80, 90
Raleigh, Sir Walter, 280
Ratcliff Charity Trust Papers, 282
Rates, Books of, 287, 291
Rating and Valuation (No. 2) Bill (1931–2), 221
Rating (Scotland) Amendment Bill (1927–8), 221
Raynham Hall, co. Norfolk, 278
Reading, co. Berks., 274
Reading Clerk, H.L., 181, 182
rebellion of 1715, 284
recognisances [in Appeal Cases, H.L.], 118; Books, 119
[in trials of peers], 112
Reconstituted Cream Bill (1928–9), 221
Record Commission, 99, 102

Record Office, H.L., 3, 5–7, 182, 193
records, keeping of, in offices, evidence concerning, 55
Records of H.C. (Catalogue), 298
Records, Papers concerning, H.L., 193
Redesdale, John Thomas (Freeman-Mitford), 2nd L., letters of, 278
Redford, P. J., Clerk in the House of Commons, precedent book, 192
Redmond, John Edward, drawings of, 295
Redrow Road Bill (1827), 50
Referees, Courts of, H.C., 224
Reference. *See* Books of Reference
Refreshment Department Papers, H.L., 193
Regicides, 8, 152
Register of Claims [Irish Peers], 168
Registers of Appearances [Appeal Cases], 119
Registers of Judgments [Appeal Cases], 119
Registers of Orders of Service [Appeal Cases], 118
Registers of Petitions on Private Bills, 90
Registers of Proceedings [Appeals and Cases in Error], H.L., 119
Registration (Births, Deaths and Marriages) Bill (1927–8), 221
Rehousing Statements, 87
Relfe, John, Clerk in the House of Lords, Book of Orders of, 280
Journals of, 191
religion, Bills concerning, 59
H.C. Committee on, 219
statistics concerning (1901), 194
Renfrewshire Road Bill (1825), 50
'Repertorium sive Elenchus Parliamentorum', 298
Reports and Accounts, Government, 129–30
Reports (Departmental) on Bills, H.L., 90, 214, 229
Reports on Private Bills [H.C. Vote], 216, 229
Representative Peers for Ireland, 21, 43, 167
papers concerning, 188
records of claims and elections, 167–9
Representative peers for Scotland, 21, 29, 43, 156, 165
papers concerning, 188
records of claims and elections, 165–7

Resolution of H.C., papers presented pursuant to, 232

Respondents' Answers [Appeals], H.L., **117**

Restitution of honours and blood, Bills for, 60, 81

Resumption, Act of (1450), 276

Returns, H.C., 232, H.L., **127–8**, 136

Reversal of Attainder Bills, 60, 81

Reynolds, Owen, Under-Clerk, H.L., 181, 271

rice, 145

Rich, Sir Nathaniel, H.C. diary of, 276

Richmond Bridge, 129, 155

Rickman, John, Clerk Assistant, H.C., 245

Rickmansworth Road Bill (1830), 51

'riders', 60, 61, 65, 67

Right, Petition of (1628), 11

Rights, Bill of (1689), 9
    Declaration of (1689), 11, 152, Pl. 11

Rights of Way Bill (1931–2), 221

Rio de la Plata, province of, 194

Ritchie, John Kenneth (Ritchie), 3rd L., 295

River Bills, 73–4

roads, 82. *See also* highways *and* turnpikes

Robinson, Mrs. M., 273

Robinson, T. M., 274

Rochdale Road Bill (1825), 50

Rochester Cathedral, co. Kent, 150

Rofford, co. Oxon., 299

Roll of the Lords. *See* Clerk of the Parliaments Rolls

Rolls, Joint Keeper of the, 280. *See also* Master of the Rolls

Rolls of Parliament. *See* Parliament, Rolls of

Roman Catholic Relief Act (1829), 172

Roman Catholic (Test) Rolls, 179

Roman Catholics, 79, 179, 194. *See also* Papists Lists

Roman Republic, 194

Romsey Paving Bill (1810), 49

Roscommon peerage claim, 188

Rose, George, Clerk of the Parliaments, correspondence of, 188
    papers of, **283**

Rosebery, Archibald Philip (Primrose), 5th E. of, drawings of, 295

Ross and Cromarty Jurisdiction Bill (1843), 85

Ross's *Parliamentary Record*, 39

Rotha Levels Drainage Bill (1830), 51

Round, J. Horace, Reports of, **288**

Roxburghe peerage (1812), 52

Royal African Company, 142

Royal Assent, 30, 59*n*, 61, 66, 94, 98, 183, 204, 259
    to Church Assembly Measures, 104
    formulae for, 94, 95, 98
    by notification, **176**
    refusal of, 191
    by royal commission, 30, 94, 95, 176

Royal Commissions (Letters Patent), 127, **175–6**

Royal Family, autographs of, 276

Royal Household, 136, 251. *See also* King's Household

Royal Institution, 265

Royal Licence, 78

Royal Messages and Answers, 234

Royal Scottish Academy, 265

Royal Warrant, 130

Rubber Industry Bill (1927–8), 221

Rudyerd, Sir Benjamin, speech (1640), 296

Rugby Charity Estate Bill (1826), 50

Rugby to Hinckley Road, 193, 265

Rules, Orders and Forms of Proceedings in the House of Commons, 240

rum, 145, 153

Runciman, Sir Walter [1st V. Runciman], 294

Rushworth, John, letters, 8
    'antidote to', 278

Russell, Bertrand Arthur William (Russell), 3rd E., 113, 118

Russell, Lord John, 289

Russell, James, 269

Russia, 158, 194
    trade with, 148

Ryder, Sir Dudley, Lord Chief Justice, notebook, 278

Sachem, Chief, 147

St. Albans, Francis (Bacon), 1st V., Lord Chancellor, 109, 279

St. Katherine's Docks Bill (1825), 50

St. Mary Undercroft Chapel, Palace of Westminster, Registers, **255**

St. Pancras Vestry Bill (1819), 49
St. Paul's Cathedral, 150
Salary Books, H.C., 244
Salford, Manchester and, Improvement Bill (1828), 50
Salisbury, Robert (Cecil), 1st E. of, 211
Salisbury Cathedral, co. Wilts., 150
Salmon and Freshwater Fisheries (Amendment) Bill (1928–9), 221
salt, 145, 153
Salt, Sir William, Library, Stafford, co. Stafford, 280
Salt Office, accounts of, 137
salted provisions, 145
Samuel, Herbert (Samuel), 1st V., papers of, **283–4**, Pl. 15
Sandon Hall, co. Stafford, 278
Saratoga campaign, 138
Sardinia, 158
Sawyer, Nicholas, 193
Saxe-Gotha, 158
Schemes (Delegated Legislation), 129
School for Indigent Blind Bill (1829), 48
scire facias, Writs of, 122, 123
Scobell, Henry, Clerk of the Parliaments, *Memorials*, 245
Scotch Annuity Tax, 186
Scotch Linen Regulation Bill (1823), 47
Scotland, 145, 156–7
  Africa Company of, 142
  appeals from, 114
  arms, 155
  canal Bills for, 74
  Commissions of Teinds in, 114
  conspiracy in, 9, 156
  Constableship of, 188
  Court of Exchequer in, 114, 120
  Court of Session, 114, 233; clerks of, 165
  divorce in, 75
  East India Company of, 9, 142
  forfeited estates in, 150, 156
  Highland roads, 77n, 264
  judges in, 76
  justices of the peace in, 118
  L. Advocate, 160
  L. Clerk Register, 165
  Parliament of, 114n
  peace, commissions of the, 156
  peerage, peers of, 21, 55, 165; trial of, 254. *See also* Representative Peers

Scotland *cont.*
  plate in, 156
  poor of, 194
  post office accounts, 153
  Private Bills concerning, 77
  Privy Council in, clerk of, 165
  promissory notes (1826), 52
  Provisional Orders in, 72
  salt duties, 145
  schools in, 156
  tobacco import duties, 146
  trade with, 147, 148
  union with England, 156, 202, Pl. 2
Scottish Commissions, records of, 6, **264**
Scottish Twopence Duty Bills, 70
Scott-Milman, Archibald, J., Clerk in the House of Commons, 212
'Scribbled Books', H.L., 33, 34, 205
Sculcoates Small Tenements Bill (1834), 51
Seal, Great, 21, 112, 175, 176, 179, 297
  matrices of, 293
  warrants for fixing, 194
Secker, Thomas, Archbishop of Canterbury, 37
Second Chamber Committee of Conservative Party, 292
Second Chamber, reform of. *See* House of Lords
Second World War Records. *See* Palace of Westminster
Secretaries of State, 127, 155, 162
Sections (Private Bills), 71, 80
  H.C., **230**
  H.L., **90**
Segrave, Nicolas de, 106
Selby, Leeds and, Railway Bill (1830), 51
Selby, William Court (Gully), 1st V., 259, 276
Selden, John, *Discourse* of, 298
  Priviledges of the Baronage, 152, **298**
  Treatise on Judicature in Parliament, 270
Select Vestries Bills, 29
Semple, H.S., 282
Serjeant at Arms, H.C., 223, 244
  Deputy, 292
  history and duties, 247
  records of, 247–8
servants of peers, 124
Session, Court of. *See under* Scotland

Sessional Papers H.C., 210, 227, **232–6**
  categories, 232
  indexes, 235–6; lists of, 134, 215
  printed, 132, 133, 233–6
Sessional Papers, H.L., 47, 53, 54, 66, **127–59**, 235
  description, 127–31
  lists and indexes, 132–4
  printing of, 131–2
  subject classification, 135–58
sewers, public (1936), 55
Seymour, Sir Francis, speech (1640), 296
Seymour, Thomas, L. Seymour of Sudeley, Pl. 1
Shadwell Church Bill (1823), 49
Shaftesbury Election Bill (1775), 47
Shaw-Lefevre, Sir Charles. *See* Eversley, 1st V.
Shaw-Lefevre, Charles, 265
Shaw-Lefevre, Sir John George, notebooks of, 192
  papers of, 186, 192–3, **264–5**
Sheffield, Manchester and, Railway Bill (1831), 51
Sheffield Water Works Bill (1830), 51
Sheldon, Gilbert, Archbishop of Canterbury, 178
'Shelburne set', H.L. Journals, 32
Sheriffs or Bailiffs, Returns of, to writs of *habeas corpus*, 125–6
Ship Money, 241
shipping Bills, H.C., 216
ships, 145
Shirley *v.* Fagg (1675), 107
shorthand, charges for, 192
Shrewsbury, co. Salop, Abbot of, 30, 175
Shropshire Protestation Returns, 155
Sicilies, The Two, 158, 194
Sierra Leone Company, 143
Sign Manual, Royal, 95, 115, 121, 254
signatures, Tudor Royal, 11
Silk Manufacture Bill (1823), 47
silver plate duty, 149
Simon, Mrs. Joan, 294
sittings of H.C., returns of, 240
Six Clerks, fees of, 193
Skinner *v.* East India Company (1666), 8, 107
slave trade, slavery, 52, 145, 194
Slave Trade Bills (1788–99), 47

Smirke, Sir Robert, 254
Smith, D. W., 287
Smith, Henry Stone, 4
Smith, John Thomas, 299
Smith, Sir Thomas, Clerk of the Parliaments, 41, 181, 245, 271
Smuggling Prevention Bill (1805), 47
Soane, Sir John, 55
Solicitor General, 22, 237, 289
Somerset, Protector, Edward (Seymour), 1st D. of, 277
Somerset, Charles (Seymour), 6th D. of, 34, 277
Somerset Protestation Returns, 155
Sound Broadcasting Records, H.C., **217**, H.L., **39**
South Africa, Indians in, 238
South Australia Commission, 264, 265
South Carolina, North America, 141, 147, 269
South London Dock Bill (1825), 50
South Sea Company, 143, 233, 284
  Directors of, 193
Southampton Protestation Returns, 154
Southampton, London and, Railway Bill (1834), 52
Southwark Bridge Bill (1811), 49
Southwark, Kent Street, Lighting Bill (1812), 49
Southwold Harbour Bill (1830), 51
Spain, King of, 271
  relations with, 158
  trade with, 148
  treaties with, 10, 158
  war with, 139
Spanish coins, 141
  commercial treaty, 10
  in Georgia, 141
  rescript, 158
  ships, 152
  Succession, War of the, 153
Speaker, H.C., 5, 20, 31, 62, 94, 154, 176, 201, 204, 205, 215, 218, 220, 223, 224, 237, 239, 243, 247, 251*n*, 259, 264, 272, 278, 287, 291, 292, 295, 296, 297
  absence of, 243
  choice of, 29, 280
  Chaplain to, 247
  Department of, 237, 244
  election of, 176, 209, 243, 299

Speaker, H.C. *cont.*
list of, **298**
presentation of, 26, 29, 296
See also Abbot, C.; Brand, H. B. W.;
Bromley, W.; Glanville, J.; Grimston,
H.; Gully, W. C.; Onslow, A.; Peel,
A. W.; Shaw-Lefevre, C.; Williams,
W.
Speaker, H.L., 94, 176, 278
patent to appoint, 176
precedents concerning, 191, 192
Speaker's Warrants, **259**
Special Order Book [Private Bills], H.L.,
91
Special Orders, 45, 72, **91**
lists of, H.L., 34
register of, 192
Special Procedure Orders, 72, 91, 224
list of, H.L., 34
Speech from the Throne, 29, 30, 34, 209,
210, 213, 234, 296
Speeches delivered by Counsel [on peerage
claims], 161
speeches in H.C., 210, 234, 279. *See also*
Debates
speeches in H.L., 30, 33, 36, 234, 270. *See
also* Debates *and* Speech from the
Throne
Spencer, George John (Spencer), 2nd E.,
193, 265
Spencer, John Charles (Spencer), 3rd E.,
265
Spencer, Frederick (Spencer), 4th E., 265
Spencer, John Poyntz (Spencer), 5th E.,
record of memorial bust of, **288**
Spencer, Albert Edward John (Spencer),
7th E., 288
Spencer Estates, 186, 264, 265
spirits, consumption of, 194; duties on, 149
Stabilisation of Easter Bill (1927–8), 221
Stafford, William (Howard), 1st V., 235
Stafford *v.* MacDonnogh [in error], Pl. 9
Stafford, Borough of, co. Stafford, Poll
Books, 239
Stafford Bribery Bill (1833), 51
Stafford Peerage (1812), 52, **288**
Stafford, William Salt Library, 280
Staffordshire Protestation Returns, 155
Stamford, Thomas (Grey), 2nd E. of, 113
Stamp Act papers (1766), 141

Standing Committee Debates (Public
Bills), H.C., **220**
Standing Committee Proceedings (Public
Bills), H.C., **220**
Standing Orders, H.C., 59, 70, 74, 77, 218,
240, 241, **242**
papers presented pursuant to, 232
Standing Orders, H.L., 10, 26, 88, 131,
177–8, 255, 280, 281, **288**, 298
Committee papers on (1945), 55
on appeals, 115, 117
on committees, 41, 44, 45, 54
on conferences, 58
on cases in error, 123
on Journal Committee, 26
on Oath of Allegiance, 179
on peerage claims, 160, 164; Irish, 167;
Scottish, 165
on peers' protests, 173
on printing and publication of proceedings, 36, 124
on Private Bills, 42, 46, 55, 74–91 *passim*
on privilege, 124
on prorogation, 176
on proxies, 174
Standing Orders (Companions), H.L. **178**
Stanford Hall, co. Northants., 270
Stanton Harcourt, co. Oxon., 279
Star Chamber, 241, 279
Starkey, Ralph, 270, 297
State Trial Papers [L. Great Chamberlain],
254
State Trials Committee, 264
Statements of Proof [Irish Peerage claims],
169
States General, treaties with, 158. *See also*,
Netherlands, the, *and* Holland
Stationery Office, H.M., 5
statistics concerning H.C., 245, 248
Statute Law Committee, records of, 6,
263–4
Statute Rolls, 3*n*, 93, 99
Entwistle, 277
Statutes at Large, 102
Statutes, Chronological Table of, 103
Statutes in Force, Index to, 102
Statutes (Index), **298**
Statutes, Private, Analytical Table of, 103
Statutes of the Realm, 96, 98, 99, **102**
Statutes Revised, 99, **102**, 263

Statutory Instruments, 29, 129, 130, 132
  Annual vols., 132
  lists and indexes, 133
Statutory Publications Office, 263
*Statutory Rules and Orders, Annual Volumes
  of*, 132
steam navigation (1848), 265
Stepney, London, 282
Steyning, co. Sussex, 280
Stirling Road Bill (1827), 50
Stockton and Darlington Railway Bill
  (1828), 50
stoppages in streets, 29
Stovin, Sir Frederick, 276
Strabane, co. Tyrone, 193
Strafford, Thomas (Wentworth), 1st E. of,
  31, 96, 270, 271, 272, 276, 280
Strand Bridge Bill (1809), 49
Strangers' Book, H.C., **298**
Stray Papers [Parliament Office], H.L.,
  193–4
Stuart of Decies, Henry (Villiers-Stuart),
  1st L., patent, 164
Stutteville, Lieut., 151
Subscription Contracts, 71, 80, 83, 86, **91,
  230**
Subscription Lists, 74, **91, 230**
subsidiary legislation, 127
  papers pursuant to, **130–1**, 232
subsidies, lay, 95, 99
Subsidies of the Clergy, **178**
Subsidy Bills, 59, 178
subways, 82
'Succession de la Couronne' (1688), 296
sufferance goods, 194
sugar, 145, 147
Sugar Warehousing Bill (1781), 47
Summons, Writs of, H.L. 20–1, 29, 124, 127,
  160, 165, 167, 170, 171, 176, **179–80**
Sunderland Dock Bill (1832), 51
Sunderland, Wear and, Navigation Bill
  (1819), 49
Superannuation Diplomatic Service Bill
  (1928–9), 221
Supplement to Votes and Proceedings,
  H.C., **214**
Supply Bills, 227
Supremacy, Oath of, 79, 81, 179
surgeons (1794), 47
Surrey Protestation Returns, 155

Surrey Sewers Bills (1809, 1810), 49
Surrey and Sussex Roads Bill (1828), 50
Surveys, Parliamentary, **297**
Sussex, D. of, Prince Augustus Frederick,
  252
Sussex Protestation Returns, 155
Sussex, Surrey and, Roads Bill (1828), 50
Sutton Place, co. Surrey, 265
Swannington, Leicester and, Railway Bill
  (1833), 51
Sweden, 158
Swineshead Road Bill (1826), 50
Symonds, Richard, 285
Synodical Government Measure (1969),
  104

Table Bills, H.C., 227, H.L., 66, 84
Table Office, H.C., 243, 244
Tables of Government Orders, 133
Taff Vale Railway Bill (1837), 53
Talbot, William (Talbot), 2nd L., 278
Talbot, George, 193
tallow, 146, 147
tally sticks, 293
Tangye, Lady, Journal, H.L., previously
  in possession of, 9, 280
Tanjore, India, 149
taxes, produce of, 137
Taxing Journals, H.L., **91**
Taxing Notes, 92
Taxing Officer, H.C., 229, 230
  fee books of, **230**
  register of, **230**
  H.L., 91, 230
Taylor, A. A., 245
Taylor, John, Clerk of the Parliaments, 30,
  181
tea, 146
Teeling, Sir William, 271, 272
Tees and Clarence Railway Bill (1828), 50
Tees Navigation Bill (1828), 50
Teignmouth, Charles John (Shore), 2nd L.,
  293
Teinds, Commission of. *See under* Scot-
  land
televised proceedings, H.L., **39**
Telford, Thomas, 264, Pl. 4, 5
Temple, Richard (Grenville, later Gren-
  ville-Temple), 2nd E., 278
Temple, Hon. W., 194

Temple Bar Improvement Bill (1800), 48

Tenterden, John Henry (Abbott), 2nd L., letters of, 278

Test Act (1673), 9, (1828), 172

Test Rolls, H.C., **242**

H.L., **179**

Tetsworth, co. Oxon., 299

Tewkesbury Road Bill (1826), 50

Thames, river, 142

embankment, 238

reservoirs, 275

Thames Navigation Bill (1824), 50

Thanks, Votes of, H.C., **242**, 243, 245

H.L., 179

Theatre Censorship (1966–7), 55

Thelluson's Estate Bill (1833), 51

theses on H.L., **286**

Thirsk and Yarm Roads Bill (1823), 49

Thomas, Walter, 269

Thorne, Doncaster and, Road Bill (1825), 50

Thornton and Geldart, Land Exchange Bill (1798), 48

Thursley Common, Surrey, 274

Tickell, Thomas, Secretary of the Lords Justices of Ireland, papers of, **284**

Tickell, Sir Eustace, 284

timber, 147

Timberland, Ebenezer, *The History and Proceedings of the House of Lords from the Restoration in 1660*, 37

Time, movement for measuring (1712), 233

Times, The, complaint concerning (1831), 52

Tippo Sahib, 149

Tithe Acts, 102

tithes in Ireland, 1832, 52

tobacco, 145, 146

Tobacco Duty Bills (1789, 1790), 47

Tompson, Henry Kett, 265

'Topography of the Old House of Commons', by O. C. Williams, 290

Torquay Harbour Bill (1794), 48

Torrington, Arthur (Herbert), 3rd E. of, 125

Torrington, F. W., 131*n*

Toulon, Fleet, 153

Tournai, 202

Tower, impeachment of lords in (1675–9), 54

Keeper of Records in, 280

town improvements, 54, 71

Townshend, George John Patrick [7th M., of Raynham], 278

Townshend, Hayward, parliamentary diary, 272

version of diary, 279

Tracy peerage claim, letters, 188; tombstones, 164

Trade, Bills concerning, H.C., 216, H.L., 59; Trading and company Bills, 82; Baking Trade (Ireland) Bill (1831), 48; French Trade Bill (1690), 9; Overseas Trade Bill (1928–9), 221; Slave Trade Bills (1788–99), 47; Wool Trade Bill (1828), 48; Woollen Trade Bill (1833), 48

Commissioners of, 278

companies, trading, 142

corn trade, 52, 144, 148

countries: Africa, company of merchants trading to, 142, trade with, 144, 146, 233, slave trade with, 145; America, trade with, 143, 144, 145, 146, 147, 148; Central Asia, trade of, 238; Flanders, trade with, 147; France, trade with, 143, 147; Germany, trade with, 143, 147; Holland, trade with, 143, 147; Ireland, trade, 48, 52, 147; Portugal, trade with, 148; Russia, trade with, 148; Spain, trade with, 148; West Indies, 55, 147, 148; Turkey, trade with, 148

customs and trade, H.L., sessional papers concerning, 136, **142–9**; general accounts, **148–9**

decay of (1669), 8, 54

foreign trade, 52, 210

sessional papers, H.L., concerning, 136, 142–9

slave trade, slavery, 52, 145, 194

state of (1697), 9, 54

statistics, 47

Trading and company Bills, 82

traitors, 109. *See also* treason

tramroads, 89

tramway Bills, 71, 85

Transcripts, etc., from Lower Courts [Appeal Cases] H.L., **119**

Transcripts of Proceedings [Cases in Error], H.L., **122**

Transcripts of Record [Cases in Error], H.L., 121, **122**, Pl. 9

transport, 54

Transport Bills, 82

Transport, Ministry of, 74, 80

transubstantiation, declarations against, 29, 179

travel diaries, 273

treason, 111, 124. *See also* traitors

Treasury, the, 913, 265
   Library of, 131
   secretary to, 155

treaties, 210
   copies of, 37, 157–8

'Treaty Series', 128

Trent and Mersey Navigation Company, 79

Treves, Germany, 158

trials, 6. *See also* State Trial Papers

trials of peers, records of, **111–14**, *and see under* peers

Trinity College, Cambridge. *See* Cambridge

troops of horse, commission to command, 293

True Relation of proceedings in Parliament, 279

Truro, Thomas (Wilde), 1st L., collection of, 286, **288–9**

Trustees Acceptance Books, H.L., **92**

trustees named in Private Bills, 46

trusts, 76

Trye *v*. E. Aldborough, 276

tunnels, 82, 89

Turberville, Professor Arthur Stanley, notebooks of, **289**

Turkey, trade with, 148

Turkey Company, 152

turnpike roads, 129

Turnpike Road Bills, 71, 76–7, 85, 89, 98*n*. *See also* Highway Bills

Turnpike Road Trusts (1833), 53

Two Sicilies, 158, 194

Tynemouth election (1853), 193

Under-Clerk of the Parliaments. *See* Clerk of the House of Commons

Uniformity, Act of (1662), 8

Union Roll, of Scottish peers, 165, **166**

Unitarian Association, 276

United States of America (*see also* America) treaties with, 158

Universities (Scotland) Bill (1931–2), 221

Unpresented House Papers, H.L., **194**

Unprinted Papers, H.C., 6, **232**

Upper Lambourne, co. Berks., 274

Upwell Tithes Bill (1834), 52

Vale Royal Park, 274

Vardon, Thomas, 212

Vargas, Peter, Private Secretary to the Government Whips, papers of, **298–9**

'vellums'. *See under* Acts of Parliament

Vere, de, family of, 255

Vere, Aubrey de, 251

Vernon, Edward, Admiral, 153

Victualling Office, Commissioners of, 155

Vigo, Spain, 153

Virginia, North America, 147, 269

Visitation Papers, Archbishops', 150

Visiting Forces (British Commonwealth) Bill (1932–3), 221

vivisection, 194

Votes and Proceedings, H.C., 33, 34, 131, 205, 212, **213**, 214, 220, 222, 235, 241, 299, Pl. 16
   Appendices to, 213, **214**, 222

Votes and Proceedings Office, H.C., 244

Votes of Thanks, H.C., **242**, 243, 245
   H.L., **179**

Wakefield and Austerlands Road Bill (1831), 51

Waldeck, principality of, 158

Waldegrave, William Frederick (Waldegrave), 9th E., **194**

Wales, Prince of, 21, 253

Wales, representation of, 202

Walker, Sir Edward, papers of, **284**

Walker, John, Clerk Assistant, House of Lords, 30

Walpole, Sir Robert [2nd E. Orford], 219, 284

Walter, William, 269

Walter *v*. Walter (1641), 108

Walton division, Liverpool, co. Lancs., 276

Wandsworth, Croydon (Surrey) and, Railway, 79

War, Articles of, 139

War Memorial, H.C., Books, **246**

War Memorial, H.L., Books, **287**
War Office establishment, 194
War, Second World, records concerning Palace of Westminster, H.C., **246**, H.L., **190–1**
Warboys Inclosure Bill (1798), 48
warrants, 92
Books of orders and, 171
for Letters Patent, 278
Warrants of L. Great Chamberlain, 254
registers of outgoing, **254**
Warrington and Newton Railway Bill (1831), 51
Warrington Railway Bill (1831), 51
Warwick, Edward (Rich), 6th E. of, 113
Warwick and Braunston Canal Bill (1794), 48
Warwick borough, co. Warwick, rate vouchers, 193
St. Mary's constituency, 194
Warwick Disfranchisement Bill (1834), 48
Warwickshire, constituency, 299
Protestation Returns, 155
Water resources and supplies (1935–6), 55
Water supply and drainage Bills, 82
Waterloo Bridge, London, 292
Waterworks Bills, 82, 224
Watson, Brooke, 144
Watt, R. C., 292
Ways and Means, Committee of, H.C., 219
Chairman, of, 72, 218, 224, 244, 294
Weald of Kent (Medway River) Canal Bill (1812), 49
Wear and Sunderland Navigation Bill (1819), 49
Webster, Sir Thomas Lonsdale, Clerk of the House of Commons, 212
Weights and Measures Bill (1823), 47
Welbeck Abbey, co. Nottingham, 278
Welland Navigation Bill (1834), 52
Wellington, Arthur (Wellesley), 1st D. of, 276
Wells, co. Somerset, Cathedral, 150
Wells, co. Somerset, election (1620), 293
Wesleyan missionary, 274
West Indies, 145, 152, 153
bullion from, 143
condition of (1832), 52
courts martial in, 138

West Indies *cont.*
duties, 141
guide to records relating to, 135
privateers in, 9, 55
trade with, 147, 148
West Middlesex Water Bill (1810), 49
West Wellow, co. Hants., 275
Westminster
Abbey, 30, 253
Abingdon St., house in, 186
Bridge, 158; plans of, 190
City of, grant of arms to, 277
Hospital, 193
Palace of. *See* Palace of Westminster
St. Margaret, parish of, 255
School, 253
Streets of, 129, 158
Westminster Gazette, 295
Westminster Improvement Bill (1826), 50
Westmorland Protestation Returns, 155
Weston, Rev. Samuel Ryder, estate papers, **299**
Wetherall, William, 274
Wexford county constabulary, 194
Weymouth Improvement Bill (1810), 49
whale fisheries in Scotland, 157
wheat trade, 144
Whips, secretary to, 298
Whips' Sheets, **194**
Whitaker, Charles, 289
'White Papers', 128
Whitelock, Bulstrode, 152
Whitworth, Charles (Whitworth), 1st V., and 1st L. Adbaston, 278
Wilberforce, William, 293
Wild Birds Protection Bill (1926–7), 221
Wilkes, John, 241
Willcocks, R. M., papers of, **284**
Williams, John, Bishop of Lincoln, L. Keeper, 276
Williams, Orlo Cyprian, Clerk in the House of Commons, 278, 290
Williams, William, Speaker, H.C., 207, 211
Williamstown, Virginia, 269
Willoughby of Parham, peerage claim, 160
wills, 162
Wilmington, 1st E. *See* Compton, Spencer
Wilson's Road Bill (1829), 50

Wiltshire Protestation Returns, 155
Wimbledon, co. Surrey, estates in, 265
   tithes of, 186
Wimbledon Poor Bill (1828), 50
Winchester Cathedral, co. Hants., 150
Windlesham Inclosure Bill (1812), 49
Windsor, co. Berks., St. George's Chapel,
   195
wine, 146
Winslow, Rev. Octavius, 273
Witham Navigation Bill (1826), 50
witnesses, 60, 76
   Books of, 92
   H.C., 223, 230, 244
   H.L., 30, 33, 41, 43, 45, 46, 47, 53, 67,
      88, 109, 118
   recognisances of [trials of peers], 112
Wolsey, Thomas, Cardinal, Lord Chan-
   cellor, 3, 276, 284
Woodcock, Lieut., 52
Woods and Forests, Office of, 130
Woods, Forests and Land Revenues, of
   the Crown, Commissioners of, 137,
   141
wool, 146, 147, 149
Wool Trade Bill (1828), 48
Woollen Trade Bill (1833), 48
woollens, 147
Wooller, Mr., 130
Worcester Cathedral, co. Worcester, 150
Worcester Protestation Returns, 155
Worcester Roads Bill (1803), 48
Workers' Educational Association, 291
'working class statements', 87
Working Men's College, London, 275, 291

Works, Commissioners of, 294
   First Commissioner of, 293
Worricker, J. W., 190
Wren, Sir Christopher of, 254
   pedigree of, **299**
Wright, Elizabeth, 193
Wright, John, assault of (1832), 52
Writs in Acceleration. *See* Acceleration,
   Writs in
Writs of *certiorari*. *See certiorari*, Writs
   of
Writs of Error. *See* Error, Writs of
Writs of *habeas corpus*. *See habeas corpus*,
   Writs of
Writs of *scire facias*. *See scire facias*, Writs of
Writs of Summons. *See* Summons, Writs
   of

Yale University, 272
Yarm, Thirsk and, Roads Bill (1823), 49
Yarmouth, Francis Charles (Seymour-
   Conway), 2nd M. of Hertford,
   styled E. of Yarmouth, 253
Yate, Thomas, 186
Yatten, Thomas, Articles against, 96
Yelverton, Sir Henry, 280
Yonge, Harriet, 273
Yonge, Walter, 298
York, D. of, Prince George Frederick
   Ernest Albert, 43
York, Convocation of, 178
York, London and, Road, 77
Yorke, Charles, 293
Yorkshire, election (1784), 293
   Protestation Returns, 155